Tropical Diaspora

A view of the St. Louis surrounded by smaller vessels in the port of Havana.

TROPICAL

Markus Wiener Publishers
Princeton

DIASPORA

THE JEWISH EXPERIENCE IN CUBA

Robert M. Levine

With a new Foreword by Anthony P. Maingot

First Markus Wiener Publishers edition, 2010

Copyright © 2010 for the new Foreword by Anthony P. Maingot

Originally published by the University Press of Florida, Gainesville, Florida
Copyright © 1993 by the Board of Regents of the State of Florida

For information, write to
Markus Wiener Publishers
231 Nassau Street, Princeton, NJ 08542
www.markuswiener.com

Library of Congress Cataloging-in-Publication Data

Levine, Robert M.
  Tropical diaspora : the Jewish experience in Cuba / Robert M. Levine ;
with a new foreword by Anthony P. Maingot. — 1st ed.
    p. cm.
Includes bibliographical references and index.
ISBN 978-1-55876-521-4 (alk. paper)
  1. Jews—Cuba—History—20th century. 2. Immigrants—Cuba—
History—20th century. 3. Cuba—Ethnic relations. I. Title.
F1789.J4L48 2010
972.91004924—dc22

                                    2010022381

Markus Wiener Publishers books are printed in the
United States of America on acid-free paper and meet
the guidelines for permanence and durability of the
Committee on Production Guidelines for Book Longevity
of the Council on Library Resources.

For David S. and Ruth F. Levine

Contents

ILLUSTRATIONS

ACKNOWLEDGMENTS

Several individuals contributed generously to my effort to learn about Cuba and its history from a distance; dozens of others lent their support and advice. A few years ago Mark D. Szuchman and I produced a documentary videotape on the lives of Jewish immigrants to Cuba after World War I. I am indebted to Mark for his insights, and for his help in arranging contacts with members of the South Florida community who were interviewed for that project. These people included Osher (Jaime) Schuchinsky, Moisés Pitchón, Mark's parents, Ida and Iser Szuchman, Carlos and Uva Márquez-Sterling, Isidoro Behar, Susi Rafi, Micha Blumen, and Chalon Rodriguez. Moisés and Sara (Zoila) Levin kindly assisted me and took me with them to visit Sender M. Kaplan, who has since died. Rabbi Nesim Gambach and Dr. José Achuily provided invaluable documentation of the history of the Cuban Sephardic colony. Stanley and Rachel Wax contributed documents and useful comments about their experiences in Cuba and put me in touch with Moshe Bondar. Moreno Habif offered major insights, tirelessly throwing himself into the task and introducing me to his indefatigable mother, Ena, and her brother-in-law, Alberto Habif. I am indebted to Abe Resnick, Eva Berman, Walter Lippmann, Felix Reyler, Dr. Berta Savariego, P. S. Osorio, and Arón and Saulo Yukem for their help. Vivian Ferrin lent invaluable assistance in several ways, including putting me in touch with Mauricio Zeilic and Lucía and Humberto Suárez, who provided some lovely photographs. Natalie Lyons offered a useful interview.

More than anyone else, Hannah Wartenberg contributed to the project that resulted in the chapter in the Wyman series and to this book. She conducted research in the YIVO Institute for Jewish Research and the American Jewish Committee archives in New York

City, interviewed several subjects in Chicago and Miami, maintained correspondence with persons who provided help, and generously translated materials from German into English. Her husband, Rolf, assisted generously as well. Leah Kadden provided me with valuable comments about her experience as a child on the SS *St. Louis* and her subsequent internment in Belgium and Switzerland. Omar Cuan kindly conducted interviews and also researched Spanish-language newspapers at the special collections of the University of Miami Richter Library.

Günter W. Cohn, who was initially interviewed by Marcia Hencinski of Florida International University, provided a wealth of detail and also put me in touch with others who became helpful, most notably Norbert Adler, who provided interviews, photographs, and excellent advice. Ilsa Mittel-Ashe wrote a moving personal account of her experiences as a young refugee, mentioning things that she had never talked about before but that now she feels "should be known." Günter Kosse, Ruth G. Weitzenkorn, and Hilde Backow offered their stories. Shlomit Oz contributed interviews with Sender M. Kaplan and Osher Schuchinsky in Miami Beach; Matthew (Levi) Lemberger and his wife, Berta Sherman, provided marvelous help talking with Mr. Kaplan at length, reading him sections of the manuscript for his comments, and providing photographs. Maureen Nutting helped locate information on the role of the Catholic church in Cuba. Patricia Wickman helped instruct volunteers in interview techniques. Sara Sánchez was generous in her help. Alberto Rodriguez made useful contacts and kindly found copies of materials, including a detailed map of Old Havana.

Edmund Lipsitz of the Canadian Jewish Congress sent me information about the CJC's role in aiding Cuban Jewry after 1961 and put me in touch with Rabbi Lavy Becker, who during the 1970s and 1980s made more than a dozen trips from Canada to Cuba for his organization. Sandra Levinson of the Center for Cuban Studies provided information about Cuba during the Castro period, as did Rabbi Morton Rosenthal of the Anti-Defamation League and Jacobo Kovadloff of the American Jewish Committee. Jacobo interviewed Primitivo Ramírez at his home in Queens when I could not go because of a snowfall during a trip to New York.

Rabbi Jeffrey K. Salkin and his wife, Nina, put me in touch with Rabbi Meir Lasker, who served at the Cuban Hebrew Congregation from 1933 through 1942, and who graciously received me in his home in Philadelphia in November 1989. Margalit Bejarano of the Hebrew University of Jerusalem generously sent me translations of some of her work and put me in touch with Moisés Asís, one of the most active members of the remaining Jewish community in Cuba. Her advice has been invaluable and generous, and I doubly appreciate it because she is completing a dissertation on a similar topic to mine. Edy Kaufman of the Hebrew University's Truman Institute sent me portions of Mahmud Abbas's scurrilous *La otra cara*. Eric D. Kohler of the University of Wyoming sent me a copy of his article based on interviews with Rabbi Nathan Witkin, and Rabbi Witkin himself spoke with me several times. Following his death, his widow, Helen, continued to correspond with me. Clive Afflick mailed letters for me from Jamaica to Cuba. Bernard Wasserstein of Brandeis University offered useful advice about refugee policy and provided evidence that Britain was rather more responsive to the plight of refugees, especially children, than was the United States. Lutz Krätzschmar generously sent me from Hamburg copies of several important documents, including transcripts of *Le Télégramme du Pas de Calais et de la Sommer* and interviews with Carl Glissmann, a sailor on the SS *St. Louis*, and data about passengers on that ill-fated ship. Patrick von zur Mühlen of Frankfort also lent valuable assistance.

George Mosse of the University of Wisconsin, Madison, the noted expert on Nazism, provided moral support and some good early ideas as well as a reading of the chapter on the interwar years. Stanley R. Payne also provided useful advice on Spanish Falangism. Cuban-born Ruth Behar of the University of Michigan kindly offered insights from the perspective of a trained anthropologist who remembers vividly her Sephardic *abuelo* and Ashkenazic *zeide* and kindly gave me permission to use two of her excellent photographs taken in Havana in December 1991. Ignacio Klich of St. Anthony's College, Oxford, kindly forwarded material from the Spruille Braden Papers and information about Muslim and Jewish immigration to Latin America. Gregory Celentano read Spanish newspapers from the late 1930s as part of an undergraduate history project. Rabbi Sanford E. Saperstein, whose sermons were always as stimulating as college lectures and who in many ways influenced my choice of history for a career, kindly invited me to Longboat Key in Sarasota to speak to his interesting congregation. Shirley Cortada provided information about her job in the visa section of the U.S. embassy in

Havana during the war years. Congresswoman Ileana Ros-Lehtinen provided information about her grandfather, Jacobo Adato.

At the University of Miami, unique assistance was lent by Peter Tarjan, who chairs the Department of Bio-Medical Engineering, and Andrew Handler and Hermann Beck, my colleagues in the History Department. Robert Kirsner of the Foreign Language Department kindly conducted a number of interviews on life in Cuba and introduced me to Joseph Schraibman of Washington University of St. Louis, who lived in Cuba during the war years. Students who helped with the project included Linda Lurie, María del Carmen Rivero, Keith Frostad, and Andrew Speyer; volunteers included Karl-Heinz Mainberger, Ariel Segal, and the always generous and friendly Lenny del Granado. Peter Beattie and Henry Green provided helpful editorial observations. Julian Weinckle helped me locate Woodrow de Castro to check out the Panamanian dimension of the study, which was accomplished through the kind assistance of I. Roberto Eisenmann, Jr. President Edward T. Foote II made the initial contact for me with Abel Holtz. William E. Brown of Archives and Special Collections enlisted his staff to help find good photographs for the book. Provost Luis Glaser contributed an interview about his family's emigration to Mexico.

Hardy L. Spatz was kind enough to fly from Charlotte, North Carolina, to Miami to set me straight on a large number of things. I greatly appreciate his desire that I tell the story of the wartime refugees accurately. He provided remarkable details about the diamond industry and the ways to obtain landing permits and visas and put me in contact with individuals in the "American" and Sephardic colonies in South Florida. I am indebted to him for his insight and continual help throughout the project. Susan E. Cernyak-Spatz provided valuable help with German-language documents. The Winers provided very useful information about their lives in Cuba, José from an Ashkenazic family and Esther from a Sephardic family from Turkey. They graciously put me in touch with Primitivo Ramírez and with former residents of Cuba now living in South Florida, including Morris Rosenfeld, Joe and Hilda Robinsky, and Frieda Seleski. Bernardo Benes generously read an early draft of the manuscript and provided invaluable information about aspects of the story that needed to be covered. Elissa Papirno of the Hartford *Courant* assisted with an interview and provided valuable ideas about the project as well as editing suggestions.

Moisés Asís patiently overcame the difficulties in communicating between Havana and Miami and offered his complete cooperation. He also visited Coral Gables in November 1991, a memorable trip that yielded considerable further insight into Cuban Jewish history. Historian Maritza Corrales, whose knowledge of the history of Cuba's Jews is impressive, provided valuable help as well.

Not everyone who was asked to help did so. From the outset of the project, I had decided to circulate chapters and even whole copies of the manuscript-in-progress to anyone who might be able to comment or to help my research. Some of the survivors of the SS *St. Louis* declined to be interviewed, explaining through family members that to bring back memories of their wartime experiences would be too much to bear. I also knew that there were people who were suspicious of the effort to write about the subject by a professor who had never been to Cuba. The reaction to my offer to provide copies was interesting. Some accepted them but never replied or responded in any way. Others told me about a few inconsequential mistakes and let it go at that. Some people, on the other hand, wrote me lengthy and detailed comments; these were invariably useful. Some people refused outright either to see me or to receive questionnaires or copies of my drafts in the mail. One former German Jewish refugee who lived in Cuba during the war, and who after coming to the United States became a distinguished university scholar, explained his decision not to cooperate: "I have managed to protect myself fairly well by a rather severe amnesia about many of these matters."

Research for this book was carried out with the assistance of a grant from the Lucius N. Littauer Foundation of New York City. Portions of the text will appear in my chapter in *The World Reacts to the Holocaust: 1945–1900*, edited by David Wyman (Baltimore: Johns Hopkins University Press, 1993), the project that initially gave impetus to my research on the subject of refugees emigrating to Cuba. Encouragement to engage in research on Latin American Jewish history has long come from Judith L. Elkin, the founder and president of the Latin American Jewish Studies Association. Last but not least, I gratefully appreciate the loving support of my family: my wife, Peggy, and my sons, Joey and David.

FOREWORD

In proportional terms, Cuba offered refugee or migrant status to more Jews than did any other Latin American country. Proportionally more, in fact, than was offered by the United States. In addition, despite occasional periods of hostility by certain sectors of the Cuban elite, these Jews were generally afforded a good reception. In this scholarly and informative book, Robert M. Levine offers three reasons for this unusual circumstance. First, Cuba had an open economy and a "worldly" elite, long accustomed to dealing with strangers. This explains the relative absence of the class-based ethnocentrism and anti-Semitism often found among other Latin American elites. To be sure, prejudice and discrimination existed but, according to the author, tended to be of the "petty" rather than the institutionalized sort.

Second, because the Jews settled all over Cuba rather than concentrating in one city—much less in one neighborhood—and were involved in a variety of economic activities, their presence never engendered the "ghetto" syndrome so common in most Old World countries.

Finally, accommodation, if not full assimilation, was facilitated by the fact that Jewish migration occurred in widely spaced historical sequences, each with different settlement patterns. Twentieth-century arrivals benefited from the fact that two earlier groups had already incorporated themselves smoothly into Cuban society and the Cuban economy. First came the Spanish and Portuguese Sephardim who arrived surreptitiously with the conquering Spaniards. Later came Jews from northeast Brazil. They had settled there when the Dutch conquered that part of Brazil in 1630 and left when the Dutch were expelled in 1661. Many then settled on the Dutch island of Curaçao. Variously called *marranos*, *conversos*, *nuevos cristianos*, or simply "crypto-Jews," the Jews who settled in Curaçao were especially important given that Dutch protection since the seventeenth century had made their settlement the center of Jewish culture in the Caribbean. Indeed, the Sephardic Council of Elders (the *parnassim*) was located in Amsterdam. The next successful migration was that of American Ashkenazi Jews who followed the American military involvement in the Spanish-American War and Cuban independence. Other migrations, such as the Sephardim from the Ottoman Empire (especially Turkey), came after World War I.

Even as Levine is correct in noting the ameliorative and benign atmosphere created by the early arrival and assimilation of the Sephardim in Cuba, he deals with this only in passing. His real purpose and central focus in this book is the unraveling of the complex history of the diaspora of later arrivals: the German, Russian, and Polish Ashkenazim. As splendidly as he elucidates this explicit theme, there is a need to explain the origins and evolution of the Sephardim to convey a full understanding of the evolution of the Jewish presence in Cuba—in particular, how Judaism survived after the half century rule of the atheistic Marxist-Leninist state. A brief anecdote relating the experience of one Jewish woman will serve to introduce the topic of Sephardim in Cuba.

The daughter of Julio Lobo, owner of at least twelve major sugar factories (*centrales*) in Cuba and thus the island's undisputed "sugar baron" of the first half of the twentieth century, had only a vague idea that the Lobos were originally Sephardic Jews. This was not surprising, since Julio Lobo had arrived in Cuba from Venezuela already a Roman Catholic, and his daughter was raised as a Catholic in Cuba. Her curiosity about her family's history was piqued by a dinner conversation which led her to consult the fundamental text on the settlement of Sephardic Jews in Curaçao[1] and their subsequent spread to the whole region, including the United States. In that book, Ms. Lobo could trace her lineage to Isaac and Joseph Jesurun Lobo, related by marriage to the da Costas and the de Limas, families whose progeny spread to and became successful in Jamaica, Barbados, and Trinidad. She became intrigued by the biography of David Lobo, who migrated from Curaçao to Caracas, Venezuela, where he opened one of the better known medical clinics. David was the son of David Solomon Lobo and Clara de Jacob Haim Senior. His sister, Sarah Lobo, married Curaçao-born Daniel de Leon, Professor of Economics at Columbia University and founder of the still existent Socialist Workers Party of the United States. Fascinated by her newfound genealogical knowledge, Ms. Lobo concluded that the Cuban Lobos descended from a restless, entrepreneurial lot, and this gave her a deeper understanding of her father's own climb to the top of the sugar business, in Cuba and the world. But Lobo was only one of a wave of Sephardic sugar producers and commission agents who were much more interested in commerce than in religion. It is known that by 1880 a number of prominent Sephardim from Curaçao were settled in Cuba and New York. To cite but one relevant case, the New York–based trading company De Sola, Lobo & Co. was already trading with Cuba by the end of the nineteenth century. By the early twentieth century Sephardic names were manifest among those of the Cuban sugar planter class, for example, Leon, Levy, Machado, Salas, de Marchena, and Maduro. Lobo was simply the most successful of them all. Significantly, they had already earned the kind of reputation for hard work and entrepreneurial talent that tends to chip away at the persistent anti-Semitism so rooted in Catholic societies. So much so that historian Roland Ely notes how the newly arrived, hard-working, and thrifty Spanish Catalans were favorably compared with the Jews and became known as *"judios completos," "los israelitas de la cristianidad,"* and *"judios españoles."*[2]

So how did these Jews, expelled from England in 1290, then from Spain in 1402 and 1492, and somewhat later from Portugal, manage to travel to the New World and subsequently not only survive but indeed prosper enough to create a social cushion of sorts for later arrivals? Two facts, one historical and one theological, are crucial. Historically, the Sephardim became adept at survival through flight. In doing so, the Sephardim resorted to any and all schemes and subterfuges, explains Palóma Díaz-Mas: ". . . registering in Seville under assumed names, falsifying documents of purity of lineage, traveling as stowaways, hiding in the service of important dignitaries or undertaking the trip in ships of smugglers, pirates and privateers."[3]

The fact that they spoke Spanish and, as Seymour B. Liebman points out, shared a secular ethnicity with the Spanish helped. Iberian or Sephardic Jews, says Liebman, could scarcely be singled out from their Iberian-Christian neighbors.[4] "The Jews expelled from their fatherland, that is, Spain, in 1492," writes Américo Castro, "felt themselves . . . as Spanish as the Christians."[5] The groups that came later, such as the Sephardim migrants from North Africa and the Ottoman Empire, tended not to integrate as readily since they were religiously orthodox, poorly educated, and non-Spanish speaking. These Jews were always disdainfully referred to as *"Turcos."* The migration of American Jews occurred with the arrival of U.S. occupation troops during the War of Cuban Independence. They held important technical and commercial positions from the start but in the manner that Americans typically do abroad: they formed their own religious and social communities distinct from Cuban *criollo* (Creole) society.

Sephardic survival was also supported by a distinct theological precept. Sephardim (as distinct from German Ashkenazim) were not deterministically prone to martyrdom, because conversion was not seen as the end of the world. In addition to the instinctively developed strategies of survival over the centuries of persecution, flight, and then resurgence, there were the concessions to such strategies in the teachings of the great Sephardic scholar, Maimonides. As B. Netanyahu explains, "While hailing martyrdom, [Maimonides] did not denounce forced conversion, and thus gave a kind of moral sanction to conversion under duress."[6] This explains the precept of the *Moda'ah*, which permits Jews to separate themselves from the faith in a moment of danger and then annul that act with a counter-declaration. This theological-cum-political stratagem explains why so many *conversos* or *marranos* in Spain and the Greater Caribbean could for generations seem totally removed from Judaism only to have their descendants return to the faith without much apparent trauma. Ms. Lobo was one such case but was representative of a Latin American and Caribbean (including Cuban) phenomenon. In fact, it is a Caribbean rule of thumb that the longer a family has been in the region and the higher its social status, the greater the probability that Jewish blood runs in the family.

Later migrations of Ashkenazim (generally referred to as "*Polacos*") were not as easily integrated, but it is evident that without the success of the earlier migrations conditions could have been much worse. Those who arrived in the 1920s and early 1930s included a good number of Marxists who played a key role in the founding of Cuba's communist party. In the 1930s, especially around the years of the Spanish Civil War, these Jews became targets of a small but influential sector of the Cuban elite that had Falangist leanings. These elites also opposed the entry of the next wave of Jews, the refugees from Nazism. Levine is especially adept in his portrayal of these refugees, desperate but unable to enter the United States. Their histories provide him with his most dramatic material; clearly, the most poignant and heartrending lines are written around their stories. As distinct from the Sephardim, who came to settle, Levine explains that these refugees settled for Cuba as a safe haven—not a home but rather something of an "immigration hotel." One beneficial, unintended consequence of their aloofness was that it minimized potential confrontations with local anti-Semites. As such, Levine provides us with a powerful sense of hemispheric history repeating itself: refugees attempting to reach the United States by any means including expensive smugglers; the United States attempting to secure alternative settlements for them in several Caribbean countries; corrupt local officials and politicians enriching themselves from this sordid game of avoidance and callousness.

Thus, this book is about more than just a Jewish diaspora; it is about the many diaspora which have made the Caribbean Basin what it is. Levine passed away in 2003, so his verdict on the effect on the Jewish community of four decades of Marxist-Leninist dictatorship is harsh. From a perspective measured only in decades, these judgments are certainly true. But Jews have 4,000 years of survival behind them, and from that perspective no one should despair about Judaism disappearing from Cuba. The principle of *Moda'ah*—if not in strict theological form, at least as effective practice— is still alive. In 1994, the Chief Ashkenazi Rabbi of Israel visited Cuba and declared that the 60 percent of the Jewish population who are converts were legitimately converted. As Maritza Corrales, a resident Jewish historian, put it, "To be Cuban and Jewish is to be twice survivors."[7] There are presently only some 1,500 Cuban Jews on the island, but things are looking up for these survivors. There are now at least five major American and Canadian Jewish organizations actively involved in helping Cuban Jews restore their many synagogues and educate their children. As Eddie B. Levy of the Miami-based organization Jewish Solidarity notes, Cuban Jews have teetered for decades between hardship and the struggle for survival. Now it appears that they not only have survived but are experiencing a revival.[8] A new chapter in the more than four centuries of Jewish presence in Cuba is being written.

ANTHONY P. MAINGOT
Professor Emeritus of Sociology, Florida International University
2010

NOTES

1. Isaac S. and Suzanne A. Emmanuel, *History of the Jews of the Netherlands Antilles*, 2 vols. (Cincinnati, OH: American Jewish Archives, 1970).
2. Roland T. Ely, in his informative book *Cuando reinaba su Majestad el Azucar* (Buenos Aires: Editorial Sudamericana, 1963), p. 316.
3. Palóma Díaz-Mas, *Sephardim: The Jews from Spain* (Chicago: The University of Chicago Press, 1992), p. 66.
4. Seymour B. Liebman, "The Jews as an Ethnic Group in the Americas During the 16th and 17th Centuries," in Bhabagrahi Misra and James Preston (eds.), *Community, Self, and Identity* (The Hague: Mouton Publishers, 1978), pp. 95-114.
5. Américo Castro, *The Structure of Spanish History* (Princeton, NJ: Princeton University Press, 1954), p. 466.
6. B. Netanyahu, *The Origins of the Inquisition in Fifteenth Century Spain* (New York: Random House, 1995), p. 163.
7. Quoted in *The New York Times*, February 4, 2007, p. 12.
8. Interview, Miami, Florida, April 26, 2010. The organization Jewish Solidarity can be accessed at jewishsolidarity@bellsouth.net.

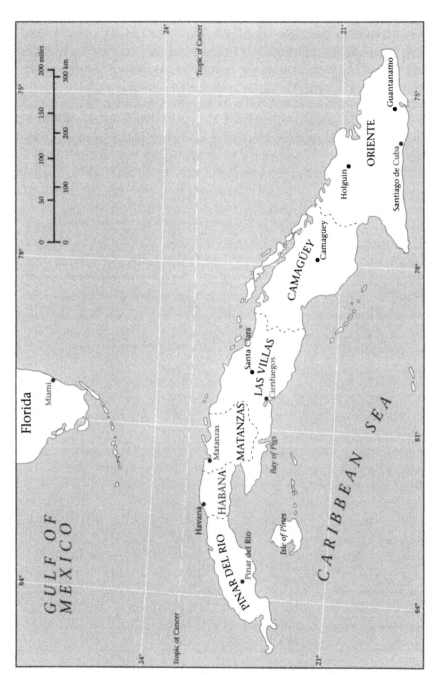

Modern Cuba, showing provincial boundaries. Map by Cartography Lab, University of Wisconsin-Madison.

1 ✡ DIASPORA
IN THE TROPICS

Until the eighteenth century, Jews scattered throughout
the diaspora shared a common bond based upon the principles of rabbinical Judaism, Jewish law (*halakhah*), and communal autonomy.
But the Enlightenment and its Jewish counterpart, the *haskalah*,
shook the ancient and well-regulated Jewish religious tradition;
post–French Revolution opportunities for political emancipation
and cultural assimilation brought even further departures from traditional patterns of behavior for those living in the countries of
Western Europe and North America. For Jews living elsewhere, however, changes came much more slowly. Some Jews (as well as *marranos*, covert Jews nominally converted) whose ancestors had been
expelled from Spain and Portugal in the late fifteenth century but
who still preserved the language and customs of Sepharad sought to
enter the Spanish American colonies, some still secretly practicing
Jewish ritual. Others went to French-, Dutch-, and English-
controlled colonies in the Caribbean. A few, tried and convicted in
absentia of Inquisitorial autos-da-fé, are known to have settled in
New Mexico, Colorado, Arizona, and California, territories distant
enough from the seat of Spanish authority in Mexico City to afford
some measure of safety for them to practice their religion discreetly.[1]

Well into the nineteenth century, Jews were barred by law from
entering the former lands of the Spanish empire, just as they had
been excluded from czarist Russia until the last quarter of the eighteenth century. Even after juridical barriers were lifted and pioneer
Jewish immigrants began to settle in Spanish- and Portuguese-

speaking Latin America, the question remained to what extent Jews would be granted legitimate status in the eyes of the majority.[2] This was all the more difficult because Latin American societies never accepted cultural or ethnic pluralism, and because the Jews who came to the region tended to be persons fleeing repression or hardship, not Westernized Jews seeking to assimilate. There was no legal separation of church and state in most of Latin America. In the United States and Canada, most Jews and other immigrants gradually became absorbed into the primary groups of the host society, receiving the same political rights as native-born citizens and earning acceptance into virtually all social contexts after two generations. This was never true for the rest of the hemisphere, a circumstance to some degree accepted both by the Creole elites and by the Jewish immigrant communities. Cuba differed from most other Latin American places because the island's indigenous culture had been eradicated; its culture became shaped by foreigners, whether Spaniards or non-Spanish immigrants. None of this took place before 1900, when fewer than 1,000 Europeans who were not Spanish nationals lived on the island. By 1907 this population would jump to more than 11,800, including 6,000 immigrants from the United States. Twelve years later, in 1917, there would be 5,619 non-Spanish Europeans and 31,442 Americans; by 1931, 10,000 non-Spanish Europeans and 121,000 citizens of the United States or other hemispheric republics.[3]

Spain authorized Jews to enter its Cuban colony for the first time in 1881, although non–Roman Catholic worship services were not permitted until after the Spanish-Cuban-American War of 1898.[4] A tiny group of families of Jewish origin—between fifty and one hundred—was present in Cuba, including the Maduros, Brandons, Marchenas, Machados, and Dovelles. Some were linked to families with the same name elsewhere in the circum-Caribbean, in Panama, Curaçao, the Virgin Islands, and Surinam. These families were wealthy and kept to themselves. Many had married non-Jews and raised their children as Catholics; most led secular lives, although they did not hide their Jewish origins. The Brandons, especially, played major roles in institutional Jewish affairs. A relative, Noble Brandon Judah, served as U.S. ambassador to Cuba after the U.S. intervention. José Martí, who became Cuba's hero of independence, enjoyed good relations with Jews in New York and attracted many to his cause. During and after the conflict with Spain, as early as 1892, some American Jews helped Martí raise funds in Tampa, Key West, and Caracas. Horace Rubens, a Jewish lawyer and member of Tampa's Junta Revolucionaria Cubana, was considered to be "Cuba's first [foreign] friend." In 1892, Jews in Key West established a Cuban Revolutionary Club, "Kehillah Isaac Abravanel," and made donations to it. Martí himself addressed the group, invited by brothers José, Max, and Eduardo Steinberg. Some funds were also raised by charging admission to a series of baseball games between teams of Cuban exiles and local players. One of Martí's most famous phrases, from a letter written the day before his death and appropriated by the Cuban Communist Youth movement (UJC), was "Mi onda es la de David" (My slingshot is David's), an Old Testament reference used by Martí, as interpreted by Castro's ideologues, to illustrate Cuba's task of "confronting the Goliath of United States imperialism."[5]

Dozens of Jews served with U.S. military forces during the brief Cuban military campaign of 1898 and the subsequent occupation of the island from 1902 to 1909. Some remained as part of the new expatriate U.S. colony attracted by the island's economic possibilities. Freedom of worship was decreed under U.S. occupation; Jewish religious services were held on the island as early as 1904. In August 1906, eleven of the American Jews who had come to Cuba established a synagogue, the United Hebrew Congregation.[6] This congregation, which was affluent from the start and which survived until the middle 1960s, conducted services in English following the liberal Reform movement based institutionally in the United States. Many of its early members were Yiddish-speaking Romanian-born Jews who had emigrated to the United States and been naturalized before going to Cuba. Other U.S. citizens, descendants of German and other Central European Jews who had come to the United States in the middle nineteenth century, gravitated to Cuba from places like Jacksonville, New Orleans, and Key West, where they had been engaged in manufacturing and commerce with Cuba from the U.S. side.[7]

Some of the members of this group attained remarkable personal success. Frank Maximilian Steinhardt, born in Munich in 1864, emigrated to the United States and enlisted in the army. He served in Cuba as a sergeant; in 1902, he was named consul general, a post he

1. City of Havana, from the casino, ca. 1887. Courtesy of Archives and Special Collections Department, University of Miami, Coral Gables, Florida.

held under the occupation until 1907. While still employed by the U.S. government, he purchased the Havana Electric and Urban Transit Company through a loan reportedly from the Archdiocese of New York. By the time he died in 1938 he had been president of Havana's electric utility, Polar Brewery, and several other businesses.[8] Another American Jew, Harry Engler, was a "wildcatter" entrepreneur working in Key West. The owner of a schooner, he was hired by the U.S. Navy to run the Spanish blockade and to carry arms to Teddy Roosevelt's forces. He was well paid, but he contracted a case of yellow fever, and his ship was quarantined when he returned to Florida waters. He established himself in Cuba during the U.S. occupation, starting a successful business exporting Cuban-grown vegetables to U.S. ports. Although his business was headquartered in Jacksonville, he urged others, including his daughter and son-in-law, Jennie and Herman L. Beller, to settle in Cuba in 1923. Beller built a successful bronze foundry and became a Jewish community leader. Several of the American Jews in Cuba were tobacco brokers. The Barouch brothers (Ernest, Marcos, and Isidoro), originally from Turkey, established a commercial house, French Brothers. They were part of a wave of thousands of adventurers, entrepreneurs, homesteaders, and people simply in search of new opportunities who poured into Cuba under the U.S. occupation from January 1899 to May 1902.[9] Some became wealthy in tobacco exporting. Eventually they branched out into retail businesses and manufacturing, becoming employers, in fact, of most of the impoverished Jewish immigrants from Eastern Europe who arrived during the 1920s.

The Jewish entrepreneurs eventually learned enough Spanish to get by, but their community remained a U.S. enclave. The U.S. Army, which pacified Cuba without engaging Cuban forces in any significant way, had attempted to make Cuba a de facto U.S. protectorate. Americans who came to settle and to invest in the economic recovery were not only welcomed but aided by protection under the Platt Amendment and by a favorable reciprocal trade treaty signed in 1903 by which the tariff on Cuban sugar exported to the United States was cut 20 percent in exchange for Cuban reduction of tariffs on U.S. goods. Despite fraudulent elections to Cuba's Congress and sporadic violence, the marines—based at the new U.S. base at Guantánamo Bay—stood ready to come in when needed, and the business climate for Americans flourished, although by the early 1920s Cuban nationalism had revived.[10]

American Jews in Cuba tended to keep to themselves. Their United Hebrew Congregation enjoyed the highest status of any Jewish religious body in Cuba, in part because it functioned as if it were located in Jacksonville or Boston, contracting English-speaking rabbis and cantors from the United States and England. The congregation welcomed as guests American Jewish visitors to Cuba and involved itself in respectable charitable and cultural activities. The American Jews did not ingratiate themselves with the less-fortunate immigrants: they did not invite them to their congregation and, according to a visiting official from the New York-based Hebrew Immigrant Aid Society (HIAS) in 1925, contributed little for local immigrant relief.[11]

The American Jews, like the hundreds of other Ninety-Eighters, Americans who had come to Cuba as investors, managers, salespeople, engineers, and entrepreneurs during the protectorate and after, established small factories, retail stores, and import-export firms. Some started cigar factories, bringing in equipment as well as skilled workers from Tampa and Key West. The children of the most affluent went to the best English-speaking private primary schools on the island: the Ruston Academy and St. George School. Others attended the Cathedral School, run by the Episcopal church. Others were sent to the most respectable public high schools, including Havana's Instituto del Vedado. Some of the American Jews ultimately gained admission to the Miramar Yacht Club, one of the Big Five elite clubs in Havana, although Ashkenazic and Sephardic Jews were always excluded. U.S. Jews never penetrated the innermost sanctums of high Cuban society, government, or business, but they became influential and considered Cuba a friendly and welcoming land.[12]

Partially in response to the military occupation command's call for immigrants to bolster Cuba's work force to accompany heavy anticipated foreign investment in the island, but mostly as a direct consequence of factors driving Jews from the lands of the Ottoman Empire and North Africa as well as from the Hapsburg lands of Central and Eastern Europe, immigrants from many countries began to arrive in force beginning in 1902. Most were from Spain, but the immigrants also included Sephardic Jews from the former Turkish empire and from North Africa, and Ashkenazic Jews from pogrom-ridden Russia, Poland, and Eastern Europe. By 1910, Cuba had three separate Jewish communities—English-speaking Americans, Yiddish-speaking Ashkenazim, and Sephardim, some of whom spoke French but most of whom spoke Ladino, late-medieval Castilian mixed with liturgical Hebrew, the language of the Jews exiled from Iberia. As World War II approached, these groups were joined by a fourth—German-speaking Jewish refugees expelled from or fleeing the Nazis in Central Europe. One of the major characteristics of Cuban Jewish life was not only that Jews sought to preserve their identity as Jews, but that there never was a unified Jewish community, not even during the 1950s, a decade of prosperity and accommodation. A final group of Jewish displaced persons, many of them concentration camp survivors, came in 1946 and found Cuba hospitable.

After World War II the Jewish colonies began to mix more readily, although differences in language, custom, and religious observance among the various elements within the community remained strong. The postwar years brought prosperity and stability for a good portion of each of the separate Jewish colonies. Few Jews were any longer impoverished; many, despite continuing hardships during the 1920s and 1930s, managed to enter successfully the privileged world of the Cuban middle class, although not all became equally affluent. Some did not succeed and remained ghettoized within the crumbling buildings of Havana's walled Old City, left behind by the more successful Jewish families who moved to elegant parts of the city or to the suburbs. Some left to take up residence elsewhere in Latin America; a few emigrated to Israel. But after the 1950s, when most Jewish Cubans left the island in the wake of Fidel Castro's Revolution, they would look back with nostalgia and longing for the amiable world they had left behind. Their gratefulness to the Cuban people for accepting them never wavered, even after they had left Cuba under Castro for the United States. Despite all of the difficulties in earlier decades and again after 1959, Cuba had been one of the friendliest and most welcoming host countries for Jews in the Western hemisphere.

The generation of Cuban Jews that came to maturity between 1945 and 1959 felt itself Cuban; its members were comfortable with the sights and sounds of their country. They also maintained strong ties to their Jewish roots; they socialized within Jewish groups and selected marriage partners from within their religious community. Their immigrant parents and grandparents had found things much more arduous. They encountered a society dominated by traditional aristocracies determined by birth. They found a weak system of public primary education that lacked both commitment to Cubanization and goals to motivate students to achieve upward social mobility. The work climate, in a country at the mercy of world agricultural prices, was harsh, although many immigrants succeeded after expending enormous energy in the form of hard work. For external as well as internal reasons, then, Cuba's Jews remained in their separate groups even as they climbed the economic ladder into the middle and professional classes.

We have good information about the lives of those who identified with the Jewish community, but we have far less knowledge about arrivals who disclaimed their Judaism, drifted away indifferently, or became lost in the general population through outmarriage. Harry Sandberg, visiting Cuba in 1917, on behalf of the American Jewish Committee, estimated the number of acknowledged Jews in Cuba at about 1,000, with perhaps an equal number of persons born Jewish also living on the island.[13] He may have missed as many as 4,000 more Jews of Sephardic background who are believed to have come to Cuba before this time (see appendix 1).[14] One can only guess how accurate were sources of information, as Jewish communal associations—except for the American Jewish colony—were only forming at the time.

Tropical Diaspora is a study of what Miguel de Unamuno called *"intrahistoria,"* or inner history. It attempts not simply to chronicle the experiences of Cuba's Jewish immigrants, a richly diverse group whose members brought with them a broad range of ordeals and cultural baggage, but to capture the flavor of their lives.[15] It not only considers Cuban Jewry as a community that shares common experiences with other immigrant groups functioning inside Cuban culture, but it pursues the meaning of Cuban Jewish life within the context of Cuban, Latin American, and world history, especially as events affected Jews compelled by circumstance to migrate and find new homes. The study is not a filiopietistic chronicle of the saga of Cuba's Jews, but an analysis of the experience of the Jewish immigrants and refugees in the Cuban context. It acknowledges Cuba's uniquely open character that, despite a rough-hewn political legacy inherited from colonialism, assured that new arrivals were treated with decency and, almost always, with respect.

The Migration

Cuba, the largest and most westerly tropical island in the Antilles, always enjoyed a singular and central status in relations between Europe and the New World, especially with the United States, only ninety miles away on a line from Cuba's northern coast to Key West. When Christopher Columbus landed at present-day Havana on October 28, 1492, he saw "the loveliest land ever beheld by human eyes."[16] Blessed with rich alluvial soil on gently rolling land, with mountains rising only 3,000 feet on the extremes of the island, Cuba became one of the most prosperous agricultural colonies in the New World.

Historical accounts of the Jewish colony's evolution on the island emphasize Jewish "connections with Cuba" by considering as Jews many people who may or may not have considered themselves members of the Jewish faith. This includes persons whose ancestors had converted to Catholicism and who were brought up as Catholics, and also persons suspected of having been marranos, or New Christians, those who maintained outward signs of Christianity while remaining covert Jews.[17] Thus even if Columbus is not claimed as a Jew, his expedition's interpreter (a *converso*, or converted Jew), Luis de Torres, is so claimed, in part because of his knowledge of Hebrew and Aramaic. New Christians associated with the Aragón court helped finance Columbus's first voyage of discovery. After the passing of the age of discovery and the transition to colonial empire, the island became one of the mainstays of Spain's economy and one of its most prized possessions.

The Holy Inquisition, to be sure, once it was established in Havana in 1519, frequently accused conversos of being secret Jews, although aside from one sixteenth-century case, Escalante, it did not issue sentences until after 1610, when Cuba fell under the jurisdiction of the Cartagena Tribunal. In 1613, a wealthy merchant in Cuba, Francisco López de León, was convicted of "Judaizing" and executed, his large fortune confiscated. During the next decades, many suspected Jews were arrested and fined, and some were burned at the stake, although in spite of this inhospitable climate Cuba also served briefly as a refuge for Jews and Calvinists fleeing Dutch Brazil after the Portuguese expelled them in 1654. Some of these Dutch Jews as well as New Christians settled in Cuba and established a thriving trade in the Antilles.[18] Some Jews were forcibly baptized in Europe before being shipped to the New World, including some Jewish women who "accompanied the armed forces that Spain sent to the island" in the early sixteenth century.[19] The last victim of the Inquisition in Cuba was a marrano sailor, a Captain Miranda, who was arrested for bringing with him a Hebrew Bible from Curaçao. Agustín Morell de Santa Cruz, the eighteenth-century bishop of Havana, may have been a crypto-Jew. He was concerned with social inequalities and abuse of political power and in this sense identified with the position of the Cuban-born Creoles, whose New World birth relegated them permanently to lesser status than that of the Spanish-born *peninsulares*. In 1764 Morell introduced bees to Guanabacoa, east of Havana, from Saint Augustine, Florida, after the English occupation of Cuba. The Inquisition accused him of Jewish activities, and he had to fight ceaselessly to deny the allegations.[20]

Chroniclers also have asserted, without hard evidence, that Jews developed the island's sugar industry. During the ten-month English occupation of Cuba in 1762 the occupiers opened the colony to international trade and permitted Jewish merchants and suppliers of goods to accompany the English fleet led by Admiral George Pocock, who had captured Havana the previous summer. One of them, Jacob Franks, a New York–based merchant, worked with other Jews from the Caribbean (including Hernando de Castro from Guadeloupe, called the father of the Cuban sugar industry) to establish trade links with ports in neighboring islands, British North America, and Europe. Thousands of slaves were imported to Cuba under the British occupation, a practice that continued after Cuba reverted to Spanish control after the 1763 Treaty of Paris. Some Jews remained, permitted to stay under the liberal trade reforms of the Bourbon monarch Carlos III. At least twenty Jewish men are known to have lived in Havana in spite of the refusal of the holy office to recognize their status legally. Although the Inquisition survived formally on the island until 1824, by that time it was too ineffectual to arrest them or drive them out.

For centuries, slavery had dominated Cuba's export economy. Some slaves could purchase their freedom, but most worked and died on the rural plantations, where treatment was harsh and frequently brutal. In 1860 Cuba produced 1.7 million tons of sugar, roughly a third of the world's sugar export supply. In the words of Herman Merivale, a leading British political economist lecturing in 1861 at Oxford University, the island was "the wealthiest and most flourishing colony possessed by any European power."[21] Its inhabitants, however, did not have easy lives. Free persons of color occupied an ambiguous place in the social equation: before the 1840s they were used by the Spanish administration as a counterweight to the slave population, but in the 1840s authorities accused mulattos and blacks of fomenting slave rebellion, with the result that many members of what Rebecca J. Scott calls the "precarious free colored middle sector" of small-scale farmers, tenants, and squatters were killed or driven from their land.[22]

Although Cuba did not receive the large numbers of European immigrants that flocked to the United States (and, later, to Argentina, Uruguay, and Brazil), Cuba did take in some 123,000 Chinese indentured laborers, almost all Cantonese, from 1853 to 1874, other workers from Jamaica, Haiti, and Mexico, as well as hundreds of thousands of Spaniards escaping from peninsular rural poverty, especially in northwestern Galicia. Cuba imported against their will hundreds of thousands of African slaves, as many as 816,000 between 1512 and 1873. More than 850,000 new Europeans, mostly

2. Rural sugar workers, ca. 1900. Courtesy of Archives and Special Collections Department, University of Miami, Coral Gables, Florida.

from Spain, came from 1898 through 1932, and some 250,000 Haitians and Jamaicans between 1913 and 1927.[23] The large numbers of Africans transformed the racial composition of the island. By the end of the nineteenth century, a high percentage of the Cuban population was mulatto or black.[24]

Through the late nineteenth century, Cuba, as Spain's major colony in the Western hemisphere, remained tightly controlled administratively from the city of Havana, located at the mouth of an excellent harbor on the northwest coast of the island. Provincial Cuba, by contrast, was overwhelmingly rural, although a relaxed kind of urban life dominated by planters characterized the capital cities of the major provinces: Santiago de Cuba on the eastern end; Camagüey in the west; and Matanzas, east of Havana. Few of the members of the rural sugar aristocracy and affluent middle class of merchants supported the Ten Years' War (1868–78), the terrible precursor to independence that cost as many as 200,000 Cuban and Spanish lives out of Cuba's 1.5 million.[25] The struggle against Spain linked the eastern Creole bourgeoisie, cattle ranchers from Camagüey, and sugar planters from Oriente province and involved soldiers from all social classes, including slaves, and volunteers from across the Caribbean. Jewish historical sources maintain that some Jewish soldiers fought with rebels led by Antonio Maceo and Carlos Manuel de Céspedes, although this claim has never been proven. There were, however, a few Jewish officers in the patriots' Army of Liberation. A handful of individual European Jews participated, including Louis Schlesinger, a Hungarian who had fought in Hungary's 1848 revolution and who ended up in the United States. Schlesinger became the chief of staff of General Narciso López's annexationist army of non-Cuban mercenaries. In 1850 he led an attack on the northern city of Cárdenas, but the invasion failed. Another American Jewish mercenary, August Bondi, was recruited by López. He survived and ultimately joined the Union forces in the U.S. Civil War. Still another soldier, Carlos Roloff y Mialofsky, known as Akiva Rolloff, a "Ukrainian Jewish adventurer," became a general in the Cuban army and the first finance minister after independence.[26]

Historians attribute the *insurrectos'* failure to their limited goals. To secure the support of prosperous sugar barons, the separatists refused to decree slaves emancipated, although some slaves were freed at war's end in 1878 when Spain amnestied all Cuban insurgents and gave freedom to all slaves in uniform at the time of the peace settlement. The motivation was possibly to guarantee the continued support of the United States for the independence effort against Spain. The separatists also avoided the type of fighting that might lead to destruction of property, as they hoped to attract foreign investment to the island after independence was achieved.[27] In all, the end of the war did not bring stability. The debate over abolition lingered until 1886. Planters clamored for increased political participation, and many chafed under Spanish rule and high tariffs imposed not only by Spain but by the United States.[28] For Cuban-born Creoles, the dream of independence did not die but simmered below the surface. It exploded in 1895 in Cuba's War of Independence. But only through U.S. intervention, egged on by that country's yellow press, was victory achieved in 1898.

On the national level, by the time the military occupation by U.S. troops ended in May 1902, Cuban independence was more nominal than real. General Leonard Wood, the head of the military occupation, called Cuba the "new California . . . a brand new country" and backed his words with decrees opening Cuba to investment. This policy flooded Cuba with new competitors for the island's resources.[29] Agriculture, transportation, mining, electric power, banks, and communications all fell under the control of foreign interests. The first electrified trolleys in Havana, for example, were installed in 1901 by a company headed by Frank M. Steinhardt. U.S. capital invested in Cuba in 1902 exceeded $200 million, with nearly another $100 million invested by the British, French, Germans, and other Europeans.[30] The island became a "laboratory" for U.S. political engineering. President Theodore Roosevelt sent troops to annul the 1905 elections and to conduct new balloting under the control of mixed U.S.-Cuban commissions. Cuban elites had little choice but to accept this paternalistic arrangement whereby the United States maneuvered to install Cuban governments able to guarantee stability, law, and order.[31]

Although the Americans built roads, schools, and port facilities and, through the aid of Cuban physician Carlos Finlay, helped eradicate yellow fever, Cubans resented the U.S. Congress dictating conditions for the withdrawal of U.S. military troops in 1902 through the Platt Amendment to the Cuban constitution. Its wording limited Cuban sovereignty and permitted military intervention when internal order was considered to be endangered. During the second intervention, 1906–9, the U.S. provisional governor, Charles E. Magoon, meddled in local politics by granting *botellas*, or sinecures, to favored individuals. The Platt Amendment also ceded to the United States a permanent naval base at Guantánamo Bay. Forced to vote for these provisions, Cubans felt humiliated. Nor were the threats of intervention empty: Washington intervened three times before 1917, invited by one or another Cuban political faction, and threatened to do so again in 1933. U.S. domination, in turn, came to be seen as the root of Cuban dependence, economic backwardness, and social injustice.[32] Many non-Cubans who came to the island after 1898 seeking economic opportunity saw the Cubans as carefree, yet some sensed an undercurrent of anger. Culturally as well as politically, Cuba's development was stunted. Cuban life during the twentieth century came to reflect its status as an American protectorate.[33] Nationalistic outrage did not originate with Castro; it had been brewing for decades.

Although Afro-Cubans, who had been emancipated from slavery only twenty-two years before Independence, made up the majority of the population, the Creole colonial elite, mostly Spanish in descent and concentrated in the cities, continued to dominate the country.

In rural areas and in the slums of the cities, Afro-Cuban culture, which was mostly Yoruba (called Lucumí on the island), remained prominent and in some ways merged with Spanish culture, but the dominant national expression remained European with a heavy dose of U.S. influence. Spanish immigrants who came to Cuba after 1900 helped preserve Cuba's European roots, especially through their participation in the rituals and festivities of the Roman Catholic church. On the other hand, among members of the lower classes, *santería* worship, imported from Africa, preserved the ethnic character of non-Christian culture.[34] Once they became accustomed to black Cubans, Jewish immigrants tended to look at them as did the Cuban elite: as simple people, meriting respect as individuals, but always expected to behave passively and never to be considered social peers. Even Sephardic immigrants, to whom blacks were not as exotic as to the East Europeans, dealt with Afro-Cuban culture from a distance. During Carnival, for example, they watched the exultant, costumed processions of blacks (*comparsas*) wind through the streets, but they did not participate directly in the revelry.[35] Cuban society separated whites and nonwhites: in towns and cities, blacks and mulattos performed manual labor or worked as maids; in the countryside, they toiled in the fields or worked as servants.

By the time of the first wave of immigration in the second decade of the century, times had been hard for residents of the island for at least two generations. Unemployment had reached desperate proportions in the late 1880s. In the early 1890s, 35,000 Cuban cigar makers were without work, and another group of roughly the same number were reduced to part-time employment.[36] The struggle for independence had left Cubans exhausted and vulnerable. Vagrancy and homelessness had increased steadily since the 1880s, when rural families had been forced to relocate to the overcrowded cities as a byproduct of the fighting in the countryside. Bandits and cutthroats roamed the interior of the island, making traveling wholly unsafe. Beggars crowded city streets, and prostitution flourished. Robberies, assaults, and petty theft increased throughout Cuba; in 1885, Louis A. Pérez notes, more than two hundred brothels were registered in Havana, most in the waterfront and industrial sections of the Old City close to where the immigrants lived; by 1900 the number of brothels had increased by half.[37] Women remained in the home and had few opportunities for formal education. The 1901

3. Horse-drawn cart taking elite children on a rural outing, ca. 1895. Courtesy of Archives and Special Collections Department, University of Miami, Coral Gables, Florida.

Constitution denied the vote to women; literacy requirements kept blacks and most mulattos disenfranchised. Foreign-born immigrants were not permitted to attain citizenship. Afro-Cubans, displaced after a war in which many had fought valiantly for independence, received neither equality nor social justice.[38]

Years of fighting had ravaged the countryside. Cuba's population had declined from 1.8 to less than 1.5 million by 1898. Hundreds of thousands perished; others fled. The brutal *reconcentración* policies of Spanish General Valeriano Weyler from February 1896 to October 1897 forcibly removed tens of thousands of rural inhabitants to towns and cities. (It is claimed that Weyler's camps were described by Spanish-language historians, and it has been alleged that in 1931 Adolf Hitler told an interviewer, Edouard Calic, that he knew about them and thought that they were a good idea.)[39] The economy and the national educational system lay in ruins. Cuba stood ready for rebuilding and in this sense was less likely to object to efforts by immigrants to settle and start businesses, although they received no direct encouragement.

Cuba differed from other Latin American countries in the large numbers of foreigners who came and went and the considerable share of the island's economy that stayed in foreign hands. Outsiders visiting Cuba viewed the American Jews who formed part of the local elite with the same disdain that they accorded Cuba's own upper classes. After all, to the U.S. soldiers of Teddy Roosevelt's San Juan Hill charge, in the words of Waldo Frank, "Cubans were 'niggers,' and they disdained them. . . . The Spaniards were the enemy, of course, but they were white, and when they were captured, the Americans lavished courtesies upon them to stress their difference from the 'mongrel' Cubans for whose freedom they were supposedly at war."[40]

In later years, high-society visitors from the United States and Europe looked down on Cuba's elite even more because of that elite's acceptance of Cuba's relaxed attitudes toward racial mixing in the lower classes, and because of their tolerance toward Jews. Foreign journalists like Basil Woon, who lampooned the behavior of Cubans at their posh clubs, described Jews and Cubans alike in a patronizing manner he considered humorous. This common treatment signaled, in a way, a perception that Havana Jews like Nathan I. Heller ("fine chap and great story-teller . . . known as 'Fat'. Sells tires and talks like a Cuban") had achieved membership in Havana's business gentry. Woon described Benhamin Projan in *When It's Cocktail Time in Cuba*: "Enterprising Jewish lad from New York on way to becoming Cuba's biggest merchant. Great favorite with the Irish. Athletic. Champion chicken-eater of Cuba. Can be seen eating his lunch at Telégrafo Hotel."[41]

The Immigrants

The atmosphere of post–World War I Cuba was unique: blacks and mulattos, immigrants from Jamaica and Haiti, Chinese, and Jews served a dual elite of Creoles and the largest foreign expatriate business community in the Americas. Immigrant Jews competed for the same jobs and chances to make a living as other immigrant groups, most directly with newcomers from Spain and, to a lesser degree, with the descendants of the Chinese coolies brought to Cuba in the mid-nineteenth century as laborers. Just as in the case of many of the Jews, the fear of onerous military service had encouraged tens of thousands of male Spaniards to come to Cuba to avoid being sent to Morocco to fight Spain's colonial wars in 1859, 1893, 1909, 1911, and 1920. They also came seeking economic betterment. Just as with early Jewish immigration to Cuba, especially Ashkenazic, men outnumbered women two to one. Most of the new arrivals from Spain were illiterate and wore rope-soled sandals because they could not afford shoes.[42] More than 600,000 came from Galicia between 1902 and 1922.

Some 300,000 Chinese landed on the island before World War II, far more than any other immigrant group except the Spanish. By 1870, Chinese peddlers and merchants were to be found in nearly every Cuban provincial town. Chinese mercantile houses opened in the larger cities, as did a Chinese bank, a theater, and, in 1885, a vaudeville company. There were also gambling dens in the Barrio Chino in which one could buy imported opium. Chinese immigrants suffered from discrimination more than any other immigrant group except the Jamaicans and Haitians, but over time many of their children prospered; by the 1950s, some had entered the professions. Upper-class attitudes toward the Chinese incorporated the usual racist stereotypes. "With centuries-old Asiatic guile," a commentator wrote, "they circumvented the immigration restrictions, got work and protection through their particular Tong, worked like beavers, saved their money and bought passage for their relatives, and paid whatever had to be paid for illegal entry."[43] Few knew or cared that most of the chinos had been imported as coolies, and that although they were often humiliated at Tiscornia, the immigrant station, not many had entered Cuba improperly. As in the United States, some Chinese opened hand laundries and restaurants and became truck farmers, supplying vegetables and fruits to urban markets. In contrast to Chinese in the United States, however, many in Cuba, especially men, married black and mulatto Cubans, a response to the friendlier racial atmosphere in the Caribbean.

The largest immigrant bloc was the *gallegos*, largely impoverished immigrants from Galicia who graduated from manual labor to shopkeeping, ultimately controlling much of the retail commerce on the island, especially in the food business, from neighborhood *bodegas* (grocery stores) on virtually every corner to shops selling dry goods and furniture. Later, the more successful upgraded their businesses, becoming importers of Spanish products that they in turn sold to gallego shopkeepers.[44] This contrasted with the pattern followed by many Jewish peddlers, who, rather than sell finished imports, purchased scraps of cloth and other remnants in bulk from foreign suppliers and then set family members or other immigrants to work manufacturing items for sale from door to door. This quickly produced commercial rivalry with the Spanish immigrants, straining relations between the two groups as time passed. Bodegas were not only all-purpose grocery stores but served a social function: patrons exchanged gossip over aperitifs (nearly all bodegas had a bar), cashed checks, bought lottery tickets, and played dice, and the shops served as offices for fixers who could be hired to work out trouble with the bureaucracy. The bodegas integrated Spanish immigrants and their Cuban neighbors and customers into a social network; peddlers remained outside. In rural areas, the thatched-roof bodegas with their wooden counters with canned goods and staples and their kerosene-fueled white refrigerators were, in the words of a visitor from Havana, "oases in the desert."[45] Peddlers and door-to-door salesmen risked provoking the enmity of these shopkeepers and always retained the air of outsiders in a social system rooted in camaraderie and lubricated by networking.

Bodegas usually extended credit to regular customers and offered small loans, but on the whole it was the immigrants—Jews, Arabs, a few Chinese—who reached out aggressively to lower-class Cubans. The peddlers hawked their goods at much lower prices than stores charged for their imported goods.[46] Immigrant peddlers in the countryside carried their merchandise on their backs or, if they could afford it, used mule-drawn carts to transport their wares of clothing, trinkets, religious objects, buttons, sandals, or anything else they could buy cheaply for resale. Their best-sellers were ties, shoes, stockings, and shirts. They visited sugar mills, small towns, and even isolated farmsteads. Shopkeepers accused them of robbing the poor. But the street vendors eventually succeeded because of their tirelessness and their willingness to sell cheap goods to virtually anyone. The commodities they sold raised the living standard of the poor, bringing them for the first time the chance to buy, on credit, items manufactured domestically.[47] Jews were not the first peddlers in Cuba. The gallegos plied merchandise on the streets as early as the mid-nineteenth century.

4. Street peddler, Havana, ca. 1897. Courtesy of Archives and Special Collections Department, University of Miami, Coral Gables, Florida.

By the mid-1920s, many peddlers would acquire horsecarts or even automobiles and sell inexpensive goods manufactured by local Jewish workshops. This development foreshadowed the intensified competition between Spaniards and Cuban Jews later in the 1920s and through the stormy 1930s. When the Jewish street vendors accumulated enough capital to open small retail stores, they sold fabric by the yard or ready-made clothing; some sold jewelry, notions, perfumes, and furs. Sephardim ran shops catering to tourists, selling souvenirs and semiprecious stones. Most of the immigrant-run shops were *quincallas*—bazaars selling every kind of sundry from buttons to candy to toilet items. These stores competed directly with the older Spanish-owned bodegas on Muralla Street, but eventually the Jewish-owned stores, willing to charge lower prices, drove the others out.[48]

Unlike the Spaniards, who could go back and forth between Spain and Cuba as they wished, or who could return permanently to their homeland, as some did in preference to remaining in Cuba, most of the Jewish immigrants had no place to return to. Few wanted to, or would have been able to, go back to their Old World countries, where they had suffered discrimination, fear, and hardship. Many of the immigrants, especially the East European Ashkenazim, had come to Cuba intending to leave for the United States as soon as possible, and many did leave before 1924. But the goal of entering the United States was unexpectedly blocked by the 1924 Immigration and Naturalization Act passed by Congress, a stronger version of the restrictive 1921 National Origin Act. As a result, the Cuban Jews would, as a common Yiddish phrase put it, "make their America in Cuba." Many would prosper, become manufacturers, and before long move up a notch on the economic scale by becoming suppliers of goods to peddlers and salesmen in small rural towns.

Jews from Turkey, the lands of the Mediterranean, and North Africa comprised Cuba's first major Jewish immigrant wave. They were Sephardim, from the Hebrew name for Spain, Sepharad. Their language was Ladino, also called Judezmo, or Judeo-Spanish, a form of Renaissance Spanish mixed with Hebrew and written in Rashi letters, a variant of Hebrew script.[49] Their ancestors had been among the more than 200,000 Jews expelled by the Catholic monarchs Ferdinand and Isabella from that newly unified country after the fall of the Muslim Empire at Granada on January 2, 1492, following four centuries of Jewish life there. A small minority were Greek-speaking Romaniote Jews, the remnant of Byzantine Jewry. In all, some 140,000 Jews lived within the borders of the Ottoman state in 1911.[50]

Some of the Sephardim were descended from Jews expelled from Portugal in 1497. Those who accepted nominal conversion became known as New Christians. The holy office hunted out anyone suspected of Jewish practices and, over the years, any remaining Jewish identity was diluted and ultimately lost. Spanish Muslims were similarly forced to convert to Catholicism, becoming known as *moriscos*. A century later, after a failed revolt, the 500,000 remaining converted Muslims were expelled. One of the few localities that offered safe haven to the exiles was the Ottoman Empire, whose monarch, Sultan Bajazet II, opened its doors. Most of the Sephardic Jews who came to Cuba in the early twentieth century were descendants of the late-fifteenth-century Jewish exiles from the Iberian peninsula.[51]

Sephardic emigration to Cuba differed from patterns elsewhere in the hemisphere in that the number of Jews from Syria and Lebanon was relatively insignificant. Syrian Jews preferred to go to Mexico or to New York, where there already were established communities. As a result, only from thirty to forty Syrian Jewish families settled in Cuba, where for at least a generation they maintained their own Syrian identity and customs.[52]

On the other hand, Cuba received more emigrants from Turkey than did any other part of Latin America, and most of these were Jews. Families from two small cities predominated: those from Silivria (Silivri), near Istanbul, who gravitated to Camagüey, and those from Kirklisse (Kilklareli), near Edirne, who tended to settle in Oriente. In 1904, Silivria had 1,200 Jews and Kirklisse about 1,000.[53] They were affected adversely by two events: first, the new policy, put into place in 1909 by the government (dominated by the Young Turk movement), to impress non-Muslim young men into the Ottoman army for twenty or thirty years; and second, economic deprivation caused by the Balkan Wars, which broke out in 1912. Some left because they were frightened by Turkish treatment of Armenians and worried that Jews could be next. Those who decided to emigrate chose Cuba deliberately, probably because of their language's similarity to Spanish. In these years, they could have entered the United States and most other countries without difficulty.

One of the earliest Sephardic arrivals in Cuba, an Algerian Jew named Hadida, established a burial society in 1906.[54] At first it was linked to the new United Hebrew Congregation, but the American Reform Jews and the Mediterranean Jews rejected each other's religious practices. In 1911, in fact, six Sephardic immigrants were refused entrance to the hotel where the Americans were holding their services. In response, the Sephardim formed their own synagogue, which opened formally in November 1914 as the Congregación Unión Israelita Chevet Ahim, accompanied by several auxiliary bodies, including a social welfare department. Sephardic religious and communal associations were established in Manzanillo, Ciego de Ávila, Camajuaní (in Santa Clara Province), Colón, Camagüey, Guantánamo, Artemisa, Matanzas, and Santiago de Cuba in Oriente province, the easternmost point of the island, 972 kilometers from Havana.[55]

Most Sephardic Jews, especially the more affluent, observed the

5. Provincial street scene, Santiago de Cuba, ca. 1899. Courtesy of Archives and Special Collections Department, University of Miami, Coral Gables, Florida.

basic tenets of Jewish law out of tradition rather than out of conviction.[56] The most affluent Sephardim from the great cities of the Mediterranean and Middle East often spoke French in their homes. They used lamb, not chicken, on the Sabbath. Before they emigrated, they had sent their children to schools run by the Alliance Française and to programs at the Alliance Israélite Universelle, modeled on the French association.[57] In Morocco alone, about 5,000 Jewish children in 1913 attended schools run by the Alliance. They were not always welcome. Some Alliance teachers called them uncouth savages "in whose minds all the world's superstitions seem[ed] to have taken up residence" and sneered at their "tiny brains" and "corkscrew curls" and skullcaps.[58]

At the height of Sephardic immigration, in 1921, the drop in sugar prices forced many of the new arrivals to abandon their small shops and other businesses and to become peddlers. The declining economy brought hardships because in the more traditional Sephardic families women did not work; the burden of earning a living fell exclusively to the men and older boys. Sephardic families sent their sons to the *meldar* (also called *hevrah* by Jews from Salonika), religious day schools dedicated to the study of sacred texts in Hebrew and to teaching daily prayers and ritual. Girls were not traditionally sent to school, but they learned reading, prayer ritual, and homemaking with the aim of raising "the condition of women to pay homage to their intelligence and to their domestic virtues."[59] Families in which girls had not been given formal education in Turkey almost always sent their daughters to schools, often public ones, in Cuba.

These descendants of the exiles from Spain and Portugal who had settled in Bulgaria and other lands of the Ottoman Empire maintained traditions that the Ashkenazim from Eastern Europe found unsophisticated or suspect. They had large families and were, in the eyes of the Ashkenazim, clannish. The East European Jews were clannish as well, of course: they tended to settle in the same places as immigrants from their old village or province. But more Ashkenazim came alone, many as young men, whereas most Sephardim emigrated in family groups, so that their tendency to cluster in families was more noticeable.

Most Ashkenazim came from nominally observant backgrounds but some, especially young men isolated from their families still in Europe, professed socialism and atheism. Their *kehillah* (religious community) was based on the European model of a loose confederation of communal groups to address common problems, but it took on a more secular than religious countenance. Being Jewish in Cuba among the Ashkenazim was an ethnic issue, not a religious one. It meant giving money to charity and belonging to the synagogue and to other Jewish organizations. (The first Ashkenazic synagogue, Adas Israel, opened only in 1925.) Even the president of the Orthodox synagogue kept his store open on Saturday.[60] Observant immigrant families strove to eat only kosher food: anthropologist Ruth Behar tells the story of her *turco* grandfather who once during the late 1930s brought home an excellent cut of beef for his wife to cook. She refused to take it, although her husband argued that they were too hungry to be choosy; ultimately she threw the piece of meat out the window into the street. But by the postwar period, Jewish families readily ate nonkosher food outside their homes, and in most cases in their own kitchens as well. Some women made kosher tamales and *caldo gallego* by substituting chicken or beef for pork, but being kosher, in Behar's words, stopped "at your doorstep."[61]

The Eastern European immigrants tended to be divided between Zionists and those indifferent or opposed to the Zionist ideal, linked internally by their Yiddish culture bolstered by a knowledge of Russian and Polish. More than half were unmarried young men, most of whom had expected to use Cuba as a way station to the United States. Virtually the only place they mingled with Sephardic Jews was in the Jewish Market in the Old City. The language of exchange was Yiddish, and even some Cuban and Chinese vendors selling their wares from behind wooden stalls in the market learned Yiddish phrases to deal with their customers. Many of the immigrants were terribly poor. In a country where extended family ties often meant the difference between finding and not finding work, immigrants fresh off the boat speaking little or no Spanish had to take the most menial and demanding jobs offered to them. One, an electrician from Lithuania, was turned down at every electric-supply shop he visited, presumably because no one could understand him, for there was a shortage of skilled labor in Cuba at that time. He was finally hired by a sugar mill to haul wood on a six-hour-on, six-hour-off, around-the-clock work schedule, but was forced to quit after a few days when his shoulders became so sore he could not walk. He was paid in coupons, redeemable only at the refinery's store, and earned barely enough to eat. Many remained poor for years. The Cuban office of the HIAS helped some, but most had to fend for themselves or rely on charity from the Froien Farain, an association formed by Ashkenazic women.

By World War I, the only institutional link between the East European and Mediterranean Jewish communities was the Asociación de Jovenes Hebreos de Cuba, the YMHA. It was founded in 1916 by Polish-born David Blis, who studied for the rabbinate at the theological seminary at Breslau and later at Hebrew Union College in Cincinnati but had never completed his studies. Blis's career was unusual. After wandering through South America and Mexico, he had arrived without resources in Cuba. Eventually, he came to serve Havana's United Hebrew Congregation as elected lay leader, functioning as a rabbi while he made a living working for a jeweler. He spent an enormous amount of effort on Zionist activities, although his English-speaking congregation tended to be less enthusiastic, not wanting to risk embarrassment by speaking out on Jewish issues. Blis attempted to organize a public demonstration of support for Jewish Palestine, writing columns for *El Día* and other newspapers, but both the Syrian Arab colony and Cuba's American Jewish community opposed the effort. Blis was not very tactful. In a 1918 article in the prestigious literary journal *Bohemia*, he charged Jewish immigrants to the island with denying their Jewish origin, complaining that there was "no compulsion [for them to] live like marranos."[62] His larger goal was nevertheless achieved. On January 20, 1919, he addressed the Cuban Senate, whose Foreign Relations Committee drafted a friendly resolution declaring its "keen interest and sympathy" for the efforts of the Jewish people to achieve self-determination and national independence. The resolution was adopted unanimously by the entire Senate.[63] (Blis met with less success in his own community. The 1930 summary report from the Keren Hayesod, a Zionist charity, on contributions during the seven years of its existence since 1922 listed Cuba at the bottom of the list of fifty-three countries worldwide, with total donations of less than £800.[64] Still, as Haim Avni has pointed out, Cuba's Jewish community was small and impoverished. Its £800 contribution nonetheless exceeded that of Hungary, which had some 445,000 Jews.) The YMHA was doomed by an internal division between young men of the Sephardic and Ashkenazic colonies. After a brief period of activity, the association disbanded in mid-1919. (Blis also attempted to drive out the rings of East European Jewish prostitutes who had been brought to Havana with the wave of Ashkenazic immigration. Because single men predominated in the migratory stream, prostitution prospered on the fringes of the Jewish colony in its early years.)[65]

The Ashkenazim and Sephardim continued to carp about each other, and the American Jews looked down on both. When a young immigrant girl from Russia announced her intention to marry the son of a successful Sephardic Jew, her brother objected vehemently, asking her sarcastically, "How can you marry an Arab?" The couple persisted and were married by the Sephardic rabbi in the home of the bridegroom's family.[66] Sephardic women were said to be addicted to astrology and liked having their palms read by gypsies. One Sephardic mother was said to have spent an entire week in bed because a hostile planet was menacing her star, and she was afraid to get up lest a disaster occur. Ashkenazim were surprised that some Spanish Jews used local healers as often as they called physicians. American

Jews scoffed at the practice among both Sephardim and Ashkenazim of arranging marriages by negotiations between families; allegedly, the choice of a bridegroom usually depended on the size of the dowry the girl's parents could offer. Young men sent to the Americas to make their fortunes courted their intended brides by mail, with weeks or months between letters. In cases where dowries were not large, many wed second or third cousins for convenience, for these unions kept the community together.[67]

The East Europeans and the Sephardim seldom mixed. Just as the East Europeans disparaged the Sephardim as turcos (Cubans tended to call them *moros*, or Moors, confusing them with Arab immigrants), Sephardim disliked the Ashkenazim. "They scrimp and save and are terribly cheap," said one prosperous Sephardic woman, "and their women work; they don't even have maids."[68] Sephardim, who were more observant religiously than their East European counterparts, called the Yiddish-speaking Jews *polacos*, the same faintly anti-Semitic term used by non-Jews.[69] Sephardim, who tended to be apolitical and to withdraw within their family groups, were alarmed at the left-wing ideology of Yiddish-speaking socialists, Communists and labor organizers, and at the willingness of the radicals to remonstrate in public. Each group over the years disparaged the other. An irony not lost on the influential English-speaking American Jewish colony was that both groups were much alike in that they maintained Old World customs considered archaic and even embarrassing. In each group, marriages were often arranged by family members or through brokers; young men or their families frequently sent for young women from their villages back home to marry. The majority of both groups were impoverished, came from ghettoized origins, and within their family circles clung to their old ways. Neither group sought Cubanization, preferring to preserve their ethnic and linguistic identities, even as each disparaged the other group for doing the same in its own way.

Cuba's Jewish colony grew to nearly 5,000 by 1923, although the community remained in constant flux: thousands entered Cuba each year as thousands left for the United States. Most of these entrants were Ashkenazim, a good portion of whom had come during the peak years of Cuban immigration, 1919–21.[70] Horace Kallen, the U.S. social activist who visited Poland in the mid-1920s, had found half of all Jewish skilled and unskilled laborers out of work

6. Arch of Triumph at entrance to Obispo Street, Old Havana, 1910. Courtesy of Archives and Special Collections Department, University of Miami, Coral Gables, Florida.

there, "outcasts of the economy." The number of Jewish businesses in eastern Poland declined by 60 percent. New licenses were issued only for street peddling.[71] Out of these conditions the Ashkenazim streamed to the New World. During the postwar boom caused by high sugar prices on the world market, some of the immigrants who had managed to consolidate and enlarge their fortunes became manufacturers. They hired other immigrant Jews for vaguely philanthropic reasons but mostly because they would accept low wages. Many of their employees endured sweatshop working conditions, especially during the early 1920s when particularly destitute Ashkenazic Jews began to arrive in large numbers and would take virtually any jobs. But there was little alternative. Cuban industry was narrowly based, concentrated in sugar refining, cigar making, and other agricultural products; workers were badly paid, and foreigners were excluded at first from the trade unions. As a result, the immigrants had to carve out entirely new industries, accumulating capital on their own and for the most part hiring fellow immigrants as workers.[72]

Roots were put down even among the Ashkenazic Jews, most of whom had come to Cuba seeking to reemigrate to the United States. The community sponsored a contingent of Jews to march in Havana's Armistice Day parade on November 11, 1918, constituting the first display of Jews as an ethnic-religious group in Cuban society. Life was hard for the immigrants, but they were aided by communal self-help organizations and in some cases by assistance from relatives in the United States. The Sephardim found Cuba comfortable and did not seek to leave, and the East European Jews, although disoriented by the heat and tropical conditions and the fluid, lethargic pace of Cuban life, remained deeply grateful to their Cuban hosts, for Cuba was almost without exception better than the cold lands from which they had been driven. Cuban Jewish life until 1924, when the doors to the United States slammed shut and immigrants could no longer use Cuba as a place of transit, was characterized by a relatively large number of immigrants compared to the receiving Jewish population.[73]

2 ✡ THE IMMIGRANT GENERATION

Most immigrants, especially the East Europeans, brought nothing with them in their small suitcases except clothing, often garments suited for winter, and stifling in tropical Cuba. The Ashkenazim were as diverse as their origins, although most were from small towns and villages in the old Russian Empire's Pale of Settlement, the area of forced residence out of which more than a million fled during the troubled years between 1880 and 1914. Others came from cities and centers of learning. Nearly all were destitute, unskilled, and linked to their fellow Ashkenazic immigrants by their use of Yiddish. There had been terrible economic hardship in Eastern Europe, and Jews suffered doubly because anti-Semitic laws restricted possibilities for employment. One man's father left his village near Minsk in White Russia because there was so little food that he had to forage in the forest for roots to boil for soup for his family.[1] From 1910 to 1917, nearly 4,000 of these economic refugees passed through Cuba to ports in the United States; only several hundred had remained on the island.

Postwar Immigration

After World War I, immigration to Cuba from North Africa and the Mediterranean slowed, while immigrants from Eastern Europe arrived in ever greater numbers. On the island, both Sephardic and American Jews enjoyed the postwar prosperity, which reached its height in 1920. Thirty or so U.S. Jewish families derived their living from sugar exporting. So lucrative were the years 1918–20 for the island's elite of agricultural producers, exporters, and their clients that Cubans coined the name the "dance of the millions" for the boom. Word reached the Old World rapidly: immigration to Cuba jumped nearly ten-fold from prewar numbers (340,241 in 1920, 148,361 in 1921). These numbers fell in 1922, but rose again to 79,361 in 1923 and 85,288 in 1924, when perhaps a third of the new arrivals were Jews [see Appendix].[2]

The immigrants who arrived after World War I and in the aftermath of the Russian Revolution were no longer able to gain entry easily into the United States and settled in large numbers in Latin America, especially in Argentina and Brazil.[3] They came to Cuba only when other doors began to close; in 1919, there were only 2,000 Jews in Cuba, many more having entered and then left. Those Ashkenazim who did settle in Cuba did not maintain the Orthodox religious observances that characterized life in the shtetl. The immigrants tended to be young, single men, subject to immense pressures both from the relaxed Cuban society around them and from the necessity to fight to make a living. Immigrants working eighteen hours a day in sweatshops or sewing piecework goods in their rented rooms could not afford the luxury of eating kosher food (although it was available) or observing the Sabbath. Cuban workers were paid on Fridays, and merchants, eyeing lower-class people with suspicion, felt that they had to collect the money owed to them on Saturday or the paychecks would be spent.

The Ashkenazim tended, as a result, to retain their Yiddish language and culture while relegating religious observance to nominal status. The Sephardim, in contrast, more frequently came with their entire families, sometimes with dozens of fellow immigrants from their old villages. Sephardim remained nominally observant, although they strayed from orthodoxy as time passed and in response to local conditions, especially in the provinces. The first Ashkenazic synagogue was organized only in 1925; the first rabbi, Zvi Kaplan from Bialystock, came only in 1928 (see figure 7). No sooner did he arrive than his new congregants squabbled, and he left with some of the membership to form a new synagogue, Knesset Israel. Rabbi Kaplan, who died in 1939, played only a small role in the Jewish community. It was left to his son, Sender M. Kaplan, to build on his foundation by becoming the secretary of an association of Jewish organizations in Cuba organized during the 1930s.

Even before they arrived, the Old World Jews took advantage of

7. Rabbi Zvi Kaplan, Havana, ca. 1926. Courtesy of Sender M. Kaplan.

networking. A person desiring to immigrate, usually a young man, wrote to a contact in Cuba, who in turn obtained an affidavit, or claim paper, promising to provide for the newcomer. Employers furnished the affidavit, thereby requiring the immigrant to work for them at whatever wage the employer agreed to pay and under any conditions, at least until the greenhorn figured out that Cuban officials did not care what happened to foreigners after they landed. Once established, the immigrants sent for the rest of their families, often a hardship, because sea passage cost $100, and new arrivals were required to bring with them at least an additional $10. Kosher meals were available on some ships for extra payment; in most cases, observant Jews ate only bread plus the food items they managed to bring with them on the voyage. Many who were strictly observant refused to leave Europe because they feared that they would have to eat *traif*—food that was not certified as acceptable. Occasionally, young women came alone. Generally they faced even greater hardships than young men because they could not live alone lest their reputation be sullied. Most moved in with relatives, although the Ashkenazic community supported a Maydl Heim, a residence that housed from forty to fifty young immigrant women living on their own.

Cuba and its lush tropicality were strange to the newcomers but not unfriendly. Jews who had in the Old World been cursed, restricted in their actions, and at times physically endangered found Cuba a place where ordinary people treated them with respect. Peddlers (*clientelchiks*, in Yiddish) who trudged from door to door were often offered coffee, even though their wares were usually *shmates* (shabby goods). Neighbors helped foreigners even though they did not always understand them, and even though they were often terribly poor themselves. Cubans were accepting and compassionate, and the immigrants never forgot that.

Virtually all of the newcomers entered Cuba through the immigration and customs station in Havana at Tiscornia, Cuba's Ellis Island. The rest entered at smaller ports. Some remained interned for a week or more until someone, usually from a Jewish relief agency, came to post a bond guaranteeing that the immigrant would not become a burden. Facilities were pleasant enough, with shaded outdoor pavilions in which people could wait, but the system was frightening for the newcomers, who usually found Cuba bewildering. A few Jewish shysters who had gained influence among immigration personnel visited Tiscornia regularly, fleecing arriving compatriots through a variety of schemes based on the newcomers' ignorance of how the system worked. Some were charged whatever money they had with them to expedite successful transit of the emigration process, as the new arrivals did not know that the Cubans allowed everyone to enter shortly after landing.[4]

Despite the live-and-let-live attitude shown by Cubans to the immigrants and the lack of overt discrimination in Cuban society, the initial experiences of many of the newcomers—whether they were Jews, Spaniards, or Asians—were frequently arduous.[5] Many brought with them only one or two muslin shirts or dresses; some of them had to sleep on benches in the Parque Central or in cheap flats in Havana's red-light district near the docks. Those with relatives in the United States fared somewhat better; they occasionally received money orders for five or ten dollars, small amounts that nonetheless went far. Others—single men without trades and families with children—endured great hardship. Most U.S. consular officials were not only uncooperative but considered the Jewish immigrants a "direct menace" to U.S. immigration laws. One vice-consul claimed early in March 1930 that 14,000 immigrants had entered the United States through Cuba during the 1920s and that many had done so illegally.[6]

At least 7,000 Jewish immigrants landed between 1921 and 1923 and as many as 20,000 in 1924, creating a bewildering world within the neighborhoods, mostly in Old Havana, where the Jews settled. Because so many of the new arrivals before 1924 emigrated to the United States within a few months of landing, conditions in the Jewish colony were fluid to an unprecedented degree, with almost all seeking temporary jobs to earn money for food and lodging. Most of the immigrants in this stream were from Russia and Poland. Steamship companies there, faced with loss of steerage-class revenue, began to publicize in the European Yiddish-language press Cuba's lack of immigration laws and Cuban officials' practice of permitting anyone disembarking in Havana harbor to remain. As U.S. immigration laws did not restrict immigration from Latin America, persons remaining in transit in Cuba could remigrate to the United States after a year's stay. A total of 24,000 Jews—the equivalent of about 5 percent of the Jewish population of the United States—resided in Cuba by the end of 1924.[7] Yiddish speakers among them called the island Akhsanie Kuba (Hotel Cuba), considering it a temporary home until they could enter the United States, the *goldene medine* (golden country), only ninety miles away. In 1924 Congress enacted the new Immigration and Naturalization Act, shutting out immigrants from the impoverished nations of Europe and closing the Cuban loophole. Jews who had hoped to live in the United States now found that they had to remain in Latin America permanently. Although some in Cuba emigrated to other Latin American countries and some—how many we do not know, although there were probably several thousand in this category—entered the United States illegally or by marrying U.S. citizens, the rest chose "to make their America in Cuba."[8]

Cuban elites did not seem to resent the thousands of immigrants, although they acted to turn back unwanted blacks who had come from Haiti and Jamaica, attracted during agricultural labor shortages. Immigrants from the Old World clustered mainly in the cities: nearly a third of Havana's residents were foreigners. Almost 85 percent of all of the Ashkenazic immigrants were males, most of them unmarried. Only a fifth were skilled workers. Most were lower-class, poorly trained artisans. A Polish consular official remarked that the emigrés were forced to live in extreme penury and received treatment "worse than blacks."[9] Unmarried men worked fourteen to eighteen hours a day as pieceworkers sewing in sweatshops.

Most had to start out as street sellers, and at the lowest rung of even that occupation: as *klappers* (door knockers), their merchandise received on credit.[10] The indignity of having to sell on the street grated on the immigrants, however relieved they were to be in a land characterized by indifference, not centuries-old hostility. Some of the Ashkenazim had studied in Polish or Russian yeshivas and had expected to subsist, as they had in Eastern Europe, as wards of the Jewish pious community. But in Cuba, secular life predominated, and in any case there were not enough resources in the Jewish immigrant community to support these religious men. The minority of immigrants who had been skilled artisans were unable to find work. Personal disorientation was common. The Cuban Yiddish press, Judith L. Elkin notes, "abounded in stories of Jewish peddlers enticed by fishermen and 'taken for a ride' in the shark-infested waters surrounding the island."[11]

> Yet every ship, reminisced a Jewish newspaperman later, speaking about the early 1920s, brought 600–800 Jews, and they all became peddlers. He added: We lived twenty or thirty families to a house, and candle-lighting on the Sabbath gave out that we were Jews. But where were our horns? Then Eskimo Pie hit Cuba, and we all carried ice boxes around Havana resting on our stomachs, bound with a cord to our shoulders. Since the name "German" had by now worn out, the Cubans began calling us "Eskimo Pie."[12]

The immigrants' work ethic set them apart from most of the rest of the population. This was true not only for the Jews but for other new arrivals, especially the Syrio-Lebanese and Chinese. Immigrants drove themselves mercilessly to establish themselves and to improve their lot. Itinerant salesmen trudged the streets, singing out in broken Spanish, cajoling, smiling at children, and haggling over price when this would spur sales. Peddlers made a dollar or a dollar and a half on good days, virtually nothing on others. A wooden box with goods to sell cost ten or twelve dollars, a steep investment for near-indigent newcomers. On the street the peddlers were often robbed, set upon by vagrants, or beaten by the police when they did not pay protection money to claim their territory. Violence against itinerant vendors peaked during the late 1920s, when city merchants tried to drive them from the streets. New arrivals who could not afford even carts or pack animals carried their wares on their backs or on outstretched arms. When they entered restaurants at lunchtime—usually a good time to sell—seated diners would sometimes throw crusts of bread or wadded up paper at them. The mortified peddlers, desperately attempting to make ends meet and to get started in their new country, plugged on.

That the overwhelming majority of Jewish immigrants sought to leave for the United States, and that counting was carried out in the form of rough estimates by agencies representing small entities within the Jewish community (Sephardic, American, and Ashkenazic institutions remained completely separate), meant that no one really knew how many Jews were in Cuba at any given time (see Appendix). More importantly, Jews who drifted beyond communal borders, who married Catholics, or who assimilated by failing to maintain any formal links to the community were simply not counted. In Judith L. Elkin's words, they "got themselves free." The nominally Orthodox Jews were not interested in conversion; intermarriage in Cuba, therefore, became overwhelmingly a one-way street.[13] As a result, the number of immigrants and residents of Cuba counted as Jews dropped dramatically as soon as the immigration-emigration turmoil stabilized. Between 1925 and 1935, Cuba's Jewish colony was counted at about 5,000, roughly the same as it had been in 1917. Thousands more, the products of Europe's Jewish ghettos, assimilated into the Cuban landscape and vanished from community sight.

Conditions were made more difficult by the foundering economy. Prosperity proved to be short-lived, as sugar prices crashed to prewar levels by the end of 1920. Banks called in loans that had been based on anticipated high prices. Many banks were forced to close, including Cuba's largest, the Banco Nacional. The First National City Bank of New York took over sixty failed Cuban sugar refineries. High unemployment persisted until the government acted to shore up prices by cutting sugar production.[14] General Gerardo Machado y Morales, a hero of the War for Independence, won election as Cuba's fifth president in 1924 by promising continued economic progress through continued price supports. Many hoped that Machado's administration would be an improvement over earlier corrupt regimes, and many of his projects were popular with voters. Machado supported women's suffrage and spoke in favor of broadening the democratic base, although some believed these positions to be a ruse simply to enhance his popularity. Machado's 1927 constitutional convention extended his presidential term from four to six years, permitting him to succeed himself, but on a legal pretext it refused to grant the vote to women. Disappointed feminists participated in the formation of an anti-Machado opposition that organized in 1928 and that ultimately helped bring down his tyrannical regime in 1933.[15]

Cuba's economic fortunes did not improve as President Machado continued in power. He used the economic crisis as justification for extending the presidential term, and "through bribes and threats," in historian Jaime Suchlicki's words, he subordinated Congress and controlled the election.[16] The bottom had dropped out of the international sugar market in 1926, and merchants lost customers, suppliers defaulted, and wages dropped. Tens of thousands of rural *precaristas* (squatters who worked on land they did not own) migrated to Havana, taking up residence in thatched-roof shantytowns with walls of corrugated aluminum dubbed *llega y pón* (come and squat), seeking jobs on the docks or as day laborers, or becoming beggars.[17] Others swarmed into *solares*, old unoccupied tenements subdivided into tiny single rooms rented to entire families. Day-old bread cost five cents; a restaurant meal, forty-five or fifty cents. Immigrants lived alongside mulattos and blacks, many of whom practiced santería, the exotic spiritist religion imported from Africa. Among the native poor, women made up most of the heads of households, often sending their children to church-run orphanages when they could no longer support them. Still, not all were affected equally by the downturn. Cuba may be suffering an economic crisis, editorialized the newspaper *Comercio* in August 1927, but $80 million is collected annually in tax revenue, there are a "fabulous" number of expensive automobiles in the capital, Cubans are "crowding transatlantic steamers in search of recreation in Europe," Havana has scores of shops selling luxury items, and its citizens spend in excess of $2 million a month on lottery tickets. "Only Cubans are to blame for the invasion of foreign capital," remarked the editor, "because they prefer the easy life of the Capital and safe mortgage investments to the vicissitudes of commerce and industry.[18]

The 1926 fall in sugar prices interrupted the government's price support program, which was replaced with a production control arrangement based on reducing the harvest season from 136 to 87 days. This effort to force prices up by limiting output applied a brake to the Cuban economy. Living standards, which had been rising since 1923, suddenly dropped, especially in the rural provinces. These circumstances had a negative impact on immigration. Jewish organizations in Europe began advising would-be emigrants to Cuba to make other plans, but the island remained the most attractive option for East Europeans so destitute that even raising money for a ship passage was a heroic achievement.[19]

In spite of economic constraints, as many as a thousand Jewish immigrants found employment in the shoe and clothing factories owned largely by the American Jewish businessmen in Cuba. The rest still had to make their living as peddlers selling neckwear, aprons, engravings of Catholic saints (estampas), or ribbons, or by performing odd jobs. But the formerly tolerant atmosphere deteriorated rapidly in the wake of Machado's reelection campaign in 1928, which, unlike that of 1924, was characterized by strident nationalism. Police in Havana, as well as Machado's secret police, the Porra, usually used to combat street demonstrations and to attack his enemies, harrassed peddlers, arresting them for blocking traffic. In addition, the fee for peddlers' licenses was raised from $6.25 to $125 per year, although in Havana the peddlers formed a protective league (Shutzfarain far Peddler) that succeeded in having the fee reduced; the league broke up when some of its more stalwart members were able to leave street vending behind.[20]

Worse, new labor laws enacted in Havana under Machado and extended to the entire nation under the revolutionary regime of his successors reserved a majority of jobs to the native born, forcing many immigrant workers who had gained a toehold in manufacturing or artisanship to become pieceworkers at home. This pressure transferred them, in Judith Elkin's words, "from the domination of the foreman to the tyranny of the supplier of their raw materials."[21]

8. Obispo Street, Old Havana, ca. 1910. Courtesy of Archives and Special Collections Department, University of Miami, Coral Gables, Florida.

Hundreds of immigrants lost their jobs. Yet a new wave of some 4,000 East European Jews came to Cuba between 1925 and 1935, mostly working-age males but also women and children. They came for political reasons, to seek economic improvement, and in some cases to reunite with family members. Cuba was for them a land of opportunity, but they found themselves subject to worldly temptations. In some cases, mothers arranged for overseas Jewish brides to be sent from the mother country for their sons who had begun to go out with Cuban women.[22]

Cultural Adaptation

Culture shock was great for the Yiddish-speaking Jews, whose language was totally unlike Spanish and who were utterly unaccustomed to the tropical climate. Many of the immigrants were given new, Cuban-sounding names by officials when they arrived, so that Moishe (who became Moses or Morris at Ellis Island) became Máximo at Tiscornia. According to one source, observant Jews anxious to keep kosher but unable to pay for kosher meat lived on bread and bananas when they first arrived.[23] Newcomers, especially those from Northern Europe, were tormented by the noise and infernal heat and humidity; they slept huddled beneath mosquito nets or, worse, kept the wooden shutters closed to prevent swarms of biting insects from invading at night. They found local Catholicism incomprehensible, blended into daily life in a myriad of ways. Public spaces were dotted with shrines, for example, and in such sacred locations as the *ceiba* (kapok) tree in the corner of the Plaza de las Armas the ground was strewn with coins and food and the soil bulged with buried offerings; strollers passing by circled the tree three times and made a wish.[24] Such colorful practices made an impression on the immigrants, who took them as signs that they would never be able to feel entirely comfortable in a place with such beliefs.

9. Prado promenade, Havana, ca. 1910. Courtesy of Archives and Special Collections Department, University of Miami, Coral Gables, Florida.

As time passed, the immigrant generation was caught up in a classic dilemma: they continued to speak their native tongue to their spouses and others of their generation, but to their children and to strangers they often spoke Spanish, because their children insisted. Anthropologist Ruth Behar's description of her relationship with her Russian Yiddish grandfather, "a man of the Jewish European old world," is touching: "My relationship . . . was lived entirely in Spanish. To be more exact, it was lived in a combination of Spanish and silence. My grandfather did not talk very much. He was suspicious of people who talked very much. He spoke telegraphically. His most memorable utterances were his jokes, tellable only in Spanish." The " 'sound' of a colonized voice," she observes, carries traces of the effort to resist speaking.[25]

The Sephardic immigrants fared better than the Ashkenazim. They came from lands where the climate was similar to Cuba's, and their language, Ladino, was close enough to modern Spanish that they learned it fairly easily. Some had been well-to-do or even wealthy. The Mediterranean Jews established shops adjacent to sugar refineries and in provincial urban centers. By extending credit to peasants, they made it possible for many to purchase manufactured goods that they could never have acquired previously. The merchants permitted them to pay off their accounts in amounts of twenty, twenty-five, and thirty cents a week. Unlike the East European Jews, who were almost all poor when they arrived, some of the Sephardim came from prosperous backgrounds. These families integrated without too much difficulty into provincial life. The father of Sara Bembenaste (on the right in figure 10) owned a shoe factory in Constantinople before emigrating. In Havana, Chevet Ahim's first *Jajam*, or rabbi, Gershon Maya, arrived in 1923 from Silivria in Turkey. His son settled in Camagüey to serve the community there, and Santiago de Cuba's congregation imported its own rabbi from Edirne. At home, these Jews spoke Ladino, a blend of medieval Castilan, Hebrew, Turkish, and Greek, written in Hebrew script.

Sephardim represented a continuation of the Babylonian tradition, whereas Ashkenazim followed the tradition of Palestinian scholars. Worshippers in the Sephardic Old Temple faced the rabbi's pulpit from three sides, and the Torah scrolls were kept behind the rabbi near the wall. Women walked up two steps to their special

10. Sara Bembenaste and cousins, Sagua la Grande (later, Las Villas) Province, ca. 1925. Courtesy of Lucia Suárez.

section, although they remained in full sight of the men. *Kohanim*, men descended from the traditional priestly caste, prayed with their heads and upper bodies completely wrapped in prayer shawls. In wedding ceremonies, the bride and groom faced the audience, their heads covered by a single prayer shawl. In the *bishola*, a naming ceremony for infant girls, the godmother, who was by tradition a virgin, dressed in a wedding gown complete with veil and held the child in her arms to be presented to the rabbi. Women held a protected place in Sephardic society. When a family's resources reached the point where they no longer had to work, they remained in the home. Ashkenazic Jews (and some Sephardim) complained that Sephardic women were too sheltered. Isidoro Behar, who came to Cuba from Turkey in 1915, recalled that "if a Sephardic man became ill, his brother would have to take care of him because his wife would not know how."[26] Although improbable, the example reflects the memories of at least some of the more elderly members of the Sephardic community. Within most Sephardic families, customs brought from the Old World survived for decades. In some cases, marriages for daughters and sons were arranged by family elders as late as the 1950s.[27]

Many immigrants, especially Sephardim but also Ashkenazim, Arabs, and Chinese, chose not to live in Havana but took up residence in interior towns. Chinese immigrants were almost invariably men, many of whom settled in the rural interior and married black Cuban women; their offspring were called *chinitas*. Later many relocated in Havana, where a Chinatown (Barrio Chino) developed. Although relations between Arabs and Jews were generally cordial, the two groups rarely intermarried. Neither Arabs nor Jews condoned intermarriage with blacks, although most immigrants eventually adopted the relaxed attitudes of the Cubans and generally became tolerant of Cubans of all shades of skin coloration.

Because they seemed able to adapt more readily to Cuban life and because they had a more tightly knit family structure, the Sephardic Jews, although poor, received less attention from international Jewish welfare agencies than did the Eastern Europeans. Of the Eastern European Jews in Cuba in May 1924, 90 percent were found to be without work by a study conducted by the U.S. National Council of Jewish Women. The council provided charity through the offices of HIAS, which opened a branch in Havana in 1921 after efforts by the women's auxiliary's Ezra Society of the United Hebrew Congregation (UHC) were seen to be insufficient. The HIAS Cuban branch organized in New York the Jewish Committee for Cuba to Help Jewish Arrivals, funded by HIAS and the National Council of Jewish Women and assisted by the Emergency Relief Committee of the JDC. The committee then opened a Havana office on Calle Cuba. Its codirectors were Americans, and it engaged an American nurse and an office staff hired in Havana. Board policy was set in New York. The committee established ties with the U.S. consulate and others and with Cuban government agencies. It furnished medical aid and also channeled funds to Adas Israel. It subsidized the Sephardic Talmud Torah (religious school) Theodor Herzl School, ran an employment agency and a library, and dispensed loans. More than half of the Herzl School's pupils were sons of poor Ashkenazic immigrants, who were not charged tuition. Further responsibility for providing relief for the needy was delegated to the Ezra Society.

David Blis and the leaders of the UHC then took steps to form a new cultural association to serve the flood of East European Jewish immigrants. In September 1925 they opened the Centro Israelita (Hebrew Cultural Center) on Calle Egido, with Blis as president. The

HIAS in New York offered a monthly subsidy of $300. Blis then suggested that the center take over most of the tasks of the Jewish Committee for Cuba, which was hoping to wind down its activities, and a formal merger took place in March 1926. The group functioned as a multipurpose cultural, educational, and welfare society, sponsoring activities ranging from youth and sport clubs to orphanages and an antituberculosis league. Blis also edited a short-lived publication in Yiddish and Spanish.[28] A year later, the center sponsored a successor Yiddish-language journal, *Oifgang* [Exit], which published from 1927 to 1930 and 1933 to 1935. It generally favored Zionism, although except for an anti-Communist stance it took no firm ideological position. *Oifgang*'s editorial position was assimilationist. This represented a significant shift in the attitudes within the Jewish colony: for the first time, Cuba was seen not merely as a stepping-stone to emigration to the United States but as an acceptable host, stable and welcoming enough to become a permanent home.

The Centro Israelita also absorbed the Chevet Ahim's Theodor Herzl School, which grew from 34 Sephardic children enrolled to 125, most of them Ashkenazic. The Jewish Committee for Cuba and, ultimately, the Centro Israelita paid virtually all of the costs for the school. Borrowing from the model of other Latin American Jewish communities, especially Mexico's, its curriculum was secular, its teaching mostly in Spanish. Yiddish was also used, but never Ladino, and Hebrew was taught not as a conversational language but for liturgical purposes. Although fees were not high, many of the students had to work. Starting at the age of eight, Felix Reyler peddled newspapers two days a week after school, and on Fridays with his brothers sold lottery tickets, making the rounds of restaurants in Havana's Old City, Habana Vieja.

The school's decision to use Yiddish was in response to the demands of the East European immigrants that their language be maintained at least partially, although the New York–based Jewish Committee for Cuba's representative turned up his nose at the concession to the "'Yiddishistic' elements."[29] Sephardim, whose children spoke Spanish as well as Ladino, stayed away because their lack of Yiddish made it impossible for them to participate. Sephardic Jews continued to stay in the background and had little contact with the emerging coalition of Yiddish-speaking Ashkenazim in league with their English-speaking benefactors. Although UHC officers sat on the Centro board, most of the Americans remained "completely aloof from their Eastern European coreligionists."[30]

The leftist Ashkenazim, indifferent to worship and sympathetic to socialism, gave more support than did the other Cuban Jews to the communal cultural associations that sprang up within the colony. Yiddish culture flourished. In the early years, even before Yiddish-language newspapers and magazines began to appear, immigrants wrote poems and pasted them or nailed them to the high, thick seventeenth-century walls of the Old City; most were handwritten. A mimeographed Yiddish-language newspaper, *Dos Fraie Wort*, appeared in 1927.[31] Clippings from Yiddish newspapers sent from the United States were also posted, so that news could be shared. Wall writings included statements and commentaries on political and economic matters. Many Ashkenazim joined the Yiddishe Kulturgruppe, which met in the Parque Central. The Kulturgruppe put on plays and sponsored lectures and debates, usually in Russian but also in Yiddish. Fare ranged from traditional plays— Sholem Aleichem's *Chanuke Gelt* and Stuchko's *Herkules*—to farces like Silberzweig's *Ir Shwester* and Ornstein's *Mein Weib's Meshugas*. The year 1927 saw the first book published in Cuba in Yiddish on a Cuban theme: *Oif Inseksher Erd* (On Insular Soil), a book of songs. The author was N. D. Korman, a member of the Farain. During the 1930s he wrote another book, *Oif Zergliter Erd* (On Red-Hot Earth). Eliezer Aronowsky wrote *Tropish Licht* (Tropic Light).[32] During the late 1920s in Havana, East European immigrant children were taught Yiddish culture on Sundays by a Lithuanian-born immigrant teacher who barely spoke Spanish (fig. 11).

New social welfare programs were organized. Most of these were *Landsmanschaften* (mutual aid societies), just as had been the case in the larger cities of the United States.[33] Ashkenazic mutual aid (*Leihkasse*) societies, formed by more settled members of the East European Cuban colony, helped the most recent arrivals set themselves up as klappers. Groups of ten men each pledged cash for immigrants to allow them to buy fabric or other goods to hawk. Immigrant jobbers also supplied the peddlers with materials they and their families produced in small workshops or sweatshops. The system prospered because in Cuba, unlike Eastern Europe, most

11. Ashkenazic Sunday school class, Havana, 1928. Courtesy of José Winer.

transactions were made for the short term, in cash, and because once a salesman opened a store or a factory he could get a loan, usually from successful Jewish businessmen. Later, during the Great Depression, the mutual aid societies broadened into formal loan societies; subscribers deposited amounts ranging from $20 to $100 to be drawn upon by needy families in time of crisis.[34] There were also burial societies—*Chevra Kaddisha*—which accepted any Jewish person for membership unless they were considered "unclean" religiously—that is, profaned because of connection to illicit activities such as prostitution.[35]

Other associations included the Froien Farain, later renamed the Asociación Femenina Hebrea de Cuba, led by the wives of the first Ashkenazic factory owners and successful merchants.[36] The agency provided medicine, food, furniture, clothing, and other assistance to needy immigrants. To care for orphans within the colony, the Froien rented an apartment, which they turned into an orphanage and staffed with women who were alone and who had no jobs. From ten to twelve children were cared for at a time; some lived there through their school years and until they married. As a measure of the orphanage's success (and the spurt in the community's affluence), within a few years the enterprise was moved to larger and more sanitary quarters, and lice-infested mattresses and furniture were disposed of. Havana's Sephardim maintained a similar organization called Buena Voluntad during the late 1920s.

A permanent Ashkenazic cultural organization with a socialist orientation, the Yiddisher Kultur Tsenter, opened in Havana in May 1925 with classrooms and a theater. A year later it needed larger quarters and, with its move, adopted a Spanish name, the Centro Hebreo. Classes were based on the Workmen's Circle curriculum, and the center obtained a subscription to the Warsaw socialist newspaper, *Folkszeitung*. It maintained a lending library and brought Jewish entertainers and artists from the United States to perform. Yiddish-language broadsheets advertising performances were posted on the center's walls. As it flourished, it became evident that the Centro Hebreo's doctrinal independence would not last long. Bitterly opposed to the center's left-wing orientation, the American Jews' UHC board took steps to sponsor the center financially on the condition that if David Blis were made president, he would be allowed to purge its leftist leadership. Blis and another UHC candidate narrowly defeated two Communists, Naum Marmorstein and Josef Grinberg, members of Havana's Jewish subdepartment (Sección Hebrea) of the Communist party.[37] Blis set out to expand the center's role. The efforts to exorcise communist sympathies, however, failed, and for the second time a Blis-led organization was unable to smooth over internal divisions in the Jewish colony. The center's doors closed in August 1925 after only three months. Its left wing reorganized under a new name, the Kultur Farain–Unión Cultural Hebrea, which returned to the Workmen's Circle curriculum, sponsored another Yiddish theater group, and flourished, although its membership was relatively small. Most members belonged to the Sección Hebrea of the Cuban Communist party, itself subsidized by the Comintern's Latin American Bureau.[38] The Kultur Farain opposed religion and made a point of scheduling meetings and events on the Sabbath and on Jewish holidays. It held its first annual Yom Kippur Ball in 1925, a sacrilege for observant Jews.

Cuban Nationalism and Economic Depression

Although the Jewish community grew steadily, reaching a total population of around 13,000 at the end of the 1930s despite a stream of reemigrants (legally before 1924, illegally after), the country sending the largest numbers of emigrants to Cuba was Spain. Spaniards constituted more than two-thirds of all immigrants arriving in Cuba since 1902. Most Cubans felt comfortable with these arrivals, although they insulted them for their greenhorn ways and their language, which was Galician, not Spanish. The large numbers of Jewish immigrants during the 1920s, however, provoked an anti-foreign reaction among some members of the elite, who saw the continued influx as a barrier to the growth of Cuban patriotism. Other intellectuals, notably the Grupo Minorista (1924), took a broader approach to the goal of achieving pride in the *patria*, or nation. The writers and intellectuals in this group embraced José Martí's vision of a racially and ethnically united independent nation and turned to Afro-Cubanism for cultural inspiration. (In the early 1940s, one influential writer and member of Congress, Fernando Ortíz, proposed a model of Cuban society as a clearinghouse or melting pot, praising the contributions of all of the components of Cuban culture and criticizing the use of ethnic and racial slurs, including the terms *judiada* for Jews and *gallegada* for Spaniards, thus becoming a public voice for tolerance.)[39]

Republican Cuba in the 1920s and 1930s was wrestling with the need to establish autonomous political and economic institutions while maintaining law and order and a milieu pleasing to foreign investors and their governments. Members of the elite came to understand that public administration was the way to guarantee access to the foreign interests that controlled the economy. Government, as Louis A. Pérez reminds us, was the only Cuban enterprise during those years that remained wholly Cuban. Political parties vied for their share of elective offices and the patronage that went with them. Parties especially resisted incumbents' efforts to get reelected, because long-term incumbency blocked the source of livelihood for those out of office. This political fact of life explains the angry resistance in 1927–28 to Gerardo Machado's nomination to a second presidential term, although foreign observers—including the U.S. State Department—did not appreciate the rising tide of Cuban hatred for Machado and accompanying anti-U.S. nationalism.[40]

Functional unrest fed the discontent that had welled up during the early 1920s among the younger generation of Cubans born under the republic. They sought to do away with improbity in government and supported a greater measure of social justice, as well as nationalistic, antiforeign economic policies. Students, intellectuals, and labor leaders led this movement, and in 1925 the Cuban Communist party was founded. Some of its first members were Ashkenazic Jewish immigrants who had brought their combative socialism from Eastern Europe, where they had belonged to socialist unions affiliated with the Jewish Social Democratic party. Others were Communists who sought, in the words of Boris Sapir, a sociologist who lived in Cuba during the war, "social rebellion and . . . a better world."[41]

Not all Machado-era legislation hurt. The 1927 Custom Tariff Act aided newly created industries by granting government protection. This import-substitution measure made it possible for hundreds of small manufacturers, a large portion of whom were Jewish, to enlarge their output and to transform their workshops into factories producing shoes, clothing, jewelry, and other consumer items that previously had to be brought in from outside at high cost. Many Jewish immigrant factory workers displaced from their jobs because of the nationalistic laws started their own factories, hiring Cubans as well as other Jews.[42]

Trouble deepened after 1928 when Machado took his manipulated reelection as a mandate to rule despotically under martial law and disbanded Congress. Opposition politicians were assassinated. In December 1928 the Havana City Council banned peddlers from standing at street intersections, directly affecting the five hundred Jewish peddlers in the capital although not the three hundred estimated to be in the provinces. Fifteen peddlers were arrested and jailed for violating the ordinance two weeks later and were released after the Centro Israelita posted bond. Although Machado's tactics united political opposition against him, his appeal to xenophobic nationalism won him support in the streets. But he could not control the economic slide, and a quarter of a million salaried workers, responsible for the well-being of a quarter of the nation's population, lost their jobs as the prices of export commodities continued to plummet. Wages fell by half; in 1930 a general strike of 200,000 workers paralyzed the island and was extinguished only by repressive tactics, police brutality, and killings carried out by *porristas*—

members of a government death squad—and by a new secret police. Rural cane workers burned fields and destroyed harvests. Student protests led to violence and the closing of the university. Machado declared a state of siege throughout Cuba. Both he and opponents to his regime resorted to even more violent-sounding nationalistic slogans to rally public support, catching foreigners in a verbal crossfire. Cuba stood on the brink of chaos.[43] The conservative daily paper, Cuba's oldest, *Diario de la Marina,* called in a front-page editorial on January 5, 1930, for Machado's resignation, characterizing the political situation as "a fiction, a farce, a comedy without a joke, applauded by a clique that is beginning to tire of its sorry role."

All of this provoked great anxiety among all immigrants, who had little recourse but to toil harder and longer. Their presence in Cuban society had never fully been accepted by nationalists eager to blame someone for the economic crisis, and antiforeign sentiment rose as the Cuban economic depression intensified. The American Jews had always acted as go-betweens for the Yiddish-speaking newcomers. Virtually all contacts with Cuban society for the Jewish peddlers and craft employees came through Ashkenazim who sold cheap goods and trinkets. "Vendo corbatas baratas" (Cheap ties for sale) was a phrase heard so frequently in the streets of Havana that in later years Cubans remembered it in jokes, the phrase always spoken with an exaggerated Polish accent.[44] Another common phrase was "They earn little and sell much," alluding to the peddlers' low profit margin. Some of the more successful immigrants started up small businesses with capital borrowed from the American Jews. As long as there was a surplus of immigrant workers, Jewish businesses tended to hire them, not native Cubans. The most successful scraped together enough resources to manufacture simple goods: buttons, scarves, mirrors, neckties, cheap furniture. In some ways, Cuba's economic dependency helped the growth of home manufacture, for imported goods, always favored, were now priced too high. Not a few manufacturers from the United States moved their factories to Cuba during the early 1930s to take advantage of cheap labor and the domestic marketplace. Jewish employers usually paid less than their Spanish counterparts—six or seven pesos (dollars) a week during the depression, compared to ten—but the Jewish immigrants felt more secure working for a *landsman* even though they could eat only once or at best twice daily.

The more established Spanish-born merchants resented the business practices of the polacos and turcos (Sephardim as well as the Syrio-Lebanese Arabs), as they were called, some of whom opened small general stores. Immigrant tailors charged five dollars down for a suit of clothes in a city where men had to dress well but where many could not afford store-made goods; the tailors' profit was low, but they offered consumers an alternative to the Spanish-owned retail stores, where merchandise was imported. More than half a million Spaniards lived in Cuba by the end of the 1920s, 16 percent of the country's population.[45] Merchants from Spanish families in Cuba since colonial times dominated retail stores in the larger cities, while in the interior, immigrants from Spain opened combination dry goods–grocery stores. Shopkeepers lived in their stores with their families and employed only fellow Spaniards. Most merchants kept their establishments open for long hours. Often they reopened after the siesta time at 2:00 P.M. and remained open until 6:00 P.M. or even 8:00 P.M.; proprietors habitually remained until midnight to clean up and to prepare for the following day. Jewish-owned stores stayed open six days a week, including Saturday, the Jewish Sabbath.

The owners of El Encanto, Havana's most prestigious emporium, joined with others to protest the growing numbers of polacos wandering the streets.[46] The street vendors, of course, undercut the merchants substantially in price, although in many cases they created a new market: lower-class consumers who rarely had been able to afford the high prices of imported manufactured items in stores. Prices were forced down; for instance, the price of blue zephyr cotton shirts used by workers dropped from about $5.00 (a week's wages) to $1.50.[47] Credit selling also created lucrative opportunities for domestic manufacturers to produce and sell lower-priced clothing and accessories on the island. A Sephardic immigrant who had established a wholesale firm on Muralla Street won the contract to supply the Cuban armed forces with fabric for its drill uniforms.[48] All of this aggravated tensions between Jews and Spanish immigrants, and it set the stage for a confrontation with the Spanish store owners and the immigrant-baiting rabble rousers, loyal to General Machado, who coursed through the streets.

In other crafts, the immigrant Jews protected themselves by organizing affinity associations—not really trade unions. Borrowing from the tradition of European socialism, Ashkenazic Jewish workers organized associations in at least eight trades, from street photographers, painters, and mechanics to barbers and shoe-makers.[49] The Centro Israelita also organized businessmen's groups, the most long-lasting being the Yiddisher Sochrimfarain (Association of Jewish Merchants). The center helped lobby for better treatment of peddlers, although it did nothing to improve conditions for immigrants working for Jewish employers. As a result, relations between workers and employers were heated, the atmosphere of enmity contributing to the continued ethnic-based divisions within the Jewish colony.

As early as mid-1926, the left wing Kultur Farain led strikes against the Jewish industrialists. It won partial support from non-Jewish shoe workers affiliated with the older Cerro shoemaker's union, with good and bad effects. Employers agreed to improve working conditions, but the Machado government moved against members of the trade unions. During Machado's second term numerous Jewish trade union activists were arrested and the Kultur Farain harassed and, in 1930, shut down—a year after the University of Havana was closed. Five Jewish workers active in organizing labor unions were killed and more than sixty arrested, many of them deported. Many Cuban intellectuals and politicians of that era believed in the so-called Jewish-Bolshevik conspiracy whispered about but rarely mentioned publicly.

The depression was felt doubly in Cuba because in mid-1930 the United States passed the protectionist Hawley-Smoot Tariff Act, raising the duty on Cuban sugar imports. The effect was to drop sugar prices by another 60 percent. The harvest was reduced again, to 62 days, only two months' work for tens of thousands of sugar workers on the island.[50] This affected the Jewish immigrants in several ways. Peddlers and merchants who had pioneered selling cheap goods on credit to lower-class Cubans suffered, for customers could not continue to make payments. Manufacturers, in turn, were affected by the larger economic crisis. Newspaper editorials began to attack immigrant groups they considered undesirable. Spanish immigrants were generally accepted, but arrivals from other Caribbean locales were attacked, especially Jamaicans (jamaiquinos) and what was called the "Haitian element" imported for field labor in the countryside and to work on the railroads and new Central Highway.[51] Few newspapers openly advocated curtailing immigration for other groups, but undercurrents of hostility to Jews and Chinese surfaced from time to time. In the wake of this disquiet, government regulations required that all immigrants post $30.00 on entry, a measure aimed at unwanted West Indian and Caribbean arrivals (formerly, $7.50 was required, $10.00 for laborers). The profits usually went into the pockets of immigration officials, but this new financial obstacle symbolized the volatile atmosphere.[52] Havana's pro-Falangist newspaper, *Alerta*, began to publish translations of the Nazi Julius Streicher's anti-Semitic diatribes. In May 1932, as the tide of nationalist agitation mixed with antigovernment opposition neared its height, Machado outlawed all Jewish cultural, social, and religious activities. Panic briefly ensued. A few Jews, mostly labor organizers and Communists, went into hiding or fled to exile in the United States.

Revolutionary Transition and the Law of the 50 Percent

Open warfare and social unrest plagued the island in the 1930s until the downfall of General Machado's eight-year dictatorship and the five-month period of transition that became known as the 1933 revolution. The United States reacted to signs that Machado was weakening by sending its new ambassador, a former assistant secretary of state, Benjamin Sumner Welles, to ease Machado from power. The Cuban president, opposed by the Left as a "vile instrument of the Yankee Treasury," no longer served U.S. interests and therefore would have to step down.[53] Five days after he arrived in Havana in May 1933, Welles forced Machado to put into effect the steps that would turn the government over to the opposition. He accomplished this by maneuvering behind the scenes, by applying blunt pressure to Machado privately, and by secretly backing and manipulating opposition political groups. He forced Machado to curtail his presidential term by a year and promised economic concessions if Machado would speed up the election process. Machado's inability to establish order and control Cuba's economic plight forced him to cooperate. Raging, he was forced into a corner. Welles's mediation also manipulated the opposition by forcing underground groups to surface and organize legally and by supplying them with a vested interest in seeking U.S. backing for a new regime. A strike by bus drivers spread to other workers and paralyzed Havana for days.

By the end of the first week of August, the strike had taken on the impact of a revolutionary offensive. Machado attempted to rally popular support against the United States and its interventionist policies, but the armed forces did not back him. On August 12, he flew to exile in the Bahamas.[54]

When the provisional government headed by Welles's own choice, Carlos Manuel de Céspedes, failed to move decisively enough to restore stability, Welles withdrew his support and backed a new coalition of opposition groups. Céspedes brought to office his historic family name, but he was little more than a compromise candidate linked to neither party nor program. The political system was collapsing around him, and he lacked the means to deal with entrenched interests and the old-line political parties. Labor strife continued unabated, even though the new government curbed the repressive measures instituted under the Machado dictatorship. Cane workers seized sugar mills, declared "workers' soviets," and demanded sweeping revolution. Machado partisans returned to their government jobs, inflaming public opinion further. One of Céspedes' collaborators, Sergeant Fulgencio Batista y Zalvidar, led a protest on September 3 against deteriorating conditions within the army. The demonstration quickly turned into a mutiny. Two days later, on September 5, a civilian-military junta proclaimed a new provisional revolutionary government. For a time, Batista remained in the wings.[55]

The five-man junta took up the mantle of reform. One of its members was a physician and popular university professor, Ramón Grau San Martín, who quickly emerged as its chief spokesman. Antonio Guiteras, Grau's protegé, was perhaps a more determined social reformist, but he remained behind the scenes in Grau's cabinet.[56] The junta declared as its goal the establishment of democracy and a march "toward the creation of a new Cuba" and plunged ahead with a program of reform laws. It unilaterally abrogated the hated 1903 Platt Amendment that had preserved U.S. hegemony over the island, and it took measures to distribute public land to the landless. Foreign investors watched all of this with apprehension. Promises of nationalistic labor legislation and pledges for agrarian reform worried foreign employers and landowners. "So thoroughly had the United States penetrated Cuba," writes Pérez, "that it was hardly possible for any social or economic legislation to not affect U.S.

12. Fulgencio Batista embracing Grau San Martín, 1934. Courtesy of Archives and Special Collections Department, University of Miami, Coral Gables, Florida.

capital adversely." Welles, angered by the turn of events, warned the administration of Franklin D. Roosevelt that "radicals" had taken control of the Cuban army and government and that the new leaders were "frankly communistic."[57]

President Grau held steady to his regime's reformist policies and refused to cave in to Welles's threats of destabilization and the possibility of intervention. Hardly a Communist, he was linked to the right-wing newspaper *Alerta* and was considered personally sympathetic to the Spanish Falange. His championing of social reform was nationalistic and popular. He selected a cabinet made up of civilians known for their reformist orientation. His new regime struggled to cope with the strikes and sugar mill seizures and issued a number of nationalistic decrees that regulated and limited the freedom that foreign investors had enjoyed in Cuba for decades.

Although the United States opted not to intervene militarily, President Roosevelt and the secretary of state, Cordell Hull, supported their emissary Welles's advice to undermine Grau by withholding diplomatic recognition. Welles counseled opposition political groups to continue to resist and encouraged Cuban army officers to remain away from their commands. From September to November 1933, President Grau outmaneuvered the opposition and crushed a revolt of dissident military elements. In the aftermath of the revolt, the army was purged and reorganized.[58] Sergeant Batista was promoted to colonel and solidified his hold as chief of the army. The gap between civilians and military widened. Welles told Batista that he was the "only individual in Cuba today who represented authority."[59] Backed solidly by Welles and his successor, Jefferson Caffery, Batista constructed an alliance of anti-Machado forces, foreign businessmen, traditional political parties, and the U.S. embassy. In January 1934 he ousted Grau, sending him into exile and transferring army support to the more pliable Carlos Mendieta, Machado's old nemesis. As before, the United States manipulated the situation from behind the scenes.[60] In return for the Cuban government's compliance, Welles signed a treaty in May 1934 abrogating the Platt Amendment. Standing over his shoulder during the ceremony was Manuel Márquez Sterling, who had been his link to the Cuban government.[61] For the rest of the decade, Chief of Staff Batista y Zalvidar ruled Cuba from behind the scenes, fronted by successive figurehead presidents: José A. Barnet (1935–36), Miguel Mariano Gómez (1936), and Federico Laredo Brú (1936–40).

Martial law had remained in effect from 1930 until early 1934. Government-run agents had infiltrated opposition groups and carried out assassinations. Machado's secret police, the Sección de Expertos, had extracted confessions to alleged political crimes by brutality and torture. People were arrested randomly for such vague charges as communist sympathies and threatening public security.[62] Terror had become the principal means of government, and all citizens and residents were kept under surveillance.[63] The University of Havana had been closed along with many secondary schools in which students had led opposition to the regime. Machado's porristas had murdered hundreds suspected of subversion.[64] Armed underground opposition groups had organized. Scapegoats continued to be sought even after Machado's ouster. The Havana City Council enacted a nativist regulation that on November 8, 1933, was adopted across Cuba by the new revolutionary government. This law, the 1934 Cubanization Law, Decree 2583, became commonly known as the Law of the 50 Percent because half of the workers in every firm had to be Cuban born. The ruling also mandated that all vacancies and new jobs were to go to native-born Cubans, although later it was amended to include naturalized citizens as well.

Domestically the result of the Cuba for the Cubans campaign was to drive many immigrant workers into illegal home industries working under contract to manufacturers for piecework, the lowest paid of all garment industry work arrangements. Using U.S. methods rather than the more careful, elegant methods demanded in Europe, teams of sewers working sixteen to eighteen hours daily produced twelve to fourteen jackets a day. Gradually, although Cuba had been hit hard by the depression, some of the hapless tailors, young men who were paid barely enough to pay their rent and to eat, were able to hire others, sometimes Spaniards. These so-called *chalupniks*, part laborer and part subcontractor, gradually moved into the ranks of the self-employed. Their prosperity depended on working to near exhaustion and concentrating on bargain goods, thereby avoiding competition with Spanish businesses.[65]

Members of the Cuban Jewish colony saw the nationalistic campaign as economic and political, not as anti-Semitic. American Jewish leaders worried that the leftist Kultur Farain would instigate more labor unrest and may have been instrumental in encouraging the regime to crack down on Communists. On the eve of the Day of Atonement, 1931, police invaded the sixth annual Yom Kippur Ball and closed the Kultur Farain headquarters, arresting fifty-seven of its members. The Yiddish library was burned, and the organization banned. Forty-nine were arrested and jailed for fifteen days with fines; the Kultur Farain remained closed. Following the ugly incident, efforts were made to organize a watchdog committee to speak for all Cuban Jews in case of specific need, culminating in the organization of the Federación Israelita de Cuba in 1932. This group, like all others formed within the community, was not concerned with assimilation into Cuban life. (Note the portraits of Yiddish cultural greats I. L. Peretz and Nachman Bialik in figure 13.)

Jews were not the primary target of the protective labor laws, although a Polish-Jewish immigrant, Noske Yalom, was the first trade unionist killed by Machado's police. He was a house painter who walked slowly because of an infirmity and was therefore an easy mark. Far more numerous among immigrant workers were the true gallegos, Spaniards from Galicia, the destitute northern region that provided almost half of all emigrants from Spain between 1911 and 1958.[66] Other Spaniards, called *isleños*, came from Asturias and the Canary Islands. Most of the Spanish immigrants were illiterate or semiliterate peasants, predominantly men by a two-to-one ratio,

13. Cultural Committee, Centro Israelita, Havana, early 1930s. Courtesy of José Winer.

and impoverished. Gallegos, like many immigrants, sacrificed so that their children could go to school and aspire to higher-level careers.[67] By the early 1930s, Spanish-born nationals made up nearly 10 percent of the Cuban population. They organized communal organizations, including *centros*, societies based on the regional origin of their members. Some of these were attached to clinics and offered health care to anyone who wanted to join. Many Jewish Cubans in the 1930s affiliated with these clinics, thereby bringing the two communities of immigrants into contact.

The nationalistic 1933 immigration law was directed mostly at these workers, who depressed the wage structure by accepting jobs under the worst of conditions. By requiring that half of all employees be Cuban-born, the law struck a blow at both Spanish and Jewish immigrants. Community-based associations provided relief, but the atmosphere turned ugly.[68] Some of the new Spanish arrivals took out their frustrations on the Jewish immigrants who had displaced them in Jewish-owned textile and shoe industries in the Calle Muralla in the old quarter of Havana. Other Jews were accused of being *chivatos* (stool pigeons) and strikebreakers, in competition with Cuban-born workers who demanded slightly higher wages than the immigrants were willing to accept.

All of this was unfolding in an atmosphere of unprecedented change and growth. Cuba's population increased some 152 percent between the end of the Spanish-American War and 1930, a greater jump than that experienced by the United States during the same period. The political environment remained volatile throughout the 1920s and 1930s. The events culminating in the August 11, 1933, coup against General Machado left twenty-two dead and seventy-four injured in the streets of Havana not far from the Old City where most of the Jewish immigrants still lived. The policies of the administration that succeeded Machado, especially those of President Grau San Martín (1933–34), ushered in dramatic improvements for workers but at a high cost: the new legislation was xenophobic and nationalistic. Many Jewish employers were forced to fire most of their immigrant employees under the 1934 Cubanization Law. As many as a thousand Jewish heads of households lost their jobs under the new regulations. Nationalistic legislation was codified as the 1930s progressed and ultimately incorporated into the 1940 Constitution. Spanish merchants were affected by the same law, as were hundreds of businesses run by foreigners. Although naturalized Cubans legally shared the same job rights as the native-born, many Spanish immigrants who had acquired citizenship were still dismissed from their jobs; some bus and tram drivers who had become naturalized Cuban citizens were physically beaten and thrown out of their vehicles for being "foreigners."[69]

Cuba's 1933 revolution was not a failure. It managed to pressure the United States to abrogate the Platt Amendment in 1934, thereby ending that country's formal protectorate over the island. The revolutionary government enacted a flurry of reforms that facilitated labor organization and strengthened efforts by Cuban sugarcane growers to protect their interests. Political reform was less successful. In the end, the 1933 revolution's democratic goals were subsumed under a new government apparatus that suppressed its opponents, a dictatorship in democratic clothing. Administrative corruption continued to flourish. Fulgencio Batista opted to emphasize social reform, creating a populist-style multiclass coalition that governed while he remained in the background. Batista did not dominate absolutely or demand total obsequiousness from his underlings. The government was nominally independent, although he remained effectively the most powerful figure in Cuba. The government suffered internal division at its uppermost levels, especially during the presidency of Federico Laredo Brú, whom Batista put into office in 1936. After a constituent assembly in 1940 enacted a progressive and nationalistic constitution, Batista would be elected president "legally and democratically in his own right."[70]

The Machado-era Law of the 50 Percent, when enforced, prevented large numbers of immigrants from legally earning a living. A visiting commission of the Foreign Policy Association from New York estimated that from 25,000 to 30,000 had lost their jobs owing to the law. It also caused problems for manufacturers, who faced complaints from labor unions that some of their members—mostly Spanish immigrants—were adversely affected.[71] Jews who had emigrated in hopes of continuing on to the United States were barred from doing so because the transient loophole had been closed, and the combined impact of the Law of the 50 Percent and the deepening economic depression caused hardship for many.

In all, the notorious law drove hundreds of Jewish immigrants from their regular employment, requiring them to enter the much more poorly paid underground economy of home sweatshops or to bribe officials willing to overlook regulations. Many other employers were affected throughout the decade by labor strife stirred up by militant unionists and by Cuba's strong tradition of unionization. Cuba's economic environment in general, however, favored employers. When Israel Sarovich and Izaac Zark decided in July 1939 to move their plant's operations to Marianao and the Cerro from Guanabacoa, 150 Guanabacoa employees protested vehemently but were ignored.[72] In spite of these conditions, Cuba continued to be seen as a haven for foreigners. Some 380,000 immigrants arrived between 1934 and 1942, mostly Spaniards (178,871), but also Haitians (66,221), Jamaicans (41,000), Chinese (29,761), English (26,986), Americans (9,551), French (2,070), Venezuelans (496), and Yugoslavians (108).[73]

The Pax Batistiana

Conflict stemming from Communist-led strikes and generalized labor agitation increased during the transition period. A Soviet cell established in a sugar mill in Oriente province was dispersed by the army. By mid-1936, a commission of foreign observers reported, "anarchy reigned over the island."[74] Batista, still merely a colonel but firmly in control of the government at Washington's pleasure, replaced president after president with no attempt to cloak his behind-the-scenes power; newspapers frequently published comments acknowledging it.[75] The United States approved this Pax Batistiana because Batista had restored stability. European fascist ideas were making considerable inroads among the Cuban elite, especially among those who considered themselves of Spanish origin. At the same time, the U.S. presence, exercised through the embassy in Havana, was stronger in Cuba than in any other sovereign Latin American country.

Cuba's singular environment profoundly influenced the reception given arrivals from foreign shores, especially when they were not Roman Catholics. The Spanish crown had excluded Jews from Cuba, and even though Madrid had endorsed religious tolerance in 1881 for Spain and its colonies, until 1898 Jews in Cuba could pray at home but not in synagogues.[76] Even so, there was no modern tradition of institutional prejudice against Jews, and cultural and economic links to the nearby United States were great, so that Cuba's post-1920 Jewish population was able to maintain close contact with Jewish groups in the United States and Canada.

Vicious anti-Semitism, when it erupted after the nationalistic revolution of 1933 until it was suppressed by President Batista during World War II, was principally an imported phenomenon, brought to Cuba by Falangist Spaniards as well as by Fascist agents in the form of crude racist tracts. Since most nonelite Cubans supported the Spanish republic, their sympathies remained with their Jewish compatriots, especially after news of the Holocaust reached Cuba. This was true even if in elite circles affinity for Spain's General Francisco Franco and the Axis powers afforded fertile soil for anti-Semitism and right-wing nationalism.[77]

Jews were not permitted to become citizens until the late 1930s, although apparently it was fairly easy to purchase Cuban birth certificates illegally in and around Havana.[78] One reason for Cuba's reluctance to grant Jews nationalized status was that the U.S. State Department pressured Havana not to change its policies lest the Jewish immigrants seek entry into the United States as Cubans. Sender M. Kaplan's Yiddish-language *Havaner Lebn*, founded in April 1933, claimed five months later that more than 5,000 petitions for citizenship had been held back by officials of the Machado government.[79]

Although Cuban authorities moderated their position on immigration after 1934, when political stability returned, many Cubans continued to oppose Jewish immigration because the Jews organized unions and tended to be on the political Left. Ironically, the obstacles placed in the way of Jewish immigrants to Cuba in the 1920s and 1930s—the nationalistic laws restricting work opportunities and the refusal of Cuban labor leaders to ally with Jewish workers—drove the Jewish arrivals, especially those from Eastern Europe who had been forced to work in manual trades, into the middle class. Employers by and large accepted the Cubanization Law's incentives to hire Cuban workers. Once self-employed, many if not most Jews who had held socialist beliefs gradually began to take on the views of those who they had formerly denounced as "reactionary and bourgeois."[80] The strong current of nationalism that discouraged the foreign born from competing economically acted to encourage Jews to move into new occupations and, eventually, to send their children into the liberal professions. They also learned the lesson of political neutrality: it was unwise to take a public stand, less dangerous to maintain a collectively low profile. Even after they became citizens, the former immigrants remained wary. "We voted on the basis of arrangements made with people we knew," one recalled. "We didn't trust elections. We knew that most elections were a farce. People were paid for their votes. And nothing would change, no matter who won."[81]

That many of the early labor organizers and some of the founders of Cuba's Communist movement were Jews alerted Jewish leaders during the 1930s to the need for a public relations effort to show that Jews were progressive and civic minded, not extremists. To demonstrate their loyalty, Jewish merchants and professionals in 1936 organized a Cuban Jewish Chamber of Commerce. Community leaders met behind the scenes with politicians to assure them of support when appropriate; editor Sender M. Kaplan on more than one occasion gave free newspaper advertising to candidates for office with whom the Jewish colony sympathized. The Jewish leadership almost always worked behind the scenes, preferring to stay out of the public eye.[82]

The Cuban labor movement during this period took what a

scholar has termed a "remarkable and ironic twist."[83] Behind the scenes, Batista had urged the government to smash the great 1935 general strike, which involved as many as 500,000 workers: constitutional law was suspended, with military governors placed at the head of each province. But by mid-1937, Batista changed his position, perhaps because even as an ally of the conservative republican elite who had supported efforts to break the labor unions he had never felt comfortable in an antilabor position. Batista worked out a tacit alliance with Communist party leader Blas Roca; in July 1937, the government embarked on a three-year plan to bring sugar and tobacco exports under state control. The plan also promised paid vacations, unemployment compensation, and health care to workers, and the Communist party moved toward legal status and full rights, which were granted in late 1938. The Communists took control of the Confederación de Trabajadores de Cuba (CTC), which worked closely with the new Ministry of Labor. Batista avoided censure from Washington because the State Department applauded his efforts to restore Cuba to economic stability as the depression wore on, even if it did not appreciate the new socialist-sounding rhetoric that accompanied the formation of the CTC as a state trade union along the lines of similar entities in Mexico and Brazil during the late 1930s.[84] Batista became popular among Latin American leftists and with the Soviet Union. After Pearl Harbor, he found himself "in the advantageous position of being a loyal friend of the Allies at a time when other Latin American leaders were often suspected of being pro-Nazi."[85]

In spite of the inroads of labor and economic depression, the upper class remained well entrenched in the 1930s, comprising the old aristocracy as well as some new arrivals who made their fortunes in the post-1917 sugar boom. Some of the old families traced their ancestry to the colonial period and considered themselves to be Spanish, a badge of prestige in Cuba even after the promulgation of the republic. After the presidency of Mario García Menocal (1913–20), the old aristocracy was replaced by a new group of businessmen, professionals, and intellectuals who came to power with links to foreign commercial and business interests. Membership in the new elite was principally based on marriage and birth, not inherited property. *Compadrazgo*, the kinship system whereby loosely defined networks of extended family members looked out for one another and helped one another in all realms of life—political, legal, economic, and social—blended into *personalismo,* whereby those attaining office were considered to have the right to exploit it for their personal gain and in the interest of their *compadres* and clients.[86]

Even if the old aristocracy generally yielded to the new elite, many members of the upper class boasted of their Spanish ties, purchasing titles of nobility and other honors conferred by Madrid, but the new upper-class groups tended to be oriented socially and culturally to the United States. Members traveled frequently to Florida and to the Northeast and gave social importance to intellectual achievement and, especially, to philanthropic activity. This created a uniquely Cuban phenomenon: at the top of the social ladder, most elites displayed tolerance and open-mindedness, whereas lower down, principally among the large Spanish immigrant community, which comprised more than 15 percent of the population in 1931, paternalistic values and even pro-Fascist sentiments flourished.[87] Cuba's lower classes lived in poverty. They were courted at election time by opportunistic politicians, but they generally received little. Few poor children stayed in public school through the upper grades, and there was little available health care or adequate sanitation. Skin color determined to a large degree one's social as well as economic status: blacks and mulattos stood at the bottom of the ladder, in both rural and urban Cuba. This prejudice may have been one unstated reason why Jewish immigrants were able to succeed in as few years as they did.

Cuba's urban middle class during the early 1930s fell into two distinguishable segments. The technical and professional sector, mostly *criollo* (Cuban born), depended on fees and salaries for income. These people tended to be graduates of secondary-level schools and universities and often sought jobs in government service, which in Cuba became a vast source of employment for graduates. Some came from lower-class families; others were middle-class Cuban-born sons of Spanish parents. The commercial sector was mostly comprised of self-made Spaniards who had risen through trade "by the use of their elbows," as the saying went. They were nationalistic Cubans, usually practicing Catholics. But plagued by an underdeveloped industrial sector, the middle class suffered unusually high levels of unemployment. Unresolved tensions lived on after Machado's fall. The University of Havana, which Machado had

14. Outing of family and friends, La Tropical, Havana, 1936. Courtesy of Lucia Suárez.

closed from 1930 to 1934, was closed periodically between 1934 and 1937 along with its secondary school accrediting affiliate and school, the Instituto de Habana. Some student political activists spent as much or more time in jail than in class.[88] For those who were well-off, however, life was good, and domestic life flourished amidst Cuba's natural beauty. Many families went to *La Tropical* on weekends and on holidays (fig. 14), a large urban site owned by a brewery, with a stadium, picnic grounds, and gardens adjacent to the factory. Families could make reservations to use the facilities and were given free beer (and soft drinks for the children).

For immigrants as well as for the emerging urban middle class, the political climate in the mid-1930s permitted unprecedented freedom of political expression, especially on foreign affairs. New factions surfaced: among the large Spanish colony, groups supporting the various sides in the Spanish civil war; among East European Jews in Cuba, arguments between socialist factions endorsing Zionism and others that opposed it. The Sephardic colony remained more placid, although between 1930 and 1935, Moreno Habif and other Sephardic leaders took steps to organize an umbrella agency, Sociedad Bikur Holim, dedicated to aiding the sick and providing other forms of philanthropy, including free health care for the indigent.[89]

Cuba's middle class during this time became unusually politicized. Closely linked to the U.S. press as well as to news of current events in Europe, public opinion was buffeted by competing ideologies and blueprints for political society. In Cuba, as in Mexico, a sizeable bloc supported the Spanish republic, although a strident minority admired Mussolini, Hitler, and especially Francisco Franco. Anti-Semitism flooded in through German and Falangist propaganda channels. Observers blamed the immigrants from Spain for bringing bias against Jews with them: native-born Cubans were considered much more tolerant, lacking the strident anti-Semitic attitudes prevalent in Europe and to some degree in the United States and Canada.[90] At the same time, the *Havana Post*, the American-owned English-language newspaper, warned its readers regularly of Nazi brutality toward German citizens, especially Jews, almost as soon as the Nazis came to power.[91] But the *Post's* circulation was less than 5,000, and, like all other English-language newspapers in Latin America, it was read by foreign residents and visitors, not by the public at large.

Relations between Cuba's Jews and the government nearly became violent when an editorial on the eve of Yom Kippur (September 29, 1933) in *Alerta* accused left-wing Jewish strikers of firing on soldiers from rooftops during an antiregime demonstration that had turned into a forty-minute street battle. The newspaper charged that Jews would close their businesses in opposition to the army and to its role in suppressing the demonstration. As "predicted," Jewish-owned stores remained closed, and on Yom Kippur morning the army attacked the Ashkenazic portion of the Jewish colony. Homes were invaded and searched, several dozen Jews were arrested, and police forced some Jews to open their establishments. Sephardic Jews, who were not considered sympathetic to labor causes, were left alone, as were the "American" Jews, who even received government permission to break the evening curfew in order to attend services.[92] The Reform congregation's new rabbi, Meir Lasker, quickly established cordial relations not only with Batista but with the U.S. ambassador, Jefferson Caffery. Rabbi Lasker had been sent to Havana by the president of Hebrew Union College after previous work in Holland, Poland, and Germany and was to remain in Havana nearly ten years, becoming a valuable link among Jewish interests, the U.S. embassy, and high Cuban officials.

Nonetheless, hostility toward the East European Jewish immigrants continued unabated. Fingers were pointed at a few who became involved in criminal activities—including arson schemes and confidence games—and in the nightclub and entertainment industry, which included managing Cuban call girls. Some became engaged in the "white slave trade," importing prostitutes—some Jewish—from Poland.[93] The procurers were not immigrants in the traditional sense, as they had first gone to Argentina to ply their business, then had moved to Cuba. Many of the women recruited to the business had been trapped in the Russian and Polish Pale and throughout the Hapsburg Empire, by force or by fraud, and the human dilemma was great. Although there were likely not more than a handful of Jewish "white slavers" in Cuba, fighting the trade, as Jewish communal leaders attempted to do quietly, was difficult. "If we admit the existence of this traffic our enemies decry us," wrote a German-Jewish feminist about the worldwide problem, and "if we deny it they say we are trying to conceal it."[94] In Cuba and elsewhere, the colony as a whole was made vulnerable by association. This proved to be the focal point of a smear attack in the October 5, 1933, edition of Havana's *Mañana*, which printed a front-page interview with the city's police chief, who charged Jews with "infringement of public morals" and warned that further Jewish immigration would be stopped if such activities were not curbed. In response, the heads of all of the major Jewish organizations in Havana met and formed a body, the Comisión Jurídica, to speak for the colony. Its leaders sought and received an audience with President Grau San Martín to air their grievances. This was not to say that all Havana echoed the negativism of *Alerta* and *Mañana*. Some newspapers, in fact, supported the prorefugee position.[95] Ultimately, Grau quietly apologized for the Yom Kippur incidents; he asked that Jews still held in prison be released and that the commission report any further problems to him.

The commission remained active for a while, determined to assert the patriotism of the Jewish colony and to protest the increasing numbers of anti-Semitic articles published in the venerable *Diario de la Marina* as well as *Popular* and *Información*. The *Diario* was controlled by the family of Count Nicolás Rivero, most of whose members lived in Spain, and edited by José Ignacio Rivero (Pepín), an ultraconservative journalist personally sympathetic to the Franco forces in Spain.[96] The commission became increasingly disturbed at the pattern of anti-Jewish sentiment expressed in the *Diario,* but its editors were sophisticated enough to cloak their anti-Semitic views in pragmatic language—opposing accepting refugees from Nazis, for example, because they might displace Cubans, themselves suffering from lack of jobs during the depression. The *Diario,* with its eight-to-ten page, sepia-toned rotogravure section devoted to high-society news, was immensely popular and successful and therefore unassailable.

Commission members also worried about the newly aggressive posture of Cuba's German colony. Throughout Latin America, in fact, German expatriates and businessmen founded schools entirely Nazi in philosophy, catering not only to German children but to members of the elite who found this form of education attractive. The Escuela Alemana in the Vedado section of the city flew the swastika from its wrought-iron gate and in the evenings provided facilities for the paramilitary exercises of the teenage auxiliary of the Nazi party, the Asociación Nazista de Cuba.[97] Although the commission attempted to cooperate with a boycott organized in the United States against German exports and worked informally with the U.S. embassy under Jefferson Caffery, as tensions ebbed, indifference and the old centrifugal forces operating within the Jewish colony reasserted themselves, and the commission disbanded in October 1934. The UHC board had never formally endorsed the effort, and although its rabbi, Meir Lasker, presided over the commission, he did so as an individual, not as a representative of his institution. The rabbi claimed in later years that his congregation took only a passive role because its board wanted to keep religious and communal functions separate.[98] This institutional attitude was the leitmotif of the Jewish community, especially of its more prosperous members. Each of the major groups within the Jewish colony remained apart from the others, even during bad times, and no individual or single group ever emerged to speak for the whole.

Improving economic and political conditions reduced tensions, and the Cuban Jewish colony recovered its sense of security.[99] By the mid-1930s, nearly 150 workshops and factories owned by Jewish immigrants produced two million pairs of shoes annually. They employed between 6,000 and 8,000 workers, at least half of them native-born Cubans, in compliance with the Law of the 50 Percent.

The fact that Cuban Jewish firms achieved a 60 percent share of all clothing, fabric, and shoe manufacturing on the island sharply reduced Cuba's dependence on outside suppliers and helped ameliorate to some degree the devastating impact of the Great Depression, which was felt more keenly in Latin American countries where exports furnished virtually all sources of revenue. In less than a decade and a half, the immigrant peddlers and artisans had become an entrepreneurial class rivaling the Spanish, who also had arrived as immigrants and gained a tenacious hold on retailing and commerce. Cuban Jewish brokers dominated imports of goods that could not be produced domestically. Many immigrants who had started by peddling on the streets now owned *tiendas mixtas*, dry goods stores selling shoes and clothing items, although the Spanish Cubans still controlled the grocery chains and most other kinds of shops.

A Family's Story

No two families, of course, underwent the same experiences. Indeed, although the major Jewish groups in Cuba mostly stuck to themselves, some mixing took place as time passed. A tiny percentage of Jewish marriages in Cuba as early as the 1930s but more frequently later were made up of one Sephardic and one Ashkenazic partner. Bridegrooms in these couples were generally Ashkenazic. For one thing, there were more single Ashkenazic than Sephardic men in Cuba because of the different nature of the two immigrant streams. For whatever other reasons, the barriers between the two groups began to break down, although they never disappeared.

The Winer family offers an example. José (Josef) Winer was born in 1912 in Ostrog, in the Wolyn province of the Russian Ukraine. Settled by Jews in the sixteenth century, Ostrog had 45,000 inhabitants and was considered a site of Jewish learning. But Jews, as elsewhere in the Pale of Settlement, were marginalized, restricted to certain trades, and always made aware of their second-class status. They could attend city schools but were segregated. Visitors to the imposing sixteenth-century community synagogue had to descend nearly two dozen stairs because the building was required to be no taller than any church in the city and therefore had to be built partially below ground. Inside, the synagogue was splendid, with murals painted in the 1500s by Italian artists contracted by the congregation.[100]

Like all Jews in the Ukraine, the Winers faced recurrent pogroms and often had to hide in cellars. José's father, Isaac, who had been a corporal in the czar's army (the highest rank to which a Jew could rise) and a decorated sharpshooter, was a Bundist and before his son was born was sent in chains to exile in Siberia for life. In the gulag he became close to some of his fellow prisoners who had been sailors involved in the 1905 revolt of the battleship *Potemkin*. In his absence, the family was supported mainly by José's grandmother, who traded in bolts of fabric that she purchased in Lodz and Warsaw.[101] After the Bolshevik revolution in 1917, the prison camp was liberated, and Isaac Winer made his way back to the Ukraine with other leftists, many of them Jewish, when the reactionary Whites retreated. He saw his son for the first time when the boy was nearly seven. Even in his father's absence, José followed in his footsteps: he recollects that he was the youngest member of the Zionist Hashomer Hatzair youth group in Ostrog. In 1921, the region was ceded to Poland, and Polish troops entered. In 1912, José's paternal grandfather, a *mohel* (one who performs ritual circumcisions), had gone to the United States while emigration was permitted. A decade later, in the face of growing hardship under the Polish occupation and economic difficulties in the Soviet Union, the grandfather sent $1,000—a fortune at the time—to bring the rest of his family to the West. But by then, in the early 1920s, U.S. quota numbers were hard to obtain. Shipping company representatives advised prospective travelers to buy passage to a Latin American country and wait there for the quota numbers to be issued. In some cases, especially for Jews who came to Mexico, these specialists in illicit traffic arranged for their clients to be spirited across the border. Once in Cuba, immigrants learned that it was almost impossible to acquire visas, and some took advantage of smugglers who sold passages on small fishing boats across the Florida Straits for $150. These schemes often failed, however, with the would-be emigrants finding themselves stopped by U.S. customs officials on arrival and sent back to Cuba at their own expense.[102]

Relatively well financed, the Winers could have sailed for any Latin American port, but because José had studied geography in *cheder* he fancied Cuba, an island that on the map appeared close to the U.S. mainland. His father decided to book passage to Havana. The family took a horse-drawn cart seven kilometers to the train station at Ostrog and journeyed on to Warsaw, then to Berlin and to Holland. After a fortnight there, they boarded a Dutch ship, the SS *Spaarendam*, to Belgium, then to France, then to Spain, and then, after a twenty-four-day crossing, to Cuba.

The twelve-year-old boy entered Havana's harbor at daybreak on November 24, 1924, and was astonished to see black soldiers guarding the harborside fortress, the Castillo de la Fuerza, as the ship glided by. He had read about black Africans in schoolbooks but like virtually all of the East European arrivals had never seen one in the flesh. The family was met by Isaac, who had gone ahead ten months earlier to prepare things, working aboard ship shaving fellow passengers for five cents, a skill he had learned in Siberia. The family rented a room for seven dollars a week in a boardinghouse for immigrants on Calle San Ignacio, in the old part of Havana. With a partner, Isaac opened a store, which failed, and then a small cafeteria, which soon became a gathering place for East Europeans and for some Americans who worked at the nearby consulate. The restaurant offered Russian-style tea and European black bread, which was unknown in Cuba, and eventually added such delicacies as yogurt, which Isaac made himself, and herring, pickles, lox, and other European specialties that they purchased from a grocery store run by two immigrants from Transylvania. At one point the restaurant faced a scare when a health inspector refused to certify as sanitary the food products, which were unfamiliar to him, but things were fixed in the "Cuban way," through the help of a friendly customer who worked at the U.S. consulate.

The cafeteria did not make much money. Rent was fifteen dollars a month. Profits had to be divided between two families, and many of the patrons were permitted to eat on credit. Some of the single men who took their meals there got construction jobs with the Cuban railroad only to disappear into the interior, some dying of malaria or tuberculosis, others remaining in the rural provinces to earn a living as peddlers. Some gave Isaac Winer their passports to secure loans of five or ten dollars. Twenty years later he still had them: their owners had never returned to claim them or to pay off their loans. José, at twelve, was sent to the Chevet Ahim school with his two sisters. Spanish was spoken there, and the Ashkenazic children had to learn quickly. The Winers lived in a single room in the tenement on San Ignacio Street, cooking over a charcoal stove, salting chickens purchased at outdoor markets, not ritually slaughtered, and having chunks of ice delivered daily by horse wagon for their icebox. They shared the building with eight other tenant families, four on each floor. José recalls walking after Machado's inauguration as president with two friends on the Campo Marte (later the Plaza de la Fraternidad) in front of the capitol. They stopped to watch a photographer take the picture of a couple. When the photograph was developed underneath the cameraman's black cloth, the photographer turned to the boys, who had apparently appeared in the composition, ruining it, and shouted "Judíos!" at them, waving his fists. José, who knew that the photographer was a Polish immigrant, cursed back in Polish before the boys ran away.

Without realizing that he was proceeding differently from most of his fellow immigrants, José took steps to integrate himself into Cuban society. He recalls being invited by Cuban friends to roasted suckling pig dinners at Christmas, tasting just enough of the pork to be polite. He used his friendship with an English-speaking boy whose family had come to Cuba from British Palestine to learn rudimentary English. His father received packages of old newspapers sent by relatives in New York, and José pored over them—*Novo Ruskoye Slovo*, the Yiddish-language papers *Forward*, *Tog*, and *Ruskoye Golos*, and *Freiheit*, a Communist newspaper. He also read copies from time to time of the city's English-language paper, the *Havana Post*. Relatives visiting from the United States occasionally brought exotic foods as gifts: corn flakes and Rice Krispies. When his aunt poured milk over the dry cereal and sliced bananas into the boy's bowl, Cuban neighbors who were watching from their balconies shrieked that the boy would be poisoned, because according to their custom the two foods were never eaten together. After the 1926 hurricane, when floods killed thousands of people, José at the age of ten or eleven joined a Cuban Boy Scout troop with only one other Jewish boy; all of the other scouts were Catholic. As a teenager he joined the Cuban Sea Scouts, one of only two Jewish youths in the organization (fig. 15).

Because he worked out regularly in a gym and developed a strong physique, José was recruited to appear in boxing matches. He backed

15. Sea Scouts, Havana, 1929. Courtesy of José Winer.

out before the first public bout but learned enough pugilistic skills to become a highly effective street fighter (fig. 16). His boxing teacher was Lalo Rodríguez, a world-class Cuban professional pugilist. José also wrestled competitively and played saxophone in an orchestra. He attended theater presentations performed in East European languages—Yiddish performers of international stature made trips to Cuba—and in Russian, but he also frequented the Spanish-language theater and, like all of the immigrants, cinemas. He fit into his new life comfortably and felt exhilarated by his new experiences. When he was about fourteen, his parents sent him to Havana Public School #1, although for social events he continued to frequent the Centro Israelita, relocated to a handsome building on Zulueta Street, near the capitol. He also attended Sunday school classes conducted in Yiddish on Calle Cuba by two Lithuanian brothers, the Bernickers. In public school, he learned to play the violin—he had brought a three-quarter-sized instrument with him from Poland—and was deeply influenced by Dr. Oscar Ugarte, the school's principal and a lover of music. All during his life, José Winer would remember his public school days with fondness.

José's temperate integration into Cuban life was typified by his experience a year later on the occasion of the centenary of Cuba's first revolt for independence against Spain. Fifteen hundred students

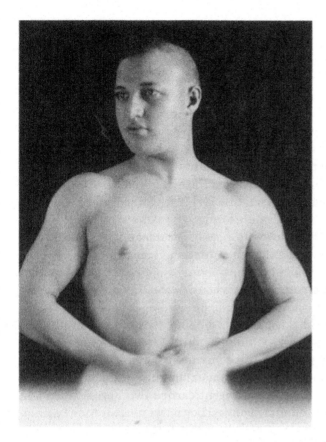

16. José Winer as fighter, 1931. Courtesy of José Winer.

from Havana schools were invited to attend a patriotic ceremony at the National Theater. José, who had been selected by Dr. Ugarte to play a selection of patriotic music in a string trio, performed on the stage before an audience that included virtually every leading political figure in Cuba. President Machado himself embraced the youths after their performance: José, another East European, Myron Levitt, and a mulatto, Ulpiano Carrillo, whose father was a stevedore foreman. In his accolade, the master of ceremonies, in Machado's presence, said with pride to the enormous gathering: "In this trio, two of the boys are immigrants." José maintained a close friendship with Ulpiano and his family until the Winers left for the United States after the Castro revolution. Not all foreign immigrants saw their children eat meals with Cubans, especially mulatto families, but José did not consider it an issue. He also maintained a friendship with a black man, Primitivo Ramírez, a social columnist for local papers during the 1940s who wrote about Jewish society and who later married a Jewish woman and converted to Judaism.

Isaac and Regina (Rachel) Winer, José's father and mother, prospered after they sold their interest in the restaurant and began to manufacture bow ties, renting a sewing machine for a dollar a month and employing a bow tie sent by an uncle in New York as a model. Their first wares were made out of a black satin dress Regina Winer had brought from the old country. Later, they imported remnants from clothing manufacturers in the United States; they also imported cases of ready-made bow ties, which they sold wholesale.

José Winer's memories of his formative years are positive. He did not recollect any troubles with Spanish merchants. A youthful acquaintance, an immigrant named Matias Handel, joined Batista's army simply as a way of earning a living, and he rose to the rank of captain. Winer remembers that when Machado was inaugurated as president in 1925, Jewish immigrants were enticed to work as strikebreakers in the dock shutdown, but they refused despite their desperate need for work. Children from Chevet Ahim, dressed in white, wore blue sashes with the name of their school written in Hebrew letters and set out to march to the presidential palace. Youths at the head of the contingent carried two flags, Cuba's and the blue-and-white Zionist banner. They never made it to the palace. It was raining torrentially, and there was intense smoke from a fire at the offices of the *Havana Post*. But even in the mid-1920s many of the immigrant children, few of whom attended public schools, considered themselves Cubans, not Poles or Russians or Moroccans. The Centro Israelita and other organizations furnished children with enough cultural exposure to preserve their Jewish identities. No little effort was put into such events as the annual Queen Esther festival at Purim (fig. 17) and other celebrations in the religious calendar, although the parties were secular, reflecting the Ashkenazic families' generally secular lives.

During the 1930s, José married and divorced twice. He embarked on a series of business ventures involved with tourism and entertainment, at one point selling jukeboxes imported from the United States, at another founding a music company that recorded popular music on phonograph records, including that of Manolo Fernandez, "El Rey del Tango" (the Tango King). He also headed the Partagas

17. Queen Esther Festival, Centro Israelita, early 1930s. Courtesy of José Winer.

cigar company's sales department for tourists. He felt at ease with Cubans and consorted with them: one photograph taken of him at a night club shows him relaxing with men who were prominent in the army, the police, and the entertainment industry (fig. 18). His livelihood took him to cities across Cuba, where he mingled and dealt with businessmen of all colors and races. He remembers setting up several blacks and a Chinese man in business. By wartime he had acquired a handsome open Packard touring car, which he sold during the war for $600. The tires were worth $400, and he gave the remaining $200 to his black driver, who would have to be laid off because gas rationing had made owning a car too expensive.

To illustrate how other Jewish immigrants were becoming involved in aspects of their adoptive society from which they had formerly been excluded, José Winer describes the way some of them developed close personal ties with the men around Batista and the head of the Cuban army, Eulogio Pedraza, after Machado's ouster. In 1934, Batista and Pedraza were living in Marianao, at army headquarters. They became cronies with the Greenstein family, Ashkenazic immigrants, while Jaime Greenstein, a younger brother, be-

18. "Tourist Industry" meeting at Havana nightclub, 1936. Courtesy of José Winer.

came involved in an anti-Batista plot. When the youth was caught carrying a bomb, he identified himself with a pseudonym, "Terry," before he was shot. José maintains that had he admitted he was Jaime Greenstein, he probably would have been spared.[103]

José's two sisters acculturated to Cuban intellectual life in different ways. The elder, Sonia, went to public high school after finishing the Yiddish-language curriculum at the Centro Israelita and became an accomplished poet in Spanish. A socialist Zionist, she published in the late 1930s a book of poems, *Compañera y Otros Poemas*, advocating social reform and support for the Soviet Union and attacking the British for their role in Palestine. The younger sister, Esther, became a kindergarten teacher at the Centro and later an accomplished pianist and piano teacher. José's third wife, Esther Behar, whom he married in 1949, came from a Sephardic family of fourteen children who emigrated to Cuba's Matanzas province from Turkey in 1920. Sephardim infrequently mixed with Ashkenazim, but José Winer was an unusual man, and he married Esther after they had both been in Cuba two and a half decades. Her family, like his, had been dominated by the maternal side: her mother had been a successful importer of goods from France to Turkey, and she had

19. Esther and José Winer, Miami, 1991. Photo by the author.

wed after lending her husband's family money to pay his way out of being recalled into the Turkish army, an act intended to save his life that also led to their marriage. When Esther's mother came to Cuba, she carried her family's wealth in gold coins sewn into her undergarments.

The family made a home in the small commercial town of Unión de Reyes, in Matanzas province, where her mother sewed clothing, which her father sold. About forty Sephardic families had come to the town, the later ones coming because they were related one way or another to families that had arrived earlier. The families were interrelated by marriage and by economic activity. Esther, like José, went to public schools, except for one year in a Presbyterian school that turned out to be less rigorous than the local public school, something that in Cuba was usually not the case. She was a popular young girl and mixed easily in Cuban society. At one point in her girlhood she was elected queen of the annual Carnival celebration. Esther entered school in the first grade but was soon advanced to the third, where her teacher was the mother of her best friend, a Cuban; she was an excellent student and later became an accomplished painter. All of her art work, however, was left behind when the Winers abandoned Cuba for the United States.

Unlike many Sephardic families from Turkey who came to Cuba speaking Ladino, Esther's family spoke mostly Turkish and French and therefore had to learn Spanish in the same manner as the other immigrants. Esther understood Ladino but did not read Judezmo, the language's Hebrew script. Her family members were traditionally religious even though they lived far from any synagogue. At holidays, Jews from several surrounding towns in Matanzas—Palos, Cabezas, Nueva Paz, and others—gathered in their house, where her grandfather led prayers, men and women sitting together, against Orthodox practice. When the family moved to Cárdenas in 1936 and later to Havana, they became more conventionally observant.

When Esther was fifteen, she married a Turkish Jewish man more than twice her age from another small village in Matanzas. They had a daughter two years later, but the marriage did not work, and they divorced. After about five years on her own with her daughter, Isolina, she married a Cuban who had converted to Judaism before they met. That marriage failed as well. Esther and Isolina ended up in Havana, where she worked as a seamstress before she met José. Esther and José had two children together, both born in Cuba before the Revolution. When they abandoned Cuba, they left behind everything that they owned and sent their two boys, nine and fourteen, to Jamaica, where they were cared for by a Jewish welfare agency. They were united in Miami in May 1962. Figure 19 shows them in Miami in 1991.

The Winers' Cuban experience was unusual for many reasons. Until the late 1930s, marriages between Sephardim and Ashkenazim had been considered scandalous. It would take the anxious 1930s and 1940s before such attitudes would dissipate. Only after the Second World War did the children of the immigrants in Cuba finally begin to become part of Cuban society.

3 ✡ REFUGEES FROM NAZISM

> *The Holocaust may even be seen as a deliberate*
> *lesson or project in philosophical redefinition:*
> *"You religious and enlightened people . . . you think*
> *you know what a human being is. We will show you*
> *what he is, and what you are. Look at our camps*
> *and crematoria and see if you can bring your hearts*
> *to care about these millions." And it is obvious that*
> *the humanistic civilized moral imagination is*
> *inadequate. Confronted with such a "metaphysical"*
> *demonstration, it despairs and declines from despair*
> *into lethargy and sleep.*
> —Saul Bellow, *To Jerusalem and Back*

Hitler's Impact in Cuba

Events in Europe, starting with the Nazi accession to power in 1933 and accelerated by the successes of the Spanish fascists under Generalísimo Francisco Franco, abruptly colored the ways Jews in Cuba came to be considered by their island hosts. The new German flag, emblazoned with a black swastika, was displayed in Cuba not only at German offices and businesses but, in a few cases, by sympathizers. Without precedent in Cuban history, a propaganda assault was launched in the news media, spearheaded by Dr. José Ignacio Rivero's three newspapers and by the radio. The attacks focused on stopping Jewish immigration and called Jews fleeing from Europe "human garbage." During the late 1930s, the attacks mounted almost daily, aimed at the thousands of pro-Falange Spaniards living in Cuba. Anti-Semitism, which had rarely flared up publicly, now became a conspicuous part of everyday life.

Rivero charged the biweekly *Havaner Lebn* with disseminating leftist and anti-Cuban views. Sender Kaplan, the Zionist newspaper's editor, was arrested in late March 1936. The charge was that *Havaner Lebn*'s press had printed copies of a clandestine student newspaper. The printing had been done without Kaplan's knowledge by his Cuban apprentice, who had been paid secretly to do the work and, when caught, denounced Kaplan to the police. Kaplan was questioned roughly—at one point the police struck him when he denied complicity—and held for four weeks before he was found innocent by the special political tribunal at the Capitolio.[1] The UHC sent a representative to meet privately with Fulgencio Batista to protest rising anti-Semitism, and Batista promised to stamp it out, but the attacks continued, now channeled through the Anti-Judea Society of Cuba. Although in the absence of a broader-based community entity, the Centro Israelita took up the fight, it was denied support from the UHC, and its efforts proved ineffectual. Attempts in 1936 to organize a communitywide association of Jewish organizations to combat growing anti-Semitism from Spanish interests failed when the more prosperous (and assimilated) American Jews refused to deal with the syndicalist-minded, Yiddish-speaking East European immigrant leaders, many of whom they considered Communists.[2]

In mid-1937 an incident occurred that embodied the patronizing attitude of the United States and that further fueled the anti-Semitic campaign. Without any previous indication to any Cuban-Jewish group, a Jewish U.S. member of Congress, Dr. William I. Sirovich, met with the Cuban president and proposed that at least 100,000 German Jews be resettled in Cuba, and that Louis B. Mayer, chair of Metro-Goldwyn-Mayer Studios, head the project. Although Cuba lacked any restrictive immigration laws, Cubans reacted with hostility, and the legislature angrily rejected the plan. The rising crisis in Europe and the need for desperate actions to rescue refugees led major U.S. Jewish organizations to increase efforts to involve Cuba in resettlement plans, principally the American Jewish Joint Distribution Committee. The Joint, a major refugee relief organization in both Europe and the United States, opened a Havana office in early 1937 as the Jewish Relief Committee. Not only was there no coordinated worldwide relief effort, but conflicts arose among the organizations involved in relief work—between the Joint, which was believed by many East European Jews to be anti-Zionist, and other groups, including the World Jewish Congress.[3] Cuban Jewish groups, given their history of internal divisiveness, did not become directly involved in support efforts, although many individuals helped when they could.

By late 1938, the rising tide of Jewish refugees from Central Europe had started to flood Latin American consulates in Europe. Some 25,000 poured into France, with thousands more taking refuge in Holland, Switzerland, and Belgium. The Nazis had barred Jews and "non-Aryans" from universities and public employment and now were placing more and more restrictive prohibitions on their right to operate businesses. Nazi policy until late 1941 was to expel Jews, but not to arrest them unless they broke Nazi "non-Aryan" laws. Jewish citizens of Germany and of the countries that came under Nazi control were not permitted to transfer money outside. Jews, at this stage mostly men, were capriciously interned by the Gestapo, although in a few cases individual Nazi officials sometimes privately warned Jews they knew personally to flee to avoid arrest, in the words of one refugee, "probably for old time's sake."[4]

At the same time, the overseas democracies had made it clear that they would not permit refugees to enter except under existing quota procedures.[5] U.S. quotas made no distinction between refugees and ordinary immigrants. Canada, South Africa, and Australia had racial preference policies that produced a similar outcome. The waiting list for immigrants from Germany and Czechoslovakia filled the quotas for the next six years; for Hungarians, for the next twenty-five years. Word quickly circulated that some Latin American countries were willing to offer visas, although usually under stringent conditions. Some accepted only agricultural workers; others, including most of the Andean republics, issued visas only to Roman Catholics. But some 20,000 refugees from nazism gained entry to Latin America in 1938. Some managed to obtain papers from U.S. consulates to permit them to leave for the United States, especially if they had relatives there who could assume financial responsibility, but most had to stay in the countries in which they landed for the duration of the war. Cuba's response was cooperative. By mid-1938,

5,000 mostly German-speaking refugees had landed in Havana. Within a year, that figure had doubled.

U.S. State Department officials encouraged Latin American countries to take in refugees with so little grace that their comments had the opposite effect. The assistant secretary of state, Sumner Welles, attempted at the July 1938 Conference on Political Refugees at Evian-les-Bains, France, to convince the governments of Peru, Argentina, Chile, Mexico, and Brazil to open their doors, but the U.S. delegate, Myron Taylor, the former head of the U.S. Steel Corporation, bluntly declared that his country would not open its own. The Latin American countries took this as a convenient excuse and announced that they would shut their doors more tightly. The Evian meeting produced nothing but an agreement by the Dominican Republic to accept "agricultural" refugees to a farm colony at Sosúa.

Nor did the Lima Conference of February 1938 help, despite oblique lobbying by Secretary of State Hull on behalf of the Roosevelt administration to attach a rider favoring more liberal immigration policies to a Cuban resolution condemning persecution of minorities. The ploy backfired when the majority of delegates passed a resolution declaring incompatible with the sovereignty of the American nations any attempt to colonize racial or national groups within any country. Dominican Republic dictator Rafael L. Trujillo publicly said that he would take 100,000 colonists, but few believed that he meant it. More likely he used this promise to attract attention and to permit him to raise funds to finance agricultural development. The Joint Distribution Committee invested $1,423,000 in the project, hoping that the colony at Sosúa would succeed and encourage other countries to permit Jews to enter as farmers. A second project, the Sociedad Colonizadora, was initiated in Bolivia in 1941, and 142 refugees were admitted, although most drifted away from the agricultural project. In February 1939, Argentina, Uruguay, and Paraguay, meeting to discuss trade, signed a convention placing greater restrictions than before on refugees and promised to cooperate among themselves to keep out undesirables.

The only German Jewish refugees in Cuba who held U.S. transit visas were a small number who had gained entry to the United States under the German quota of the 1924 Immigration Act, which numbered 25,957 each year, but who had journeyed to Cuba to attempt to aid relatives whose high quota numbers disqualified them. By the late 1930s, several hundred thousand refugees from every European country occupied or threatened by the Nazis held entry quota numbers, but Washington's refusal to differentiate between refugees and ordinary nationals seeking to emigrate meant that most Jews, especially German citizens, would have to wait for years.

The sheer numbers of refugees threatened to overwhelm the situation. In 1938, 1,500 Jewish refugees came to Cuba from Central Europe, and the arrivals were continuing at a monthly rate of 500 after January 1939. Some received visas to go on to the United States, but by April 1939 an estimated 5,000 Central European Jewish refugees remained in Cuba. Not permitted legally to work, their welfare was handled by the tiny office of the Jewish Relief Committee headed by two staff members sent from the United States, Milton Goldsmith and Laura Margolis. German Jews arrived on virtually every regularly scheduled transatlantic liner from Europe that docked in Cuba. The landings did not differ from the arrival of tourist ships: vendors came aboard the night before disembarkation and sold linen *guayabera* shirts to passengers; the Havana Chamber of Commerce sent fresh pineapples.[6] But only sixteen slots a month were allocated for Cuban visas to the United States, leaving refugees arriving in Cuba in 1939 with at least a three-year wait, even though half of them held U.S. visa registry numbers.[7] Opposition came from labor unions and from businessmen who feared that some of the refugees were socialists or Communists. The leaders of Cuba's Spanish colony protested that the refugees would cause economic dislocation, although only 300 Jews were destitute, the rest supported by refugee organizations or by their families.[8]

In the end, two entirely distinct streams of Jewish refugees from fascism arrived in Cuba.[9] The first peaked in 1938–39, then slowed when the Cuban government refused to any longer honor landing permits issued by its own Immigration Department. The second wave started in mid-1941 and ended in early 1942. Perhaps 3,000 refugees entered during this period. These were Jewish refugees waiting for quota numbers for the United States as well as for regular visas for Cuba, which were made available in Cuban consulates in Europe for those paying a $500 bond (to assure that they would not become a burden) and possessing a $2,000 letter of credit. Some refugees were victimized by foreign consuls or by unaccredited persons posing as consular officials to whom they paid large bribes, only to learn on arrival that their documents were worthless.

The experience of the family of Adolph Mechener, a Romanian-born physician from Vienna, was typical of the most fortunate among the refugees: those who were able to rescue their families and enjoy a good standard of living in exile. With the Nazis closing in on Austria's Jews three months after the Anschluss, the Mecheners managed to obtain passage to Cuba because relatives who had bought tickets for Cuba decided to remain in France a bit longer. In exchange, the Mecheners paid for a ticket for their relatives' son and his wife to go to India. They fully expected to stop in Cuba only briefly and then enter the United States, where they had relatives, and where they had shipped as many of their furnishings as they could manage.

Those who escaped before the outbreak of war had little difficulty disembarking in Havana, but they found that they would have to remain indefinitely. In his unpublished memoirs, Dr. Mechener remarks on the strange sensations he felt walking in the streets—the noisy crowds, the mulattos, the vendors, the handsomeness of the architecture, especially the Malecón and the capitol. With foresight, he and his family had studied Spanish while still in Vienna, so adjustment for them was easier than for others. But they had with them only $420, which soon ran out. Dr. Mechener was prohibited by law from practicing medicine, but his acquaintances among other refugees soon sent him private patients, whom he treated at their residences for a dollar or two—in league with a cooperating druggist who filled his prescriptions for his patients. Other relatives and friends earned small sums in similar ways. Some of the women gave piano lessons; an engineer worked as a bookkeeper—of course, off the books.[10]

They kept in touch with European affairs and with German Jewish communities elsewhere in exile by subscribing to the newspaper *Aufbau*, published in New York. By their first New Year's Eve the Mecheners were prosperous enough to be able to rent tuxedos and go to the casino. They rented a house overlooking the harbor, from which they could see the daily boats coming from Florida, and the train ferries. The family's main problem was that their seven-year-old son, Franzi, had been required to remain in France with Dr.

Mechener's sister. They ultimately bought a visa for Franzi and his aunt, although by 1939 the price had risen precipitously and no transportation was available. It took two more years for the boy and his aunt to arrive in Havana on the SS *Villa de Madrid*. They were among the last Europeans able to flee nazism to the New World.[11]

Dr. Mechener's mother and father were arrested on October 10, 1942, for the crime of being Jewish. Before being transported to the camps, they managed to send a registered letter to a friend in Vienna, who later mailed it to Cuba. It was the last message from them the Mecheners would have.

My most heartily loved children:

We are writing these lines to you in great uncertainty about our fate and we also don't know *whether* and *when* these lines will reach you! But we want to assert [to] you that we are facing our fate quietly. We are happy—it is a paradox—that you are not here. God has helped me to know that you are far away. . . . I know that all of you will be very happy, because my whole life was a prayer for you. The thought of us should not burden you. We were well off up to the end. We were held in high esteem by *everybody,* especially Papa. . . . We put our future destiny in God's hands. It is possible that we will have to leave tomorrow, on the 11th of October at 5 in the morning. It is also possible that we will still survive and will see each other again! Then our gladness will be still greater. So farewell, my beloved children, let us always be among you, even if we are not alive anymore.[12]

Most of the first wave of Jewish refugees who landed in Cuba seeking transit to the United States were able to depart for the United States or Mexico relatively soon after arriving. Some had to wait months, others a few years. Nazi decrees banned Jews from operating businesses in June 1938 and encouraged acts of violence culminating in the Kristallnacht of November 9–10, 1938, when Nazis throughout Germany and Austria smashed or burned 191 synagogues and 7,500 Jewish-owned shops, killed 1,000 men and women, and took 20,000 Jews, mostly heads of families, into "protective custody" in concentration camps. The pogrom, the worst in Central Europe in five centuries, precipitated an atmosphere of "panic emigration" and played right into the hands of Nazi propagandists.[13] Jews, many of whom had steadfastly refused to budge, believing patriotically that Germany was just as much theirs as the Nazis and hoping that things would improve, were now threatened with physical violence.

Ilsa Mittel-Ashe, a twenty-two-year-old living in Unsleben, near Würzburg, Bavaria, remembers:

> In earlier years, I had tried to get a permit to what was then Palestine, but nothing happened, and after the annexation of Austria by Germany in Spring 1938, the need to go elsewhere—anywhere on the face of the earth—became imperative. The noise of the giant trucks that rumbled by our windows at 4 A.M. on the way to the secret underground factories had gone on for years. The political propaganda on the radio became more and more foreboding by the day. In the Fall of 1938, the crisis on the Czechoslovakian border over the Sudetenland spilled over into our village and jolted our family in a very personal way. Drunk Sudeten Germans, housed in an inn across the street, stormed our house, led by local Nazis, dragged out my father and beat him half to death.[14]

Voices of alarm over the fate of Europe's Jews were now being raised in the United States not only by spokespersons for Jewish groups, but by a fairly broad spectrum of non-Jews. The usually cranky H. L. Mencken wrote in his Baltimore *Sun* column on January 1, 1939:

> It would be much more honest and much more humane to tackle the problem at once, and settle it without further ado. Either we are willing to give refuge to the German Jews, or we are not willing. If the former, then here is one vote for bringing them in by the first available ships, and staking them sufficiently to set them on their feet. That is the only way we can really help them and that is the only way we can avoid going down in history as hypocrites almost as grotesque as the English.[15]

But President Roosevelt did little, and State Department officials simply folded their hands and refused to budge. A *Fortune* magazine poll in April 1929 listed 83 percent of Americans opposed to permitting more refugees to enter, although Eleanor Roosevelt held a press conference in June to urge passage of the doomed Wagner-Roberts bill, which would have increased quotas. President Roosevelt obviously had decided not to risk a confrontation with Congress. It now became extremely difficult to obtain a U.S. quota number at all, even a high one. Success or failure depended almost entirely on the attitude of individual U.S. consular officers in European cities. In many cases, would-be emigrants were turned away because they could not produce certified documents attesting to their good character and other personal qualities; the Nazi officials in charge of such paperwork laughed at Jews applying for them. Many of the Jews who did secure proper exit papers did so through the help of individual bureaucrats who, although some were Nazi party members, did favors for old friends or took bribes.

The desperation of Jews attempting to escape came at the worst possible moment. Many had nowhere to go, and insufficient means to transfer assets into cash to buy tickets even if they held immigration papers. The Nazis mocked them: Jews received standard khaki-colored German passports stamped with a large letter *J* in red ink (fig. 20); sometimes photographs were defaced with swastikas. Jewish applicants were required after a certain date to add the name Israel to each document issued to males and the name Sara to papers issued to females.[16] The passport of fourteen-year-old Helmut Brandt, who did manage to enter Cuba, included a quota immigration visa number issued by the U.S. consulate general in Hamburg (fig. 21). For would-be refugees, the worst battle was to come up with hard currency to purchase round-trip ship passage, to book available space, and to obtain Cuban landing papers. The vast majority of Jews in Germany and other countries overrun by the Nazis were not able to do this; most perished, it was learned after the war, many in camps or in the crematoria.

In the depression-ridden United States, nativist and isolationist sentiment so dominated public opinion that even had President Roosevelt wanted to accept large numbers of refugees he would likely have been overwhelmed by opposition in Congress. In Canada, anti-Semitic outbursts from French-speaking Quebec pressured the prime minister, William Lyon Mackenzie King, to bar refugees. Neither country would budge on the issue. Both clung to their outmoded quota systems with a stubbornness that commentators would later call "blind and ignoble."[17] Between 1933 and 1939, Canada accepted only 4,000 Jews, mostly refugees from Czechoslovakia. A proposal to the London-based Intergovernmental Committee, the agency established at Evian-les-Bains in 1938, made by the director

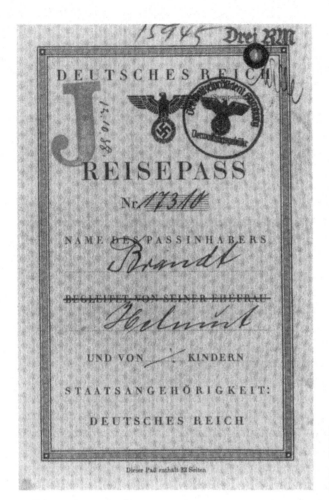

DEUTSCHES REICH

REISEPASS

Nr. 17310

NAME DES PASSINHABERS

Brandt

BEGLEITET VON SEINER EHEFRAU

Helmut

UND VON _____ KINDERN

STAATSANGEHÖRIGKEIT:

DEUTSCHES REICH

Dieser Paß enthält 32 Seiten

20. Helmut
Brandt's passport
with "J" for Jew.
Courtesy of Ilsa
Mittel-Ashe.

of Germany's Reichsbank in late 1938 to allow 150,000 refugees to emigrate in return for a loan of 1.5 billion reichsmarks in foreign currency to be provided by a corporation financed by "international Jewry" did not succeed.

In mid-May, Britain responded to the continued Arab revolt in Palestine, which had broken out in 1936, by curtailing drastically the number of immigrants permitted to enter Palestine, although through the end of 1939 it admitted more than 50,000 to the British Isles. A May 1939 white paper limited Jewish emigration to Palestine to 10,000 a year from 1939 through 1944, a policy expected to

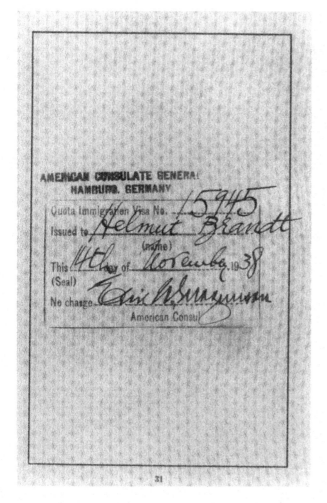

AMERICAN CONSULATE GENERAL
HAMBURG, GERMANY

Quota Immigration Visa No. *15945*

Issued to *Helmut Brandt*
(name)

This *14th* day of *November* 19*38*
(Seal)

No charge *Eric M. Wagnusson*

American Consul

31

21. Passport visa
page. Courtesy of
Ilsa Mittel-Ashe.

bring the Jewish population there to 75,000, or one-third of the total.[18] Nearly a quarter of a million refugees from the Spanish civil war passed through France, and more than 150,000 stayed. Thousands of refugees, almost all of them Jews, crowded into Belgium, Holland, Luxembourg, France, and Switzerland holding only transit visas. President Roosevelt appealed for a remote place somewhere in the world where refugees in large numbers could be settled and contacted Mussolini about Ethiopia; the Soviet Union proposed Alaska. The U.S. State Department suggested Angola, but Portugal demurred; Nazi diplomats proposed Madagascar. Jewish organiza-

Unterschrift des Paßinhabers

Helmut Brandt

und seiner Ehefrau

Es wird hiermit bescheinigt, daß der Inhaber die durch das obenstehende Lichtbild dargestellte Person ist und die darunter befindliche Unterschrift eigenhändig vollzogen hat.

Hamburg, den 29. Sep. 1938

Der Polizeipräsident.
Abt. VII.

22. Passport photo page. Courtesy of Ilsa Mittel-Ashe.

tions and national governments investigated such possible sites as the plateaus of South-West Africa, Tanganyika, Nyasaland, the Philippines, Northern Rhodesia, Venezuela's Orinoco River Valley, and British Guiana. The Dominican Republic offered to take large numbers but demanded millions of dollars in immediate payment; in the end, only a few Jewish settlers arrived at the Sosúa colony, not the thousands that had been discussed. Cuba pledged to cooperate with the International Refugee Committee in London, but nothing was done to formulate a coordinated policy on immigration and the reception of refugees.[19]

Because the Cuban government felt obliged to demonstrate that the newcomers would not drain already depleted resources in the depressed economy, those who managed to enter Cuba faced severe restrictions. They could not work, and they had to post bond to guarantee that they would not become public charges. As refugees were not allowed to depart Nazi-occupied Europe with more than a few dollars and a suitcase, Cuba became little more than a holding pen for Jews who held relatively low U.S. quota numbers. Some had traveled directly to Cuba; others had sailed from European ports to New York. Barred from entering the United States, they then booked passage to Havana, where they waited until their quota number came up. While in Cuba they often had to be supported by Jewish relief agencies in the United States. Once the U.S. consulate at the foot of Obispo Street in Havana granted entry papers, they were permitted to purchase ship passage from Havana to Key West or Miami; they continued by train or Greyhound bus to their final destination. Those with a $500 deposit in the Cuban Finance Ministry could petition the ministry to return the money, which was then delivered by messenger to the departing vessel. Before June 1939, relatives of German and Austrian Jews in the United States worked through individual members of Congress to cut through red tape and encourage Cuban officials to issue landing permits. Rep. Samuel Dickstein of New York, for example, helped twenty-three members of one family obtain Cuban visas.[20]

Ilsa Mittel-Ashe describes her experience:

Still waiting for our Cuban entry papers, I spent the night of November 9, 1938, Kristallnacht, hiding in a Christian neighbor's barn, together with my uncle's family. Some of our non-Jewish employees had loosened some slats to provide a hiding place, and all of us found safety that night. I had not been able to return from our office because threatening crowds appeared and milled about in the street. The cries we heard throughout the night from those rounded up in the village were heartrending.

Finally, our Cuban papers came through toward the end of November. At that time we were still able—against 100% taxation of value—to pack my parents' household goods and ship the container to New York harbor for storage, in preparation for whatever future time we would establish a household again.

Only 19 of the 23 visa holders were able to leave Unsleben. We sailed across the turbulent Atlantic for three weeks on the German ship *Orinoco*, in a cabin that held 16 passengers. To say it was crowded is an understatement, but nothing mattered. On touching Cuban soil, the feeling of exhilaration was overwhelming. We were free! The American Consulate in Havana was immediately most helpful in getting us out of Tiscornia within a day or two. We found temporary quarters in a third-rate hotel where the bedbugs made short shrift of our nightly rest, but within a few days we secured an apartment in downtown Havana. It was built, Spanish style, around an inner courtyard. Each family occupied one room and we shared the kitchen facilities. My 'family' consisted of four cousins, all single, aged 17 to 22 years.[21]

Some European Jews managed to buy papers attesting that they were subjects of one or another Latin American country, but there were too few ships, and many Jews were captured by the Nazis before they could depart.[22] Vienna-born Morris Branfman was told by the Cuban ambassador in Geneva that he would have to come up with the equivalent in Swiss francs of half a million dollars at the prevailing exchange rate; Branfman obtained 105,000 francs in Swiss Treasury bonds and was granted entry visas for himself and his pregnant wife. But when they and forty other German-speaking Jews disembarked from the SS *De la Salle* in Santiago, at the far eastern end of the island, they were declared illegal immigrants and interned for twenty-one days. They were finally released when local Jews interceded and arranged for the refugees to pay a bribe of $200 to the immigration officials. The next day the refugees were transported overland by bus to Havana.[23]

Nazi and Falange sympathies reached their peak in mid-1938, when Fascists held a series of outdoor masses in Havana Cathedral's plaza, and when a host of Fascist front organizations were organized. There were direct links to Hitler's Reich. Admiral Walter Wilhelm Canaris, the head of the Abwehr, the German Military Intelligence Service (and later one of the major figures in the resistance against Hitler), recruited a cadre of Cuban spies, among them Enrique Augusto Lunín (Lunning), a businessman who was to provide reports about merchant marine activity in Cuban waters.[24] The Abwehr also recruited agents from crews of the major German shipping lines as couriers for spies and to report secretly on superior officers whose

Nazi sympathies were suspect. The Abwehr network in Cuba was directed by Robert Hoffman, the assistant manager of the Hamburg-Amerika Line office in Havana. Much of this was known to U.S. intelligence agencies operating inside Cuba, but all they could do in prewar Cuba was watch and wait.[25]

The Jewish Relief Committee office in Havana, headed by Jack Brandon, handled the influx as best it could. It agreed to stand behind the costs for all refugees who arrived without funds.[26] Hundreds pressed into the committee's tiny office seeking money to live on and help for relatives still stranded in Europe. The Relief Committee also endeavored to combat the continuing anti-Semitic propaganda. The government's legalization of the Cuban Nazi party and the National Fascist party on October 20, 1938, accompanied by a call from both groups to boycott Jewish firms and inciting Cubans to "rise up against the Jewish menace," escalated the atmosphere of crisis. Relief Committee board members and their colleagues worked behind the scenes to influence Cuban authorities to admit more refugees.

Sensitive to U.S. pressure but also sympathetic to Franco's side in the Spanish civil war, at the end of the 1930s the Cuban government bestowed its Order of Merit on Nazi ministers Joachim von Ribbentrop and Vico von Bulow Schwant. The New York *Herald Tribune* estimated the number of Cuban Nazis and Nazi sympathizers at 5,000. The Cuban Falange party, legalized in July 1936, continued to work closely with Nazi agents and with Spanish consular officials in Havana and in the provinces. Considerable Spanish-language anti-Semitic material was imported and distributed through these channels. The Falange party was primarily influential in three sectors: commercial associations, elite secondary schools (especially the Colegio Belén), and the newspapers *Alerta*, *La Discusión*, *Sí*, and, particularly, *Diario de la Marina*. Some anti-Franco Spaniards sought refuge in Cuba during this time, creating some tensions in the Spanish immigrant community, but their numbers were small, and they remained overshadowed by the Falangists.[27]

Pro-Nazi Cubans became increasingly bold in their public behavior. Newspapers printed photographs of handsomely dressed men and women giving the Nazi salute. Opposition to further Jewish immigration mounted, centered in labor and business groups who feared that the newcomers would displace native workers and place a burden on the still-depressed economy—even though the Law of the 50 Percent would have protected most workers.

The director general of immigration, Manuel Benítez González, Sr., opened an office in the Hotel Plaza in the fall of 1938. (His son, Manuel Benítez Valdés, had aided Batista during the 1933 sergeants' revolt; as a result, Benítez, Sr., had been made director general of immigration when the post was insignificant.) He sold the immigrants landing certificates, typed on Immigration Department stationery and personally signed by him (fig. 23), for $150. This was not an inconsiderable amount of money; a family could live comfortably on $1.00 a day at the time. Benítez himself did not see anything wrong with the arrangement; his family said later he had considered it a "business deal."[28] On January 13, 1939, President Laredo Brú reacted in support of the rising tide of anti-immigrant arguments and decreed for the first time a distinction between immigrants and tourists.[29] Henceforth all foreigners would be required to have an entry visa approved three times: by the secretaries of state and labor and by the director general of the Immigration Department. When the chief of immigration decided not to cooperate, virtually no visas were issued through regular channels.

Although Benítez's landing permits were perfectly legitimate, the way the Cuban system worked was that much of this money was split up as the revenue moved up the ladder, ultimately to the presidential palace. The refugees knew nothing of this; they simply thought that they were paying the official charge. The morality of the system of graft, however, was never an issue. This was wartime, and people needed help at any cost. Nor did the refugees complain about Cuba's low-key and pervasive corruption. Bribes and payments for "favors" lubricated the system and made it work efficiently. Graft was handled through a chain of command that ended at the presidential palace or the army high command as long as Batista was chief of the army, regardless of who was president. The system worked according to informal rules. Everything revolved around whom you knew: privileges that went with having friends in high places ranged from invitations to closed clubs and parties to fixed traffic tickets and the opening of officially closed doors for relatives to find refuge. Some unusually compassionate functionaries felt pity for refugees or their families and helped them beyond the call of duty. Benítez's secretary, Gloria, helped a young German,

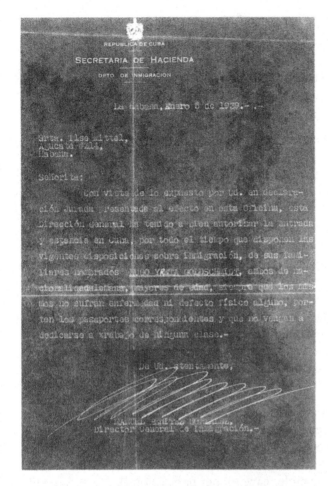

23. Landing
permit. Courtesy
of Ilsa Mittel-
Ashe.

Walter Lippmann, obtain a landing permit for his parents, who came
on the *Orinoco*, the last ship with refugees to be permitted to dock
in Cuba. Gloria's mother also helped Lippmann rent an attractive
house in Vedado.[30]

Many other refugees shared similar experiences. They were grateful for the willingness extended to them by the Cuban government,
even though they were not permitted to work and they had to play
according to the system, which required bribes at opportune mo-
ments. But these were generally small, and few complained. Most
had to leave all their bank savings and other assets behind. Ninety
percent of a person's net worth was confiscated on departure. Much
of the rest went for currency conversion, if that were possible at all,

Refugees from Nazism   95

for trumped-up fees, and for taxes. A handful managed to smuggle out funds: one man supposedly put his assets in a barrel of pickles and followed the barrel to England after his arrival in Cuba.[31]

Allegations have been made about a sordid side to the process. Ilsa Mittel-Ashe remembers what happened to her when she attempted to help relatives who were still in Germany.

> Many a morning I found myself [waiting] with five and ten peso bills, as a small, necessary bribe to the underlings in order to get into the inner sanctum. . . . [The official there] was a portly, handsome man of about 55 or 60. He greeted those who came to see him in his office, especially when they were young women, with a macho approach. Young women, in fact, were invited to his country home for the weekend. I guess the $150 fee was waived then, but although I smiled and swallowed my pride, I paid the $150. When I stated that one of the relatives I wanted to bring out of Germany was blind, the official exacted an additional payment: he demanded that I minister to his genitals, swelling under his pants. This was disgusting, but even this did not matter as long as I could obtain the coveted papers to bring freedom to a dear one. These ministrations to his person were by no means a one-time occurrence. That day they had to be carried out in a particularly fierce manner, a price to be exacted.[32]

Allocating the precious landing permits to Cuba and other destinations involved agonizing family decisions. Men and women who had spent their lives building up businesses or professional practices held on, praying that the Nazis would vanish. Ruth Goldschmidt's grandmother, for example, gave up her passage on the *Orinoco* and the permit that had been obtained for her to her son-in-law. She died in 1943 at the concentration camp in Theresienstadt.[33]

In Cuba, officials and others became wealthy dealing in visas and other immigration papers. During and after Benítez's time, permits were sold to wholesalers and even to German shipping companies. Some of the brokers were Cuban politicians with connections within the Cuban Jewish colony, including Oscar Caíñas Milanés, the brother of a senator and himself a former member of Cuba's Congress. The Cuban permits carried with them the written proviso that the holder would only stay on the island "for such time as necessary to obtain a visa for the United States."[34] They affirmed that the bearers were of good health and would not participate in any

24. American Travel Company, Havana. Courtesy of Hardy L. Spatz.

kind of employment while in Cuba. Travel agents obtained bunches of permits at $150 each and resold them in Europe for much higher prices, generally from $500 to $750. After mid-1939, the system changed. Agents received names of stranded Jews from family members (and from U.S. lawyers and travel agents representing them) and obtained individual permits on a case-by-case basis. Individuals who went to the Immigration Department and asked for permits were stalled, but those who had connections or knew how the system worked could still get them. Also, permits were handed out as political favors, based on business. The travel agencies continued to function until the attack on Pearl Harbor, when most ships stopped. Some of the Havana travel agencies trading in permits were Jewish owned. One of them was an agency owned by two Ashkenazim, Gabrylewicz and Volpe, founded before the troubles in Europe. Another was American Travel Inc. (fig. 24), opened on the centrally located Prado in mid-1941 by Arnold Spatz, a Jewish refugee from Austria.[35]

For Jews still trapped in Europe, the process of getting visas was extremely difficult because no non-German ship company would accept payment in German reichsmarks. Even most German shipping lines demanded payment in dollars or other stable foreign currencies. One former member of the Cuban government later stated that some Jews paid as much as $50,000 or $100,000 under the table for legal entry visas. Most permits were obtained for the standard fee by relatives or agents working for people who wanted to enter. If the reports about large sums being charged is accurate, it must have applied only to a handful of people who did not work through the regular system.[36] The Hamburg-Amerika Line offered package deals to passengers able to pay for both the ship passage and landing papers, which presumably were valid. In May and June 1939, more than 1,300 permits were purchased and paid for.

The reason for the sudden exodus of refugees seeking entry to Western hemisphere countries was the direct result of a joint effort between the Gestapo, under Reinhard Heydrich, and the Propaganda Ministry, headed by Joseph Goebbels, to embarrass the democracies by showing that no country wanted Jews. The Germans also wanted to exile as many Jews as possible from Central Europe, to "cleanse" the region of Jews. At the beginning, Jews were told to abandon their possessions and leave the country. Reich officials encouraged them to purchase visas and landing permits from Latin American consulates, even if the papers turned out to be worthless. The policy created havoc. Those who did manage to obtain valid visas and to find their way to the Western hemisphere were caught up in the plight that affected the 500,000 German Jews and the millions of other Jews in soon-to-be-occupied territory throughout Europe. After the Anschluss in 1938, 45,000 of the country's 186,000 Jews were driven out of Austria in eight months. The refugees who reached Western hemisphere countries during this period represented a cross-section of this displaced persons' population, but they were on the whole more affluent than most. It took considerable ready cash to make the necessary arrangements for the trip.

In retrospect, they were also more prescient regarding the approaching dangers than the hundreds of thousands who remained behind hoping that life under the Nazis would improve. Many, if not most, German-speaking Jews were economically comfortable in the 1930s. Those who did manage to leave did not necessarily have any specific foreknowledge of the coming horrors; they perhaps simply acted on their hunch that things would soon worsen. Some had to leave children or brothers and sisters behind; in other cases, parents sent children ahead. Often one family member went first, hoping to arrange for the rest to follow, only to find soon after arriving in safe haven that the doors had swung shut. Nearly every Jewish refugee who came to Cuba in the late 1930s and early 1940s lost one or more relatives in the Holocaust; some lost dozens, or their entire families.

Norbert Adler was a young single man who had been in the advertising business in Berlin. This is how he remembers his departure:

When the pressure to leave Germany became almost unbearable, I tried to secure an entrance visa to somewhere in the world. The waiting lines at all public agencies, both Jewish and Nazi, were so long that I would have had to wait several years to get . . . any permit or visa. In January of that year, my regular passport for international travel was called in and limited for travel within Germany only. That was my signal for starting to plan for my departure.

In December 1937, the police notified me in writing that I had to bring in my passport for cancellation of the foreign travel privilege. I still had a month. . . . But we could not dare simply to pack up and leave on such short notice, and there were no permissions available for us to just travel to another country and stay there.

That's when I seriously started to prepare for my emigration. I signed up for a course in window dressing at a local Jewish retraining school, and also assembled a toolbox to take along to wherever I might be going in order to be prepared for a menial occupation somewhere in the world, if I ever could get out at all. Thousands of emigration applicants stood in mile-long lines at all consulates, Jewish assistance organizations, and Nazi administration offices, and there was little hope to be able to get away from Germany in a regular manner. No country in the world opened its doors, and even the U.S. had a strict policy against job-seeking immigrants. Through good fortune, I heard about the possibility of immigrating to the United States via Cuba, by first securing a tourist visa at the American consulate. It was possible to buy a "vacation" round trip from Europe to New York, plus an additional "cruise" from New York to Havana, and pay for all this in German marks. The plan would be to get a visitor's visa from the U.S.

Consulate in Berlin, find an American in New York to sign an affidavit to guarantee I would not become a public burden, take these papers to Cuba, and magically get my immigration visa.

The many-months-long preparations for this "round trip," not recognizable as emigration, had to be done in secret, as you could not tell anyone what you were planning. You never knew whether someone, somehow, or something might interfere. . . . A careless word, an unfounded suspicion, a person you did not even know with a grudge against you, could block the way to your freedom. When I went to the American Consulate in Berlin to get my tourist visa, I had to prove that I was essential in Berlin and would return for sure. I also needed to bring in proof that I had substantial means. The irony, of course, was that as a Jew in 1938 Germany, you would not want to come back, but I and the consular official had to play the charade. Thanks to a long-time friend of my father's at the German tax bureau, I got a statement showing an inflated income. The man was now a card-carrying Nazi, but his heart was still in the right place, and he helped me. Since our finances were limited, I took our total family fortune and deposited it [and withdrew it] in quick order in three different bank accounts within one or two days, making the total look impressive.

When I went to the consul for my follow-up visit, he had forgotten about me. But, fortunately, his secretary remembered me, and upon his question, she nodded "yes" and I received my important stamp. My passport was reinstated, the tickets were paid for, and on July 25, 1938, I left with pounding heart and trembling limbs for my flight to Amsterdam. We were permitted to take only 10 marks in cash with us, plus an advance deposit of 50 additional marks to be used aboard ship. I took along three cameras I had brought especially with the idea of selling them for cash in America. In order to pass through United States customs without a problem, I handed two of the cameras to fellow refugees whom I met on the boat. But I did not have to worry, because my ticket to Cuba meant that I was only a transient and could have had with me anything without fearing a customs duty bill.

One of the cameras entered the United States with a young man who had received his immigration visa on the basis of an affidavit from his aunt, a Miss Rothschild in New Rochelle. When I went there to retrieve my camera, I asked Miss R. whether she would give me an affidavit too, and she said yes. I mailed it to the American Consulate in Havana for a preliminary examination. They sent me a wire saying I needed a supplemental affidavit, and I went to work on that task. After a few weeks, I got it from an American friend of an immigrant friend from Berlin, and mailed it on to Havana. A wire then came asking me to come for my visa.

I took the next boat to Havana and, right on arrival, rushed to the American Consulate. It was closed for Columbus Day. The first thing next morning, I went again to the Consulate and was the first on line. This time, I learned that their quota of 65 visas for October had been used up, so I could not return to New York. I was placed ninetieth on the waiting list. This meant that my turn would only come in December, but I was only slightly disappointed, because the climate was nice and the people friendly. . . .

The only problem was that on December 1st I did not get the visa either, and was destined to spend the next two years in Cuba because the entire quota system had been revamped. It made sense, because now they would hand out visas on the German quota in Germany where thousands of Jewish refugees were waiting, had in fact been waiting for years, while we, who had already left Germany, at least were safe. So who could complain? . . . .

Yet it was difficult for me to adjust to the longer waiting period. I had never lived alone, and now I was in a foreign culture. But people took care of me. The Havana office of the Jewish Relief Committee, which had helped me in New York, gave me $7 a week to live on. I didn't like accepting a dole, but under the circumstances I had little choice. Refugees who came directly from Europe received only $4 a week. I was, at age 25, the only person in our family to flee in 1938, leaving my parents behind. Much of my two years in Cuba were spent trying to get them out of Germany. . . .

Smart people knew from the beginning that the jig was up for Jews in Germany and left early. Others, like myself, who were too young, inexperienced, and afraid of the unknown, hung on longer. It was by pure intuition that I happened to leave three months before the Kristallnacht. There were [also] those Jews who were too German to leave, and they died for their "loyalty."[37]

4 ✡ THE SS ST. LOUIS INCIDENT

By the end of 1938, Cuba faced an agonizing dilemma regarding refugee policy. The scene of dozens of refugees fleeing Nazi Europe landing at Havana was repeated nearly every time a transatlantic steamer arrived in port. A rising tide of opposition confronted officials, who had never before objected to granting permission to land. Representatives of the U.S. government issued contradictory signals. Before the July 1938 international meeting on refugees from Nazism at Evian-les-Bains, the State Department had informed all of its diplomatic personnel to be sensitive to the dilemma of "political refugees" from Germany and Austria, specifically persons forced to leave Europe because of their religious faith. Another confidential memorandum in the form of an "urgent circular" from Secretary of State Hull in late November 1938 noted that "many countries may be prepared to accept larger numbers of involuntary emigrants than they are willing publicly to admit."[1] Letters and confidential reports sent by U.S. diplomatic personnel to the State Department often seemed to sympathize with the refugees, noting that the Fascists and Nazis were working to make their plight more difficult and thereby implying that failure to assist in some way would aid the Fascist propaganda cause.[2]

On the other hand, Under Secretary of State Welles in December 1938 personally advised individuals working to aid Jews fleeing Europe not to send "more refugees than Cuba could handle at any one time."[3] U.S. officials noted what they termed the "divergence of views between the Cuban Immigration Bureau and the [Cuban] State Department" but did not endeavor to interfere, although they issued pointed warnings regarding Nazi sympathies among Cuban newspaper editors and career foreign service officers. The U.S. ambassador noted that the Cuban consul in Hamburg, "the only career foreign service officer in Germany," was "Nazi in sympathies and not in favor of any Jewish refugee movement to Cuba."[4]

On January 25, 1939, Berlin cabled to all German embassies and consulates throughout the world a report on the emigrant situation, adding that expulsion of destitute Jews would lead to increased anti-Semitism in the countries of destination, and thus, according to the Foreign Ministry, to a "better understanding of German anti-Jewish policy."[5] Three months later, in early April, Joseph Goebbels, the Reich propaganda minister, set in motion the events that would forever alter prospects for refugees gaining entry into Cuba and the rest of the Free World. Fourteen agitprop agents were ordered to infiltrate Cuba with the explicit task of stirring up public opinion against the Jewish refugees already there, whom they painted as parasites and human garbage. The plan was simple: permit a large new group of Jews to leave Germany, trumpet their undesirability, and then pressure countries not to take them in. The principal vessel selected to carry out this scenario was the Hamburg-Amerika Line's handsome, 575-foot luxury liner SS *St. Louis,* one of the fastest and largest motorships in Europe.[6]

Cuba presented itself as a logical theater of operations to probe foreign willingness to accept refugees because on May 5, 1939, under a storm of domestic political pressure and agitation in the pro-Fascist press, Havana abandoned its former pragmatic immigration policy under which virtually any arrival at a Cuban port would be admitted on showing minimal means of support. President Laredo Brú asked Congress to prohibit "repeated immigrations of Hebrews who have been inundating the Republic and . . . permits that are being issued for the entrance of such Jews to Cuba."[7] Congressional Decree 937 restricted entry of all foreigners except U.S. citizens, requiring a bond of $500 and authorization by the Cuban secretaries of state and labor. Permits and visas issued before May 5 were invalidated retroactively.[8]

For a period of about a year afterward—when the plight of refugees was greatest, and when they still could manage to escape—Cuba's doors remained closed to them. No one knew exactly what had happened, but one explanation that circulated publicly, and that many Cuban Jews heard, was that Pedro Mendieta, a friend of President Brú's, asked Benítez, the head of immigration, for his support in elections for the constitutional assembly. Mendieta allegedly demanded $25,000 in cash and jobs in the Immigration Department for fifty of his henchmen. Benítez was said to have refused, saying "My balls are bigger than yours." Mendieta then went to Brú and argued in favor of retroactively canceling the affidavits for all entries into Cuba.[9]

The decision to use Cuba as the port of destination was fortuitous for the Nazis. The United States, which refused to change its immigration policy, had in effect placed unreasonable pressure on Cuba to absorb thousands of arrivals, but once Cuba started to balk at accepting any more on the basis of the former free-for-all arrangements, Washington turned unsympathetic. Cuban law, established by Decree 1021 of March 23, 1937, had simply required that any foreigner entering Cuba not as a tourist post a bond of $500, usually collected by the shipping company.[10] On March 18, 1939, in fact, a consular official, Harold S. Tewell, had sent a long "strictly confidential" memorandum to Washington on "European Refugees in Cuba," with four copies. In it he warned that "Cuba has long been a base from which aliens are smuggled into the United States" by means of "false visas, Cuban citizenship documents, passports, and birth certificates; by smuggling as stowaways on vessels; by smuggling in small boats hired for the purposes; and attempts have been made to smuggle by airplane."[11] Tewell cited antirefugee editorials in the *Diario de la Marina*, "the leading Havana daily newspaper," to underscore his point that Cuban public opinion opposed, in the newspaper's words, "the invasion of Israelites." Under these conditions it was understandable that some Cubans in the prewar atmosphere were disturbed at prospects of a continued flood of unwanted arrivals. The atmosphere was ripe for rumors and for a revival of Machado-era xenophobia.

Three ships that regularly traveled to Cuba would carry expelled Jews—the SS *Orduña* of the British Pacific Steamship Navigation Company, the French Line's *Flandre*, and, the largest of the group, the Hamburg-Amerika Line's 16,000-ton luxury cruiser *St. Louis*. This vessel, commanded by a captain with thirty-seven years of seafaring experience, Gustav Schroeder, would be infiltrated by six Gestapo agents headed by an *Ortsgruppenleiter*, Otto Schiendick, who would keep Captain Schroeder in line and personally carry espionage materials from the Abwehr station in Havana back to Germany. The line agreeably cooperated; revenues were down, and the refugees would guarantee full bookings. The four hundred first-class passengers would be charged 1,130 reichsmarks ($452 1939 dollars) each, the more than five hundred tourist-class passengers, 830 reichsmarks ($332). Both fares included a "contingency fee" of 230 reichsmarks ($92) for the return voyage in case of "circumstances beyond Hapag's [the line's] control."[12] Details for the "special voyage" were supervised by the *Reichssicherheitshauptamt*, RSHA, the bureau under which Adolf Eichmann's Department IVB4 would ultimately assume responsibility for the extermination of Jews in Germany and in occupied countries.

The *St. Louis* would carry 937 refugees, the smaller *Orduña* 72, and the *Flandre* 104, all due to arrive in Cuba during the first week of June. To extort the greatest amount of revenue possible, passengers were required to purchase round-trip passage. Of the 937 men, women, and children booked on the *St. Louis*, 734 held U.S. immigration quota numbers authorizing them to enter three months to three years after landing in Cuba. More than 1,200 Jewish refugees were scheduled to land during a twenty-four-hour period. What none of them or even Captain Schroeder knew was that the Cuban government had retroactively invalidated the passengers' landing permits eight days before the *St. Louis* had sailed. The voyage, then, was a deliberate attempt to test the willingness of other countries to accept unauthorized refugees. What the Germans were banking on was that they could stir up enough suspicion and revulsion for the "subhuman" refugee cargo that no country would accept it.[13] Cynically, pursers made the passengers pay a round-trip surcharge, as the pretense was that they would return.

The *St. Louis*'s journey involved a mixture of desperation, courage, pathos, and irony. Its passengers were treated with contempt before they boarded, but once on the ship they were treated like privileged tourists (figs. 25–27). "You feel perfectly at home on board," proclaimed the bilingual ship's program distributed to each cabin, "and in addition enjoy the gay life on a ship devoted to relaxation and pleasure."[14] Although the passengers were allowed by law to bring with them only ten reichsmarks, and this as *Bordgeld*, money that had to be spent aboard ship, Berlin's Ministry of Propa-

25–27. From *St. Louis* publicity brochure. Courtesy of Lutz Krätzschmar.

The finest thing about a voyage is life on deck

HAMBURG-AMERIKA LINIE

Hamburg / Amsterdam

Verbland Dining-room

Hier schaut Sie in behaglicher Tischrunde Ihre Mahlzeiten ein.

Here you take your meals in congenial company.

You are well looked after on board. Your steward soon becomes acquainted with your individual habits and requirements and carries out your wishes before they are expressed.

ganda dispatched press notices claiming that the passengers were "fleeing with stolen hoards of money, and much else."[15] Photographs of the most stooped and disoriented refugees boarding the ship at Hamburg were circulated worldwide to accentuate the image of the passengers as refuse.[16]

Even before the ship had sailed from the port of Hamburg, some officials publicly expressed concern that the passengers might not be permitted to land. The British consul in Havana communicated this warning to the Foreign Office, which forwarded it to Sir Herbert Emerson of the Intergovernmental Committee on Refugees. In haste, Emerson cabled Claus-Gottfried Holtusen, the shipping line director in Hamburg, not to permit the ship to leave. Holtusen, under heavy Gestapo pressure, assured Emerson that the passengers would be permitted to land, claiming that he had the "personal guarantee" of Cuba's immigration director.[17] Rumors spread through refugee circles as well. Rachel Koeppels, who had arrived in Cuba in October 1938 with her husband, sent telegrams to her father and brother to take not the *St. Louis* but the *Orinoco*, which was scheduled to leave earlier. Her niece and sister-in-law also were expecting to depart on the same ship.[18]

Allegations issued by the Cuban Nazi party claiming that the refugees were Communists were reprinted in virtually every Cuban newspaper. Daily reports about the ship fanned the crisis and led to the largest anti-Semitic demonstration in Cuba's history. Batista's old nemesis, deposed President Grau San Martín, was now leader of the Cuban Revolutionary party (*Auténtico*). From the Senate, he called for a "rally against the Jews" on May 8. The rally drew 40,000; tens of thousands more listened over national radio. Grau's main spokesman, Primitivo Rodríguez, called for the people to "fight the Jews until the last one is driven out of the country" and allegedly went to members of the local Jewish community asking for $50,000 as payment for refraining from attacking Jews any further.[19]

Jewish welfare officials in Cuba expressed their exasperation. "We have had practically daily visitations from newspapermen, 'Cuban friends,' who come with messages from Col. Benítez," wrote Laura L. Margolis on May 23 in an urgent and confidential letter to the National Coordinating Committee in New York. She wanted to know "why the Joint Relief Committee does not take any active steps in fighting the anti-Semitic propaganda and why we are so passive about all this proposed immigration legislation." She assured the committee that she and her colleagues,

> of course, receive all suggestions very politely and ask them to send us written memos about their propositions as to how we can act and what it will cost. So far we have received no written memos with any propositions.

Probably too inexperienced in Latin America to understand that this was not the Cuban way, Margolis suggested that

> The President and some of his secretaries are getting very tired of having Col. Benítez get all the graft, so the Presidential decree of May 6th was a means of stopping immigration on the landing Permit basis and at the same time they were hoping to strike a bargain with the JRC or a blanket guarantee for all persons coming in with the Five Hundred Dollar bonds and visas. The proposition is of course ridiculous because there isn't enuf money in the whole USA to take care of any such proposition. On the other hand, Col. Benítez and his crowd were trying to hold on to the graft as long as possible and indirectly sending us messages to us on the basis of pure love for the Jews, in order to get us to help them fight against the Presidential decree and the anti-Semitic propaganda. Of course, as you know we have not played ball with either side and the result has been that Benítez has really resigned [as Commissioner of Immigration]. . . . we are in a complete deadlock.[20]

Locally, officers of nineteen Cuban-Jewish groups met to organize cooperatively, the first time representatives from all segments of the Jewish community had gathered under one roof to discuss common action since the failed effort in 1936 to create a central association of Jewish organizations.[21] They established the Fareinigten Komitet Zum Bakemfn dem Antisemitism in Kuba (the United Committee to Combat Anti-Semitism in Cuba) and shortly afterward the Comité Central de las Sociedades Hebreas de Cuba (Central Bureau of Jewish Organizations in Cuba). None of their efforts succeeded in securing permission for the *St. Louis* passengers to enter Cuba, and bickering flared up as tensions grew. Socially prominent Jews simply did not trust their Yiddish-speaking East European counterparts.[22] A director of the Joint Relief Committee complained that "the unfortunate feud between German Jews and Eastern Jews has been carried over into the ranks of the refugees here." The East European Jews consider us "a German-Jewish outfit," he wrote. "Various members of this Executive Committee have expressed to me, at different times, the most violent opinions regarding the German Jews. . . . I am sure you will appreciate with what degree of objectivity [our] committee can judge refugee matters when I tell you that of the executive committee of ten members, six are relief recipients and eight of the ten are Polish Jews." The observer put his finger on at least one of the sources of the enmity: almost none of Cuba's Polish and Levantine Jews, he noted, had established themselves in small businesses. Most were "poverty-stricken peddlers" living on a standard below that of the $4.50 per person provided by the Joint Relief Committee to the 1,100 Central European Jewish refugees classified officially as "destitute" residing on the island.[23]

On May 24, 1939, less than three weeks after Decree 937 had been promulgated, Cuban newspapers printed a report distributed by the German embassy that the *St. Louis* had left Hamburg on May 13 and was transporting nearly a thousand Jewish refugees to Cuba, ranging in age from infants to a ninety-three-year-old man. The ship docked at Cherbourg on May 15, passed the Azores four days later, and headed for Havana, its regular cruise destination.[24] Many of its passengers were professionals: there was a high percentage of physicians and lawyers, who, as Jews, had been barred from public practice by the Nazis. Most of the passengers had lived for some time holding transit documents in Belgium or France; some, coming out of the Reich, had been in concentration camps but had managed to be freed. More than three hundred were children, many of whom had one or both parents waiting for them in Havana. Crew members treated the passengers well—Captain Schroeder had insisted on this. Elegantly clad stewards served foods that by 1939 had been rationed in Germany; there was a full-time nursemaid to care for small children when their parents sat to eat.[25] There were dances and concerts, and the captain allowed passengers to hold Friday evening religious services in the dining room and even permitted them to throw a tablecloth over a plaster bust of Hitler that sat there. The weather on the seas was beautiful most of the time, although some passengers suffered bouts of seasickness. Photographs of the Karliner family on board the ship (fig. 28) and of their son with other boys (fig. 29) reinforce the impression that the Jewish passengers were relieved to be leaving Germany. Children were given swim-

28. Karliner family
on board *St. Louis*,
June 1939.
Courtesy of
Herbert Karliner.

ming lessons in the on-deck pool. Passengers felt that they were, in the words of Lothar Molton, a boy traveling with his parents, on "a vacation cruise to freedom."[26]

But when President Federico Laredo Brú heard that the ship had departed despite Cuba's official notification to the Reich and to the Hamburg-Amerika Line that only passengers with valid visas would be allowed to enter, he set into motion steps to force immigration authorities to turn the passengers away. He dismissed Benítez from his post; the immigration chief claimed that the motives were political, and many Jewish Cubans believed the dismissal sprang from Benítez's refusal to cut in the president, who was considered to be an anti-Semite, on his racket. Benítez claimed that he had gone to Batista to ask that the *St. Louis* passengers be allowed to enter Cuba—promising that they would be the "last boat of Jews" he

29. Boys on board *St. Louis,* June 1939. Courtesy of Herbert Karliner.

would bring in—but that Batista had refused. Benítez's son in later years maintained that Cuba had acted to stop further admission of refugees at the behest of the U.S. State Department.[27] Batista, whose relations with Laredo Brú were reportedly strained, chose to remain silent, in keeping with his decision to maintain a low political profile. Jewish group leaders hoped that Decree 937 would not be enforced or that some kind of exemption could be arranged for the passengers. But the government did not back away. Captain Gustav Schroeder, personally enraged at crude acts of defiance among the Gestapo agents in his crew, attempted to reach Havana ahead of the two smaller (and faster) refugee ships.

Whether or not Manuel Benítez knew that the permits he issued to the *St. Louis* passengers would be considered invalid, he had sold them wholesale, accumulating a personal fortune estimated at more than $600,000 at prewar values from the proceeds. Relief officials blamed Benítez for instigating a racket through which refugees who had posted the required $500 bond could get it back by paying from $100 to $125 for the "service," in clear violation of Cuban immigration law. Cuban officials also allegedly took bribes from Hamburg-Amerika agents. Laredo Brú reportedly demanded $250,000 from the line to change his mind and let the *St. Louis* passengers disembark. Hamburg-Amerika agents paid lesser sums to permit the ship to dock at least long enough to allow Otto Scheindick ashore to be able to retrieve the Abwehr spy documents from Robert Hoffman.[28]

Cuban public reaction continued to be unsympathetic to the *St. Louis*'s plight. Prodded by Cuban Jews, the Chamber of Commerce and some foreign firms (including Pan American Airlines) urged that "tourists of all nationalities" be permitted to enter Cuba but stopped short of speaking to the specific case at hand. Newspaper editorial writers argued that the humanitarian aspect of the dilemma was overshadowed by the fact that Cuba, mired in economic depression, was being asked to do what all other countries had rejected. National sovereignty became the issue, over and above sentiments fired by the barrage of anti-Semitic propaganda that emanated from pro-Nazi sources. On May 25, Reich diplomats in Havana dispatched a gleeful telegram to the Foreign Office in Berlin documenting what they described as a recent "intensification of the anti-Jewish campaign" in the local press. Excerpting examples of anti-Semitic articles in *Alerta, Avance,* and *Diario de la Marina,* the cable noted that the articles "state that the Jews are forcing their way into local business, that they exploit the Cubans unscrupulously, and even begin to push them out of business; further, that they violate and circumvent the laws of the country and cheat Cuban authorities." The articles predicted that "soon they will dominate all commerce in Cuba, and the Cuban people will have to suffer under capitalists of a new kind, who speak another language and believe in another God, and do not care about the problems of the country." The cable's authors added: "The newspaper demands that the Cuban government speedily expel the Jews as undesirable and troublesome elements, and characterizes them as polyps who drain the blood of the Cuban people."[29] Even the Communist newspaper, *Hoy,* urged curtailment of immigration in the wake of the *St. Louis* visit.[30]

Dr. José Ignacio Rivero wrote in a *Diario de la Marina* editorial reprinted in *Avance:* "Against this Jewish invasion we must react with the same energy as have other peoples of the globe. Otherwise we will be absorbed and the day will come when the blood of our martyrs and heroes shall have served solely to enable the Jews to enjoy a country conquered by our ancestors."[31] He added that the question of Jewish emigration carried with it a danger of communism. "Not that every Jew is a communist nor every communist is a Jew," but "every Jew is a potential communist." "Such elements," he added, "never fully assimilate in any country but retain their own customs and habits, constituting a danger for the nationals of the countries to which they come." We should be very careful to consider permitting any more free emigration, he wrote, especially since economic conditions in Cuba are so difficult.[32] Other newspaper voices were less strident but equally unsympathetic. *El Mundo* remarked that the "initiative of the United States in taking steps to assist" Jewish and other refugees was "highly praiseworthy" but that "it would be ridiculous for Cuba to attempt to receive any further emigrants without making a scientific study of the entire question, which, if entered into blindly, might possibly disrupt the economic life and social organization of the country."[33]

On May 26, armed guards barred Benítez's office and prevented any further permits from being issued. Refugees arriving on any ship would only be permitted to land if they had official Cuban visas. Cuban Secretary of State Remos cabled the *St. Louis*, refusing landing permission; he also told the press that Cuban consuls in Europe "found guilty" of extending visas without permission "will be punished."[34] At that point, neither the local Jewish colony nor the Joint Distribution Committee in New York was able to do anything to block enforcement of the decree. The *St. Louis* dropped anchor at 4 A.M. on May 27 at the far end of Havana harbor and was denied permission to come to the usual docking areas. Refugees ashore, anxious but still hoping that disembarkation would be permitted, watched the steamer in the harbor. The *St. Louis* passengers were awakened early to prepare for disembarkation; health inspectors came aboard, and all preparations were made for normal docking. Hours passed. The harbor smelled foul, the result of unchecked discharges from shore.[35] A photograph taken from the ship after it dropped anchor shows the passengers' view of the harbor from the ship rail (fig. 30). At midday, the passengers were told by loudspeaker that disembarkation would be delayed indefinitely. The six days that followed were tumultuous and pathetic. Moored far out in the harbor under a broiling sun that registered 102° F. on the ship's

30. Havana from deck of *St. Louis*, June 1939. Courtesy of Herbert Karliner.

deck, the *St. Louis* was surrounded at all hours by boats and small launches carrying relatives and friends of the passengers (fig. 31), who leaned over the railings to catch a glimpse of their loved ones and to shout encouragement at one another. One girl was able to take aboard ship a pineapple that her mother had brought from shore. Some passengers managed to send out letters telling of their despair and hope. Ironically, not a few mailed postdated postcards to relatives in the United States stating that their senders had "arrived safely in Havana."[36]

Captain Schroeder, accompanied by two Cuban attorneys, attempted to deliver personally a memorandum from the passengers to the president at the palace but was told that the president was attending a cabinet meeting and would be unable to receive him.[37] Fearing disorder on board, he requested that twenty-five port police officers be posted on his ship; his request was granted. No one else from the island was permitted to board the vessel except, at various times, medical officers, Hamburg-Amerika representatives, the Jewish Relief Committee's Milton D. Goldsmith, and the American congregation's Rabbi Meir Lasker. The body of ninety-two-year-old Professor Mendelsohn from Würzburg, who had died aboard ship, was to be brought ashore for burial. Cuban officials demanded payment of $250 for a lead coffin, for which a collection was taken up

31. Relatives on launches in Havana harbor, June 1939. Courtesy of Herbert Karliner.

from among the passengers, but the officials changed their minds; Mendelsohn was buried at sea by the captain and twelve men wearing prayer shawls.[38] Hilde Rothold, a young woman who had come from Breslau to visit relatives in Norfolk, Virginia, in 1932 and who had been sponsored by them six years later and therefore admitted to the United States, had traveled to Cuba to await her parents who were arriving on the ship. She pleaded with the dock administrator in his home to permit her to board the ship to be with her parents. He authorized a brief visit to the ship's bridge, accompanied by two Cuban officers. Rothold, along with a few dozen others who had come from the United States to meet members of their family, voluntarily gave up her reentry visa so that the number could be assigned to a refugee still caught in Europe. For this act of generosity, she and the others had to remain in Havana for another six months until new papers could be issued.[39]

Some passengers became hysterical. Others fell into deep, disoriented gloom. They now had little to do but wait at the railing. In photographs, many seem anxious (fig. 32); a few smile wanly at the launch from which the photographs were taken; others stare; some prop themselves up by their elbows, as if they had been standing for a long time. One man, Max Loewe, became so distraught over the delay that, in full view of other passengers, he slashed his wrists and jumped into the harbor. A lawyer from Breslau, he had been arrested during the Kristallnacht and sent to Dachau before he managed to gain his release and find passage on the ship. Despite the efforts of his wife and fifteen-year-old daughter to help him, he had become deeply despondent. A ship's crew member immediately jumped in and rescued the flailing passenger, who was taken by police launch to the Calixto Garcia hospital. Sharks circled the spot where the bleeding man had fallen. His family was not allowed to join him, and he became the only passenger holding only a landing permit to reach Cuba from the *St. Louis* alive.[40]

Cuban public opinion, stirred up by the propaganda barrage, emphatically supported the decision to refuse to permit the ship to land its passengers. The U.S. ambassador at luncheon at the American Club asked an intermediary, Mario Lazo, to find out the disposition of the Cuban government and was told later in the day on May 31 that the cabinet had "voted unanimously to exclude the Jewish refugees and require the *St. Louis* to sail with all on board." The Cuban president, the ambassador was told, had listened to humanitarian

32. *St. Louis* passengers, June 1939. Courtesy of the National Archives of the United States.

arguments but had remained steadfast, feeling that "a lesson must be dealt to the Hamburg-Amerika Line which had brought these passengers here with documents obtained through bribery after they had been categorically informed that passengers brought under such circumstances would not be allowed to land."[41]

The only other passengers permitted ashore were the twenty-two with regularly issued visas, a few of whom were non-Jewish refugees from the Spanish civil war, and six anonymous passengers sent for at the last minute after personal negotiations between the Annenberg publishing family in Philadelphia and the Cuban ambassador in New York, Pedro Fraga. Fraga somehow authorized their passports to be stamped with legal visas while the ship stood in the harbor. Another story went that officials had agreed to permit all Christians to land, and they should wear crosses around their necks on disembarking; four passengers supposedly accepted the offer. A claim about payments of bribe money in behalf of some passengers by the U.S. Jewish gangster Meyer Lansky, who in the 1930s spent considerable time in Cuba investing in casinos and a race track, has never been documented.[42]

A single Cuban newspaper, the English-language *Havana Post*, pleaded for compassion: "Witness the care-worn faces of old and young, their once-bright eyes grown dull with suffering, and your heart will go out to them. Witness the stark terror in their expression, and you will realize that they cannot be sent back to Germany."[43]

Heywood Broun wrote in his New York *Journal-American* column an emotional plea to reason, arguing that had the *St. Louis* struck an iceberg, an immediate international rescue effort would have ensued. Some U.S. journalists showed less understanding. "How could the refugees have been so careless about ascertaining whether and where they would be allowed to land?" wrote the editor of the Columbia (South Carolina) *State*. "Cuba had not invited them, had not even been asked if they would be received as residents; and harsh as it may seem, Cuba's President Laredo Brú perhaps had no alternative but to deny them admission," concluded a Seattle *Times* writer.[44]

The Joint Distribution Committee had flown attorney Lawrence Berenson, a prominent New York lawyer, former president of the Cuban-American Chamber of Commerce in the United States, and one-time personal legal adviser to Batista, to Havana to negotiate the landing of the refugees with President Laredo Brú. At least one meeting was held at the president's home, Párraga, and at least $290,000 was deposited. Records show that Berenson was aided by Dr. José García Montes, secretary of agriculture, and one of his aides, Dr. Eisenstein, identified as a Jew who had been in Cuba for fifteen years, "never interested in Jewish matters" until the *St. Louis* incident "roused his soul." During the meeting with the president, Dr. Eisenstein "burst into tears, went to the bathroom to wash his face, but came out still in tears."[45]

The Joint (that is, the JDC) knew that there would be financial constraints if the Cubans demanded more money: in this year of the *St. Louis* crisis, 1939, the entire budget of the committee was $8.1 million. But Berenson was prepared to offer cash, and for a time it appeared as if the matter would be dealt with simply. The reaction to Berenson's high-profile mission was mixed. Accompanying him was Miss Cecilia Razovsky of the National Refugee Service of New York, an affiliate of the Joint. Her presence drew criticism later on the grounds that "there is the unanimous opinion that a woman, in the first place, and Miss Rakovsky especially, could do no good and probably did some harm."[46] The newspaper *Flecha* editorialized that the Jews on the ship should be permitted to land lest there be an "international scandal," but most of the rest of the press expressed approval of statements made by the labor secretary and other officials standing firm in the determination not to allow any foreigner with documents unadjusted to the recent decree to set foot on Cuban soil. *Discusión*'s editor wrote that in spite of Berenson's presence, if the law prohibited the passengers' entry, they should be turned away. The secretary of justice instructed his underlings to expedite investigation of "forged passports" held by German nationals already in Cuba, and the Cuban Department of State declared that as many as five consuls who had issued improper visas would be prosecuted. The president ordered police officials to capture twenty-five "Chinamen" who had been allowed to disembark from the SS *Siboney* earlier, on the grounds that they were reported to have landed in violation of the Immigration Law. A storm of controversy erupted, most of it negative, on the issue of whether Cuba should suspend further immigration in light of the difficult times.[47]

The efforts on the scene to aid the *St. Louis* passengers were coordinated by Milton D. Goldsmith, the able director of the Joint, who was a former navy officer and graduate of Annapolis. Rabbi Lasker kept in contact with all parties, including the U.S. ambassador. When Berenson pledged to pay to free the passengers, the local Jewish Relief Committee Advisory Board voted unanimously to forbid Berenson and his party from representing them to the Cuban government, arguing that the case should be handled only on humanitarian grounds. In any case, despite early optimism, Laredo Brú refused to see Berenson a second time.

Instead, Berenson was told by two intermediaries (Major Bernardo García, Havana's chief of police, and Colonel Manuel Benítez, the immigration director's son) claiming to represent President Laredo Brú that a bond of $453,000 would suffice to permit the refugees to land. Pleading lack of time to obtain more funds, Berenson rejected the offer, and the *St. Louis* sailed northeast out of Cuban waters for a week while Berenson continued to talk with other Cuban officials.[48] García had been authorized by Laredo Brú to negotiate for him, but Berenson had been given no proof and did not seek another meeting. When final negotiations fell through days later, the Cuban government acknowledged that Berenson had offered to fund the sustenance of the *St. Louis, Flandre,* and *Orduña* passengers to be housed on the 1,180-square-mile Isle of Pines, but that he had waited too long, and that the matter was closed. *Discusión* expressed its editors' pleasure, reminding readers that the Isle of Pines had been kept out of the clutches of the Yankees by the bitterly negotiated Hays-Quesada Treaty, and that turning it over to Berenson for a Jewish colony would render Cuba's victory hollow.[49]

During the last days that the ship was still in Cuban waters, other strenuous efforts were under way. The Cuban branch of the crypto-Jewish Maduro family, also represented in Curaçao and Panama, attempted without success to obtain visas for at least some of the passengers.[50] Hints that Honduras and the Dominican Republic would take passengers evaporated. Rabbi Lasker, who played a central role in the negotiations and who was one of the few persons to be permitted to board the *St. Louis*, maintains that the ship actually headed for Panama, where officials bribed by relatives of the Maduro family there allegedly permitted about forty refugees to be landed quietly. This is a highly perplexing assertion, although Rabbi Lasker is adamant that the story is accurate.[51] Nearly fifty years later, Rabbi Lasker (fig. 33) maintained that a brother-in-law of one of the pas-

33. Rabbi Meir
Lasker. Courtesy
of Meir Lasker.

sengers, a man from New Jersey, acted in behalf of the Cuban Jewish
Maduro family and hastily flew to Panama to make the arrangements, aided by members of the Panamanian branch of the Maduros.
But Rabbi Lasker has no notion of how the passengers were selected,
how they disembarked, or what happened to them after they entered
Panama. No other survivor from the ship with whom I had contact
can vouch for this story, nor does Captain Schroeder's book, which
describes everything he did to aid the passengers, mention such an
effort. Unless further evidence comes to light, the story will have to
be considered false. Most likely, Rabbi Lasker confused the episode
with the saga of another ship, the *Orduña*. He may never have been
as close to the events as he maintained in hindsight.[52] Tragically, the
one offer that would have saved all of the passengers was turned
down because at the time it looked like the Berenson negotiations
might still succeed. The Joint Distribution Committee in New York
received a telegram from a quarantine station at Balboa in the U.S
Canal Zone offering to house the refugees at a cost of $1.50 per day.
Weeks later, these facilities were used by the refugees from the *Orduña*, which rather than returning to Europe had crossed the Panama Canal and gone from port to port in search of safe haven.

For the *St. Louis*, nothing more could be done. Huge spotlights were installed by port officials to illumine all sides of the ship, to forestall unauthorized attempts to board or disembark. On June 2, President Brú ordered the Cuban navy to accompany the ship beyond Cuba's jurisdictional waters, and to tow it if it did not move on its own. Twenty launches filled with marines escorted the liner from the harbor and a short distance beyond Morro Castle, so that no one would jump overboard.[53] Passengers leaned over the ship's railings and attempted to converse with relatives and friends who had hired launches to approach the ship in the harbor; many became hoarse because they had to shout to be heard. Mothers held their children over the rails and threatened to throw them into the water unless they were allowed to disembark. But the die was cast. The frantic telegrams sent by passengers to world leaders—President Roosevelt, the British prime minister, Neville Chamberlain, the king of England, the Dutch royal family—went unanswered. Wires from influential persons ranging from U.S. trades union chief John L. Lewis to members of the U.S. Congress were ignored.[54] On June 6, after twenty-two days at sea, the heartbroken Captain Schroeder, at all times in control, ordered his crew to start the slow journey back across the Atlantic. The tense but optimistic atmosphere that had characterized the cruise on its westward crossing was replaced by an air so grim that the passenger committee named by Captain Schroeder carried out an around-the-clock suicide watch. The sea, which had been as motionless as a mirror, became turbulent. Passengers were violently seasick, many until the ship reached the Azores. Passengers discussed with the captain and some of his sympathetic crew the possibility of beaching the ship at Southampton or setting it afire.[55] Rumors circulated that the Gestapo was planning to board the ship at Cuxhaven to organize the transport of the passengers to concentration camps.

President Laredo Brú personally cabled James N. Rosenberg, chair of the National Council of the Joint Distribution Committee, arguing that the matter was one of Cuban internal governmental policy, not financial guarantees.

IN REPLY TO YOUR CABLE REGARDING REFUGEES ON BOARD S.S. *ST. LOUIS* YOU KNOW DEAR MR. ROSENBERG THAT CUBA HAS CONTRIBUTED IN RELATION TO ITS RESOURCES AND POPULATION TO A

GREATER EXTENT THAN ANY OTHER NATION IN ORDER TO GIVE HOS-
PITALITY TO PERSECUTED PEOPLE BUT COMPLETELY IMPOSSIBLE TO
ACCEDE TO THIS IMMIGRANT ENTRY INTO NATIONAL TERRITORY.
SUBJECT *ST. LOUIS* IS COMPLETELY CLOSED BY THE GOVERNMENT.
REGRETFULLY REITERATE THE IMPOSSIBILITY OF THEIR ENTRY INTO
CUBA. WISH TO ASSURE YOU OF MY SINCERE FRIENDSHIP.[56]

On board, the captain ordered that the ship sail as close to South
Florida as possible, hoping that U.S. officials would give permission
for the passengers to disembark. The ship anchored briefly off
Miami Beach, but no permission came, and orders came over the
radio to raise anchor. Herbert Karliner, a twelve-year-old passenger,
spent much of his time gazing at the shore through binoculars. He
estimated years later that the ship anchored roughly off Fourteenth
Street.[57] A Coast Guard patrol boat out of Ft. Lauderdale closely
trailed the ship in the early hours of the morning as it sailed parallel
to the Florida coast to be sure that no one plunged overboard and
swam to safety. Coast Guard aircraft also flew overhead. Just in case
a breakthrough in negotiations occurred, Captain Schroeder ordered
the liner to sail slowly in a southeasterly direction, marking time.

It has been noted that after the *St. Louis* departed Cuba, the German embassy in Havana requested the Foreign Office to send a protest that, although Berlin understood that Cuba did not want to accept any Jews, the "treatment" given to a German line ship had been
objectionable. Berlin sent an expression of displeasure (*Befremden*)—
less than a formal protest. The U.S. Department of State sent no
protest of any kind.[58] Grudgingly, lest the Nazis win a full-fledged
propaganda victory, U.S. and British officials met at the Home Office
to devise stopgap measures to prevent the passengers from having to
return to Hamburg and face transport to concentration camps. The
U.S. ambassador to Britain, Joseph Kennedy, cooperating with representatives from the Joint and other agencies, worked to find alterna-
tives. The Joint team, headed by European director Morris Troper,
pledged $500,000 to cover costs incurred in taking in the refugees. In
France, Baron Robert de Rothschild consulted with Colonial Office
officials to allow the passengers to be transferred to French Guiana
or Tangiers. The *St. Louis* passengers sold their jewelry, cameras, and
even clothing to crewmen to pay for cables to be sent to leaders all
over the Free World, begging for asylum lest "acts of desperation"

occur on board. Interviews with members of the crew years later suggest that the crew did not understand the significance of their ship's voyage. Carl Glissmann claimed that en route back to Europe, he spoke with "one of the Jews," a lawyer, holder of the Iron Cross from the First World War, "a Nordic type, blond, blue-eyed, and nothing Jewish around the nose or mouth." The passenger allegedly told Glissmann that, in light of the ship's rejection by Havana and by the United States, he was glad to be returning to Germany, that if they guaranteed that nothing would happen to his family, he would prefer to "sweep the streets in Hamburg than to be a peddler in Cuba."[59] Jewish organizations throughout the world pleaded for help. "What we have gone through," wrote Adolph H. Kates in Havana, acting as spokesman for the Jewish colony, "can be compared to a tropical cyclone with all its horrors."[60]

On June 10, the deadlock was broken when the Belgian minister of justice, Paul Emile Janson, and the prime minister, Hubert Pierlot, within an hour of being asked formally, agreed to accept 214 passengers.[61] Queen Wilhelmina and the Dutch government offered to take 181 more. Pressed by Sir Herbert Emerson over the arguments of more junior Foreign Office spokesmen that the passengers should be returned to Germany, Prime Minister Chamberlain's permanent undersecretary at the Home Office recommended that up to 350 passengers be accepted, as long as the Joint pay for their maintenance. Lots were drawn aboard ship to determine to which of the four countries each family would go. A total of 287 were earmarked for England. The French government agreed to take the remaining 224. The news was communicated to the ship on June 13; the telegram from the Joint was read, in Captain Schroeder's presence, to cheers and sobs of joy. More than anyone, Schroeder and his sense of correctness and resolve to stand up to the Nazi members of his crew had prevented chaos and hopelessness from descending on the ship through the course of its tense, five-week journey.

The next day, the French national chief of police in Paris told the press that he "regretted . . . that our American friends, to whose country the majority of the refugees were eventually going, stopping at Cuba only en route, were not able to direct them to one of their ports instead of sending them back to Europe."[62] The *St. Louis* landed at Antwerp on June 17, where passengers were met by a flock of customs officers, police, and refugee organization officials who ignored the ugly demonstration near Pier 18 by the pro-Nazi (Rexist) National Youth Organization protesting the landing. Its members later distributed handbills stating that "we too want to help the Jews. If they call at our offices each will receive gratis a piece of rope and a strong nail."[63] A planned Rexist parade did not materialize, but the police took no action and would have permitted it had it occurred.

The passengers selected to enter Belgium were taken by bus to a special train, third class, with windows barred and nailed shut for the passengers' "security," they were told. Otto Bergmann, one of the passengers who hoped eventually to get into France, noted in his diary: "In order to get permission to enter France we had to come to Antwerp in Belgium. And to get to Belgium, we had to travel to Cuba." The Joint and HIAS paid for the upkeep of the *St. Louis* refugees in Belgium until the country was overrun by the Nazis. A few of the ship's passengers whose quota numbers came up fairly early were able to emigrate directly to New York.[64] When Belgium fell, its government continued supporting the remaining Jews in secret, never revealing them to the Germans. Some escaped, taking the old sea passage from Dunkirk. A handful managed to survive through the war, including Hilde Rothold's parents, who paid a local family to hide them in an abandoned, boarded-up store during the five years of Nazi occupation. If Hilde had not managed to give them $1,700 in cash when the *St. Louis* was in Cuban waters, they would likely have been unable to pay for their later escape. Her uncle, also a passenger on the ship, who was transported to the internment camp at Gurs in Vichy, France, did die. The grandparents of Dr. Luis Glaser, whose Viennese son and daughter-in-law had managed to obtain a visa from the honorary Mexican consul in Zagreb, Yugoslavia, were hidden in an attic for the duration of the war by two successive Belgian families whom they did not even know. But in spite of the heroic gestures of individual Belgians, most Jews interned in Belgium died in Nazi concentration camps.

Leah Kadden, however, was one whose story had a relatively fortuitous ending.

My brothers and I were enrolled in the public schools in Brussels. When the Germans invaded, our odyssey began. My oldest brother, 16 at the time, was interned by the Belgians and sent to Camp Gurs. He was able with the help of relatives in the United States to leave there and enter the United States in April 1941. My mother, other brother and myself remained in Brussels under German occupation until 1942, and then had to go into hiding because our name was on the list to report for work camps. With the help of the underground and other connections, we were hidden by a Belgian family until papers could be gotten to enable us to flee to Switzerland. Many people were refused entry [but] after being interrogated by Swiss police at the border, we were placed in reception camps: my brother, 14, in a youth camp, I, age 11, in a children's camp, and my mother in a camp for women. Camps in Switzerland were hotels in small villages, requisitioned by the government to house the refugees. I was allowed to attend the local one-room school, and enjoyed civilized life under the circumstances.[65]

The *St. Louis* passengers apportioned to Holland went by steamer, the *Jan van Arckel*, to Rotterdam. They were interned at the Heij-plaat quarantine station with hundreds of other German refugees. Most remained for weeks, and, little more than a year after their release, most would be picked up by Nazi soldiers and transported east to camps in Germany and Poland. Others were interned in the Westerbork transit camp under deplorable conditions. In 1942 it was taken over by the Gestapo. Jews were removed via cattle truck and shipped to the gas ovens. Before that happened, one of the members of the passenger committee, Dr. Fritz Spanier, was put in charge of the camp hospital, and he continued in that position until the end of the war. In 1944 he and his staff were ordered by the Gestapo to sterilize all Jewish women in the camp, or they and the doctors would be deported. When Holland was liberated, he returned to Germany, where he worked with survivors at Bergen-Belsen. He stayed in Germany until his death in 1967.[66]

Passengers destined for Britain and France sailed on the *Rhakotis*, an aging, overcrowded freighter with portable lavatories on deck. It disembarked 224 passengers in Boulogne; the next day the group was split into two, half taken to Le Mans, half to Laval. The elderly Baron Rothschild addressed the French contingent of passengers in broken German during a two-hour stop at the Paris train station. He concluded with a warning: "Think about this: never spit on the street. When a Jew does this it will always be said, all Jews spit on the street."[67]

Most of the passengers stayed in France, only to be captured when France fell. Members of at least one wealthy family, who had been able to transfer $25,000 in assets out of Europe, managed to secure papers that permitted them to travel from France to Montreal.[68] The Arons were able to gain entry to Cuba in the last months before its doors closed in 1942. Herbert Manasse, the youngest member of the *St.Louis*'s passenger committee, fled to Italy with his wife and their two young children after the Germans took France; they were captured and sent to Auschwitz, where they were gassed. Refugees unable to obtain emigration papers were forced to huddle in cities such as Limoges, whose normal population of 100,000 had swelled to 600,000 by late 1939. People slept on the floor on burlap bags filled with straw. Children were permitted to attend schools but suffered from lack of food, head lice, and stress. German Jewish children, most of them brought up in comfortable middle-class homes, had to beg for scraps of bread. People waiting in long lines to buy food would come to blows. The lucky few managed to escape over the mountains to Spain and ultimately to Portugal, where—at least until the shooting war started—they could board ships for the Americas.

The final contingent of 287 sailed on to Southampton. They became the fortunate ones: of the one-quarter of the *St. Louis*'s Jewish passengers who survived the war, most were those sent to Britain.[69] The refugees disembarked to a spectacular water and fireworks display, a rehearsal for the arrival of King George VI and Queen Elizabeth, due the next day from the United States. The passengers then proceeded by train to Waterloo Station; some families were housed in local hotels, while the sixty unmarried men were taken to the Kitchener Camp at Richborough, Kent, where refugees awaited transport to Palestine, the United States, or South America. They were instructed not to talk with reporters about their experiences under Hitler.[70] Three months later, when Germany declared war on Britain, all German nationals in the British Isles, including the *St. Louis* passengers, were declared enemy aliens, and many of the men were interned.[71]

Captain Schroeder and the most loyal members of his crew remained on the *St. Louis*, which was scheduled to leave for New York. They were afraid to return to Germany, where they would likely be punished for having acted compassionately toward their

Jewish passengers. Among those not sympathetic to the captain, Otto Scheindick signed off at Antwerp, carrying with him a Cuban walking stick, some magazines, and some fountain pens, in which Abwehr agents in Havana had hidden microfilmed U.S. defense papers.[72] Ironically, Scheindick, who had bullied passengers throughout the trip despite the captain's strenuous efforts to protect them, nearly missed making his connection with his contact because of the successful Nazi propaganda barrage that kept the ship anchored at bay.

In spite of the emotional nature of the unfolding story and the Reich's attempt to use the refusal of the democracies to take in more Jews, the story of the *St. Louis* was often reported in a matter-of-fact way in the world's press. Many stories, moreover, proved to be false, yet they were never corrected in print. Although readers of Swedish newspapers, for example, were told on June 3, in stories based on dispatches borrowed from the European news agency Havas, that the Jewish passengers of the *St. Louis* were "gripped by panic" when the ship sailed from Havana, three days later, they were served up a Reuters-based story that was completely untrue, stating that the Dominican Republic had accepted "all 922 refugees," and that in fact the refugees had disembarked safely in Santo Domingo. Not a single Swedish newspaper, even the *Goteborgs Handels* (whose editor, Torgney Segerstedt, was so anti-Nazi that publication of his paper was suspended under Sweden's policy of neutrality when the war broke out), ever retracted this false report. *Goteborgs Handels* did report, twelve days later, that refugees from the *St. Louis* were due to disembark in Rotterdam.[73] Stockholm's main daily newspaper, *Dagens Nyheter*, never ran any story after it reported, incorrectly, that the passengers had landed safely in Santo Domingo. An earlier version of the story—that refuge would be provided by Trujillo—was published in Havana's *Diario de la Marina*.[74] When this soon proved false, no Cuban newspaper printed any follow-up story reporting the passengers' fate. Nor has the passage of time improved historical accuracy. As recently as June 1992, a letter to the *New York Times* comparing the *St. Louis* affair to the post-Aristide coup plight of the Haitian boat people seeking refuge in Florida claimed that in the *St. Louis*'s case "almost 1,000 people" had been "saved."[75]

The refusal of Western governments to open their doors to any additional Jewish refugees—and the even harsher stance taken by Washington and Ottawa—did yield a propaganda victory for the Nazis. One of the reasons that the *St. Louis* story did not stir up more attention in the press was that thousands of refugees were caught up in similarly harrowing circumstances all through 1939 and 1940. Eichmann's functionaries loaded Jews on ships in Austria and sent them wandering from country to country up the Danube.[76] On the day the *St. Louis* entered Havana harbor, a Greek line steamer, the SS *Liesel*, carrying 900 Jewish passengers, was turned away from Haifa by the British, bringing the total of Jews turned away from Palestine to more than 2,000. European newspapers reported, based on dispatches from Buenos Aires, that 200 Jewish refugees on board the liners *Caporte*, *Monte Olivia*, and *Mendoza* docked in Buenos Aires had been refused entry to Paraguay and would be returned to Hamburg even though they held consular visas.[77] On the same day, the Costa Rican Supreme Court denied appeals from 20 Jewish refugees who had managed to enter on ninety-day permits and ordered all of them expelled except for Gertrude Hirsch, who gave birth to a baby boy while in San José.[78] Bolivia and Chile admitted 520 Jews, but officials warned that no more would be taken. The *New York Times* reported on June 8, 1939, that after six weeks of wandering from port to port in the Mediterranean, eight German Jews attempted suicide by taking poison while their steamer languished at anchor in the port of Alexandria. They had been denied permission to disembark in Alexandria, had continued on to Jaffa, then to Turkey, then returned to Alexandria. Near death, they were finally taken off the ship and treated at Alexandria's Jewish hospital.[79]

An enduring measure of the tragedy was that the deaths of 667 of the 907 *St. Louis* passengers who were returned to Europe and perished as part of Hitler's "final solution" could have been avoided by more skillful negotiation or by accepting the offer of the Panama Canal authorities to take the refugees.[80] The *St. Louis* incident was all the more tragic because of the trajectory of its route—it came so close to shore that passengers standing on deck at night could see the lights of buildings and residences both in Miami Beach and Havana, and in some cases they spoke with officials and even relatives who were given brief permission to board before the ship ultimately was forced to return to Europe. The atmosphere could fairly be described as sordid. All of the time in which the *St. Louis* sat at anchor at the far end of Havana harbor, the anti-Semitic fusillade continued, even in the Cuban Congress, where rival political factions speculated on how families of the hapless refugees could be made to pay millions of dollars for the right to land.[81]

While the ship was anchored at Havana, *Información* editorialized that Jewish immigration would be stopped because of likely detrimental effects on the Cuban economy. *El País* declared that all immigrants except those from Holland and Spain should be forced to leave. The *Diario de la Marina* reported that a petition had been submitted to the Cuban House of Representatives to prohibit all further immigration from Poland, Hungary, Czechoslovakia, Yugoslavia, Lithuania, Bulgaria, Germany, Turkey, Romania, Russia, China, Japan, Jamaica, and Haiti. All immigrants in Cuba engaged in occupations or activities other than those in which they declared they would engage on entry would be deported, and all those who had been in Cuba for less than three years would be prohibited from engaging in commerce or industry.[82]

During the *St. Louis* ordeal, tensions ran high in Havana. José Winer remembers standing outside of Sloppy Joe's, a popular bar catering to tourists, with two Cuban friends while the *St. Louis* was docked offshore. A young street tough who often hung around the same place made an anti-Semitic remark to José and his friends. José, who had taken boxing lessons and who knew street fighting, punched him in the stomach and then in the jaw, which was sagging from the first blow. Had José's friends not caught the man as he fell, they later realized, he might have cracked open his head on the cement curb.[83]

The first of the other two refugee ships to reach Havana, the *Flandre*, gave up and returned to France when the initial Berenson negotiations failed. The British vessel, the *Orduña*, did not give up that easily. Like the *St. Louis*, it arrived in Havana on May 27 and was not permitted to approach a regular landing berth. Tearful passengers lined the ship's rails, watching at a distance the hundreds standing on shore, including many relatives.[84] The British ambassador in Havana tried to win entry for the ship's seventy-two passengers, and, when his efforts failed, the ship's captain weighed anchor and headed south. The *Orduña* then proceeded on a frustrating journey through the Panama Canal, docking at ports in Colombia,

Ecuador, and Peru. The Joint representative in Guayaquil managed to find sanctuary for four of his passengers in Ecuador, and the rest of the passengers were taken to Lima, where they were transferred to the *Orduña*'s sister ship, the *Orbita*, which was scheduled to sail back through the Panama Canal and return to Europe. From Ecuador, the captain sent a telegram to Rabbi Nathan Witkin, Jr., the field representative of the Jewish Welfare Board in the Canal Zone and Caribbean region and a former army chaplain in the Canal Zone since 1935, who had succeeded in gaining permission from Canal Zone authorities to offer to house the *St. Louis* passengers. The Joint and the Pacific Steamship Navigation Company also were instrumental in convincing the Canal Zone authorities to extend their help.

The sixty-eight refugees were disembarked at Balboa on June 12. Rabbi Witkin arranged for a special train and for buses to transport the refugees to the Panama Canal Quarantine Station at Fort Amador. All but seven, who managed to obtain entry visas for Chile and therefore departed, stayed at the base hospital for more than fifteen months, through September 1940. At that time, Colonel Morrison C. Stayer, the chief health officer of the Canal Zone, informed Rabbi Witkin that his charges would have to leave, for the quarantine station had to be used for other purposes. Working arduously through the Joint and through HIAS, arrangements were finally made for a transport ship, the *American Legion*, to take the quarantine station refugees, whose number had grown to 134, to the United States.[85] Rabbi Witkin remained in the Canal Zone for some years after the end of the war (fig. 34).

The *St. Louis* affair shook Jews living in the Free World, although in 1939 no one could know how fatal the act of turning back Jewish refugees and forcing them to return to Nazi-occupied Europe would be. The vessel, a French journalist for the German-language *Pariser Tageblatt* reported on June 24, 1939, "is neither the first nor the only 'ghost ship' that has wandered from harbor to harbor. More than 800 people have been rescued by the HICEM during the first five months of 1939 from being shipped back to Germany." But there were two reasons for the uproar the *St. Louis* had caused, he added: first, it contained almost a thousand people, and second, the responsible authorities had been warned in time, quite officially, from Hamburg. Only the passengers "knew absolutely nothing."[86]

34. Rabbi Nathan Witkin in Canal Zone. Courtesy of Helen S. Witkin.

In the context of the history of the efforts of Jews to flee from Hitler, however, the memory of the episode, which after the war gained international attention as the subject of a book made into a Hollywood film, *Voyage of the Damned*, has obscured the fact that Cuba's overall record in permitting Jewish refugees to enter was among the best in the world.[87] As many as 8,000 Jewish refugees came to Cuba between 1933 and 1942, despite the retroactive cancellation of Benítez's entry permits in 1939 and despite the outburst of anti-Semitism, which was short-lived and for the most part suppressed once Cuba entered the war on the Allied side.[88] Prominent members of Cuba's Jewish community later suspected that pressure from the United States against permitting the refugees to land had been the determining factor in the Cuban government's decision to close its doors suddenly, because in the past, personal contacts lubricated by bribery had always worked.[89] The new U.S. consul general, Coert du Bois, a former aide to conservationist Gifford Pinchot in the Forest Service, privately expressed sympathy for the refugees, calling them "these unfortunate people," but he held fast to his instructions from the State Department not "to warrant any drastic changes in the present quota distribution." In a letter to a colleague who had asked for help for the refugees in Cuba awaiting visas, he warned that the Cuban government, "as usual, hard up for money," was said to be planning to confiscate the bond money put up by the refugees who already had arrived. "The [legal basis] for the scheme," he wrote, "is pretty thin, but I put nothing by these people when there's $1,000,000 in sight."[90]

For Jews around the world, the SS *St. Louis* episode dashed hopes for further rescues of Jews trapped in Europe.[91] The crisis signaled the triumph of neoisolationism in the hemisphere and gave a major propaganda victory to the Nazis, who used the incident to affirm that no country wanted Jews. For Jews in Cuba after 1939, restrictive labor legislation made it difficult to earn a living, although the laws were not enforced consistently. Those who did not take advantage of this laxity, avoiding forays into personal entrepreneurship, were supported by private philanthropy, much of it from the Hebrew Immigrant Aid Society (HIAS) and the Joint Distribution Committee in the United States. The luckier ones had cousins or other relatives in the United States, who sent payments via Western Union or bank transfers whenever they could.[92] Most refugees from Europe who were able to obtain entry to Latin America after 1939 were wealthy individuals who could pay large, sometimes extraordinary, sums of money to private agents acting in behalf of government officials willing to look the other way.

Dominican Republic and Mexican Immigration

The most important offer of concrete help from a Latin American country came from the Dominican Republic. The three-man Dominican delegation to Evian expressed optimism that many settlers could be welcomed, and later in London the remarkable figure of 100,000 refugees was suggested by members of the Trujillo family.[93] Many, though, doubted the dictator's sincerity. His brother, Virgilio, represented the Dominican Republic at Evian but attended few of the working meetings.[94] One story had it that he would ask $500 each for the visas, which would yield $10 million not to mention millions more paid by relief organizations for sustenance.[95]

According to analysts, Generalíssimo Trujillo, better known in the past for the exiles he had created than for those he was willing to accept, sought to offer a humanitarian gesture to improve his regime's image and as a possible bargaining chip to encourage the

United States to relinquish its control of Dominican customs. Trujillo also thought the Jews would be good workers; for years, in fact, the Sosúa colony would produce almost all of the milk in the Dominican Republic. Upper-class Dominicans also favored immigration of Europeans to whiten the population. Trujillo had accepted 2,000 Spanish republicans for much the same reasons. When asked by a journalist why the dictator had taken in so many Spanish radicals, a Loyalist refugee replied, without rancor, that "we are white and we can breed." The irony did not escape the interviewer: Dominican race prejudice created a haven for victims of a different race prejudice in the Reich.[96]

Trujillo's initiative had not been the first time that Jewish refugees had been invited to come to Santo Domingo. An attempt had been made a half-century earlier by General Gregorio Luperón (1839–97). As a cabinet minister and as provisional president in 1879–80, he had advocated liberal social reforms, broad-based immigration, and, to entice would-be settlers, religious toleration.[97] After a visit to Paris in late 1881 on a diplomatic mission, the general made contacts with Victor Hugo, Léon Gambetta, Ferdinand de Lesseps, and other liberals and learned about the plight of Jewish pogrom victims in Russia. He also read accounts of "inhuman persecution of the Jews" written by Alfredo Herrera, a Dominican writer living in Paris. He visited Herrera and took steps formally to invite Jews to come to live in Santo Domingo. Notices were placed inviting Jews to locate in the Dominican Republic, "a vast and fertile country which has every prospect for the future . . . [where] your coreligionists will be received with open arms."[98] Luperón also admonished others to emigrate to the Dominican Republic, which he characterized as underpopulated and striving for greatness. One of those who did, attracted by the general's liberal civilizing visions, was Eugenio Hostos, the Puerto Rican sociologist and educator. Jewish groups across Europe enthusiastically accepted Luperon's invitation, but somehow the project became mired in details about costs, visas, and other practicalities. Two hundred families from the Russian Pale prepared to sail for Santo Domingo, but, abruptly, the undertaking fell apart. It is unlikely that any Jewish refugees ever did arrive.[99]

At the Evian conference, Virgilio Trujillo Molina had assured delegates that not only had his nation for years sought to promote agricultural development by importing settlers, but that it would grant "specially advantageous concessions to Austrian and German exiles, agriculturists with an unimpeachable record who satisfy the conditions laid down by the Dominican legislation on immigration."[100] The mechanisms of Trujillo's immigration and resettlement invitation were worked out in London through the Intergovernmental Committee for Political Refugees, and in the Dominican Republic by representatives of the U.S. Department of State. The Dominican Republic Settlement Association was established, headed by James N. Rosenberg and Joseph A. Rosen, both former officials of the Agro-Joint Commission, which settled 300,000 Jews on three million acres of land in the Crimea between 1922 and 1936. They were offered several tracts of rural land in the Dominican Republic, finally selecting among sites offered on former United Fruit Company land now owned by the Trujillo family. In response to the Dominican initiative, the Refugee Economic Corporation of New York, working with President Roosevelt's Advisory Committee on Political Refugees, embarked on a full-scale study of prospects for emigration to the island. The study included an on-site visitation by soil, agricultural, and forestry experts selected by President Isaiah Bowman of the Johns Hopkins University and concluded in 1939 that the location was suitable. Jewish philanthropic groups, working through the Agro-Joint Commission, received an appropriation of $200,000 from the Roosevelt administration to cover initial expenses. The puppet Dominican government agreed to waive the $500 entry fee for the initial colonists, and funds were raised to pay for relocation of 500 refugee families. Trujillo then donated the deed for the land to the Settlement Association, which sent representatives to camps in Germany, Norway, Sweden, and Holland seeking settlers trained in agriculture or engineering and suitable for emigration.

A tract of land bordering the Atlantic at Sosúa, in the northern province of Puerto Plata, was turned over for colonization on January 30, 1940. A total of 500 Jews and non-Jews were to be brought in; the first group of 37 arrived in Santo Domingo in May 1940. Handsome wooden homes were constructed at Sosúa. Trucks, automobiles, and farm equipment were donated and imported from the United States, and gestures were made on the part of officials and their families from the municipal capital in Puerto Plata to welcome the newcomers. The farm colony fared well. On December 7, 1941, a Portuguese freighter, *Serpa Pinto*, arrived at Cuidad Trujillo bringing relatives of Sosúa colonists, one of the last such boatloads of refugees to make the transatlantic voyage. The quickening pace of the war doomed plans for large-scale colonization. Within months, sea lanes were cut off, and it became impossible to transport any further refugees from Europe. Altogether, 352 settlers came, two-thirds of whom were men, less than 1 percent of the promised 100,000. Sosúa continued to operate well beyond the end of the war, although most settlers ultimately left for the United States.[101]

The initial willingness of the Dominican government to cooperate was not duplicated on any significant scale elsewhere in the hemisphere. There were small efforts, but no continuing, extensive rescue plans. In 1940, for example, the Venezuelan government under the dictator López Contreras gave permission for Jewish passengers on two ships (one of them the SS *Caribea*) to disembark at Puerto Cabello, under the ruse that they were agricultural immigrants. The small but prosperous Mexican Jewish colony, which dated from the mid-nineteenth century, was divided between the traditional Ashkenazic and Sephardic groups. Perhaps owing to tense relations between church and state before and after the Mexican Revolution, few Mexican Jews applied for citizenship. The Sephardim, however, put down deeper roots: in 1917 the Sephardic community established a *kutab* school after five years of irregular functioning, a traditional religious academy analogous to the European *cheder*.[102] A small but steady stream of new arrivals came from Eastern Europe during the 1920s, Jews who were unable to enter the United States but who thought they would have a better chance in a neighboring country.[103]

The early years of the Great Depression were difficult for Mexico's Jews. On June 1, 1931, a mass demonstration of as many as 20,000 marchers in the nation's capital, led by retired general Angel Ladrón and greeted by the mayor of Mexico City, chanted anti-Semitic slogans and demanded the expulsion of Jews from Mexican territory. Earlier, Ladrón had forced the removal of about 250 peddlers from Mexico City's La Lagunilla market and had been awarded a gold medal by President Pascal Ortíz Rubio.[104] Perhaps as an index of how tenuous the pre-World War II Jewish colony felt about its host country, a self-study of the colony in 1940 found nearly two-thirds of

Mexico's economically active Ashkenazim engaged in commerce, in contrast to only 2 percent in the professions.[105] In any case, German Jews with possibilities of finding transport to the Western Hemisphere preferred Mexico over Cuba, in part because there was a more active anti-Nazi movement there.

During the gathering refugee crisis, Mexican Jews had little influence on immigration policy. In 1938 the administration of President Lázaro Cárdenas imposed a quota of 5,000 German immigrants a year.[106] Preference was given to Catholic Germans who wanted to settle in Mexico, and to some Protestant religious communities whose members feared persecution under the Nazis. The revolutionary government accepted large numbers of refugees from civil-war-torn Spain and in 1939, feeling overburdened, placed severe limitations on the kinds of immigrants who could enter the country, favoring agricultural and industrial workers. Some 1,600 Spanish refugees from the civil war arrived in Veracruz on June 13, 1939, on the SS *Sinaia* and were welcomed by the interior minister. During the same week, the SS *Flandre*, carrying 98 Jewish refugees, was turned away from Mexican shores. The government acted to bar the entrance of all tourists, students, and visitors from Europe; the entrance of *rentistas* (persons living on their own sources of income) was prohibited, and visas were restricted to those who could show assets of 50,000 pesos ($10,000).[107]

No more than 700 German-speaking Jewish refugees entered Mexico during the crisis period, although a small additional number were admitted in 1942 on condition that they leave Mexico at the war's end, and President Cárdenas personally arranged for the admission of twenty famous German writers and intellectuals, some Jewish, who had escaped to southern France. Less well known applicants were turned away. Presumably some of these were refugees who had carried landing passes for Cuba. Labor leaders, including the prominent Vicente Lombardo Toledano, spoke out vehemently against Fascist atrocities in Europe, but did little to encourage Mexican authorities to relax immigrant quotas. In late August 1940, ninety-eight Jewish passengers on the SS *Quanza* holding transit visas for Guatemala were not allowed to land, although some others on board with Mexican investment permits—those who had brought with them assets of $50,000—were granted entrance. In one case, a customs official used his own discretion to allow members of "one

Goldschmidt-Rothschild family," the Marquesa de Casa Forte and her children, to enter on the grounds that they were not Jewish.[108]

Mexico's established Jewish community took it upon itself to support the refugees: virtually every Jewish family contributed a fixed sum each month, which was collected by a community official who went from door to door, although in most cases Mexican Jews were not noticeably affluent. The ways refugees managed to enter Mexico varied, but the case of Luis Glaser's father was typical. He was a Viennese physician who managed to escape with his wife and five-year-old son to Belgium. After a year, they obtained a somewhat spurious Mexican visa from the honorary Mexican consul in Zagreb and sailed to Veracruz and then to Tampico. When they experienced difficulties entering the country, they were aided by a local Jewish family, not acquaintances, who offered to act as their legal custodians. Unlike Cuba, where all refugees were officially prohibited from working, and the United States, where foreign-trained medical personnel had to recommence their formal education to obtain certification, in Mexico those who had been physicians in Europe were permitted to practice medicine under a blanket law enacted principally to help doctors who had left Republican Spain. In April 1942 Mexico stopped issuing entry visas to anyone who was not a citizen of a Western Hemisphere country.

Although there was little overt anti-Semitism in Mexico, the Jewish colony remained largely self-contained. Mexicans were considered by the refugees to be antiforeign, not pointedly anti-Semitic. Although Mexico City was cosmopolitan to a degree, foreigners stayed in their own groups. Nearly all non-Mexican children in the capital attended private schools taught in their native languages—French, Italian, German, and English. Jewish children matriculated at the Colegio Israelita de Mexico. Classes were taught in Spanish during the morning and in Yiddish and Hebrew in the afternoon, but the overall curriculum was secular. As elsewhere, the refugees found themselves positioned between the Ashkenazic and Sephardic colonies, and even though their own group was small, as time passed it further subdivided into clubs and cliques based on places of origin: Hungary, Poland, Czechoslovakia, and so on. The refugees, most of whom spoke German, avidly read the *Aufbau*, published in New York, and therefore were very much aware of the tragedies of the gathering Holocaust, probably in much greater detail than was the

Mexican public at large. They also organized professional study groups: the eighteen or so physicians from Germany and Austria who were practicing in Mexico City met weekly to review medical journals mailed to them from the United States.[109] When the war ended, most of the refugees emigrated to the United States.

Refugee Efforts in Latin America and Europe

The lucrative enterprise by which Manuel Benítez sold hundreds of Cuban entry permits to would-be refugees brought a flurry of hope to those in Europe who grasped at any means to escape. The circumstances under which they were sold caused strains among friends. Günter W. Cohn, who escaped with his wife and whose parents were on the ill-fated SS *St. Louis*, asked Norbert Adler after he had arrived in Cuba to obtain some of Benítez's landing permits, which were being sold in Germany. Adler at first refused but later went along on a limited basis. He wrote to Cohn, years later:

> If I had grasped the urgency of the situation, I would have engaged in this project with more enthusiasm. Things in 1938 did not seem as bad as they became, and all I could see was the huge profits which others made when reselling the permits in Europe at double and triple the cost, and I did not want to be part of that abuse. However, I wanted to bring my parents out of Germany, and for them, I'd spend the bribe money if I had it. Therefore I wrote to you that I would agree to buy ten permits at $150 each providing that each purchaser add $30 to his payment, to give me the $300 I needed to buy two permits for my parents. I wanted the purchasers to know that they were contributing to my parents' liberation.[110]

As was the case for many would-be Jewish emigrants, the Benítez permits proved worthless to Adler's parents. They could not find a ship available to take them, and the *St. Louis* affair seemed to bar further routes for escape. Adler then used his new contacts in Cuba to find help.

> [My friend] suggested that I see his buddy in the government, who promised to help me as a political favor for my contact. I still remember the bright sunny morning when I went up to the politician's office, full of expectation and anxiety. By this time I spoke pretty fluent Span-

ish and was proud of my linguistic ability. He received me cordially, listened to my request for a visa for my parents, and asked "Are they Jewish?" I did not know the reason for his question but answered truthfully, "Yes," whereupon he replied "In that case I cannot help you." I was too crushed to do anything but pull in my tail and leave. In retrospect, I concluded that the reason he could not give me a permit for Jews just like that was that Jews were reserved territory for someone else to make money from. Or, perhaps, he expected me to offer him a bribe. A little while later, another man filled the immigration post and began to accept bribes, and I bought the permits.[111]

The *St. Louis* was not the only "errant vessel"—the term given to ships carrying refugees seeking safe harbors at which to land—to ply the coasts of the nations of the Caribbean and Latin America. Slightly under 2,000 Jewish refugees arrived in Cuba during 1940 on sixty-seven different ships, some en route from other Latin American countries where they had failed to gain permanent status.[112] The Italian ship *Conte Grande* and two Hamburg-Amerika Line passenger ships carried refugees to Uruguay, but they were refused landing rights; local Jewish community refugee aid societies ultimately gained entrance for these and other ship passengers in Chile and in Paraguay, even though Chile had formally stopped issuing visas to anyone in German-occupied territory in December 1939.

The history of the errant vessels involved bribery, swindles, and clandestine landings.[113] Three thousand Jews who had been sold counterfeit documents in Europe promising visas to Bolivia were turned away, although the Jewish refugee aid group, HICEM, worked out a compromise through which most were admitted. At one point, the German Foreign Office announced that it might permit 5,000 Jewish children to emigrate to Palestine, but the Nazis canceled the plan after exploiting it for propaganda purposes. Their stated reason for refusal was that they did not want to have "the noble Arab people . . . settled with such inferior stock."[114]

One craft caught up in the refugee tragedy was the *Navemar*, a Portuguese freighter. It sailed from Lisbon with 1,100 Jews who had paid up to $1,500 each for emigration documents. The ship was not fit for a sea voyage; some passengers had to sleep on deck, huddled in life rafts on which they had to bribe deckhands $300 for places (fig. 35).[115] Some contracted typhus, which led to mass quarantine for a

35. Passengers on board *Navemar*. Photo by Jim Strong, provided by Leo Baeck Institute.

lengthy waiting period. Virtually no community support was extended. Held over at Tiscornia—Cuba's Ellis Island—on Yom Kippur, some Jews with access to the island arranged for a post–Yom Kippur "dinner" for the passengers, which cost $400. In the end, the Joint Relief Committee paid the bill, because the Cuban Jewish community, made up mostly of immigrants, was still on the whole very poor.[116]

When authorities accepted the landing permits of only 300 of its passengers, the *Navemar* was expelled, just as the *St. Louis* had been. Only a handful of passengers were permitted to remain. The ship eventually arrived in New York on September 12, 1941, after a harrowing journey of twenty-five days, and its passengers disembarked.[117] Representatives of Jewish agencies in the United States were appalled at what they considered the lack of interest shown by members of the Cuban Jewish colony. A Joint Distribution Committee representative remarked bitterly that to help serve a turnover of approximately 8,000 refugees during its work in Cuba, the Jewish colony of Cuba contributed "the magnificent sum of $1,500" in 1940.

One rescue effort in the region that has not been generally known was carried out in El Salvador by two brothers, Hungarian Jews named Joseph Mandel (originally József Mandl) and Georges M. Mantello (born György Mandl). They were born either in the Transylvanian village of Nasaud or in Beszterce. Joseph was a businessman in Geneva. Arriving in Switzerland in December 1941, Georges became employed by the San Salvadoran consulate in the Swiss capital and apparently asked for (and was granted) Salvadoran citizenship. He succeeded in getting himself appointed as first secretary of the consulate general of El Salvador. Aided by his brother, he began immediately to help Polish Jews escape and turned to Hungary after that country fell to Nazi occupation in 1944.

The procedure was simple. Anyone who wrote to Georges with a physical description and photograph would be issued a passport as a national of the Republic of San Salvador, and thus, as far as the Germans and Hungarians were concerned, a neutral alien.[118] Their rescue program eventually came to the attention of the Swedish diplomat Raoul Wallenberg, who was working feverishly to mobilize public opinion in the Allied nations against German atrocities and in favor of efforts to evacuate more Jews.[119]

Georges Mantello's rescue program was bold. Rather than relying on protective passes (*Schutzpaesse*), which many others did, including the Swedes, El Salvador simply claimed that the persecuted Jews were citizens and issued travel papers to them. At first Mantello did this himself without prior approval from San Salvador, although the consul general, Colonel I. H. Castellanos, cooperated. Several hundred "nationality" certificates were sent by the consulate to Hungary, conferring foreign national status on their recipients and therefore exempting them from Hungary's anti-Jewish laws.[120] Their informal program was legalized some time later when Salvadoran officials concurred with it.

The Hungarian historian Jenö Lévai notes that Salvadoran interests in the Fascist countries were generally represented through Switzerland. Before the war, no Salvadorans resided or did business in Hungary, so there had been no Salvadoran presence there, but now that Mantello had conferred citizenship on Hungarian Jews, he worked through Wallenberg in Switzerland to help. Mantello also kept in touch with Rabbi Stephen Wise, the president of the World Jewish Congress, in New York. Through Mantello and Wallenberg, the Swedish government pledged to accept responsibility for any

Salvadoran "citizens" if Swiss officials for any reason failed to do so. We have no precise information on how many refugees were saved through the Salvadoran-Swedish connection, but there are indications that efforts initiated by Wallenberg to place under Argentine protection several hundred—perhaps 300—Hungarian Jews may have succeeded. Mantello also worked independently to publicize the Vrba-Wetzler version of the Auschwitz protocols in April 1944, an action that helped raise public alarm against what was happening in Hungary and elsewhere, although it was ignored by most governments and by the Vatican, which had received copies.[121] Mantello associated with Wallenberg and Walter Garrett, the Zurich representative of the London Exchange Telegraph Company, who used their social and business contacts to publicize what the Nazis were doing at a time when few knew many details, much less believed them. They wrote to leading Swiss clergy, journalists, academicians, and public officials, urging a press campaign to inform the world.[122]

The example of El Salvador was not repeated elsewhere in the region. Costa Rica's attitude was more typical. Although some scholars maintain that many early colonial settlers were conversos, there is no hard evidence for this. Sephardic Jews arrived in the late nineteenth century.[123] Some Alsatian Jews emigrated after the Franco-Prussian War of 1870–71, and another group came at the turn of the century from Silesia, near the Polish border. An Ashkenazic Jew from Austria, Enrique Yankelewitz, who initially settled in Argentina, played a major role in Costa Rica's post–World War I economy by starting a department store, Mil Colores, and by supplying cloth and inexpensive merchandise to peddlers (buhoneros in Spanish; klappers in Yiddish) on consignment. These peddlers were part of a group of 210 Polish Jews who emigrated during the mid-1930s, mostly from Zellowchow, a shoemakers' village outside of Warsaw, and Ostrowiecz, a larger city. Most claimed on their visa applications that they were farmers, but as soon as they could they gravitated to urban centers. They were shtetl products, uneducated but skilled technically and commercially. Their practice of selling on credit to lower-class residents became known as pagos a lo polaco (Polish payments), and the term polaquear entered the language as a colloquial verb.[124]

Some Costa Rican politicians found it opportune to attack the presence of the polacos and to criticize the incumbency for permitting "undesirable" elements to enter the country. Some claimed that the Polish Jews were communist agitators. As in Cuba, one element of this hostility was the commercial competition offered by the newcomers. Another, probably the main factor, was the internationalization of anti-Semitic sentiment during the 1930s and 1940s, a potent ideology that of itself encouraged acts against Jews.

The anti-Semitic opposition gained the presidency in 1936 under the conservative León Cortés, who named a German citizen, Max Effinger, as immigration director. Despite his efforts to exclude non-Aryan applicants for entry, Polish Jewish residents in Costa Rica did manage to gain visas for 159 family members. In 1939, facing the rising tide of panic among European refugees seeking entry to any safe haven, the Costa Rican government managed to limit entry to only fourteen immigrants, and only two in 1940. The government also decreed that Jewish residences and businesses must be registered, but few cooperated, and the policy was never enforced. The incoming president in 1940, Rafael Angel Calderón Guardia, accused his predecessor of having been *too* lax on the Jewish issue, reacting to pressures from retail merchants, who were largely Spaniards, Lebanese, and Germans, to suppress peddling.[125] Anti-Semitic political campaigning continued after the end of the war. It took the form of a continuing "anti-Polish" campaign, spearheaded by a right-wing provincial politician and newspaperman, Otilo Ulate, who was a candidate for the presidency in 1948. Following an eighteen-month interlude in which José Figueres's revolutionary movement triumphed, Ulate became president.

Ulate's resentment was summarized in a 1946 editorial he wrote for the *Diario de Costa Rica:*

The [Polish Jews] have a separate social life, they marry without the contamination of creole blood, and even in death they prefer that they be covered in their cemeteries by a dirt different from that which covers other mortals. Those are racial distinctions, and Costa Ricans are not the ones who are making them. . . . They have not come to create wealth but to drain it away and to try to take over national and long-standing foreign trade. . . . They have undertaken mass naturalizations, not out of conviction nor love for the land which shelters them, but out of calculation and with the intervention of the local Communists. . . . [They] constitute one of the greatest plagues which we suffer. . . . Go to the countryside, as you promised when you entered the country; work the land, give evidence that you want to be productive elements.[126]

Things quieted down in Costa Rica after the early 1950s. A major calming influence was the local Roman Catholic hierarchy, which always had refused to be drawn into the anti-Semitic campaigns, and which was led by a call by the archbishop of San José, Rubin Odio Herrera, for an end to the anti-polaco polemic.[127]

Before June 1939, the practice of obtaining landing permits from third-party nations—not only Cuba but Haiti, Panama, the Dominican Republic, and other Latin American countries—had been the best that the Joint Distribution Committee and HICEM could do to aid refugees to escape from Europe. The Joint helped arrange for the permits and paid for sheltering the refugees in Lisbon, Seville, and other ports while emigration transport was arranged. Everyone had tacitly cooperated, including both Washington and Berlin. Now, suddenly, the rules changed, likely the result of pressures applied by both the Americans and Germans. Haitian officials legally sold Haitian citizenship to the few individuals who could afford to pay the exorbitant fees.

Cuba had found itself caught in the middle, exposed to unusual pressures. Franklin D. Roosevelt's administration probably could have applied sufficient pressure on Havana to permit the passengers to disembark and also could easily have responded to Captain Schroeder's frantic appeals to allow the *St. Louis* to disembark passengers at Miami. The failure to find willing nations to accept the ship's passengers signaled a new and frightening escalation in the pressure on European Jewry: now individuals and families could not afford to worry about shipping their household goods or assets; now the only thing they could do was try to escape. On September 19, 1941, the Nazis forced Jews in Germany and in the Western occupied countries to wear the yellow Jewish star in public, as they had done earlier in Poland and in Eastern Europe. The decision for the "final solution" had been made, as Yehuda Bauer reminds us, six months earlier.[128]

A few refugees from German-occupied lands managed to gain entry to Latin American countries (and ultimately to the United States) by working on the edge of the formal visa system. Rolf Wartenberg, some of whose relatives had gotten into Guatemala and El Salvador, obtained a tourist visa to Salvador. He managed to stay for two years; prohibited from working, he lived by his wits. He held a U.S. quota number, which he had gotten in Berlin on the advice of a friend—just for contingency's sake—and, after telling his story in a hotel lobby in Salvador to a friendly U.S. consular official, was given an entry permit to the United States, where he had other relatives. For Wartenberg and a handful of others, fortuitous circumstances converged on their behalf. In the sweep of events, though, these successful cases proved the rare exception.

Rolf Wartenberg writes of his emigration:

When Hitler came to power in 1933 I was employed in Bremen as assistant buyer in a department store. On April 1, 1933 I was fired because I was a Jew. My father took me into his business, and I worked there until the factories were *aryanized,* forcibly sold to a non-Jewish buyer. My father died in 1934 and I could not leave Germany immediately because I had to protect my family's interest in the enterprise.

After the sale I contacted my half-brother who had emigrated to El Salvador in 1935. He promptly arranged for an immigration visa for me, and I sailed on the SS *Schwabenland,* a German flag vessel, for La Libertad, El Salvador's entry port. I would have preferred to sail on a Swedish vessel, but would have had to wait in Germany for an additional two weeks. With the constantly-deteriorating situation for the Jews, I took the first available ship. I left Germany with the equivalent of $2.50 in my pocket.

I arrived in El Salvador 40 days later. The authorities at that time changed my visa from immigrant to visitor's status. My brother was manager of the Hotel Nuevo Mundo, and I stayed with him until my departure for the United States. As a visitor, I was not allowed to work. However, after having learned some Spanish, I assisted my brother unofficially in his duties as manager of the hotel.

After about a year I decided to apply for a working permit. This was denied by the Salvadoran authorities, and I was notified that I had to leave the country within 60 days. It was arranged for me to become a trainee as a tractor driver in one of Salvador's agricultural areas near San Miguel. I was to go to Honduras where no special visas were required for agricultural workers. After I had been on the farm for about a month, my brother notified me that I could return to San Salvador, but I should assume a low profile.[129]

He eventually obtained an affidavit from a friend of his brother's in New York attesting that Rolf was a cousin and managed to sail for New York. He had to stay overnight on the ship under guard, was taken to Ellis Island for a hearing, and finally was admitted as a legal immigrant.

In Wartenberg's two years in the tiny Central American country, he knew only two German Jewish families admitted as visitors to the country—they stayed at the Hotel Nuevo Mundo. A third man came as a refugee; they had been apprentices together in 1929 in Breslau. He was not aware of any of the others who came in via Georges Mantello's efforts. This is an arresting reality that suggests we should not assume that the refugee stream flowed in a single channel or even a visible one. Even many of the Jews who went to Cuba, where their numbers were far greater, claimed not to have been aware of the plight of fellow refugees, or even, in a few cases, of such events as the arrival of the SS *St. Louis*.

On the whole, Latin American nations made it easier for non-Jewish refugees from the Axis nations to enter than for Jews. Mexico permitted thousands of Spanish Loyalist refugees to enter from Vichy, France, and even remnants of the Polish army marooned in Iran. German Jews and half-Jews who had been baptized petitioned the Ecuadoran government to accept them as Catholics.[130] There were some heroes. One was the future Pope John XXIII, Angelo Roncalli, who, as apostolic delegate to Turkey and Greece, personally issued thousands of baptismal certificates without religious ceremony to Jews whose only chance of emigrating—in this case, to Colombia—was to prove that they were Roman Catholics in good standing. Some 3,000 refugees entered Colombia under these conditions.[131] Jamaica accepted 152 Polish Jewish refugees, and Curaçao took 86, all paid for by the Joint Distribution Committee.

But at the same time, the desperate efforts to save refugees, now not by the thousands but only by the dozens, kindled increased anti-Semitic activity, especially in Mexico, where a resolution of the Federation of Mexican Farmers protested against admitting any more refugees because they "become merchants and gangsters."

Mexico closed its doors in early 1942. The Bolivian legislature received a resolution that would have prohibited "Jews, Mongols, and Negroes" from entering.[132] Other Latin American nations warned that admitting refugees would pose security risks. The F.B.I. and U.S. State Department did not help dissuade foreign states from making these arguments; in fact, both agencies were sympathetic to the security-risk excuse. In all likelihood, few spies succeeded in infiltrating by posing as refugees, although Rabbi Lasker maintains that two Abwehr agents were exposed posing as Jews but identified by other refugees. The U.S. embassy also asked Rabbi Lasker regularly to examine dossiers of Jews seeking entrance to Cuba under special circumstances, to help weed out spies. Others, including Hardy Spatz, were also asked to do this by U.S. officials.[133]

The process of obtaining visas in Europe to any safe haven was arduous and haphazard. Conditions varied greatly from city to city, depending on the attitude of individual consular officials. The United States would only grant visas according to its rigid quota system, and few exceptions were made. The stated policies of most Latin American countries made it difficult, if not impossible, for refugees to gain permission to land, although throughout the late 1930s and into the early 1940s individual arrangements were made. This was only a tiny portion of the hundreds of thousands who were desperately trying to flee from Nazi control.

Individual Latin American consuls, of course, permitted exceptions. A Brazilian consular official in Hamburg, Caio de Lima Cavalcanti, accepted bribes in the form of silver, gems, cameras, Dresden china, furniture, and works of art in exchange for visas for Jewish refugees.[134] Cuban officials seemed mainly interested in cash, usually asking for a few hundred dollars. These were very hard to come by in Europe, especially after the war started. Most refugees had to buy them on the black market, at rates as high as six times the official rate.[135]

Vatican diplomacy during the war attempted to aid Jews who had converted to Catholicism, the so-called Catholic or Christian non-Aryans. In late March 1939, German Catholic officials asked the newly elected Pope Pius XII to petition the Brazilian government for 3,000 immigrant visas for German Jews who had converted, but despite two years of negotiations few were helped. Some German Jews were able to enter Brazil and ultimately become citizens, but only before 1938. Some who arrived without visas married acquaintances who had arrived earlier, and who were permitted to board the refugee-carrying ships in port. Most of the German Jews remained in the large cities, although at least one agricultural colony was permitted to be established in the northern part of the coffee-growing state of Paraná.[136] The American Jewish Committee even contributed $50,000 to pay for saving refugees who had been born to one or two Jewish parents but who were practicing Catholics.[137] Diplomats from other Latin American countries watched the negotiations with interest and were likely influenced by the fact that Brazil remained unyielding. Before the war broke out and during its early stages, the Vatican, caught between Communists and Nazis and emphatically opposed to both, was generally reluctant to take political initiatives or even to participate in mediation. Pope Pius XII did not acknowledge this. His aide remarked in 1939 that the pope was offended that critics never acknowledged the material aid the church was providing to refugees.[138]

5 ✳ THE WAR YEARS

When Washington closed its consulates in Axis countries in June 1941, Cuban consulates remained open for another year, during which Cuban consular officials either legally issued or sold large numbers of travel documents, many of which were later pronounced invalid for landing.[1] By this time, most of the Jews who managed to escape from Europe did so through bribery and the use of false papers available at very high cost. Werner Stahl's family, for example, which had been wealthy, paid off the Spanish foreign minister as well as Cuban consular officials in France and Spain. The family also obtained false health affidavits from a cooperating French physician, attesting to the need to travel in order to recuperate from illness. At the French border, the women of the family were permitted to pass; the father and his teenage son were apprehended and interned until they paid additional bribes to pertinent officials.[2] Other European Jews, especially those in Nazi-occupied countries, sought to buy legitimate passports and other kinds of identity papers from foreign consuls acting from humanitarian, not mercenary, motives, but these were available only sporadically.[3]

The Last Refugees from Hitler
Cuba did not enforce the immigration provisions of the 1940 Constitution. Of the Jews who arrived in Cuba after 1937, 8,000 did not have documents permitting them to enter the United States or other countries, and most of these spent the war on Cuban soil in limbo, not allowed to work, waiting for the war to end.[4]

Jewish immigration virtually stopped a year later, although a small stream continued through 1942 with a trickle in 1943 and 1944. A total of 68,000 Jewish refugees during the Holocaust period managed to enter Latin America. By contrast, the United States during 1938–39 took only 65,000 as well as an additional 20,000 holding tourist visas who refused to leave. Another 65,000 came into the United States before 1941. From 1933 through 1945, the United States, with a population of 130 million, took in 250,000 refugees from Hitler; 55,000 found haven in British Palestine.

Only the most fortunate got through after 1940. Among them was Michel Mendelson, a Latvian who as a boy had been shipped with his family in a cattle car to Siberia as a result of anti-Jewish political persecution; at nineteen, he was allowed to return to Latvia. He then escaped to Belgium, where he established a successful electronics distribution business. When he arrived in Cuba on a false passport he again had to start over. He got a job selling light fixtures in the interior of the island. He knew no Spanish, but he managed by speaking to prospective clients in French.[5]

The experience of Leonhard (Hardy) Spatz was typical of members of the last of the refugees who managed to escape:

> I was 18 years old and arrived with both my parents on March 19, 1941. The name of the ship was the *Magallanes*. It and its sister ship, the *Marques de Comillas*, made regular crossings from Vigo or Bilbao to Lisbon and on to Havana. We sailed from Lisbon, where we had stayed six months trying to obtain a U.S. visa. The trip to Cuba was intended to be a stopover, but we never got our papers straight and remained in Cuba for nineteen years. I had left Vienna in September 1938, after my father had been in *Schutzhaft* from the first day of the *Anschluss*. He was held for 142 days, and then released. I spent a year in Switzerland at the Swiss Hotel School in Lucerne—this was a way that entry documents could be obtained for me—then joined my parents in Paris in May 1940 where I was arrested as an "enemy Alien" and almost immediately converted into a "Prestataire." When rumors started that the Vichy government intended to extradite their Austrian and German Prestataires to Germany, I escaped from the camp to Marseilles where I remained for several months after having been reunited with my parents. We went on to Portugal via Spain, travelling over the mountains by train.[6]

In April 1942, the Cuban government announced that it would no longer accept transmigrants born in Axis countries. By then the fate of Jews and other peoples determined undesirable by Hitler was sealed.[7] (Only Brazil, the Dominican Republic, and Ecuador continued to accept Jews beyond 1942, and in extremely limited numbers.) Despite President Batista's decree, Cuba issued new visas after April 1942 to 257 refugees on two Portuguese ships, the SS *Guinee* and the SS *Saint Thomé*, although by this date it was virtually impossible for Jews to escape Axis-occupied countries. Forty-seven who were not citizens of Axis or Axis-occupied countries disembarked immediately, while the remaining 210 had to wait ten days at Tiscornia until the Joint convinced the Cuban authorities to permit them to land by pledging $480,000 per year maintenance. Persons who called publicly for the refugees to be admitted despite rumors that there were Nazis among the passengers included the archbishop of Havana.[8]

Individual Jews who were able to make contact with Cuban consular officials in Europe were required to have available more than $3,000 for each person desiring a visa, a small fortune in those days, payable in hard currency, not German marks.[9] From early 1939, German Jews knew in considerable detail the type of life they would lead (no regular employment, living on grants from the Joint, details about rents) if they managed to get into Cuba, because newspapers like the *Berliner Jüdische Rundschau* published detailed reports from subscribers on the island.[10] Among the arrivals during those years were diamond cutters from Antwerp, who started the Cuban diamond industry.[11] Belgian Grand Rabbi Srul Sapira was allowed to enter to join Temple Beth Israel when Rabbi Lasker departed for the United States. A number of German-born professors obtained university positions, and Jewish writers and artists plied their crafts.[12]

Cuban citizenship saved the lives of a small number of Jewish Cubans in Europe, mostly Ashkenazic immigrants who had come to the island in the early 1920s, done well, and then traveled to France—especially to Paris—during the 1930s. Some were businessmen; others worked in the Parisian entertainment industry. When France fell, a few escaped, but most were trapped in Paris and were rounded up by the Germans. They were held in concentration camps but not transported farther east because of their passports. In 1942, they were sent by the Germans to San Sebastián in Spain, in exchange for Germans who had been living there before the war. These Jews spent the remainder of the war interned in Spain, sustained by payments from the HIAS and Joint, and in 1945 were permitted to return to Cuba. But the Nazis did not honor foreign passports at all in Eastern Europe—those holding them were usually transported to the death camps when captured there, and even in Hungary, some holders of Swedish passports issued by Raoul Wallenberg were arrested and transported or murdered on the spot. Earlier in the war, many Jews who had managed to obtain Latin American citizenship papers and similar documents were saved.[13]

Although formally in the war on the Allied side, most elite Cubans did not concern themselves with the war in Europe or with the refugees in their midst. The wife of one of the island's most distinguished politicians of the 1940s later commented sarcastically that "we Cubans danced our way through World War II."[14] Measured another way, when wartime newsprint shortages forced papers to reduce their number of pages, the *Diario de la Marina* allotted nearly half of its space every day to news of weddings and social benefits and to gossip columns.[15] German Jewish refugee children who attended elite private schools found prejudice against East European Jews, which to some degree they shared.

With the German Jewish refugees who did manage to land in Cuba came others, including non-Jewish Europeans. Many were Social Democrats or Communists, and therefore political refugees. There were German citizens as well as Poles, Ukrainians, and Ruthenians—about a thousand in total. Ironically, because these immigrants suffered from the same restrictions against working as the Jewish refugees, a few became dependent on their Jewish colleagues and in some cases learned Yiddish, which came more readily to them than Spanish. Many were single men, and their social life revolved around the Jewish colony rather than larger Cuban society.

Most Cuban Jews had found their non-Jewish neighbors friendly and sympathetic. As war in Europe had approached, however, a rising number of anti-Semitic articles had begun to appear in the Cuban press and on the radio. Radio Prensa Nacional broadcast "mortifying accusations against Jews," and the political magazine *Campaña Autentica* followed suit. *Hoy* regularly ran stories charging specific Jewish businessmen and industrialists with underpaying or mistreating Cuban employees.[16] *Alerta* continued to be the worst

36. Uniformed high school students marching, Havana, ca. 1941. Courtesy of Norbert Adler.

offender, with regular pro-Falange, anti-Semitic articles. The *Diario de la Marina* also published articles arguing against the admission of Jewish refugees, although in more muted language. Nazi propagandists sent reams of anti-Semitic materials through the mails via German-flag shipping lines and diplomatic courier. During a three- or four-day period in August 1939, the *Havana Post* received anti-Jewish printed material that measured a foot and a half in height. Many smaller newspapers, unable to afford their own wire services, regularly used this material.[17]

Culture Shock

With the Cuban Jewish colony now relatively stable, the major Jewish world organizations turned their efforts to helping the refugees from nazism. For the first time, the U.S.-based ORT Federation, a leading Jewish social service agency, established a Havana branch, headed by Hugo Semler, devoted to vocational training through trade schools, farm colonies, and nonprofit industrial workshops.[18] In November 1942, all refugees were asked to register and were permitted to sign up for classes. Through the New York–based newspaper *Aufbau* and its network of community groups, German Jewish refugees in Cuba kept in close touch with refugees who had gained admittance to the United States. In 1942, ORT funds were provided for a newsletter, *Unterwegs*, which appeared with articles in three languages—German, Spanish, and (occasionally) English.[19] *Unterwegs* combined news with advertisements by German-speaking Cuban firms, Spanish-English language academies, jewelers, and a full range of commercial services. It also ran a weekly series of phrases for those learning English. The list for June 19, 1942, typical of the series, comprised a mixed assortment of practical and rhetorical sentences and reflected what must have been a baffling environment for the refugees: "That's lucky that you have so much money with you"; "That hits the nail on the head"; "She was hit by a bullet"; "We shall have to wait whether his prophecies come true"; "Does the express train arrive earlier than the local train?"; "After being separated for two years, they met again at Tiscornia"; "The pilot missed the bridge"; and "The Dutch took measures to prevent an invasion."[20] The newsletter provided detailed information about the war, including articles describing the plight of the surviving Jews in Europe. Because of close ties with Jewish organizations in the United States and because Cuban print journalism was closely linked to the North American press and wire services, newspaper audiences in Cuba learned about events in Europe at the same time as did readers in the United States and Canada.[21]

Some of the refugees experienced wrenching culture shock. Formerly wealthy German Jews found themselves in some cases crossing the ocean in third-class quarters that usually carried sheep and freight. New arrivals, recalling where they first stayed in Havana, would speak of "dumps," where rooms were partitioned cubicles with no windows.[22] Those managing to find rooms in boarding-houses run by Central Europeans ate meals familiar to them, but most clustered in hotels and pensiones, where they found the fare exotic. Typical of Old Havana were courtyards built at right angles from the street entrance, centers for family activities, food preparation, and laundry activities (fig. 39). In such open-air settings, the refugees had contact with their neighbors. The refugees had only the woolen clothing they had brought with them. Heat rash was rampant, for it took time to adapt to the climate. As many had unlimited free time at first, shedding their heavy clothing and going to the

37. German-Jewish
refugee on balcony,
ca. 1940. Courtesy
of Norbert Adler.

beach took care of this problem. Europeans used the beach even
during winter months, when the temperatures dropped into the 70s
and low 80s, driving away native-born Cubans, who considered this
much too cold (see figure 40). Many refugees complained bitterly
about the Cuban mentality, which was certainly different from
theirs, and argued about how things in Germany were more effi-
cient, more civilized. Some refugees were disoriented and dazed by
their separation from family members. Günter W. Cohn, who ran a
boarding-house, remembers that a twelve-year-old boy lived there
who had come to Cuba alone. Some relatives, especially older ones,
decided to wait just a little bit longer; then they were trapped in
Germany and unable to join their families in Cuba.[23]

Natalie (Nena) Beller Lyons, daughter of the U.S.-born president

38. View across Old Havana rooftops. Courtesy of Norbert Adler.

39. Living quarters in Old Havana. Courtesy of Norbert Adler.

40. Beach on outskirts of Havana, ca. 1940. Courtesy of Norbert Adler.

of the United Hebrew Congregation, Temple Beth Israel, remembers that, as a thirteen-year-old volunteer teaching English to a group of middle-aged German Jewish men and women in a pensión near her school, she heard so much carping that she exploded, yelling at her pupils that they should go back to Germany if things were so much better there. She told them that they stank, that they should wear lighter clothing and bathe more frequently.[24] If she was right, her students must have been unusual, for German Jews brought with them their penchant for cleanliness, which Cubans found at times astonishing. "Our neighbors," Ilsa Mittel-Ashe recollected, "looked benevolently and with a sense of distant friendship upon this new element in their midst who kept the places very neatly and even learned to wet-mop the floors every morning to exterminate the ubiquitous giant cockroaches."[25]

More hostility came from East European Jews, who called the German refugees "Daitch" (a Yiddish bastardization of "Deutsch," or German) and bridled at what they perceived to be the refugees' attitudes of superiority, although some worked at menial jobs illegally, even on the docks, to supplement their income (fig. 41). "The Cuban Jews never made any attempt at social contact or help, unlike the American Jews," recalled a woman who had arrived in 1939. "I never met a Cuban-Jewish teenager much less was invited for anything."[26] Some Cuban Jews insulted the refugees by offering to buy for very little whatever goods they had managed to ship, although East European Jewish merchants did attempt to win the refugees as customers. "Einziger Juedischer Optiker von der Universitaet Habana Graduiert," proclaimed Isaak Yawitz's advertisement for his "Optica Orbe" in *Unterwegs* ("The only Jewish optician who graduated from the University of Havana.")[27] Some of the East European Jews complained that the payments of relief money to refugee families was more than they themselves earned, and they resented the many refugees who lived in comfortable neighborhoods, especially Vedado, Havana's most elite. "Most of the Yiddish-speaking Jews could not afford to have telephones before the war," one recalled later, "but the refugees not only ended up in Vedado but they all rented apartments with telephones."[28] Some refugees who evaded the laws restricting them from working earned a good deal of money. Norbert Adler purchased a 1939 used car with earnings from the "alternative economy" printing business he ran during his two-year stay in Cuba (fig. 42).[29] The refugees who lived well were more

41. Docks employing European workers, Havana, 1940. Courtesy of Norbert Adler.

42. Norbert Adler's used car, ca. 1941. Courtesy of Norbert Adler.

visible than those without resources; the success stories and the persistence of at least some poverty within the permanent Jewish colony discouraged its members from contributing. Organized Cuban Jewish institutions gave an average of only $300 per month to refugee relief; the vast bulk of the funds came from the United States.[30]

For some refugees, the experience was bittersweet. Ruth G. Weitzenkorn remembers that

> having lived almost half of my life under Nazism, where friends and classmates ostracized me and later even physically attacked me . . . Havana was a free and glorious place for me. We were poor as church mice. In order to save the few pennies for the streetcar, we walked downtown. I had plenty of shoes, especially sandals, and also new clothes bought for the tropics. We lived in a two-family house, with a Cuban family upstairs. It was very crowded since we took in other refugees as boarders. The architecture of the house was very strange, the decor refugee-style (crates made into wardrobes and cupboards), as was common. Our neighbors, non-Jews, accepted us. . . . The kitchen had a charcoal stove and no hot water. Nor was there hot water in the bathroom. The first summer I suffered physically from the heat. That probably would be the worst thing I can remember.

> One of my fondest pleasures was going to the beach. Never in my

life had I been to an ocean beach. In the second year, one place gave refugees a reduced rate on one day during the week. There was always a big crowd. We teenagers met there and had a wonderful time. When I sported a great tan, the neighbors advised my mother to keep me home, since my beautiful white skin was turning too dark.[31]

Among the Sephardic Jews who had fled from Fascist Spain was Rabbi Nesim Gambach of Barcelona, who had been Spain's first rabbi since the expulsion of the Jews in 1492. The Turkish-born rabbi, who spoke Turkish, Hebrew, and Catalán but not Spanish, arrived in Cuba in September 1941 and spent a year in Camagüey. He then moved to Havana to become rabbi at Chevet Ahim, although he continued to minister to small Sephardic communities in the interior, where Jews were not prospering nearly to the degree that they did in the capital, and most continued to be isolated in towns and small cities with only a handful of correligionists.

The German speakers fared best. The U.S. consulate was located on the bay, and refugees found it pleasant to come and sit in front of it almost every day waiting for news that new quota numbers would be announced and that they would be able to leave for the United States.[32] Although it was fairly easy to overcome restrictions on employment, refugees who disdained extralegal work did little but sit and wait. Some women took off-the-books jobs in U.S. firms as janitors, just to learn English. Some made adjustments that must have appeared comical. One man decided to start a butterfly collection, but as he had no net, he used his stiff straw hat to swipe at the creatures and stun them, after which he kept them in a cigar box. He sent specimens of butterflies to his seven-year-old son stranded in France, although the insects arrived completely squashed.[33]

Refugees who took steps quickly to get around restrictions on formal employment soon established themselves in their former occupations or as entrepreneurs of one sort or another, relying on petty bribes to keep authorities at a distance. Others simply ignored regulations and talked their way into jobs as salesmen, especially in the interior. Still others earned money by giving piano lessons, or by tutoring in European languages, or by setting up small, unofficial businesses. Norbert Adler, for example, worked in his hot boarding-house room to supply promotional literature for businesses. It kept him busy, and he earned enough not to have to depend on the dole

43. Günter Cohn and Norbert Adler, Havana, ca. 1941. Courtesy of Norbert Adler.

from the American Council of Jewish Women (see figure 43, Adler with his old friend Günter Cohn). If they did not have other sources of supplementary income, members of almost every German Jewish family found work in the diamond trade established by the refugees from Belgium who were able to gain admission to Cuba during the first months of the war.[34]

The Wartime Diamond Business

The remarkable story of the wartime diamond business testified to the ingenuity of the refugees as well as to Cuba's live-and-let-live atmosphere. A great number of the refugees who arrived in 1941 were Polish Jews who had migrated to Antwerp, and who had managed to buy visas or other documents from Cuban consular officials or from other sources well after the *St. Louis* incident, fleeing from the Nazi occupation of Belgium. They were able literally to bring the diamond industry with them because it required little equipment beyond cutting and polishing machines, which could be manufactured anywhere; prototype machines were imported from Brazil and then copied. The labor was manual and precise. Diamond splitters (*Saegers*) earned forty cents per stone and could do up to a hundred stones a day or more, depending on how many machines they had at their disposal and on their supply of stones (fig. 44). Some of the workers took rough (*brut*) stones and split them; others, mostly women, worked as *Schneiders*, who were paid less, usually fifteen to twenty cents per unit, rounding and shaping them. There were four categories of *Schleifers* (polishers), depending on the type of facet being worked on.

Each of the approximately sixty diamond firms needed dozens of workers and machines. In each factory the employees were directed by several foremen, called *Mijstergast*, as well as workers who weighed, counted, and distributed the rough and finished products. Virtually all of these people were Jewish refugees. The industry also employed many native Cubans, who continuously swept the factory floors, sifting the debris in search of stones or diamond chips discarded by the machines. This detritus was valuable because it could be mixed with castor oil and used in polishing. The system by which the stones were exchanged and handled utilized a network based on such trust and honor among its participants that transactions rarely involved cash.

The diamond people had contacts all over the world. Most of the

44. Diamond technician, Havana, ca. 1942. Courtesy of Hardy L. Spatz.

rough stones originated in South Africa and were exported from New York into Cuba under a strict quota system. Brokers then reexported them to the United States for sale at the retail level. Practically overnight, as many as 6,000 men and women, mostly European refugees, went to work and prospered in the industry, manufacturing nearly all of the world's *Achtkant* gems, the small diamonds used in jewelry settings. The Antwerp Jews also brought over their chief rabbi, Srul Sapira, who affiliated with the UHC and who conducted separate Conservative services, alternating between French and German, serving the needs of the refugee community.

Although legally restricted from earning wages, refugees found work in the burgeoning diamond industry because Cuban officials didn't really care what they did. Diamond production was explained to them as being part of the Allied war effort, which it wasn't. Novices paid from $200 to $500 to the Belgian technicians or to other refugees who had learned the trade by doing the same. The apprenticeship lasted from five to six weeks, during which time the apprentice's production was taken as further tuition by the "master," who was always called "Rebbe," but enough money was left over in many cases to permit the student to open a small diamond factory.

Diamonds were exchanged every Saturday morning through an informal ritual that operated on the grounds of the Hotel Plaza underneath its arcades, the Corso. It functioned as a kind of stock exchange, its unwritten rules understood by its participants. The workshop owners, *Fabrikanten*, as well as the workers (some of whom were also traders on the side) engaged in a brisk trade in *briefkes*, small envelopes containing finished stones. The business flourished and evolved so quickly that strikes broke out over wages as well as over demand for greater numbers of stones—the more stones furnished, the more money made. The odd nature of the industry was illustrated when the striking workers and the Fabrikanten, who in private life were usually the best of friends, went to the beach at Varadero together "to wait it out."[35]

The diamond industry was open to men and women, young and old. Most of its members left for the United States if their papers came though while the war was still going on; when the war ended, most returned to Belgium or Holland or emigrated to Israel, where the diamond trade was transferred. The Cuban authorities wanted very much to keep the industry and made strong efforts to do so, forbidding the departing former refugees to leave with their machinery.[36] But the diamond workers took their sources of diamonds with them, and in any case few Cubans had been trained in the more skilled aspects of the trade; moreover, Cuba was out of the way geographically, and the industry there could no longer be cost effective.

Politics and Anti-Semitism

Some members of the refugee colony devoted considerable effort to showing their support for the war effort and to thanking their Cuban hosts. An umbrella organization, Loyalty Action, was organized to link the myriad of refugee groups, which arrayed themselves along national lines: the ORT Foundation's *Asociación Democratica de Refugiados Hebreos* (ADRH), *Asociación Italo-Cubana Antifascista*, Free Poles, Free Yugoslavs, Free Hungarians, Free Austrians, Free French, and so on.[37] The anti-Franco Spaniards tended not to organize, suggesting that the Free Europe groups may have been financed by the Allied war effort, less concerned about Spain than about Hitler-occupied Europe.

The Free Peoples groups in Cuba were anti-Fascist associations, organized to complement the Freies Deutschland (Free Germany) movement, which was a Communist front with member groups throughout the hemisphere, notably in Mexico. Gerhard Kaden, a Protestant refugee who funded the Cuban Alexander von Humboldt Society, associated freely with members of the Jewish refugee groups until it was discovered that he was a Soviet spy. (When the war ended, it was whispered that he was picked up by a Russian freighter outside of Cuba's territorial limits.)[38] Some of the non-Jewish European refugees married Cuban women, usually of the upper class: Edgar Von Russ, for instance, the head of the Free Austria association (and formerly Austrian consul in Havana), married into the Padrón family. A few of the Central European Jewish refugees also married Cubans.[39] One such couple's son was Otto Reich, who later became U.S. ambassador to Venezuela. His father was Viennese, his mother a Cuban Catholic.

Most who in the late 1930s heard allegations about the Holocaust either did not believe them or considered them exaggerated war propaganda. Those who did believe the stories about mass killings and starvation felt helpless in the midst of a two-front world war. Among the Jewish community in the United States, reaction to the news of channels for refugees being closed down included anger and dismay. Fear that "we Americans will lose our own right to life, liberty, and the pursuit of happiness" unless restrictions on immigration were lifted was expressed in 1939 by R. W. Harrison to a gathering of 1,500 of Miami's Bayfront Park, according to the Miami Herald.[40] But the incident was buried under many more tragic tidings as the years passed.

Yet the memory of the St. Louis affair could not be eradicated. In June 1939, Fernando Ortíz, the veteran of the Grupo Minorista of the 1920s and a university professor and editor of Ultra, a review of the world's press, used the St. Louis trauma as a rallying cry against anti-Semitism, claiming that it was foreign to Cuban soil and should be rejected as a European disease.[41] Ortíz worked strenuously to support the Allied war effort, reprinting in nearly every issue short pieces in translation extolling the bravery and preparedness of the French, British, Americans, and Russians. Readers of Ultra would not be surprised at the revelations of Nazi atrocities made later, because as early as 1939, Ortíz published articles warning of the grave danger posed to Jews by Hitler.[42]

Others avoided the issue. Manuel Benítez's family in later years claimed that the U.S. ambassador had delivered a personal message from President Roosevelt asking that the St. Louis not be permitted to land. Others—including Florida congressman Claude Pepper—claimed this to be false. President Roosevelt's aides denied that any telegrams from ship passengers pleading for help had been received, although we know that dozens, perhaps hundreds, were sent and that the Joint had worked nonstop but fruitlessly to gain aid from the United States, from Cuba, and from British officials in Trinidad. The State Department denied the undocumented claim that 743 of the 930 passengers had held official U.S. entry quota numbers, meaning that they should have been eligible for immigration under the German quota, if not in 1938 then later. In January 1944, Randolph E. Paul, counsel to the Treasury Department, accused the State Department of failing to use the governmental machinery at its disposal to rescue Jews fleeing from Hitler, and of concealing its guilt by issuing false and misleading statements.[43]

Even after the St. Louis steamed back to Europe, the anti-Semitic barrage continued in Cuba. Congressman Tirso Domínguez Fumero introduced a bill on July 3, 1939, calling for a census of all Jews who had entered Cuba after January 1, 1933, as a prelude to expelling them. The Labor Department recommended legislation barring immigrants from starting businesses that would compete with Cuban-owned firms. The Polish consul general in Havana issued a statement pointing out that the polacos were not "genuine" Poles but Jews, for whom he had no concern. In Polish scholarship on emigration to Cuba, the fact that more than 90 percent of Poles entering Cuba were Jews has been virtually ignored. Polish writers either concentrate on the tiny percentage of Roman Catholic Poles who went to Cuba—most of them miners ending up in the Matahambre mine in Pinar del Rio—or further minimize the Jewish presence by lumping together non-Catholic emigrants as "Jews and Ukrainians." At the time, Polish writers avoided commenting on why the Jews left except to say that they sought to "make better money." They expressed anger at Jews being called polacos and at the term's meaning someone "dirty, miserable, and lazy."[44]

The Cuban Constitution written during 1939–40 contained provisions introduced during the stormy controversy over Jewish immigration, including a prohibition against immigrants practicing law or medicine and regulations forbidding entry to political or religious refugees. A massive public rally was sponsored by the Juventud Fascista de Cuba on the spacious Paseo del Prado in December 1939. At the harbor entrance, at the juncture of the Prado and Malecón, bands played, speakers attacked "fifth columnist Jews," "Yanqui imperialists," and "communist fellow travellers."[45] The German-American Bund (Amerikadeutscher Volksbund), headquartered in New York, sent representatives to participate. According to the U.S. embassy, about 500 German nationals residing in Cuba were Nazi party members. They were directed by the German minister, Hans Hermann Voelckers, with headquarters in the German legation. The party was legal, and members wore swastika insignia or emblems on their clothing, never bashful about their sympathies.[46] The Communist party was also legalized, in 1939, but it never assumed an influential role.[47]

When the new Constitution went into effect on September 15, 1940, Fulgencio Batista assumed the presidency of the Republic of Cuba. Batista, although a personal friend of individual Jews, never interceded against any anti-Semitic propaganda, but in late 1939, even before the United States entered the war, he outlawed the Cuban Nazi and Fascist parties.[48] Two years later, in the week following the Japanese attack on Pearl Harbor, sweeping measures were implemented against Axis interests. These included the confiscation of Axis property in Cuba and a series of police raids on December 17, 1941, to arrest known Fascist sympathizers. The head of the old Fascist party, Antonio DiGregori DiVivanco, an Italian national and supporter of Mussolini, was detained, as was a German engineer named Hahn who was accused of Gestapo activities. Four thousand German citizens and a hundred Japanese nationals were rounded up as "enemies of the nation" and held at prison camps on the inhospitable Isle of Pines.[49] At least one Nazi in Havana became disillusioned with the movement: Joachim Wirkenstaedt, the manager of the German firm Quimicas Schering, who worked closely with some of the German Jewish refugees, was shot to death in mid-1940 when Gestapo spies found out about his conversion.[50]

Other fringe front groups were permitted to continue to function but were kept under surveillance. An extensive Nazi espionage network operated, its existence providing a continuing pretext for the Latin American Division of the U.S. State Department in June 1940 to advise Caribbean and Central America nations not to accept German Jewish expatriates on the grounds that spies had infiltrated the refugee stream.[51] There is a controversy over to what degree these fears were rooted in anti-Semitic undercurrents within the State Department, fanned by wartime anxiety.[52] Many high U.S. administrators did look down their noses at Cuba, not only at the refugees but at venal Cuban officials and their henchmen. The U.S. embassy in Havana cabled the following message to the State Department on April 21, 1942:

> The Cuban government has issued a decree canceling the visas of nearly all the refugees on board the *S.S. San Thomé* then at sea. While the decree's ostensible purpose was to prevent entrance of possible Axis agents, the real purpose was believed to be an attempt to extract more money from Jewish relief societies which were anxious that the refugees land. The Embassy received from several independent sources, including consulates of other United Nations, repeated accounts of how these refugees were being held at the Tiscornia immigration center un-

til such time as they were willing to make payments to secure release. The Ambassador vigorously protested this situation to the Prime Minister, who was reluctant to take action, explaining that it was a "very difficult situation involving politics."

U.S. Consul General Tewell, accompanied by British and other consular representatives, visited Tiscornia and "thwarted the attempted extortion." The refugees were allowed to enter Cuba on May 5, 1942. The embassy received the thanks of Jewish organizations for its effective work in this case.[53] Norbert Adler's parents had faced a similar difficulty. When they disembarked in early December 1940 with "legitimate" landing permits that their son had purchased for $150 each, they were sent to Tiscornia until they came up with $1,000 landing money. They demanded to be taken to the U.S. consulate in Havana and were escorted there by a policeman three or four times until, a month later, their U.S. visas were issued and they were allowed to proceed to Brooklyn, arriving January 14, 1941.

The State Department's Breckinridge Long, who saw his role as "not only to protect the United States from its declared enemies but also from all who might adversely harm the war effort," constantly blocked efforts to bring in additional refugees. A State Department official stated to Cordell Hull in June 1941 that he had advised the Cuban minister in Washington to make Cuban immigration laws more restrictive.[54] In 1943, the U.S. ambassador, Spruille Braden, warned that "a high-ranking official of the Cuban government has tipped off a member of our staff that Col. Jaime Mariné and Batista have a little plan under way to import into Cuba 2,000 Jewish refugees at $2,000 a head. Having heard of Trujillo's activities along this line, I naturally wonder if Mariné's visits to Santo Domingo may not also have a bearing on this racket."[55] Ambassador Braden regularly fired off telegrams to Foggy Bottom attesting to his vigilance against "well-organized racket[s] to sell visas to European refugees of unknown reliability and also Cuban passports to those not legally entitled to them."[56] A 1945 State Department memorandum referred to Mendel Schachne, a New York attorney, as "a visa racketeering lawyer who represents several visa applicants in Cuba, one of whom has a very bad reputation."[57]

To be sure, wartime Nazi infiltration of the Caribbean was significant, especially in Cuba and in the Dominican Republic, where Dr. Adolf Meyer—an acquaintance of General Trujillo—controlled a network of agents in contact with German submarines, aircraft, and telegraph installations. Gestapo agents carried out murders of turncoat former Nazis.[58] Right-wing front organizations funded by the Axis flourished, such as the Legión Nacional Revolucionaria Sindicalista.[59] After Pearl Harbor, Cuba declared war on the Axis. Nearly 2,000 Cubans volunteered as individuals for service in the U.S. armed forces, although Cuba itself did not send soldiers.[60] The F.B.I. worked closely with Cuban police and military authorities to ferret out Axis spies, especially those seeking information about Allied shipping.

One of the consequences of Cuba's wartime stance was that U.S. armed forces were permitted to construct bases on the island. There was a large air base outside Havana, and the U.S. Navy used Cuba as a center for antisubmarine surveillance. The presence of so many officers and soldiers helped reinforce the influence of U.S. culture on the island, which already had been strong, and helped the tourist industry (some of which was run by Cuban Jews) as well as the ancillary flesh trade. Members of the American Jewish community hosted Jewish servicemen stationed in Cuba and provided Passover seders, parties, and religious services.

Havana's Jews also participated in a six-hour anti-Germany demonstration in December 1942 following news of the suicide, in London, of Arthur Zielbaum, the Polish Bund's representative to the World Jewish Congress, who anguished over the failure of the democracies to help East European Jewry under the Nazis. As many as 10,000 people, including non-Jewish factory employees of Jewish firms, marched from the Centro Israelita to the presidential palace. President Batista at first refused to meet the delegation's leaders, but a sympathetic senator, Eduardo Chibas, was asked to intercede, and Batista dutifully appeared before the crowd by the end of the day.[61]

The Batista presidency (1940–44) was accompanied by increased Cuban-U.S. trade. Washington sent lend-lease arms in exchange for the right to operate military bases in Cuba. Sugar production increased under U.S. guarantees to buy the crop at a price higher than depression levels. Economic conditions improved in some sectors but worsened in others, affected by the wartime interdiction of shipping. The threat of German submarines forced sugar producers to haul sugar by rail to Havana for shipment under convoy.[62] Shortages of consumer goods caused grumbling to spread, and some expressed the hope that Batista would intervene and seize dictatorial power.

This did not happen. His candidate in the 1944 presidential election, Prime Minister Carlos Saladrigas, lost to Ramón Grau San Martín, former president and Batista's antagonist. Some worried that Grau might restore the reformist initiatives of 1933 and with them the nationalistic policies that discriminated against the non-native-born Cubans. They remembered Grau's 1933 slogan, "Cuba for the Cubans." But only one member of Grau's Auténticos, Primitivo Rodríguez, publicly engaged in anti-Semitic activities. Rodríguez bitterly opposed anything to do with Jews or Jewish refugees, and after the war he attempted to block Cuban government support for the state of Israel. During the war, there were a few isolated incidents: Jewish peddlers were temporarily barred from the Parque Trillo Market, and Jewish tourists were not welcome at Varadero Beach hotels.[63] But Fulgencio Batista had cracked down on imported anti-Semitism during his presidency as part of the war effort, and Cuban society remained on the whole open and tolerant.

Grau's Auténticos, the Cuban Revolutionary party, promised economic and political independence and pledged to remove corruption from government. But Grau's presidency made things more difficult for foreigners. Batista had governed in a progressive manner, not permitting corruption to get out of hand, but Grau's Auténtico politicians and officials, especially his cronies in the Education Ministry and in the state-run lottery agency, not only stole and extorted millions but intimidated opponents and directed violence against them. Most Auténticos had been out of power, some in exile, for years. The opportunities for personal gain once they returned to take over the government were too great. Office seekers with "voracious" appetites took control of government posts and privileges. Thousands poured into the civil bureaucracy, paralyzing it. Historian Louis A. Pérez, Jr., describes the results:

The opportunity was not lost. Embezzlement, graft, corruption, and malfeasance of public office permeated every branch of national, provincial, and municipal government. The public trust was transformed into a private till. Politics passed under the control of party thugs, and a new word entered the Cuban political lexicon: *gangsterismo.* Violence and terror became extensions of party politics and the hallmark of *Auténtico* rule.[64]

Astute observers who watched the chain of petty gifts and other special payments made to facilitate business knew that it ended at Grau's sister-in-law, Paulina, Cuba's First Lady. Making payments of this kind was so common that many accepted it as a standard component of the system, just as well-placed Cuban youths who graduated from college expected to receive, if they wanted one, a public job that required little or no work.

Preserving a Jewish Identity
Because most of the Jewish immigrants who arrived in Cuba had hoped that their stay would be temporary, they related to their tropical island in a very different set of ways than they would have had it been their final destination. Many of those who had come before 1940, especially those from the towns and cities of Eastern Europe, were initially stunned, not only by the heat and lush tropicality and brilliant colors, but by the society's worldliness and by the presence of mulattos and blacks, who made up a good

45. Tropical Havana. Courtesy of Norbert Adler.

portion of the island's population. Sender Kaplan likened Cuba's Jews to Robinson Crusoe, stranded on a faraway island that would become their home for many years.[65]

Others drifted away from the colony's clubs and synagogues and married Roman Catholics.[66] Some accepted religious conversion voluntarily: Oscar Ganz, prime minister under President Carlos Prío Socarrás (1948–52), was fully accepted by the Cuban establishment after he gave up his Jewish identification. Even men and women who remained religiously observant faced pressures from a society that was so different from theirs. Young single men often adopted the practice, common in middle- and upper-class circles in cosmopolitan urban centers, of engaging prostitutes or taking mistresses. So did many married men, who rationalized their behavior by saying that "at least we came home for dinner every night." Brothels such as Casa Marina thrived in the red-light district and were inexpensive, part of the fast life-style of the celebrated capital and tourist center.[67]

Cuban Yiddish literature and poetry, which flowered during the 1930s, told stories of immigrants who had become entranced with their exotic new land. Many were bittersweet tales of suffering and attempting to be understood by Cuba's unpretentious people, to whom the immigrants' exotic tongues made them seem strange beings.[68] There were two main reasons that the East European Jewish immigrants chose to pour their energy into Yiddish culture rather than attempt to assimilate. First, Cuban society, although tolerant, did not endorse cultural or religious pluralism. There was no public school network devoted to Cubanizing immigrants, as public schools Americanized them in the United States. Second, most of the Ashkenazic Jews in the 1920s and 1930s did not intend to stay but sought to emigrate to the United States. Communal organizations remained inclusionary, preserving Yiddish culture for the hoped-for transfer to the United States even though immigrants to that country were rapidly shedding immigrant culture, behavior, and identity, especially the younger generation.

Although Zionism initially attracted adherents from the Sephardic community, by the 1940s it interested mainly Ashkenazim, especially teenagers who joined one of the many Zionist youth groups. But Zionism's appeal in Cuba was not universal; in fact, a barrier separated the Unión Sionista (founded in 1924), which preserved the

46. Unión Sionista de Cuba Tree Fund certificate. Courtesy of Stanley Wax.

use of Yiddish and its members' prewar socialist views, and the other leading community associations, anchored by the Centro Israelita and its Colegio Hebreo, the UHC, the Sephardic Unión Hebrea Chevet Ahim, and, during the 1950s, the Patronato. By the late 1940s, these organizations played mostly cultured and social roles, separating them ever further from the activist Zionists. Marco Pitchón, a Sephardic Jew who headed the small Cuban B'nai B'rith organization, neither religious nor Zionist, tried to mediate between the Zionists and non-Zionists but was largely unsuccessful.

The Zionist groups ranged from the far Left to the far Right and were often rent by still smaller internal factions. Nonetheless, funds were raised continuously (see figure 46, a certificate for a tree to be planted in the Holy Land). Zionist fund-raisers and publicists regularly visited Havana, including, on one occasion immediately after the war, Menachem Begin. The Keren Hayesod organization's annual fund-raising campaign, emphasizing Jewish settlement on the land in Palestine, was the major institutional vehicle for these activities, and, unlike other Jewish organizations, the group received support from most segments of the community; Cuban Sephardic Jews, less directly affected by the stunning news coming out of Central Europe about the Holocaust, did not participate as much as the Ashkenazim. The American congregation, the UHC, cooperated with the movement, sponsoring concerts and rallies in support of a Jewish Palestine. At a public program in 1936, for example, guests in the Teatro Principal de la Comedia sang the Cuban national anthem and "Hatikvah," heard a congratulatory message from the president of the republic, listened to speeches by David Blis, the old Jewish community leader, by Rabbi Meir Lasker, by four members of Congress including Dr. Radio Cremata, secretary of the House of Representatives, and by a representative from the Jewish agency, Manuel Gravier, who came in 1936 to raise funds; they heard a concert featuring works in Spanish, Yiddish, Italian, and English, with a final recital by Cuban soprano Maruja González of the classic Hebrew chant "Eli Eli" ("My God, My God") and the "Song of the New Palestine" sung in Hebrew.[69]

The fragmentation among Cuban Jews over language and national origin meant that there never was a single, united Cuban Jewish community. Of Jews in Cuba at the time of the outbreak of the war, 80 percent had arrived between 1922 and 1930 but, like the later arrivals, had come from diverse national groups, many as different from one another as they were from the Cubans. Jacques Rieur identified thirteen distinctive communities, ranging from the descendants of the earliest Sephardim (the French Jews whose ancestors came from Martinique and Guadeloupe during Havana's occupation by the British in 1762–63) to the small but self-contained group of fifty Arabian Jewish families from Iraq and North Africa, isolated from other Sephardic Jews because they spoke Judeo-Arabic, not Ladino.

Adaptation and Acculturation

Out of 4.25 million Cubans in 1938—a million of whom lived in humid but stately Havana—Jews numbered about 13,000, subdivided into a settled population of about 10,000 and the rest refugees or immigrants in transit. The vast majority lived in Havana, the rest scattered in the provinces: 300 in Pinar del Rio, 600 in Matanzas, 900 in Santa Clara, 800 in Camagüey, and 900 in Oriente. The isolation of most of these communities resulted in a high rate of intermarriage and eventual assimilation outside Jewish life, although families traveled from long distances to attend communal activities in the provincial capitals on Jewish holy days.

Most Cubans with whom the refugees had contact treated them in a matter-of-fact manner and were pleasant. Norbert Adler encountered some young Cubans who had returned from volunteer service against fascism in the Spanish civil war; they sympathized with him because he was a victim of nazism. Other Cubans, he found, considered him some kind of American on whom they could practice their English.[70] Ordinary Cubans were confused by the presence of the refugees and about foreigners in general. Their world included, for the most part, four principal categories of people: Spaniards, Americans, upper-class Cubans, and lower-class Cubans; Jews did not fit into the puzzle. One young Cuban woman told Lisa Fittko that she thought Jews were non-Catholic Christians, like Protestants. Other evidence suggests that many people did know about the refugees and why they were in Cuba. Fittko also remembers that black homeless men who sat on park benches, sometimes drunk, harassed the refugees, mocking them and calling out that "they're finally going to kill you."[71]

To nominally Roman Catholic Cubans, the great majority of the population, Jews were Jews, even if they had never seen one. But Cuba's Jewish colony on the eve of the war represented a panoply of small groups, whose members clung to one another, offering help only to their own and separated by cultural, language, and religious differences reinforced by the feeling among the immigrants of the 1920s and by the German-speaking wartime refugees that Cuba was only a temporary place for them, not their home. There were the French and the Dutch Jews, those who were descendants of West India Company merchants (as well as some representing Hamburg banking firms) who had come from the Netherlands and from its Caribbean territories after Havana was restored to the Spanish crown, which at that time exercised sovereignty over Holland. There were citizens of every Nazi-held country in Europe who had arrived in Cuba with U.S. visas in 1939 to find that the national quotas for immigration to the United States from their places of origin had been filled. Some thirty Italian Jewish families came in 1940, and another group from Belgium, many of whom—nationalized Belgians born in Lithuania, Poland, Hungary, or Romania—could not emigrate because their country of national origin quotas were filled by others. There were also the three major branches of the Jewish population: the American Jews and the much larger groups of Sephardim and Ashkenazim. After the war, internal barriers within these groups would erode, and Cuba would become, in their minds, their permanent home. Jewish culture would survive, but with less intensity than before the war, more as an expression of nostalgia than as a means to keep the community together.

The social and cultural institutions that had flowered during the 1920s for the most part survived the war, especially among the older members of the community. Their children, although not shying away from Judaism, felt much more comfortable in the Spanish-language environment of Cuba. The four Jewish newspapers had a total circulation of 1,200 at war's end. *Havaner Lebn* published bi-weekly, the others less frequently. Ten books about Jewish life had been published after 1928, four of them translated into Spanish or written in that language.[72] There were a few Jewish restaurants, including the celebrated Moyshe Pipik (literally, Moses's Belly Button), which catered to tourists. This Havana coffee shop's bilingual sign (fig. 47) spelled out Sweetshop—*Dulceria* in Spanish and *Konditorei* in Yiddish. A cooperative cafeteria, the Kitchen Cooperative, opened in 1933 under the auspices of Cuba's Communist movement; it employed twenty-four workers, charging lower prices than regular commercial restaurants. A share of the profits went to charity, the rest to members.

Later, when the refugees began to arrive, German-speaking Jews opened two restaurants, Annie Stein's and Siboney, on the Prado, within walking distance of the U.S. consulate. Siboney specialized in German and Hungarian food. Lucerna, near Woolworth's on Avenida Italia, offered Swiss pastries, chocolates, and pralines.[73] There were also several Chinese restaurants (two were Charlie Sing and Pullman) where the new arrivals liked to congregate. Meal coupons here, when purchased in booklets, cost about thirty-five cents. Central European refugees also frequented Reissmann's, a restaurant on the corner of Twenty-first and K Streets in Vedado. Everybody who was anybody among the refugees could be found at Reissmann's having their Wiener Schnitzel or their Viennese pastry with their *Kaffee mit Schlag* (coffee with whipped cream).[74]

Residents could choose from an ample selection of high cultural events mixed with mostly U.S. popular entertainment. The Cine

47. Jewish restaurant, Old Havana. Courtesy of Norbert Adler.

Gris in Vedado offered German- and French-language films on Mondays, "Montag des Emigranten." On other days standard movie fare ranged from Robert Taylor in *Waterloo Bridge* to Humphrey Bogart in *The Wagon Rides at Night* to *The Lone Ranger Rides Again*. The famous Tropicana Club in Marianao offered admission for a cover charge of twenty-five centavos. The Montmarte Casino charged no cover at all. More pedestrian bars and nightclubs offered a variety of nightlife characterized by lively music, good food and drink, and women. One club featured an all-female orchestra (fig. 48) and probably catered to foreigners.

Through the war, the East European Jewish associations continued to sponsor theater, musical recitals, lectures, and poetry readings in Yiddish and sometimes in Russian. One resident of the community remembers that as a youth he attended his first play,

48. Night spot, Havana. Courtesy of Norbert Adler.

Hamlet, in Yiddish—he did not realize that the work was Shakespeare's.[75] There were several serious music societies, including Conciertos Daniel, which in order to win consent from authorities to perform publicly had to verify that all its Jewish musicians were regularly employed and not immigrants working illegally. Ashkenazic essayists and poets combed Cuban history for heroes. Eliezer Aronowsky wrote an epic poem on Antonio Maceo; others wrote about José Martí, finding common ground in the Liberator's abhorrence of religious prejudice, the fusion in his writing of Christian and Judaic thought, and his statement that "Moisés no ha muerto, porque Moisés es el amor" ("Moses has not died, because Moses is love").[76] *Havaner Lebn* implored its readers to accept Cuba as a "substitute America."[77] Its editor, Sender Kaplan, cultivated an Americanized Yiddish writing style, carefully excluding Spanish variants, and urged in editorials that Jews "make their America in Cuba." Abraham Dubelman, who became an associate editor in 1937, wrote short stories emphasizing the immigrants' culture shock and frustrations in adjusting to Cuban life. The newspaper also reported on the difficulties faced by Jews in the provinces. Dubelman, Osher Schuchinsky, and others recounted poignant stories of Jews attempting to assimilate but never really fitting into racially mixed, small-town Cuban life.

The adaptation problems of the German Jewish refugees were more acute than those of the Ashkenazim. Many arrived bewildered, having left relatives behind, and unsure of what would happen to them. Perhaps in defense, many continued to express their preference for the German way of doing things, raising bitter resentment among the other members of the island's Jewish colony, most of whom felt little nostalgia for the countries they had left under duress or in poverty. The German Jews in Cuba echoed the sentiments of Kurt Hahn, the exiled educator and founder of the elite school at Schloss Salem, the home of the Margrave of Baden. Of Jewish birth, Hahn sought refuge in Britain, founding the Gordonstoun School in Scotland for boys from the upper classes, including the royal family, destined for national leadership. Hahn's prescription was as blunt as his educational outlook: "One must love one's fatherland even when it does not love one back."[78]

That the refugees from nazism had a better possibility of emigrating to the United States than the Jews who had arrived earlier provoked jealousies among members of the Ashkenazim who had not become prosperous and who still wanted to leave for the United States but could not do so. Although grateful, most of the German Jews developed few ties to Cuba and left as soon as they could. They had come to Cuba for the simple reason that it was the first country to offer them refuge.[79] Lisa Fittko, who with her non-Jewish husband was a member of the Nazi resistance in Berlin, tells in her autobiography how she reacted when her husband, Hans, told her that the Centre Americain de Secours in Marseilles was arranging Cuban visas for them:

"Where is Cuba, actually?" I interrupted him.

"I don't know exactly either, somewhere between North and Central America. Why do you have to know that now?"

"Because it does not sound like a real country—Cuba. Like those visas for China or Panama, a piece of paper, but no place where one can go.

"Do you know what language they speak there?"

"It doesn't matter—probably Spanish."[80]

Because all Germans were suspected of Nazi sympathies and could be interned, Hans Fittko's landlord told the police that Hans was a Jew in order to save him. Lisa, although Jewish, thought of herself primarily as an anti-Fascist and associated mainly with anti-Nazi Germans and Cubans. Perhaps more than the other Jewish immigrants who had preceded them, some of the Germans took umbrage at the corruption of the Cuban system. Among themselves they called President Fulgencio Batista a "bandit," complaining that corruption was so pervasive that "one cannot get [even] a death certificate without a bribe." Lisa Fittko described her reception at Tiscornia in 1941: "There are hundreds of refugees in the Camp. . . . [The Cuban officials] try extortion: we should pay more money. Since we don't have any, they release us after about ten days. Most of the others are gradually released. The validity of the visa is not particularly relevant; bribes are more important."[81]

The wartime refugees fortunate enough to gain entry to Cuba before the government changed its policies in mid-1939 lived reasonably comfortably. Initially many were put up in Máximo's Hotel, a large, graying building that looked like a penitentiary and that was run by a Polish Jew. Rates were cheap. The refugees were signed up for weekly restaurant vouchers and for relief agency grants of from seven to twelve dollars per week, more than double the amount given refugees who came later. For most of the refugees, who had been allowed to take only ten German marks with them, this stipend was a godsend. One of these who arrived with virtually nothing, Walter Lippmann, set himself up as a photographer. He soon found himself making a comfortable living at his craft, and volunteered to the relief board that he didn't need the weekly seven-dollar allotment. The board representative accepted his offer gratefully, then asked him to provide the names of other refugees who also could be cut off the dole. He took umbrage at this, refusing to spy on others.[82]

The German-speaking arrivals paid special attention to cultural events, securing from patrons as diverse as the U.S. ambassador, Spruille Braden, and the Inter-American Commission's Nelson Rockefeller support for the Havana Philharmonic Orchestra, whose director was a non-Jewish Austrian refugee, Erich Kleiber, one of Europe's eminent conductors.[83] Maurice and Jeanette Schechter, he from Rumania and she from Palestine, U.S. citizens (and members of the United Hebrew Congregation) who had come to Cuba in 1903 among the estimated 100 American Jews who had taken up residence following Cuban independence, invited members of the refugee community to Saturday afternoon concerts at their Vedado estate and served refreshments. Among the musicians who performed was Arthur Rubinstein, himself a Polish Jewish refugee who had been admitted to the United States.[84] Musical performances, in fact, were almost the only events that attracted interest from all parts of the Jewish colony, and therefore they served as vehicles to break down, if only briefly, internal barriers. Old enmities, of course, were strong. German Jews before Hitler customarily referred to the Eastern Jews with disdain, and many carried these opinions with them across the Atlantic.

Occasionally, a member of a Jewish family who had managed to emigrate was non-Jewish or had converted to Christianity. Some of these individuals did not have the red J stamped in their German passports and as a result were technically considered enemy aliens and subject to arrest and internment. The police came for Lisa Fittko's husband, Hans, at their transient hotel but were dissuaded from taking him to jail by an acquaintance, Máximo, who paid a bribe. Presumably they had come looking for payment. Some other non-Jewish resistance fighters who had fled occupied Europe with the aid of the Emergency Rescue Committee in New York turned up at Tiscornia. Some of them were allowed to come to the mainland; others were arrested and held on the Isle of Pines together with known Nazis arrested after Cuba entered the war on the side of the Allies. The administration of the Isle of Pines camps was left to the Germans, who made life hell for the anti-Nazis caught in their midst. One man lost his teeth from repeated beatings.[85]

The refugees admitted to Cuba had enjoyed a comfortable standard of living in Europe and now had to rely on their wits (and the underground economy) to maintain themselves. Most were ignored by the resident Jews, few of whom spoke the same language, although the American Jews, who shared the refugees' cultural interests to some extent, did accept the German-speaking refugees on an individual basis. Economic and psychological stress affected refugees in different ways. Rabbi Meir Lasker recalled later that a few of the unmarried young women stepped out into Cuban society, angering community leaders because going out alone implied (but did not always mean) sexual promiscuity.[86] Some elegant and comely young European women became the mistresses of politicians and members of society and through these connections were of help to their families and friends. Refugee men often took Cuban mistresses. According to one then-unmarried member of this group, this relationship was the ideal way to learn Spanish.[87]

The UHC's Rabbi Lasker raised some funds for a vocational academy, Finca Paso Seco, established by American Friends from Philadelphia outside Havana to give young men and women training in trades and in English, for their eventual emigration to the United States. Sponsorship for the academy came from the dean of Bryn Mawr College, who visited Havana during the early 1940s, and from other U.S. sources including the Joint, and the school was created. Nearly a half-century later, many of the men and women who had been tutored there, on almost a one-to-one basis, continued to speak with admiration and thankfulness for the considerate treatment they received from the Quakers.[88] Later during the war, the New York–based ORT Foundation provided vocational classes and orientation sessions for refugees headed for the United States. The UHC provided a room for the Quakers to use to teach refugee teenagers, although none of the volunteer teachers, who were mostly wives of non-Jewish U.S. businessmen in Havana, spoke German. Nonetheless, they taught English, mathematics, geography, and U.S. history as best they could.[89]

By 1942 the now-permanent Jewish community had institutionalized certain practices to facilitate a self-sufficiency that, given Cuba's lack of well-defined laws, was considered to be necessary. There were no banking statutes before 1942, for example, so court judgments could not be enforced nor could liens be placed on property. Instead, Jews turned within their community to traditional ecclesiastical forms of adjudication—the Bet Din, religious courts in which an Orthodox rabbi acted as mediator and judge. Jewish businessmen often used these methods to settle their problems with other Jews and only occasionally went to the formal legal system. Lacking access to bank loans, Jews arranged to borrow money when needed from the Jewish Committee for Cuba and other agencies.

In 1942, the first small group of Jewish immigrant children graduated from the University of Havana—a physician, several engineers, and one teacher. Tuition was low—thirty-five or forty dollars per

49. Hardy Spatz walking in park, Havana. Courtesy of Hardy L. Spatz.

year; admission was based on entrance examination scores. More second-generation Cuban Jews graduated after the war, although a few of the more successful Ashkenazic families (and many more of the American Jews) sent their children to secondary school and to colleges and universities in the United States. Some of the refugees were so eager to have their children learn English that they enrolled them in double sessions, so that they would learn faster and make up for whatever time they might have lost.[90] During wartime, some community leaders attempted to bridge the "lamentable" distance between the Sephardic and Ashkenazic elements in the colony, using Zionist activities as their vehicle and even inaugurating inter-colony "Intersocial Hebrew Baseball and Volleyball Leagues." These activities did succeed in breaking down social barriers among Cuban Jewish youth, but as late as 1945, Zionist Union leaders complained that most of the Sephardim had remained untouched by the movement.[91] This should not have been surprising. Zionist Union meetings still were conducted in Yiddish, and the Zionists for the most part disparaged religious observance, which remained strong among the traditional Sephardim.

War's End and News of the Death Camps

The Fittkos first heard that European Jews were being exterminated in early 1942, but they found the news unfathomable and did not want to believe it. When the details became public knowledge later, most Cubans were sympathetic, although marches by Jewish groups through the "broad, sunny avenidas of Havana," in the words of one participant, went unnoticed. As the war progressed, the sense of hopelessness grew. When Lisa Fittko's sister-in-law gave birth to a daughter, the Red Cross sent a telegram to their parents in Cassis, in occupied France. They received a response, offering congratulations and a plea: "Our imminent deportation is probable. Is there really no one in the world who can help us?"

The Cuban branch of Free Germany was created in late 1942 and early 1943, calling itself the Comité Alemán Antifascista de Cuba. Some of its members were Jewish, some not. The CAAC broadcast half-hour radio programs over the Havana station CMOK starting on July 24, 1943, at 7 P.M., transmitting anti-Hitler material, including information about the concentration camps established in Germany and in German-occupied territory and news about the resistance movement in occupied lands. The first detailed information about the Holocaust available in the Americas came from these sources, as well as from Jewish organizations in London.[92] By September 1944, news began to arrive of deportations to death camps from Hungary and Yugoslavia. Rarely, one heard that a specific family member had survived: a daughter still in one camp, an uncle in Theresienstadt. Sometimes individuals who managed to escape from occupied territory ran advertisements in the *Aufbau* and other foreign-language newspapers in the United States looking for their children or their parents.[93]

Leizer Ran, an ORT teacher who broadcast a series of radio appeals in Yiddish over Havana radio for funds to aid refugees, recalls that on the day after one of his broadcasts a man came to him saying that his mother, a seamstress, had sold her sewing machine to be able to donate something. The broadcast had been about the Warsaw Ghetto.[94] Detailed statistics about the numbers of Jews murdered in Europe were regularly reported through the Cuban Jewish Relief Committee and by representatives of other agencies, and articles written for the U.S. press were regularly translated and reprinted in Cuban newspapers and magazines throughout the war.[95] The fact that of the one million Jewish children in Europe prior to Hitler's rise, only 150,000 survived the war was emphasized in appeals to Sephardic and larger Cuban audiences, known for their strong traditional sense of family.[96] The Joint spent more than a million dollars in Cuba merely in the last eight months of the war, about 2 percent of its entire relief budget.[97]

The refugees lived on the periphery of wartime espionage activities and once in a while came into contact with them. Stories circulated that members of Cuban high society who owned homes on islands off the coast entertained German submarine captains and their officers at lavish parties. It was an open secret that German submarines received food, water, and fuel in the Cuban keys, some owned by wealthy Spanish Falangists such as the owner of the brewery that produced Tropical beer. Colonel José Pedraza, chief of police, was considered a close Franco sympathizer, a fact that, if true, may explain the government's hands-off attitude toward the Falange.[98] Hans Fittko claims to have been approached in Havana by Herr Gruber, who owned a shop in town and had been contacted by a Belgian who had asked for a loan in exchange for some diamonds he was carrying with him. Gruber had become suspicious and asked Fittko, who had been in the resistance but was not Jewish, to interview the man; Fittko discovered that he was a fairly high-connected Nazi who had escaped to the Balearic Islands, then to Spain, and then to Cuba during the last days of the war. Hans knew that he could not report the man to the police because he could be accused of entanglement with a Nazi diamond smuggler, but he advised Gruber, a Cuban citizen, to do so. Gruber reported the case at the Interior Ministry and indicated where his contact could be found. A few hours later Gruber was arrested in his store. He was interrogated for days, released, then brought in for interrogation again, then let go for good. He was told that "Herr Schuster" had disappeared.[99]

With the Axis defeat in 1945, the German Jews residing in Cuba started to leave. Restrictions were lifted, and refugees could apply for Cuban citizenship. Reminiscing about those days, Lisa Fittko took stock of their predicament nostalgically:

On the terrace of the Café Aire Libre at the corner of the Paseo there was always a light breeze from the ocean in the evening, and we cooled off after the heat of the day and before the humid night. Hans had meanwhile learned diamond cutting, like many refugees, and I had found a position in an office. So life had become somewhat easier, and we could afford to have a Cuba Libre or a sherbet in the evening. I thought, it is the same with these tropical fruits as with everything else here: at first the taste is strange, not at all like fruits: why can't they taste like strawberries or like cherries. Then one day one notices that mango and *fruta bomba* are part of our daily lives. One cannot imagine how one managed to live without them, and I have trouble remembering the taste of plums and pears. That is the way it is with everything here. Now, like everyone else, we say *mañana* when we mean perhaps soon.[100]

The German-speaking refugees considered Cuba, in the words of one, a "peaceful paradise." Young men and women studied Spanish, polished their English, attended cultural events, and went to the beach. News from Europe was never far away, but they settled into their relatively carefree interim lives, realizing that things would be serious enough when they finally entered the United States. "We were young," Ilsa Mittel-Ashe recollected later, "and so grateful to have been given freedom from oppression. That it was a gift of life itself, we only learned much later." Ilsa's visa to the United States was granted by the U.S. consulate in Havana in September 1939, shortly after the invasion of Poland. "Filled with excitement and hope (and the thrill of once again taking a hot bath)," she wrote, "I took the boat to Miami to go North from there by train."[101]

Looking back, we now know that Cuba offered life to more Jewish refugees than did any other Latin American country, and that France, Belgium, Holland, and Britain, even under the threat of imminent German invasion, all were far more generous than the United States.[102] President Franklin D. Roosevelt faced stormy opposition from an isolationist Congress in 1939, one so insensitive to the plight of refugees and stateless persons that it nearly overturned by a two-thirds vote Roosevelt's decision in late 1938 not to expel 15,000 refugees whose visas had expired.[103] Most of Cuba's German Jews departed for the United States as soon as they were permitted to, but they could have stayed in Cuba, and they would have been welcome. Some of the departing refugees expressed personal gratitude for the humanitarian manner in which individual U.S. consular officials aided them, but others were saddened by their failure to be able to bring other relatives over, and by the callousness with which they were met by consular officers carrying out U.S. policy to the letter.[104]

6 ✳ "La Gloria
Eres Tú"

When World War II ended, most of the Jewish refugees from nazism who had entered Cuba emigrated to the United States. Those who stayed for the most part were those plagued with ill health or personal problems; a few had become well-established in business and had become naturalized Cuban citizens. The few left-wing German Jews who had come as political refugees tended to go back to Europe; at least one returned to what had become East Germany. Cuba's postwar economy improved dramatically, buoyed by high sugar prices and by the rapid growth of the tourism industry, now aided by easier conditions for travel, including new low-fare air excursions, and later by a drop in airfares and the building of modern hotels on the island. Prosperity for individual Cuban Jews and its attendant visibility brought a sense of well-being and stability to the permanent Jewish community, although it was accompanied by a new surge of anti-Semitic propaganda claiming evidence of Jewish monopolistic power and economic penetration worldwide.

Cuban immigration policy from 1945 to 1949 under Grau and the first two years of his successor, Prío Socarrás returned to its pre-1939 openness, and the government accepted Jewish displaced persons who still could not gain entry into the United States. Most of the experiences of these refugees were harrowing. Rabbi Dov Rozencwaig, who lost 300 members of his extended family in the Holocaust and who had fought during the war with anti-Nazi partisans in Poland, found himself in a displaced persons' camp in Italy in 1945. Because one of his seven brothers had emigrated to Cuba years before, relief agencies made the contact for him and helped him obtain papers to emigrate.[1]

In all, somewhat less than 600 Jewish displaced persons (*Flichtling*) came to Cuba to join relatives already there.[2] The new arrivals included a small group of European Jews who had spent the war interned by the Japanese in Shanghai. Abe Resnikovitz escaped from his Lithuanian ghetto and fought with the Russians for three years, ultimately as a lieutenant in a special division in Marshal Zhukov's army, which liberated Berlin from the east; Resnikovitz escaped to the British sector of occupied Germany in 1946. Able to speak several languages, including German, he did undercover work investigating Nazi war crimes. His uncle, who had emigrated to Cuba in the early 1920s and worked his way from peddler to textile manufacturer, paid his passage after he was able to defect. As a stateless person unable to travel directly to Cuba after the war, Resnikovitz and another refugee, Abraham Rabinowitz, had to journey first to France, then via Dakar to Martinique, Antigua, and Puerto Rico before they found a ship to take them to Cuba. When Resnikovitz arrived, he had only ten dollars.[3]

Hilda Jonesh, who had spent the war in several concentration camps in Poland, including Majdanek and Buchenwald, obtained a visa to Cuba after spending two months in a Swedish displaced persons camp. That it was Cuba was accidental: someone applying to HIAS for a visa for his sister applied for one for Hilda also. When she arrived in Havana, she was given a job at the Centro Israelita. She spoke no Spanish, but within six weeks had organized Spanish classes for other refugees. She rented a room with a German Jewish family until she married. She and her husband, Joseph Robinsky, a salesman and Jewish community worker, went to the United States during the early 1950s but returned to Cuba. "The island was a beautiful place," she remembered years later. "The people were nice, and we loved it there." The Robinskys had a daughter in Cuba; they left for a second time in 1961 and went to South Florida.

Another of the displaced persons, Fanny Portnoy, a survivor of the Stutthoff concentration camp in East Prussia, worked as a seamstress in postwar Poland for two years until she was able to obtain papers. In Cuba, she got a job as a secretary until 1950, when she finally was permitted to emigrate to New York. In later years, like Hilda Jonesh, she remembered Cuba as a beautiful country with pleasant, friendly people, although she recollected that there seemed to be virtually no middle class: the rich lived well while beggars slept in the streets.[4] In fact, Cuba by this time had developed one of the largest groups of professional and related middle-class groups in the hemisphere, but foreigners continued to see the extremes of wealth and poverty.

Postwar Adjustment

By the late 1940s, the social, class, and linguistic divisions among Cuba's Jews had diminished although by no means disappeared. The Jewish immigrants who had arrived between the wars and who had made Cuba their home no longer were as poor as they had been during the decade or two after their arrival. Their Cuban-born children spoke Spanish, not Ladino or Yiddish, as their primary language. Zionists, whose factions had jousted with one another and who were never accepted wholly by the larger Jewish community, diminished in influence after the establishment of the state of Israel in 1948. There was still inconsequential socializing between Sephardim and Ashkenazim and only scant intermarriage between the two groups. Sephardim were still disparaged as emotionally volatile and tradition bound, and Ashkenazim made remarks about their swarthy skin complexion, which made them appear more like "Cubans," and about their tight-knit family life; at least one Ashkenazic Jew claimed snidely that the Sephardim "practice polygamy on the side."[5]

Most Jews in postwar Cuba preferred to belong to Jewish associations, but during the early 1940s, a handful of Jewish women joined the prestigious Lyceum and Lawn Tennis Club, Havana's most prominent women's cultural and philanthropic institution, formed in 1939 by a merger with the 1913 Tennis de Señoritas association. The Lyceum's annual yearbooks contain no clearly Semitic names during the 1930s and early 1940s. The first Jewish name (Anne Binder de Kates) appears in the 1937–39 *Memoria*, and by the second half of the 1940s members included Vivienne Rosenberg Gersona, Sara Levi de Mitrani, Sylvia Klein de Teitelbaum, Esther Rosenthal Perl, Sara Balbin, and Silvia Kaffenburgh. Some Cubans of Arab origin also joined in the 1940s, among them Haifa Chediak.[6] Hardy Spatz, who had his own television program during the 1950s, claimed to be the only Jewish member of the Havana Lions Club and of the Círculo Militar. Because neither the Sephardic nor Ashkenazic immigrants who had come to Cuba in earlier decades had brought with them particularly strong models of rabbinic authority, the array of Jewish organizations that represented the spectrum of Jewish Cubans exerted greater influence than did the synagogues. Chevet Ahim, an offshoot of the old Sephardic Temple, served religious needs and ran a cemetery and a private school. The Bikur Holim cared for ailing Sephardim. The Spanish-speaking Consejo Pro-Israel worked for the state of Israel. Adas Israel, the leading Eastern European synagogue, represented a kind of minyan community of worshippers, but it did not exert influence beyond its own congregation. Ashkenazim, most of whom lost many family members in the Holocaust, constructed two cemetery monuments after the war in Havana, unique in Latin America. One commemorated the six million Jews who perished; the other, a marble headstone, marked the spot where small pieces of soap were said to be buried, symbolizing the soap the Nazis had manufactured from Jewish flesh (fig. 50).

The community transformed itself during the 1950s. The largest Jewish organization remained the Centro Israelita, with its own primary school (fig. 51), the 500-pupil Colegio Hebreo, joined in the 1950s by a second Ashkenazic school, the Tahkemoni Israelite Center Hebrew School.[7] Middle- and upper-class urban Cubans usually sent their children to private schools, beginning with kindergarten. There was no onus to enrolling in Catholic- or Protestant-run schools, especially if they were prestigious. Most private schools stopped at the eighth grade. Parents had three options at that point: to continue sending their children to a private academy, many of which were bilingual; to enroll their children in public high schools; or to send their children to the United States to school, a more viable option when relatives could help out. Some wealthy Cuban Jews sent their children to the Spanish-speaking Edison School, and the small community of American Jews favored the Ruston Academy (at Fifth Avenue and G before moving to the Biltmore); Cathedral, run by the Episcopal church; Columbus; Lafayette; and St. George, an English-language school patterned on the lines of British schools around the world, whose students nevertheless were almost all Cuban. Ruston was considered the most prestigious private school in Cuba and charged the highest tuition fees.

50. Holocaust monument, Havana. From "Hotel Cuba" documentary.

51. Kindergarten class, Centro Israelita, 1949–50. Courtesy of Berta Sherman.

Even though changing times brought new opportunities for the immigrants, the road was not easy. Felix Reyler, who had helped his family pay for his elementary schooling at the Centro Israelita by selling newspapers and peddling, was invited by a senator to whom he had sold a lottery ticket to become a page boy at Congress because he spoke German. Felix dropped out of elementary school to work full time but was dismissed as a page when Machado closed the Congress in 1932. He then worked as a bell boy at the Hotel Plaza, studying by himself at night, and eventually passed the university entrance examination at the Instituto de La Habana when it was reopened in 1937. He worked his way through law school at the University of Havana running a tailor shop during the day and in 1946 was selected valedictorian. He was the first Ashkenazic Jew to become an attorney in Cuba.[8] Orphaned by then, Reyler taught himself how to get along on four or five hours of rest at night, sleeping without a mattress lest he become too comfortable. Because of his very high grades in law school, he won a competitive appointment, affirmed by presidential decree, as a public prosecutor. This was a lucrative and prestigious post within the judicial system, never before given to a naturalized Cuban.

Reyler spent one year in the Santa Clara provincial court and then used his friendship with politicians for whom he had made suits as a tailor to win a transfer to Havana for the final year of his appointment. In 1946 he was invited by two of his former law school professors to join their firm and during the 1950s was one of Cuba's most successful practicing lawyers, specializing in mercantile and corporate law. He never felt anti-Semitism directed at him, although he knew the prejudice was present in Cuba, especially in Catholic schools. Reyler felt that he was treated differently at first because he was a foreigner lacking a Spanish surname, not necessarily because he was Jewish, and that after some initial hostility or reticence toward him, he was able to build bridges and gain full acceptance.[9]

Second-Generation Cuban Jews

The experiences of Jewish children growing up in Cuba varied, especially after the war. Some were enrolled in one of the three private schools operated by the Spanish community: the Centro Asturiano and the Centro Gallego (fig. 52)—each with elegant buildings more impressive visually, according to some, than the

52. Centro Gallego, ca. 1910. Courtesy of Archives and Special Collections Department, University of Miami, Coral Gables, Fla.

presidential palace itself[10]—and the Centro Castellano, a more modest but well-equipped facility that had become more Cubanized than the other two. The tuition charged by the Spanish community schools was low—the equivalent of two dollars per month per child—and their health clinics provided medical care and prescriptions to the families of their students at no cost. Through the 1950s, private health clinics continued to provide comprehensive care for families for $2.85 per month per person. Expatriate Americans thought this was marvelous, although they looked patronizingly at what they considered to be the Cubans' obsession with taking medicine. "When you were sick you went to the doctor in the *clinica*," John Huff Parker wrote. "If he saw fit, you were sent to one of the hospitals they maintained and you stayed there until you were well. . . . The Cuban got his money's worth in spades. Even if there was nothing wrong with him, he got his cherished prescription for some innocent nostrum to keep him in the running with his friends and neighbors."[11]

The clinics were open to anyone, regardless of ethnicity. Although Arón Yukem became an active leader in the Jewish community and president of the Centro Israelita, because it was easier financially his children attended the Centro Asturiano school when the family moved from Pinar del Rio to Havana in the late 1930s. His son remembers that he was called a "little Polack" and got into scuffles, but on the whole the experience was a positive one for him.[12] Despite the animosity between Spanish and Jewish merchants in the Old City, the administrators of the Spanish centros did not discriminate against Jewish families who applied to their schools. In fact, in one case the director of the Centro Castellano offered free tuition and medical care to the children of at least one Jewish immigrant who had been turned away from the Centro Israelita school.

Children from the most prosperous American Jewish families—the Rosenbergs, Shapiros, Diziks, and Segals—as well as some German Jewish refugee children attended classes at Ruston with those of President Prío and of other members of the upper class. Parents so much desired to send their children to Ruston that some believed that they had to register them almost immediately after birth to gain a place on the waiting list.[13] Cuba afforded newcomers more opportunities for elite schooling and social mingling than their counterparts found in the United States, where many exclusive private academies before World War II accepted few or no Jews. In most cases, Cuban schools, no matter how exclusive, required students to be able to pay the tuition and not be too dark-skinned.[14] To enter Cuban universities, all prospective students had to be certified by the public *institutos* in their district. In some cases, students went to the reputable instituto to take the examination; in others, examiners were sent to the schools. This guaranteed uniform admissions standards for all high school graduates. In Havana, Jewish children who attended public high school went usually to the Instituto de La Habana as well as to del Vedado, Marianao, and especially la Víbora, which examined candidates for Edison School. Student career patterns began to change as well. By the 1950s, the immigrants' children had started to matriculate at the University of Havana, formerly the Universidad Nacional. When old political troubles resurfaced there, some shifted to José Martí University or Villanova University. Very few from the Jewish community attended other universities or went to the United States for college.[15]

The sons and daughters of immigrants felt as Cuban as their non-Jewish neighbors, free of the anti-Semitism their parents had faced in the Old World. "In Europe," Dr. Samuel Oberstein recalled, "it was inconceivable to be invited to dinner on Christmas Eve to a gentile home. Yet in Cuba, Jews were often invited to non-Jewish homes for celebrations—birthdays, baptisms, *los quince,* and so on. In Europe, my parents were restricted to the ghettos not by force but by choice because in the ghetto they felt secure and protected from a cold outside world. This was not the case in Cuba, and was why so many Jews loved Cuba dearly."[16]

Economic and Residential Patterns

The former immigrants, who by now had been in Cuba for almost thirty years, as well as their children, found themselves by the late 1940s much closer to the top than to the bottom of the economic ladder. Their lives centered around their families, Jewish schools, clubs, and their businesses. Almost more than any other group, the immigrants and their children formed a true middle class. Many purchased or built homes in suburban Vedado and the newer neighborhood, Miramar, considered one of the world's most luxurious and beautiful urban projects. In the 1920s Miramar was linked to the city by the magnificent Fifth Avenue Parkway, three miles long and 150 feet wide, reducing the travel time from Havana's Central Park to twelve minutes. There was enough undeveloped land along the route to permit the wealthy to build strikingly large tiled homes surrounded by banana groves. Foreigners and naturalized Cubans intermingled in these handsome suburbs. Affluent members of the Jewish community moved up to Miramar from Vedado; the more prominent American Jews built lavish homes in the Country Club section, the poshest of all.

By the mid-1950s, residential patterns within the colony had solidified. Practically all of the Western Jews (the Americans, the few German refugees who had stayed, and the more successful upwardly mobile East European Jews) lived in Vedado and Miramar, while the polacos—so-called within the community because they still retained their Yiddish culture—for the most part lived in La Víbora, Santos Suárez, and other middle-class areas. The poor and those elderly without families continued to live in declining Old Havana. The new Cuban Jewish middle class moved from the old city, but many still earned their living in retail stores located in the heart of the city on or near Muralla and Sol streets. Some ran insurance and travel agencies or worked as representatives for foreign firms.

There were hundreds of Jewish-owned businesses in Havana in 1950, probably more than 300. Nearly 60 percent sold fabric or ready-made clothes, and another 12 percent sold specialty clothing,

53. Fabric store on Muralla Street, Havana, ca. 1949. Courtesy of Lucia Suárez.

including lingerie and furs (fig. 53).[17] For the most part, Jewish-owned shops extended credit to customers and bargained over prices. Owners had learned how to deal with Hacienda Department inspectors, officials who visited businesses to examine the books and assess penalties or collect taxes. Some of the Hacienda inspectors were honest, and others were not. Dishonest ones would try to find discrepancies in a shop's records and then extort a bribe from the owner to avoid having a report filed or a fine assessed. Fanny Seinuk recalled an incident experienced by her father, Morris Auerbach, in one of his stores, Morris Photo Supply on Aguila Street:

> One day, a tax auditor came in and asked my father to see the books.
> My father obliged. The auditor feverishly went over the books and
> found nothing wrong. He kept saying "I'll find it, sooner or later,
> Morris, I'll find it. I'll find where you are hiding the money!" After two
> months, the auditor gave up. He congratulated Morris on having the
> best bookkeeper in Havana. My father was so amused seeing the audi-
> tor's frustration that he gave him a 16mm projector as a gift and the
> auditor became a lifelong friend.[18]

Some of the island's Jews had achieved substantial wealth. The Sephardic Habif family established the largest perfume factory in

Cuba, Fibah (Habif spelled backwards), and also owned souvenir stores. Herman Weinberg, a Polish immigrant, owned Herman's Store, one of the most popular and successful on the island. Several Jewish businessmen, especially the Americans, ran finance companies, investing in commercial and residential real estate. The Juricks, one of the original American families, owned The Fair, an elegant women's dress shop. Some Jews purchased franchises of U.S. firms—Hardy Spatz and his father owned the Avis car rental franchise, for example. Albert Hartman, who headed the wartime Joint, became president of Chrysler of Cuba. As businessmen, the former immigrants were no different from their Spanish and Cuban competitors. They did what was necessary to operate under the prevailing system, usually nothing more than paying bribes to inspectors, police, and in some cases union officials. A small minority operated on the shadier edges, owning buildings and other establishments that burned down at opportune times, a racket so prevalent in Cuba that anyone whose property caught fire, however innocent, faced being hauled off to jail for the night while an arson investigation was made.

Adaptation without Assimilation

Foreign visitors noted that at the start of the 1950s Cuban Jews born abroad still spoke rudimentary, heavily accented Spanish and seemed to have little desire to strike cultural roots in the country. Perhaps this resulted from the size and influence of Cuba's foreign-born population. Jews and other immigrant groups were not absorbed into the host culture to the extent they were in South America or Mexico. The proximity to the United States, where many Cuban Jews had relatives, and the ease of travel back and forth may also have contributed to the community's uniqueness. Mendel Kochanski's picture of the lack of permanent intent within the Jewish colony was exaggerated. "They steadfastly refuse to be identified as Cubans," he wrote of the Ashkenazim, "and are ready to liquidate their businesses and take their families across the Florida Straits at the drop of the U.S. Consul's rubber stamp."[19] In reality, most Cuban Jews by the 1950s considered themselves Cubans and intended to stay, and the new generation spoke Spanish perfectly.

Even so, assimilation never occurred. The East European Jews acculturated slowly. Yiddish-language newspapers continued to flourish. Spoken Yiddish, at least in the early 1950s, remained mostly devoid of Spanish admixtures. Instead, Cuban Yiddish began to pick up U.S. slang, perhaps the result of the presence of visitors or from the plentiful circulation, albeit four days late, of Yiddish newspapers from New York. Some Ashkenazic children studied for professional degrees, intending to practice law or medicine or architecture, likely within the Jewish community itself, for barriers, if always unwritten, remained between the Jewish colonies and Cuban society.

To some extent, acculturation depended on how long a family had been on the island and on individual experience. Martin Mayer's half-Jewish uncle, Hugo May, had arrived in Cuba in 1912 as an employee of a German import-export company and settled there. He married a Cuban Catholic woman in 1917, although he did not inform his family in Germany. He did not identify with Cuban Jews, but he helped some of his relatives come later as refugees, and he gave Mayer, who arrived in 1938, a job in his firm. Mayer was a salesman and already knew Spanish. When he made the rounds of Jewish businesses in Havana, he was told more than once that "we don't want to do business with that German, Hugo May." Mayer later recollected that his closest friend during the 1950s was the Cuban part-owner of the building in which his family bought his condominium apartment. Cubans, in his view, never cared about one's beliefs, only that one was not *un pesado* (a bore). His family began to be drawn into social intermixing. They belonged to one of the smaller clubs that accepted members without regard to religion, the Professionals' Club, where there was a swimming pool. They bought lottery tickets from the ubiquitous street vendors (fig. 54). They became friends with their Catholic pediatrician and his family and often went to baseball games or concerts with them. The Mayers befriended their non-Jewish neighbors as well and were invited to several church weddings.[20] But many members of the Jewish community remained within their own world. José Raij, who was born in Havana to an immigrant family, remembers that the first time he attended a Catholic wedding was in the United States. "When I walked by a church," he said, "I looked away from it."[21]

Prewar divisions among the turcos and polacos began to blur. Jews who had remained divided during the stress of wartime became more relaxed with postwar prosperity. The American Jews had

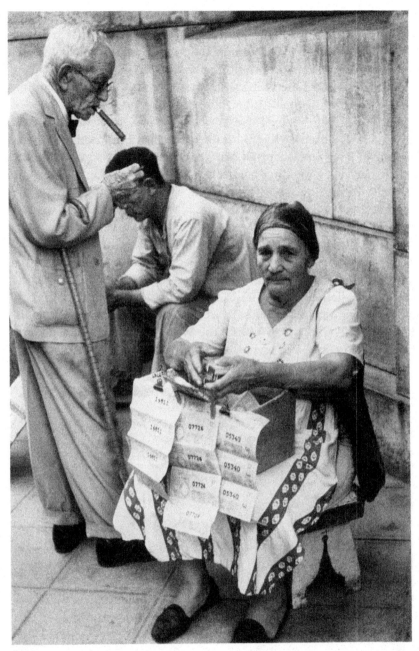

54. Lottery vendor, Havana. Courtesy of Norbert Adler.

mixed with some of the German-speaking refugees who tended to share their outlook and who were accustomed to a higher standard of living than the polacos, whom they considered uncouth. "It was not that we said that we would not associate with *Ostjuden*," Lisa Fittko said, "but there was a world between us."[22] The Sephardim, whose customs seemed to be more Cuban than Jewish in spite of their religious orthodoxy, had always appeared exotic to the Westernized Jews. Intermarriages between the East European and Mediterranean Jews now occurred from time to time, no longer creating much notice. A wedding between a Sephardic and an Ashkenazic Jew that in the 1920s was considered, according to one Ashkenazic observer, "worse than marriage to a black" by the early 1950s had become a fairly commonplace event.[23]

Nonetheless, as a result of the continued mutual feeling of separateness, efforts to organize a unified Cuban Jewish Committee among representatives from the three major components of the community failed. The American Jews remained almost completely aloof. There was, nonetheless, participation by members of the different Jewish colonies in WIZO, the Women's International Zionist Organization, and in a few other organizations (fig. 55).[24]

55. WIZO meeting, 1946. Courtesy of Rabbi Nesim Gambach.

The Prosperous Fifties

Cuba in the 1950s, lush and vibrant, brimmed with abundance. Havana was an international city with, in the recollection of a nostalgic former resident, the aura, the look, and the feel of Fellini's *La Dolce Vita*. Its beachfront called itself the Antillean Riviera. Visitors compared the view of Havana in the golden light of the late day's sun to Venice or Alexandria. The Tropicana's cabaret was the most luxurious in the world, a vast open-air musical theater regularly featuring such U.S. performers as Duke Ellington and a supporting cast of at least a hundred. Criminals, some on the run from the United States, infiltrated Havana's entertainment industry. Lucky Luciano, Santo Traficante, Jr. (the son of the numbers boss of Tampa), Dino Cellini, and other underworld figures moved to Cuba when pressed by the Kefauver investigations in the 1950s. Mayer Lansky, who had gotten involved in racetracks and gambling in Cuba during the war, used Batista's comeback to revive and enlarge his interests in high-stakes gambling; within months of the coup, Lansky had purchased a partnership in the Cabaret Montmartre, and he was asked by President Batista during the winter season of 1953–54 to clean up the casino industry. Lansky helped Batista build a gambling wing on the premier hotel in Vedado, the Hotel Nacional, which opened for the 1955–56 season. He then built his own hotel, the Riviera, the largest casino hotel in the world outside Las Vegas, which opened in March 1957. George Raft appeared as a kind of celebrity greeter and, on occasion, so did Lansky himself, who remained a confidant and special adviser to Batista, although his status as a crime boss in the United States was well-known.[25]

Legal casino gambling at the Tropicana, the Riviera, and other Vedado clubs and hotels was sedate and well managed, in contrast to the raucous smaller clubs in the city, especially in the Barrio Chino, which specialized in come-on games, drinking, live sex shows, and prostitution. Havana's specialty brothels catered to every whim, supplying young girls, boys, or (for undergraduates from Miami, who treated Havana the same way Southern Californians treated Tijuana) English-speaking, blond, blue-eyed prostitutes dressed like coeds.[26] Havana also had jai alai frontons, racetracks, restaurants, and elegant resorts, many developed under Batista's efforts to boost tourism. There was cockfighting, a national lottery, and illegal lotteries like the China and the Guanabacoa. Gambling was a national obsession. When England's King George V died, hundreds of thousands across Cuba played the number sixty-four (death) in the popular *charada* game. The number came up, and the bookies had to flee into hiding until they could scrape up enough money to pay off the winning bets.

Havana, a former resident recollected, "was a fashion sensation and a feast for the eyes": "Sitting on the Prado Boulevard in the evenings was a spectacle in and of itself, as one would watch beautifully dressed women in gloves and broad-brimmed hats and elegantly appointed men sip cocktails in cafés, standing before ornate buildings in the Italian style as pastel-colored convertibles drove by. . . . Havana resembled more a city perched on the Mediterranean coast than in the American hemisphere."[27] Even the city's slums appealed to the eye—curious places, in the words of Ludwig Bemelmans, the gifted travel writer, "friendly, with a kind of super squalor." "Places here," he added, "are painted in vivid colors and lit up so that the color blares like a trumpet. . . . There is music everywhere. The people in bars and restaurants have the coloration of cigars of various shades."[28]

Life became easy. Families in all but the lowest classes employed maids, relieving housewives of burdensome work. Employers treated servants patronizingly; the worst were foreigners, especially Americans, who had grown up without servants and who relished the power of having someone in a subservient position do all of one's manual work.[29]

Longtime Cuban Jews referred to Spaniards as gallegos, and made the same kinds of pejorative references to Cuban blacks as did the rest of the middle and upper classes. The former immigrants now were using their white skin to accommodate to the existing social system, not to challenge it. There were incentives. Havana exuded the aura of Paris, Bemelmans wrote. "The driving is awful, the natives are as much in love with it, and the mass of the people are as bourgeois as are the Parisians."[30] The new members of the middle class adapted, taking advantage of the opportunity to have their clubs and placid living quarters and cheap labor force. They adjusted to the warm and fast-flowing pace of the Cuban temperament: to one visitor, the casual encounter of two acquaintances on a street reminded him of a "meeting of brothers who haven't seen each other in years."[31] Jewish youths considered Cuba their home, mixing with non-Jews but preferring to frequent entirely Jewish clubs or ones like the highly popular Casino Deportivo, which accepted Jewish members as long as their hair was not too frizzy and therefore "negroid."[32] The casino had been founded by a Catholic, Alfredo Hornedo, a senator and editor of the large-circulation newspaper *El Pais,* who had himself been snubbed by the prestigious Big Five clubs.[33]

Prosperity was based on the rural, not the urban, economy. By 1951, the annual sugar crop yielded more than half a billion dollars. Exports to the United States of sugar, tobacco, and rum, in addition to the burgeoning tourism industry, produced a favorable balance of trade for Cuba of $50 million. As in most economically backward countries, this wealth did not filter down to the overall population, although the lower classes, especially in towns and cities, fared marginally better than much of the rest of Latin America. By comparison, most Cubans enjoyed reasonably high levels of education, health care, and public services, although a vast gap separated rich and poor. Ordinary Cubans were subject to a legal system based on Roman law and a tradition of differential justice whereby accused persons were assumed guilty until proven innocent; the lower classes received harsh handling from the police, and more prominent citizens received kid-glove treatment. Nor was much progress evident as time passed. Only 39 percent of school-age children (ages 5 to 14) attended school in 1942–43 nationwide, up only a tiny percentage from a generation earlier, when in 1919 attendance reached 35.5 percent.[34]

In Havana and in the provincial capitals, affluent Cubans and the large resident foreign population, including the American Jews, lived extremely well. Visitors compared parties given by members of high society—the Condesa de Revilla-Camargo, for example—to those of Aristotle Onassis and Don Carlos de Beistegui, with fifteen chefs cooking for two hundred, gardens lit by thousands of candles, gold-plated dinnerware, guests dressed in Paris originals and Cartier jewelry, the shrubbery around the residence and the balconies patrolled by private guards carrying automatic weapons when the president or other dignitaries were on the guest list.[35] Cuban high society made no concessions to the tropics. Mink, chinchilla, sable, and ermine furs were popular items of apparel in 1946. "Americans

56. Suburban home, Vedado. Courtesy of Norbert Adler.

think we are silly to wear furs," a society woman said, "but we like outdoor entertaining—the smartest New Year's party is outdoors at the Country Club—and *of course* we need furs."[36]

Cuba was beginning to look more and more like the United States. The posh neighborhoods outside Havana looked strikingly like their counterparts in Miami, less than an hour away by air (fig. 56). By the late 1950s, as many as fifty scheduled airline flights daily carried passengers to and from mainland airports, mostly Miami and New York. Importers brought in "vast numbers of Nordic pines" at Christmas in refrigerated ships. Entrepreneurs boasted of their connections on the mainland: Hardy L. Spatz, the owner of Havana's largest driving school, stated in his advertisements that he had studied at Yale and New York universities.[37] Baseball, which had been popular on the island since the late 1870s, when returning Cuban-born aristocrats brought it back from the United States as a preferred alternative to Spanish bullfighting, attained the same level of saturation as in the United States. The University of Havana fielded not a soccer but a football team and played the University of Miami Hurricanes in regularly scheduled games in 1926 and 1928.[38] Observed Ruby Hart Phillips a decade later:

> The United States is mirrored in every phase of Cuban life. The modern Cuban eats hot dogs, hamburgers, hot cakes, waffles, fried chicken, and ice cream. . . . The new apartment buildings could be mistaken for

those in any American city, and the new private homes resemble those of Florida. Spanish furniture is rapidly becoming extinct.[39]

The elite drove imported cars, shopped in air-conditioned department stores for a wide array of imported merchandise, frequented resplendent parks, resorts, and beaches, and received a constant flow of visitors who tied Cuba more closely to the rest of the world than to its Latin American neighbors. Now naturalized, Jewish Cubans could travel anywhere. The flights to Miami on Cubana Viscount jet-prop planes took about fifty-five minutes and were cheap enough that families could come and go on the same day, shopping in Miami where prices were much lower than in Havana. South Florida hotels ran Jewish New Year's ads in the Ashkenazic community's *Almanaque Hebreo*. So did some non-Jewish businesses, courting business from their Jewish neighbors: "I cordially wish the great People of Israel, God's chosen children, the predecessors of Christians, continued success in Cuba and throughout the world."[40] Meanwhile, pockets of poor Jews, some still making their living by street vending and peddling, continued to dot shabby Old Havana. The words in Hebrew letters on the run-down market (fig. 57) on Acosta Street read "Di nayeh yeedishe bodega" (the new Jewish grocery store)— the first three words in Yiddish, the last, in Spanish. Jewish community charities still paid the rent for poor Jews, ran the community

57. Grocery on Acosta Street. Courtesy of Norbert Adler.

58. Motor road leading out of Havana, 1947. Courtesy of Norbert Adler.

orphanage, and paid tuition for poor Jewish children to attend religious school. The Jewish Committee to Support Victims of Tuberculosis and the Mentally Ill ran a clinic for indigent Jews, most of them elderly. It also paid the costs for tuberculosis patients in a local sanatorium and for the severely retarded.[41]

The nation's prosperity during the 1950s centered in a small portion of the population and was based on at least two factors unique to Cuba: first, commerce and export of raw agricultural products (not industrial diversification), and second, progressive labor legislation that made it difficult to dismiss workers, although government social policies failed to address such problems as underemployment and poor social services, especially in rural areas. Cuba enjoyed the fourth highest rate of literacy in Latin America and the second highest per capita income ($374) after Venezuela, but prices were high— Havana was one of the most expensive cities in the world—and income very unevenly distributed. Per capita income did not increase from 1947 to 1958. The middle class was buffeted by rising inflation and artificially high housing costs. Because the economy was so dependent on the world price of sugar, much of the boom stood on shaky ground. As Louis Pérez notes, Cubans rarely invested in government securities or other forms of national investment; rather, "they preferred liquidity, principally in short-term funds in banks abroad or hoarded in safe deposit boxes at home. They preferred ventures promising rapid and spectacular returns, high profits on small turnovers."[42]

Only a quarter of the sugar workers could expect more than a hundred days of work per year. The economy boomed but did not produce new jobs. Beggars, especially women carrying small children, filled the streets of Havana amid urban affluence. Wooing support, President Batista would later lavish gifts taken from lottery proceeds on labor unions, the church, and other groups; he paid more than $1 million a month to newspaper editors and publishers. At the same time, the news magazine *Carteles* in May 1957 claimed that twenty members of Batista's government each owned a numbered Swiss bank account in excess of $1 million.[43]

More than half the population earned less than $75 monthly. The price of a small radio represented three weeks' pay for a rural worker; office clerks earned about sixty dollars a month. In 1958 an estimated 11,500 women earned their living as prostitutes in Havana, some of them in the city's 270 registered brothels. Havana, after all, was known worldwide for what novelist Graham Greene termed its "louche" atmosphere. "I was enchanted by Havana," wrote Arthur M. Schlesinger, Jr., recalling a visit in 1950 sponsored by the Inter-American Association for Democracy and Freedom, "and appalled by the way that lovely city was being debased into a great casino and brothel for American businessmen over for a big weekend from Miami. My fellow countrymen reeled through the streets, picking up fourteen-year-old Cuban girls and tossing coins to make men scramble in the gutter. One wondered how any Cuban—on the basis of this evidence—could regard the United States with anything but hatred."[44]

The tolerant atmosphere and ease of human contact nevertheless created an idyllic setting. Cubans of all classes were easygoing, friendly, and flexible. Relations between the races tended to be relaxed, and although movie theaters, restaurants, beaches, and clubs were segregated according to levels of affluence, they never explicitly barred blacks or mulattos, as happened in the United States at the time, ninety miles away.[45] The guests, at a mid-1940s wedding dinner at an elite club, however, might be expected not only to be dressed exactly as they would be at a reception in the United States in a warm climate, but also to be white and affluent, although Cuba was, of course, a multiracial society (fig. 59).

59. Wedding party, 1947, Havana. Courtesy of Hardy L. Spatz.

The Community Stabilizes

During the first two years of the second Grau presidency (1944–48), the Jewish press reported only a few isolated hostile incidents, including efforts to bar Jewish tourists from registering in hotels on Varadero Beach. Cuban Jews tended to shrug this off, accepting the dubious argument that the discriminatory hotel owners were acting not on their own but in response to the wishes of guests from the United States who did not wish to have Jews staying at the hotels they patronized. This same argument was used to exclude blacks and was commonly offered as a rationalization for barring minorities in tourist locations throughout the hemisphere, including some in Canada.[46] The Kawama, a resort hotel built by Colonel Eugenio Silva, maintained a restricted (No Jews Allowed) policy, but applied this only to U.S. tourists. The resort was extremely popular with old Havana families, who often went there for their honeymoons.[47] Cuban Jewish residents could visit clubs as guests, although they were usually not invited to be members. Because much of Cuban life functioned this way—those connected to people in high places always gained advantages—there was a perception that the absence of Jews from certain clubs and businesses was not a matter of discrimination.

The East European Jews who had come to Cuba in the 1920s hoping to leave but who had put down roots tended to disdain the American and German Jews who were willing to associate with powerful Cubans on their own terms. Even after the war ended, the old animosities survived. In 1949, the two Ashkenazic synagogues, Adas Israel and Knesset Israel, which had separated because of a rift in the late 1920s, merged to become Kehilla Adas Israel after dwindling Orthodox observance severely cut into the membership of both. The German-Austrian and American Jews worshiped at Temple Beth Israel, which during the war modified its traditional Reform liturgy and offered German-language services one week and English-language services the next. The German- and English-speaking Jews considered themselves more accomplished culturally and in the skills of adaptation.

That Cuban Jews experienced significant postwar prosperity was demonstrated by the luxurious community center, the Patronato de la Casa de la Communidad Hebrea de Cuba (Bet ha-Keneset ha-Gadol), built in Vedado in 1953. Most of the funds came from Ashkenazim who had become wealthy and, having moved to the moneyed suburbs of Vedado, Miramar, and Santos Suárez, found the Centro's location in the declining Old City inconvenient.[48] Overnight, the Patronato became the community's major voice. President Batista, his prime minister, and several high Cuban officials attended the dedication of the Patronato's community center in October 1955. Batista was considered a solid friend of Cuba's Jews; while he had not intervened in the St. Louis case, earlier in 1939 he had acted to grant asylum to seven Jewish refugees, and he referred to this intervention proudly in 1952. Several members of Batista's government from 1952 to 1958 were close to local Jews; they included attorney García Montes, who had served as lawyer and counselor to the Joint Distribution Committee during the 1940s.[49]

The boards of the Centro Israelita and of the Orthodox Kehilla had opposed the Patronato's construction at the new site, but their influence was now restricted to the older and less affluent Ashkenazim still located downtown in the Old City commercial district. The Patronato's handsome modern building was designed by one of Cuba's leading architects, Achilles Capablanca, and constructed at a cost estimated at between three-quarters of a million and one million dollars.[50] It contained a synagogue, large club rooms, a library, offices, and a restaurant. A White Russian emigré worked as chef at the Patronato as well as for special receptions in the Soviet embassy. The Patronato functioned as a pointedly apolitical entity, more social than religious; it never had its own rabbi, hiring a cantor instead to preside at religious functions. Many of its activities were ceremonial and included invited diplomats and members of the Cuban cabinet.[51] The Patronato boasted a membership of nearly a thousand families, the core the now-successful Ashkenazim who formerly had belonged to the Centro Israelita and some Sephardic and American Jews.

The opening of the Patronato in a number of ways closed the circle of Jewish immigrant history in Cuba. Before 1953, effort after effort to promote a close working relationship among Jewish community organizations failed, not only because of institutional competitiveness but because of personal friction among community leaders. After the Patronato opened, World Jewish Congress representatives convinced Patronato leaders to stop working against the interests of competing organizations and to constitute a plenum of fifty delegates from all Jewish organizations in Cuba to elect in early 1954 a representative body of all Cuban Jews.[52] By doing this, the Patronato assumed the mantle of community leadership in the name of most if not all of the factions within the larger Jewish colony. Divisions remained. A visitor in 1953, reporting on community charitable organizations, noted that one, the Anti-TB Society, ran its activities in "strong competition" with its rival, the Jewish Women's Social Welfare League.[53] Linguistic and ethnic differences still remained strong. WIZO, the largest Jewish organization in Cuba, was divided into a Yiddish-speaking section of 600, a Sephardic group of 450, and a "Vedado group" of 100, presumably Spanish-speaking, made up of women also affiliated with the Patronato. Most of Havana's more affluent Sephardic families put their energies into the construction of a handsome Sephardic community center in Vedado, but construction only started in 1957 and it was not completed until the eve of the Revolution. Had it functioned, it would have rivaled the Patronato (fig. 60) along ethnic lines.[54]

Although Cuban Jewry in the late 1940s and early 1950s seemed on its way to fuller integration and a prominent role in Cuban life, this postwar era of good feelings would last for little more than a decade.[55] In the midst of this improved climate the Jewish commu-

60. "I" Street entrance to Patronato. Courtesy of Tequila Minsky.

nity accommodated more readily to Cuban life than it had before the war. Jews in Cuba in 1951 numbered nearly 10,000, many engaged in mercantile activities, and, to at least one observer, carrying an "air of satisfied prosperity."[56] Second-generation Cuban Jews moved freely socially and felt comfortable in the friendly atmosphere. There was less self-consciousness about religious differences. Jewish businessmen, for example, began to receive invitations to attend commemorative masses in honor of civic achievements.[57]

Influences from prewar days, of course, remained. *Havaner Lebn's* political outlook, for example, represented a Cuban version of Old World socialism. In that tradition, internal schisms hindered potential alliances and cooperation within the Zionist movement. Sender Kaplan, who had served in the late 1930s as executive director for the council of forty-seven Cuban Jewish organizations as well as representative for the Jewish Agency before 1948 and as Israel's consul after that date, always resisted the effort by the Centro Israelita to speak for the Jewish community.

The Zionists never reconciled their differences with those Cuban Jews for whom religion was a matter of ethnicity and culture, not nationalism. Even though many Cuban Jews were not Zionists, the many Zionist organizations helped promote Jewish consciousness, especially among the children of the immigrants. Foremost among them was the militant socialist Hashomer Hatzair, founded in 1933 in affiliation with the umbrella Zionist organization, the Unión Sionista. From year to year, Hashomer had between 120 and 160 participants between the ages of 12 and 19. There were also a Zionist association for German Jewish youth, the Club Juvenil de la Unión Sionista, founded in 1940; a revisionist, right-wing youth group also founded in 1940 and affiliated with the Jabotinsky group in Palestine, Betar; Hatikva, founded in 1942 by Jack Beller; and Macabi, a sports-oriented social club founded by Sephardic members of Chevet Ahim in 1938. Despite all of this organizational activity, the state of Israel never made much of an impact on Cuban Jewry until the middle 1950s, although Israel's success by then further diluted Cuban Zionism. Twelve young university-age Jews affiliated with Hashomer Hatzair did leave Cuba in 1951 to help 123 other Latin American Jews to found Kibbutz Gaash on the coast twenty minutes north of Tel Aviv, an experiment in pioneering that forty years later

61. Board meeting, Zionist Youth, 1960. Courtesy of Rabbi Nesim Gambach.

remained one of the few surviving socialist collective farms in Israel.[58] A photograph of the board of the Zionist Youth Council, which functioned through the early 1960s, shows Sephardic Rabbi Nesim Gambach as the speaker; Sender Kaplan, the editor of the Jewish community newspaper, sits next to him under the Cuban flag (fig. 61).

Cuban Jews, like the other immigrant groups, including the Spaniards, did not participate in politics. They nevertheless brought with them a tradition of political awareness if not of direct involvement, and in the early 1920s recent Jewish immigrants had been active in the establishment of the Cuban Communist party. But the staunchly conservative nature of the permanent Cuban Jewish community as it evolved discouraged political activity. After the war, Jewish youths who were politically concerned sometimes joined secret organizations in order to hide their activities from their parents.[59]

On March 10, 1952, at the age of fifty-two, Fulgencio Batista, with the aid of young army officers, seized full dictatorial power. But although Batista closed opposition newspapers, occupied union offices, and arrested activists suspected of being Communists, individuals who minded their own business were not bothered. To build popular support, he made frequent speeches and radio broadcasts, always ending his addresses with the words "*Salud, salud.*" This populist appeal proved largely successful, and as a result few voices, at the outset, were raised publicly in protest. Grau's corrupt Auténticos never had won broad-based support, and many now felt that Batista would govern more efficiently. Business leaders welcomed Batista's pledges of law and order, and the United States looked with favor on the prospects for renewed foreign investment.[60]

Like most of the middle and upper classes, Cuban Jews went along. Cuba was undergoing its postwar economic upswing, and many people remembered with nostalgia Batista's first presidential term, when tourism and high sugar prices had brought a sense of energy to the wartime island.[61] Few Cuban Jews took a personal interest in politics, tending instead to accommodate to whatever faction or party took power.[62] Jews appreciated Batista's public condemnation of Soviet persecution of Jews and the Prague trials, a Soviet venue for anti-Semitism. Some Cuban Jews during the Second Batistato (1952–58) demonstrated their patriotism by volunteering for military service during the Korean War. One who had been living in the United States, Isaac Abondam, was killed in Korea; his body was brought back to Cuba for burial. Some others participated in anti-Batista underground movements, mostly led by former Auténticos as well as by members of the old Ortodoxo party. One of the Ortodoxos was a young man named Fidel Castro, who led an armed attack on Cuba's second largest military installation, Santiago de Cuba's Moncada Barracks, on July 26, 1953. The foray failed, but it signaled the beginning of a steady deterioration in armed forces morale fueled by Batista's practice, started in 1933, of naming cronies to high military posts, bypassing career officers graduated during the 1944–52 period of Grau and Prío who should have been promoted. A series of armed forces and police mutinies beginning in 1956 rent Batista's façade of stability.[63] A few Jewish students participated in Castro's Twenty-sixth of July movement, but most did not. Those looking back from within the community explain this as a result of the still-early stage of assimilation for the community in the 1950s.

Still Outsiders

Throughout the 1940s and 1950s, Cuba's Jews, riding the crest of the economic boom, on the whole continued to live in their own world, however Cuban it had become. Cubans generally referred to them as *hebreos* (Hebrews), not the more colloquial (and impolite) *judíos*. Jews continued to be called polacos or Germans by Cubans on the street, but most Jews still claimed that they did not take this as an affront.[64] The word *polaco*, Cuban historian Herminio Portell Vilá rationalized, was rooted in a sense of social difference, not in traditional anti-Semitism.[65] Sephardic Jews themselves called the East Europeans polacos, and were in turn called turcos, a term applied by Cubans without distinction to Sephardic Jews as well as to Syrian and Lebanese Arabs, who plied the same trades, mostly peddling and house-to-house sales. The use of both *polaco* and *turco* was not explicitly pejorative, but both names were rooted in the acknowledgement that the Jews were different, foreigners in a society that did not value cultural pluralism. Everything, moreover, depended on the way the name was uttered: neutrally, or with disdain.[66]

Jews understood that the average Cuban remained oblivious to their religion and to their origins. They did not experience institutional or overt anti-Semitism. Jews in Cuba tended to shrug off expressions of prejudice, expecting them to occur as part of the underlying hostility to Jews felt everywhere. On the affirmative side, numerous Cuban Jews developed lifelong business and even social relations with non-Jewish Cubans, often deepening these ties after the exodus to South Florida after the Castro takeover. Most former Cuban Jews passionately denied that anti-Semitism in Cuba was ever much of a factor in their lives, perhaps because what they understood by anti-Semitism was the far more pervasive institutional form their parents had experienced in the Old World.

Some anti-Semitic activity resurfaced over the debate in the new United Nations over the partition of Palestine. Cuban Jewish Zionists cooperated with the Comité Cubano Pro Palestina Hebrea, founded in 1944 by Rachel Sefardi-Yarden of the Jewish Agency in New York as a non-Jewish support group, which Cuban politicians and intellectuals were encouraged to join. Nominal affiliates eventually included Fulgencio Batista as well as Havana's mayor and the secretary-general of the Cuban Communist party, Juan Marinello.[67]

Some dissident Grau supporters also pledged their support. The committee's most active member was its secretary-general, attorney Ofelia Domínguez y Navarro, a former Communist party leader expelled during the late 1930s, and a feminist and human rights worker. Domínguez worked through her contacts in Mexico, where she had spent time in exile, to help the Jewish Agency organize a pro-Israel group there. She spent a good deal of time speaking to the Sephardic colony, attempting to boost support and raise awareness about the Palestinian question.[68] CCPPH members included Cubans of all persuasions, including such Batista allies as the governor of Havana province, Rafael Guas Inclán, and a number of dissenting Grauists such as Senator Eduardo Chibas and Congressman Manuel Bisbé, who in 1947 broke away and founded the Ortodoxo party. The Cuban Senate in October 1945 unanimously endorsed a resolution reaffirming the Senate's 1919 vote supporting the Balfour Declaration (promulgated two years earlier on November 2, 1917). President Grau and the presidents of the Senate and Congress received a delegation of Jewish leaders in late 1946 after a rally by Jews in favor of Israel and publicly pledged support for the Jewish aspiration for national life in Palestine.

A stream of Zionist emissaries (sheliajs) came to Havana in the postwar years. One Zionist faction, the Keren Kayemet, sent Joseph Tjornitsky, Nathan Bistriski, and Leib Yaffe (who was later killed in the bombing of the King David Hotel in Jerusalem) to plead for help and to raise funds. Cuban Jews held massive rallies in theaters and meeting halls to hear these visitors. Some Jewish Cubans purchased parcels of land in Palestine from Arab Palestinians living in Cuba. Payment was made in Cuba and the title deeds then sent to Jerusalem.[69]

During 1947 two new organizations launched a wave of hostile propaganda, accusing Cuban Jews of illegal acts including clandestine immigration and claiming that Jews in league with Communists had taken control of the island's commerce and industry. They were the Liga Nacional de Trajabadores Anti-Comunistas and Defensa Revolucionaria.[70] A book by Enrique Trinchet published in 1947 cited Jews as "national tumors" and called the Cuban Jewish polacos a "foreign plague."[71] Independent of these groups, members of Cuba's Lebanese community, including Dr. Antonio Faber and Dr. Pedro Khouri, established the Comité Pan Arabe de Cuba, which opposed the Jewish state. Some Pan Arab members during the war had supported Nazi and Falange causes, but most had worked for the Allied side, especially the Lebanese participants. Some of the group's literature, though, contained anti-Jewish propaganda, including excerpts from the notorious *Protocols of the Elders of Zion,* the forgery authored by the czar's secret police before World War I alleging that an international Jewish conspiracy dominated the world. At least one Sephardic Jew, Isaac Garazi, who had formed close friendships with Lebanese Cubans and had been elected president of the Syrian-Lebanese Society, severed these relations when anti-Semitism surfaced among its members.[72]

During the years of Batista's behind-the-scenes domination, relations between the Jews and officialdom acknowledged the political reality that Batista was de facto head of state. When anti-Semitic broadcasts from one radio station during the mid-1930s increased in bellicosity, representatives from the United Hebrew Congregation paid a visit to Batista, reminding him that Jews had donated $10,000 to build the city's José Martí monument and using the opportunity to ask that something be done about the broadcasts. Batista characteristically denied that he had any influence but reminded Rabbi Lasker that a visit to Cuba's president might help. Within a few days unknown vandals smashed the radio station, and the offensive broadcasts were stilled.[73]

The Cuban government also nominally supported the state of Israel, as did most Latin American countries, its leaders joining those who advocated Israeli independence and who publicly backed the Zionist cause. Many of these diplomats (including Guatemala's Jorge García Granados, Mexican labor leader Vicente Lombardo Toledano, and Argentina's Silvano Santander) were attacked by U.S. diplomats and by the FBI as Communists or fellow travelers at the time of partition.[74] The Cubans, of course, were never accused of such sympathies.

One contrary voice from Cuban official circles came from Guillermo Belt y Ramírez, Cuba's ambassador to the United States and titular head of Cuba's delegation to the United Nations in 1947, where Cuba voted against the creation of the state of Israel, the only negative ballot from a Latin American country. In fact, when news came to the floor of the United Nations that President Harry S Truman had unexpectedly and against the strong opposition of leading State Department officials recognized the state of Israel even while U.S. delegates were working against recognition, Belt became so enraged that he had to be physically restrained from marching "to the dais to withdraw his nation from the world assembly."[75] Staunch opponents of recognizing Israel within President Truman's circle included General George C. Marshall, his secretary of state, as well as Dean Acheson, Robert Lovett, Charles Bohlen, George Kennan, James Forrestal, Warren Austin, and Dean Rusk, the director of the Office of United Nations Affairs. Only Truman and his aide Clark Clifford supported the Zionist cause.

That most of the rest of the Cuban delegation was pro-Israel, and that Belt was considered to be motivated by personal ambition, has been used to identify his motives as anti-Semitic.[76] President Grau may have been behind the negative vote, possibly as a result of his relationship with the stormy Raúl Roa, whose wife was a member of the Khouri family. The hostility ended, however, with the election to the presidency of Grau's candidate, Prío Socarrás. His government recognized the state of Israel in early 1949 and voted in the Security Council for Israel's admission to the United Nations.[77] In response, rightists carrying the banner of the Nationalist League of Anti-Communist Workers (Liga Nacional) distributed pamphlets attacking Israel as "anti-Christian" and "anti-democratic" and its soldiers as "Jewish murderers."[78]

Many Cuban Jews strove for the independence of the state of Israel after partition. Sender Kaplan, Israel Luski, and other Zionists raised money in the Ashkenazic community, and two groups of volunteers—thirty-one in all—went to Palestine to fight. The first group left in July 1948; the second embarked at the end of that year. Cuban Jews financed a shipload of arms earmarked for the Irgun, the right-wing paramilitary organization that refused to merge with the Haganah, Israel's defense force. When the ship, the *Altalena*, docked at Haifa, the Haganah's David Ben Gurion refused permission for it to land; when the standoff had continued for forty-eight hours, he ordered the vessel fired upon. Daniel Levy and David Mitrani, Sephardic Cuban Jews aboard the ship, were killed.[79] After independence, about 150 youths who were members of the Betar group in Cuba emigrated to Israel to create agricultural settlements.

Not every Cuban volunteer fighting for Israel was born Jewish. Primitivo F. Ramírez Medina was a "handsome black man" (in the words of Abraham Luski) who had married a Jewish girl who worked at a store near where he lived. Born in 1911 in Matanzas, he initially prepared for a career in law, switched to medicine, but ended up becoming involved in politics, supporting himself as a society reporter and journalist. His desire to marry a Jewish woman during the late 1930s met with antagonism; several Jews attempted to impede his efforts to convert, although he was accepted warmly by the Sephardic rabbi who performed the conversion ceremony, and later by the Ashkenazic rabbi, Zvi Kaplan, who performed the wedding. Ramírez became an ardent Zionist, soon heading Juventud Patriótica Hebrea, a youth group, and affiliating with the Irgun, one of whose leaders was Menachem Begin, who visited Havana in 1947 to raise funds. Fearing violence, Begin's sponsors picked him up from Miami and escorted him to Havana in secrecy. During his stay, he was protected by security guards provided by the government, which did not want to risk a diplomatic incident. Begin was given almost an entire floor of the Hotel Nacional for security reasons.[80]

A newspaper columnist, Ramírez then inaugurated a radio program, "The Voice of Israel," broadcast six nights a week from 7 to 8 P.M. and on Sundays from 11 to noon.[81] When the British mandate over Palestine expired in May 1948, he and a small group of Cuban Jewish youths sailed on the SS *Jagiello* to Marseilles where they awaited orders with volunteers from many nations and received instruction in the Hebrew language and coaching about how to enter Palestine clandestinely (fig. 62). Once there they would join the Jewish Defense Forces under the Jabotinsky-Begin faction. On his return to Cuba, Ramírez was received as a hero by the Zionists in the Jewish colony. A member of Batista's political faction, he was named an inspector in the Ministry of Communications. He also tried his hand at politics and unsuccessfully ran for Congress. When Castro took power, he was fired, at which point he opened a night club, the Tel Aviv Bar. He was able to leave Cuba soon afterward, in 1961, as a delegate to the twenty-fifth World Zionist Congress. He remained in New York, convinced that it would not be a good idea to return to his homeland.[82]

Late 1948 and early 1949 brought not only anti-Semitic pamphleteering by the Liga Nacional in Havana but a daily anti-Semitic radio program produced by Eladio Cortina and Enrique Trinchet. Complaints led police to shut down the broadcasts and the pam-

62. Primitivo Ramírez en route to Palestine. Courtesy of Primitivo Ramírez.

phlets. This was one of the last times that overtly anti-Semitic acts occurred in public. The 1950s saw only a series of snide articles in the daily *Tiempo* accusing individual Jews of Communist sympathies and of abusing workers, avoiding payment of taxes, and smuggling. Ironically, one of the authors of the series was "Cabi," Rodolfo Cann-Birnholz, himself of European Jewish extraction. A "fixer" among the refugees, he worked out of the Caíñas Milanés's office in the Manzana de Gómez, a prominent office building in central Havana. He could arrange almost anything for a price. With his connections in the police, he was considered very powerful, able to fix things with the authorities.[83]

The allegations made over the radio were scurrilous. Birnholz's broadcasts charged that Jewish textile merchants were exclusively involved in illegal smuggling. In reality, corruption lubricated the entire system, with the principal culprits being the generals, customs inspectors, and higher-ups in the government; if a merchant did not cooperate, *aduana* (customs) agents would hold up shipments or refuse to release goods that they had impounded. The atmosphere created by the broadcasts grew so heated that Jewish merchants met and agreed to ask for help from Lawrence Berenson, the Chicago attorney who was a friend of Batista and who had attempted to negotiate freedom for the passengers of the *St. Louis* in 1939. Berenson came to Havana and met with Batista. Birnholz's broadcasts stopped a few days later.[84]

The Jewish community maintained its tradition of combatting discrimination by sending personal contacts as private emissaries to government officials throughout the 1950s. All of this was done quietly, to avoid public exposure lest anti-Semitism be stirred. After the war many of the members of the small American Jewish community had achieved considerable wealth and influence; they could be relied on when the need arose to ask privately for action. Sender Kaplan, the editor of *Havaner Lebn,* which by the 1950s was published in both Yiddish and Spanish, played a major role openly as well as behind the scenes. During the debate over Cuba's position on the creation of a Jewish state in Palestine, and later over the issue of diplomatic recognition of the state of Israel, Kaplan not only lobbied sympathetic politicians through the Comité Pro-Palestina but, as correspondent for the Jewish Agency in New York, wrote dozens of press releases and other articles sympathetic to Israel, which were translated into Spanish and wired to Havana's thirteen daily newspapers. This was as much a product of the fact that Cuba's press depended heavily on foreign sources of news as anything else.

Batista's return to power in his bloodless military coup on March 10, 1952, terminated the democratic system and ushered in an era of martial law. University of Havana students ceremoniously buried a copy of the democratic constitution of 1940. But Batista was popular in the business community as well as among the lower classes. He was personally charming and seen as a man of the people, not representing special interests. His personal intervention to rescue seven Jewish refugees in February 1939 had won the lasting gratitude of Cuban Jews. He always reaffirmed his sympathy to Jewish humanitarian causes. Prime Minister García Montes had worked as a lawyer for the Joint during the war and had helped defend the cause of refugees. The Cuban government staunchly supported Jewish causes, and even the old anti-Semitic newspaper, *Alerta,* modified its approach. Its editor, Ramón Vasconcelos, who had taken part in its anti-Semitic campaign between 1934 and 1946, now praised the planting of a forest in Israel named for the Liberator, José Martí.[85]

Three Jewish Communities

After the European refugees from the war left Cuba for the United States, the island's Jewish community reverted to the prewar pattern of three major groups. The first were the Americans—industrialists, developers, financiers, department store owners (Charlie Shapiro's Los Precios Fijos, for example), and, in the case of Philip Rosenberg, sugar magnates.

The English-speaking American Jews continued to live their lives as they had done before the war. They mixed little with other Jews. Rather, their lives paralleled those of other members of the rather large foreign colony of businessmen, entrepreneurs, and administrators from the United States, Canada, and the European nations. As an exporter of agricultural products and a tourist playground, Cuba was so integrated into the international economy that it functioned as a colonial dependency run by an elite partially Cuban and partially foreign. The American Jews fit comfortably into this elite. They sent their children to schools in the United States; they traveled back and forth with ease; and some of them continued to avoid the immigrant generation of Jews which by now had set down roots.

Their admission into the upper strata was likely a result as much of the Cuban upper classes' understanding of the realities of the island's special economic relationship with the outside as of inherent tolerance, although Cuban Jews firmly believed the latter to be the case. The achievements of individual members of the American Jewish colony were impressive. Philip Rosenberg, who was born in 1895 in Brooklyn, had been sent to Cuba in 1921 on a six-month assignment as an employee of the National City Bank of New York to reorganize sugar properties (nine sugar mills and assorted plantations) that the bank had foreclosed. He went with his wife and three-year-old daughter. When the six months were up, he decided to stay, becoming eventually one of the largest sugar producers on the island, heading the General Sugar Corporation. He was a prominent member of the Asociación de Hacendados and attended international meetings on a Cuban diplomatic passport. He befriended high Cuban officials and more than once opened his country house to them when they needed to hide during attempted coups. He also played a major role in the American Jewish colony, being one of the pillars of the United Hebrew Congregation during and after the war. His memberships included the Masons and Havana Country and

Havana Yacht clubs. The ease with which he circulated in Cuban society indicated the willingness of Cubans to admit him into their inner circle—something only the American Jews could aspire to. The Havana Yacht Club, founded in 1886 at the Playa de Marianao, was so exclusive that some former presidents of the republic were blackballed when they tried to join formally. Possibly the most expensive private club in the world as well as one of the most exclusive, it was said that the only way to get in was to marry the daughter of a member, which entitled the husband to automatic membership.[86]

Adolph Kates, one of the leaders of the United Hebrew Congregation and a founder of the Patronato de la Casa de la Comunidad Hebrea de Cuba was a thirty-third-degree Mason, a member of the Unión and Havana Yacht clubs, ex-commodore of the Almendares Yacht Club, founder of the Miramar Yacht Club, member of the American Chamber of Commerce and the Cuban Chamber of Commerce, member and ex-director of the Cuban Rotary Club, and the president of honor of the Pro-Israel Committee in Cuba.[87] Jews could not join most of the second-tier social clubs, even though their incomes equaled those of the Cubans who frequented them. There were some exceptions, including the posh Club Náutico, where some Jews were admitted. When Jews joined these kinds of clubs, notably in the interior, they found themselves associating with Cubans of a lower economic status than their own.[88] Yet a handful of American Jews were listed in Havana's Social Register, something which would have been less likely in the United States at the time.[89]

During the war, a few of the American Jews had received honors from the Cuban government. Jacob Brandon was knighted with the Order of Merit Carlos Manuel de Céspedes by President Laredo Brú at the Cuban Embassy in Washington. A year later, Brandon received an Award of Merit from President Batista for having helped publicize Cuba's claim that Dr. Carlos J. Finlay had been the sole discoverer of the mosquito that transmitted yellow fever. Adolph Kates was awarded the Cross of the Order of Carlos Manuel de Céspedes for his "services rendered to Cuban interests in the country and abroad."[90] Cuba's high degree of public recognition of Jewish residents was unique in Latin America, an indication of how comfortable relations had become between the community and Cuban authorities.

63. Mrs. Rosita Zeilic and son Mauricio at Adas Israel synagogue, ca. 1952. Courtesy of Mauricio Zeilic.

At a considerable distance from the American Jews, the Sephardim and Ashkenazim maintained their separate communal profiles. The Sephardic community had more or less caught up with the Ashkenazim in prosperity. This was most visibly demonstrated by the completion of the new community center, the Centro Sefaradi in Vedado.[91] Jewish women regardless of background assumed more domestic independence. Jews took their places in the prosperous urban middle class. They lived very well compared with the difficult conditions of the prewar period, but they did not approach in luxury the life-styles of the most aristocratic Cubans and Spaniards, whose lives revolved around their exclusive clubs, so much so that their children virtually grew up in them. *Habaneros* took them for granted, in a way, but tourists were dazzled by the luxury of their clubhouses and gardens. Only the most successful of the American Jews could frequent this world.

Even though Jews moved to the suburbs as soon as they could, links to the poor remained. Businessmen made financial contributions to government clinics for the poor, and charitable organizations like the Froien Farein and Bikur Holim found no shortage of

64. Main entrance
to Centro
Castellano.
Courtesy of
Norbert Adler.

needy cases.[92] In this way, Havana, to some degree like Montreal or
New York during this period, functioned on the basis of a tripartite
system of schools, clubs, and cooperative societies: one serving Cubans, one for the Spanish (including the Quinta La Covadonga clinic
maintained by the Centro Asturiano, the posh Casino Español, and
the Centro Gallego), and one run by Jewish groups. The Spaniards
were the first to build *quintas*, clinics charging membership fees of a
few pesos a month. Jews were welcome to join any of them; there
were no Jewish health clinics per se. Cooperation extended to other
areas as well. The Centro Castellano, for example, rented its facilities to the Centro Israelita for lectures and special meetings (fig. 64).

In business, and in most spheres of Cuban life, few things could be expedited without a *padrino*—someone watching out for one's interests. Collectively, the Jewish community fared well because individual merchants and businessmen learned this system and followed the well-worn path to the presidential palace where officials, just as they had done under the Auténticos but now much less blatantly, accepted bribes in exchange for preferred treatment and exemption from restrictive regulations. One of the keys to success in business was being able to get around customs duties. Most businessmen needed to pay off customs agents, who then charged duty on lesser-valued items.[93] Corruption and the purchase of "favors" flourished within the Jewish community as well as outside. Businessmen kept two sets of books to evade taxes. According to popular belief, most taxes paid would be misspent or stolen, so few had qualms about playing the game. Within the Jewish colony, there were the *machers* (Yiddish for "fixers"), who would extort money from refugees interned at Tiscornia awaiting final clearance of landing papers by claiming to be able to expedite entry visas and other paperwork. Prices were set according to the affluence of the victims and their degree of anxiety. The fixers were East European immigrants who had arrived earlier, and who maintained offices in Havana as well as correspondents at all ports of embarkation.[94] (The immigrants had always used existing laws to their advantage. In the 1920s and 1930s, immigrants in Cuba whose relatives or friends had managed to enter the United States often sent for girls for them to marry. Some of these young women were known to them; others were total strangers. But being the husband of a U.S. citizen made it possible to receive an entry permit. Thousands of Jewish immigrants of the estimated 20,000 who arrived in Cuba between 1923 and 1942 were able to depart by slipping through this legal loophole.)

We know much more, of course, about those who remained within the Jewish community than about the men and women who drifted away, or about those who managed to emigrate outside of regular channels. The desire to keep to themselves, and the close sense of shared origins and practices within the separate divisions within Cuban Jewish life, irked those who sought greater assimilation. But lack of integrative pressures within Cuban society sustained the separate identities of the Jewish groups. In the absence of a universal free public school system as in the United States, East European Jewish Cubans sent their children to private schools, where they spoke Yiddish among themselves. Communal institutions among all immigrant groups insulated them and preserved barriers between their members and larger Cuban society.

Spanish Cubans, many of them transient, sailing back and forth across the Atlantic to visit their families in Spain, banked and invested their salaries with the centros, were served by Spanish priests, and sent their children to Spanish-run schools. Members of the Jewish colony followed a similar pattern, divided between Ashkenazic, Sephardic, and American institutions.[95] Health care (including psychiatric assistance) for indigent Jews was underwritten by the Anti-TB Society, maintained by annual subscriptions.[96] In Cuba, as elsewhere in Latin America, comprehensive assimilation never occurred except for members of immigrant groups who married into the mainstream and who for all practical purposes no longer were members of the communities from which they came. This was true for Spaniards as well as for Jews, but much less so for Jamaicans, Haitians, Chinese, and members of other groups of foreign origin who for racial reasons could not so easily blend into the larger population.

Patterns of cultural expression preserved community-based traditions. For the older generation of immigrants, this was natural enough, although their sons and daughters born in Cuba developed a kind of cultural dualism by which they moved easily in both worlds. Life in Cuba more than in other parts of Latin America was intimately affected by the culture and economic power of the United States. The middle class that evolved after 1940 was cosmopolitan in tastes as well as formally well educated. Affluent Cubans made trips nearly every month to the mainland, taking the air bridge across the Gulf Stream, over the shoal-studded Florida Bay, and over the Overseas Highway spanning the sea to the Pan American terminal in Miami's Coconut Grove, or bringing their cars with them on the 230-car capacity war surplus amphibious landing craft ferry (El Ferry) the hundred miles to Key West, at the southernmost tip of U.S. Highway 1. Traveling to Cuba, all passengers, including returning islanders, went through Cuban customs on U.S. soil.[97]

Evidence of Assimilation

Within Cuba's Jewish community, institutions fostered maintenance of Jewish identity. The magazine *Israelia*, founded in 1949, presented a potpourri of articles on cultural, literary, and domestic themes and boasted a column devoted exclusively to the social life of "Hebrew-Cuban physicians." The private network of Jewish day schools strengthened after the war as the community prospered economically. This was accompanied by new evidence of assimilation, especially among the children of immigrants who had arrived before 1933, had chosen to make Cuba their home and given up on the old dreams of emigration to the United States. Students with Ashkenazic names studying at the medical faculty of the University of Havana were frequently cited in the Jewish press, evidence of how far the East European Jews had come in little more than two decades. At least sixty children of Sephardic Jews graduated in medicine or dentistry after the war.[98] Cuban Jewish youths who earned professional diplomas frequently cultivated ties outside Cuba through travel or memberships in professional associations.

In Cuba, however, where a professional degree did not necessarily earn one the position it might in, for example, the United States, many non-Jewish Cuban university graduates did not work in law, medicine, or engineering; in a society oversupplied with university graduates, they kept the title of "doctor" and took a government job. Many held two or three government jobs besides moonlighting as university professors or journalists. These were options unavailable to Jews, as the government bureaucracy remained closed to them. Similarly, the Cuban elite profited from Cuba's continued economic dependence on the United States. Cuba produced almost no agronomists, despite having an economy built on sugar, and relied on foreign technicians and professional experts, most brought from the United States at great expense. Still, high-level administrators inside and outside the government received social respect whether their jobs were meaningful or not.

The government offered two kinds of sinecures: *botellas* (no-work jobs created for the job holder) and *jamones* (patronage posts ranging as high as cabinet minister). Hundreds of teaching jobs, for example, were filled before elections; sometimes substitutes were employed at meager wages; sometimes no one performed work at all. Hundreds and even thousands of phantom workers glutted government payrolls at all levels, especially during the prosperous 1950s. As a result, Cuba's internal economic and social structure retained aspects of its old dependency on Madrid as a colony, although now other foreign nations, especially the United States, had replaced

Spain as the dominant influence. At the top of the economic ladder in Cuba sat the Cuban aristocracy, closely linked to the permanent colony of foreign nationals who ran Cuba's largest banks, agro-industrial firms, and tourist industry, and who administered foreign-owned interests on the island. The tiny, insular colony of American Jews in Cuba moved in these circles, although its members tended to be involved in retail business and manufacturing. The former Ashkenazic and Sephardic immigrants, most of whom by the 1950s had entered the Cuban middle class, by the closing years of the decade were facing some difficulties, although they were better off than they ever had been. They still lacked access to the upper echelon, governed by patronage and personal connections, but they channeled their energies into other ways of making a living, and many did very well.

Postwar Cuban life revolved too centrally around its special atmosphere to nurture an atmosphere conducive to assimilation or, in a larger sense, middle-class stability. The island retained and enhanced its reputation as a seamy tourist resort, a place where one could do anything forbidden at home. This had started at the onset of Prohibition, when travelers from the nearby United States found that they could have liquor there; by the middle and late 1950s, they could also hear Xavier Cugat and Chico O'Farrill, and they could find drugs, prostitution, transvestism, child pornography, and could obtain abortions. The "dance of the millions" of the post–World War I boom had returned in another form. Foreign businessmen also understood the ethic of corruption and believed that Prío Socarrás had purchased his election, even though the election had generally been honest. It was also understood that after Batista openly took power in April 1952, graft had risen to new extremes, and that U.S. mobsters had muscled into the action. By the mid- to late 1950s, U.S. gangsters were jockeying for control of most of the brothels, drug houses, and hotels along the 150 kilometers of coastline stretching from Havana to Varadero Beach.[99] The local elite, as well as the Cuban Jewish community, accepted these sordid aspects of life on the island as facts of life, and good for business. So did the resident colony of 6,500 Americans in Havana, most of whom lived remarkably privileged lives, and who loyally supported the Batista regime.[100]

Jews and other minority groups clustered within their own colonies, creating their own worlds, relating politely to their Cuban neighbors but rarely engaging in meaningful discourse or competition. The Jewish school system, anchored by the Centro Israelita's Colegio Hebreo (which graduated as many as 1,000 youths over the years), played a strong role in shaping Jewish identity. Jewish professionals almost always took clients from within their own subcommunities, still divided by Sephardic and Ashkenazic origins. Not holding government jobs, they lacked the opportunity for the graft that followed what earlier observers had referred to as the "Spanish tradition," by which "public office was intended principally to benefit the holder."[101] One source claimed in 1927 that the graft bill of the official lottery, derived from markups charged by lottery collectors, who were political appointees, had ranged from 13 to 18 percent of the total government receipts from all sources.[102] But Jewish residents accepted this exclusion, because there were many other ways of making a good living in Cuba's tolerant climate.

Jews had now become so much a part of the mosaic of the Cuban population that mainstream writers included them in their work. The eminent novelist Guillermo Cabrera Infante's 1979 novel, *La Habana para un Infante Difunto*, set in the postwar years, includes a fictional polaca, Sonia, who obsessively recounts her harrowing experiences escaping Nazi Europe but who makes no impact on the members of Havana's fast set to whom she spills out her story. Mentally unstable, she accuses her neighbors of being German spies. Ultimately Sonia is committed to a mental institution because she cannot deal with her past: she carries her family album with her and has become paranoid about being persecuted.[103] Darcia Moretti's novel, *Los Ojos del Paraíso*, carried this theme, Jewish dispersion as tragedy, to the second exile of the Cuban Jews—to the United States.[104]

Abel Holtz's biography illustrates the Jews' new feeling of security in the late 1940s and early 1950s.[105] His parents and two older brothers had left Litvino, a town outside Warsaw, in December 1932. His father had spent a year in Danzig waiting for permits and visas and finally gained entry into Mexico. When he was unable to obtain work, he moved to Cuba and sent for the rest of his family. He started a small shoe factory, with three or four workers, in the province of Santa Clara. Abel was born there in 1935 and spent his first twelve years there. In 1947, the Holtz family relocated to Havana. By his own description, Abel was a brash youth who did not grieve when word came that his grandparents had died in concentration camps because, in his words, he had never known them. His parents received news from Europe and often remarked that "ma harget und ma schlaegt de Yiddn" ("they are killing and beating the Jews"), but he did not feel otherwise affected by the news of the Holocaust. He reacted to his father's news about Franklin Roosevelt's death by asking if school would be closed that day; his father slapped him. When his teacher in the private elementary school he was attending heard about his attitude, she admonished him, asking the boy "if he wasn't embarrassed after all [Roosevelt] did for the Jews?"

Even newly arrived Jewish immigrants like the Holtzes felt comfortable enough and were economically able within a decade to send their children to private schools and secure enough to ask permission from school officials, when the schools were church run, to exempt their children from required classes in catechism and religion. Jewish pupils in Jesuit schools attended daily masses but did not have to pray or make the sign of the cross. As a member of only one of twenty or so Jewish families in Santa Clara, Holtz felt accepted by non-Jews, hearing not much in the way of anti-Semitic language save for the widespread use of the term *polaco*, in school and at the University of Havana, with its 15,000 students. At age seventeen Holtz was elected freshman delegate to the Law School's student government and, after a deadlock, emerged as president for three years. He maintained that there was little or no anti-Semitism in Cuba at the time, although four of the "Big Five" clubs continued not to accept Jews, and the fifth, American Jews only. As a teenager in Havana, Holtz belonged to several Zionist youth movements and organizations. His father served as president of the Centro Israelita. He escaped to Miami in 1961 after having been imprisoned four times for defending anti-Castro activists.

By the late 1950s, the American Jews mixed increasingly with the other groups in the Cuban Jewish mosaic, socially and in business, but religiously they still stood apart. On the eve of the Castro revolution, Temple Beth Israel conducted Reform services in English and liturgical Hebrew with one or two prayers or comments in Spanish. The temple's rabbis were appointed by the Union of Hebrew Congregations in New York. Although it was one of the oldest Reform synagogues in the world, the Havana synagogue was more or less ignored. Internally, it operated with scant recognition given to the host country, as if the congregation was living in a U.S. city, although services started at 9:15 P.M.—a time attuned to Cuban life.

English-speaking visitors to the American Jewish community felt right at home, although some were puzzled to find their language used in Cuba. The Honorable Lily H. Montagu, president of the World Union for Progressive Judaism in London and a former congregant of Rabbi Frederick Solomon in London's West Central Synagogue, wrote to Rabbi Solomon after he moved to Havana that she was not certain about the affiliation of his new congregation with the World Union, noting that "my geography is not very good but I think Cuba is an independent state."[106] Dr. Solomon, Beth Israel's last rabbi before the Castro era, almost never addressed Cuban themes in his sermons or talks, or even in graveside services for congregants who had lived in Cuba for decades. Addressing the British Club, which made him an honorary member, he shared his expectation that his pulpit in Cuba would be a peaceful one: "Maybe," he joked, "I shall still learn to play golf." Abruptly, however, things changed. During a 1959 Sabbath service, he asked that the congregation pray "for the welfare of Cuba, the land where some of us gathered here were born." Referring to the guerrilla conflict raging in the island's interior, the rabbi asked that members respond to the needy and "those left destitute in the wake of warlike destruction."[107]

The shock of political reality suddenly assaulted Cuba's Jews. It is probable that few members of the temple congregation imagined what the impact of the 1959 Revolution would be on their status as entrepreneurs and successful members of Cuba's foreign-based elite.

7 ✸ A Second Diaspora

Fidel Castro's Twenty-sixth of July movement took power in Havana on January 1, 1959, after two years of guerrilla fighting in the mountains and countryside. Cuba entered a period of temporary euphoria over the prospect of erasing the brutality, corruption, and special privilege that had characterized the dictatorship. For Cubans who had accommodated to the laissez faire economic system permitted by the Batista regime and its predecessors under the benevolent eye of the United States, the revolutionary rhetoric rapidly soured. Some maintained their personal commitment to the Revolution for years, championing it as a boon to the Cuban people and to Cuban national independence. Some turned cynical, viewing the Revolution as—in the words of the disenchanted French radical journalist Regis Debray—a myth, a "golden legend." Those at the bottom of Cuban society benefited almost immediately, receiving access to better health care and free education than they had enjoyed before. To these Cubans, historically excluded from the system with no hope of betterment, the Revolution promised hope and nationalistic self-pride in exchange for isolation and economic malaise.

Jews and the New Regime

Postwar Cuba had represented an anomaly in the hemisphere—not Latin American, not wholly North American. Havana was one of the world's most expensive cities, fueled by tourism; its residents found it hard to keep up with the cost of living. The standard of living was much lower elsewhere in the island. Cuba's per capita income was twice as high as in any other country in Latin America but five times lower than that in the United States.

There were 11,000 to 14,000 acknowledged Jews in Cuba on the eve of the Revolution, among more than six million Cubans.[1] About one-quarter were Sephardic, the large majority East European in origin. Most of the island's Jews in 1959 lived in the capital, although up to 3,000 resided in the provinces, especially in Oriente, Camagüey, and Las Villas. There was even a small organized Jewish community in Guantánamo City, settled during the 1940s and 1950s by Jews from Turkey and Syria. More Sephardim than Ashkenazim lived in small cities and rural towns, perhaps a measure of the Mediterranean Jews' greater adaptability to Cuban society, or their lesser degree of identification with the fast urban life of the capital.

A survey by the Jewish Chamber of Commerce—an entity created in 1936—revealed that in 1959 about 75 percent of the working Jewish population was engaged in small-scale retail trade, 15 percent owned larger stores, and 10 percent was engaged in the production of consumer goods.[2] Cuba's Jews saw their country as a place of opportunity and comfort. There is no hint that any of them would have abandoned Cuba had not the political situation soured. When they did flee to the United States in the early 1960s, most expected that they would be able to return within a few months. Many had maintained close ties with the Batista regime, which behaved amiably to them. After the Castro victory, although Cuban Jews had overwhelmingly entered the mainstream and were now considered in most cases to be bourgeois, they were not persecuted as Jews in any manner by the new revolutionary government. They were not harmed by the revolutionary trials in the first months of the new regime or by the purges of Batista regime officials, as few Jews had entered government.[3]

Comandante Fidel Alejandro Castro Ruz, now the "Maximum Leader," spoke out passionately in favor of human rights and social equality and attacked discrimination against minorities, especially blacks.[4] So frequently did he appear in public and launch into impromptu speeches on the virtues of the revolution that patterns of street behavior in Havana changed: the traditional Malecón-Prado route of the carnivalesque comparsas was rerouted in 1961 so that the revelers would pass by Arturo's bar where El Líder came to drink glasses of tiny Sagua oysters.[5] A few Cuban Jews played important roles in the heady early days of the new regime. Max Lesnick was born in Santa Clara province to a Catholic mother and Polish-Jewish father, who had as a newly arrived immigrant found work as a railroad construction worker in the provinces. Elected national president of the Cuban Students' Association, Max Lesnick, who later broke with Castro and went into exile in South Florida, claimed to have coined the phrase "Cuba Sí, Yanquis No." Carlos Mizrachi, a surgeon resident in Santa Clara, was one of the first Cuban physicians to serve with Castro.[6] Isaac Silber, a former classmate of Castro's and a former leader in the Cuban Hashomer Hatzair movement, emigrated to Israel in 1949 but kept in contact with socialist militants.[7]

Others included Martin Klein, a Czech-born flier who had joined Batista's air force but who had been court-martialed and jailed for refusing to bomb rebel positions in the Sierra Maestra. He was released when the Revolution triumphed and was made El Comandante's personal pilot. He died in a plane crash a few years later.[8] José Egozi was active in the Castro regime at the outset. Jean Contenté, a former Jewish fighter in the French resistance (and a veteran of Irgun and Altalena during the Israeli War for Independence) helped train Ché Guevara and other Cuban revolutionaries on guerrilla war in Costa Rica, under the protection of President José Figueres. In 1959, Contenté came to Cuba but had to escape with Guevara's help because he incurred the enmity of Raúl Castro, Fidel's brother.

Enrique Oltuski Osachki, of a Polish Jewish immigrant family, joined Castro in 1955, served in Las Villas province with the rebel forces, and, at twenty-nine years of age, was made minister of communications. He and Máximo Bergman, Castro's minister of the interior and a nonpracticing Jew, were the only Jews ever to hold cabinet-level positions in Cuba. He left his post in 1960. His role in Castro's government offered evidence that the Revolution, in the words of a leading specialist on Jewish life in Latin America, did not constitute a calamity for Cuba's Jews.[9] Some of the Polish Jewish immigrants had been Communists for years, including a man named Guralsky, the director of the South American bureau of the Comintern from 1930 to 1934. A few of the Jewish Communists attempted to assert themselves as speakers for the Jewish community, but their efforts were rejected.[10] One of them, a man named

Novigrad (Stolik), did play a major role in the young Castro regime; he was named Cuban ambassador to Great Britain and to India. Boris Goldenberg, a Marxist until the late 1930s, also played an important role in the early revolutionary government. Born in Russia, he grew up in Germany, attended a German university, and became a Communist, only to be expelled from the party in 1929. He was arrested in 1933 by the Nazis but fled to France. In 1941, he escaped again, to Cuba. In 1946 he became a Cuban citizen. In the early 1950s, he was hired as a teacher at the English-language Ruston Academy. He left Cuba in July 1960 for West Germany, where he became the director of the Latin American Department of Radio Deutsche Welle. During the Willy Brandt administration he served as the prime minister's major adviser on Latin American affairs.[11]

Most of the Jewish Communists wanted nothing to do with Cuban Jews, including Fabio Grobart (Abraham [Yunger] Simchowitz), one of the founders of the Cuban Communist party in 1925, although Communist activists Mordechai Epstein and Jaime Novomodi remained attached to their fellow Jews and may have attempted to recruit them. Grobart, who worked as a tailor on first arriving in Cuba from Poland in 1924, was a member of the editorial board of *Cuba Socialista*, the monthly theoretical journal of the Cuban Marxist-Leninist movement. (Many of the left-wing activists never attempted to fit into Cuban life; at early Cuban Communist party meetings, they spoke Yiddish and needed Spanish translators.) The low-profile architect of Castro's reorganization of the Cuban government, Grobart sat on the party's Central Committee for decades. He traveled in and out of Cuba, spending most of the postwar years in Eastern Europe before returning to Havana in January 1961 to take a major role in shaping the ideology of the Cuban Communist movement. Grobart shunned publicity, and his name appeared in print during the early 1960s only once, on the masthead of the first issue of *Cuba Socialista*.[12] During the 1980s, Grobart headed the party-sponsored Institute for the History of the Workers' Movement and Socialist Revolution, renamed later the Cuban Institute for Film, Art, and Industry (ICAIC).

Ricardo Subirana y Lobo (later Wolf), a chemical engineer and elderly socialist Zionist, was one of the two men who financed the purchase of *Granma*, the boat that took Castro and some of his followers back to Cuba from Mexico to begin his campaign in the mountains against Batista. In gratitude, El Líder designated Lobo minister to Israel, a post he held until relations were broken off in 1973. The six-foot Castro used to approach the five-foot Subirana at receptions and lift him from the floor in a bear hug.[13] After 1973, Subirana remained in Israel, where he created a foundation devoted to awarding prizes to scientists and mathematicians. Other non-practicing Jews prominent in official circles included José Altschuler, vice president of the Cuban Academy of Sciences (installed in the capitol building in Havana) and president of the Cuban Commission for Space Research; Belisa Warman, vice president of the State Committee for Labor and Social Security, later cohead of Cuba's polygraphic industry. Israel Behar reached the rank of general in G-2, Cuba's intelligence service. Saúl Yelin was until his death the foreign affairs director of the ICAIC. Jacobo Peisson was vice president of the National Bank of Cuba. Samuel Savariego was president of the National Institute for Computers and Automatized Systems (INSAC). Dozens more "non-Jewish Jews," in the words of community leaders, because they denied their Jewishness, held top positions in the fields of hematology, cardiology, bioengineering, cybernetics, physics, mathematics, medicine, and the arts.[14] According to the *American Jewish Yearbook* for 1962, the Castro regime employed thirty veteran Jewish Communists and about a hundred Jews, mostly students, who had worked for the Revolution or who had stepped forth to serve it.[15]

Conditions for middle- and upper-class Cubans deteriorated swiftly. Most Cuban Jews were anything but Marxist-Leninist sympathizers and found themselves embarrassed by their compatriots who had stubbornly clung to 1920s and 1930s socialism. In foreign policy, Cuba quickly abandoned the Batista regime's pro-U.S. orientation and began to champion Third World causes. Early in 1960, Raúl Castro visited Egypt's president Gamal Abdul Nasser, although Israeli visitors to Cuba still were met warmly, and the now state-controlled Cuban press covered Israeli issues sympathetically.[16] This state of affairs changed quickly as the cold war intensified and as Cuba moved closer to the Soviet orbit. The turning point came in February 1960, when the Soviet foreign minister Anastas Mikoyan visited Havana, working out the framework for close relations between Cuba and the socialist camp. In that same year, José Pardo Llada, the chief of the state radio and television corporation, visited

65. Fidel Castro, 1958. Courtesy of Archives and Special Collections Department, University of Miami, Coral Gables, Fla.

Israel over the objections of the Cuban Foreign Ministry; he soon fled to exile in Mexico. The Cuban position on Israel now became "determined primarily by considerations outside Cuban-Israeli bilateral relations," as two Israeli scholars have noted. Concurrently, Israel's options in its relations with Cuba were also circumscribed by worsening relations between Havana and Washington.[17]

Following Lenin's thesis about the existence of two cultures within a class society—the culture of the exploiters and the culture of the exploited—the revolutionary regime accepted the support of those willing to renounce the island's decades-old system of blending free enterprise with paternalism. The period from 1934 to 1958, during which Cuba's Jewish immigrants embraced Cuba as their permanent homeland, was labeled the "neocolonial" era by revolutionary revisionists; those who had prospered during these years were called lackeys of international capitalists.[18] By the early 1960s, all private holdings were expropriated—not only the agricultural lands of the multinational corporations but all factories, retail establishments with four or more employees, and banks. Those who owned property or who were identified with the prerevolutionary regime in one way or another were initially looked at with suspicion and eventually labeled part of the exploiter class.[19] Because postwar Cuba had become a showcase of luxury and visible wealth—the island, a well-traveled foreign visitor wrote in 1957, had more Cadillacs than anywhere else in the world—it became easy after 1959 to point fingers.[20] As most of Cuba's Jews had been engaged in business or commerce and had by the 1950s gained a secure place in the middle class, the large part of those who identified themselves as Jews (as opposed to those of Jewish birth who had drifted away from association with Jewish institutions) fell into the category of enemies of the revolution.

The First Wave of Emigration: 1960

The United States broke off diplomatic relations with Cuba in 1961 just after an anti-U.S. Castro speech. Castro proclaimed the socialist character of the Cuban Revolution in April, after the Bay of Pigs invasion, and Washington imposed an embargo on Cuban trade. The Organization of American States expelled Cuba a year later, and Havana introduced rationing of clothing and food. The fortunes of those leaving the island varied from family to family. Merchants whose businesses had been based on importing basic materials from the United States (as in the case of textiles and leather) were generously extended credit by their suppliers when they emigrated, to permit them to start anew. Some individuals converted their pesos into dollars in the early days of the Revolution, thereby saving at least a portion of their assets, although the exchange rate quickly fell from one peso to the dollar to ten, twelve, or more. Those who guessed wrong bought pesos, hoping that Batista's ouster would be good for business. A few were able to sell their homes; most turned them over to friends or associates who had decided, for the time being, to stay. Eventually all of the property formerly owned by those seeking exile was confiscated by the au-

66. Leaders of the 1959 Revolution. Courtesy of Archives and Special Collections Department, University of Miami, Coral Gables, Fla.

thorities. During the transition period in the early 1960s, when no one knew how far the Revolution would actually go, a few managed to have some belongings shipped to them. The Winers wrapped their family photograph albums in brown paper and mailed them to relatives. Stanley Wax asked the man who had moved into his elegant home in the Country Club section of Havana to rescue an oil painting of his children; the man took it with him on a trip to Italy and sent it to the Waxes in the United States.[21] Those who stayed were allowed to keep their homes. Moisés Baldas, for example, continued to live in his penthouse in the seven-story building that he had built, although the government nationalized his street-level store and the six floors of apartments. In addition, he was granted a pension of some 700 pesos (geared to the dollar) monthly, in compensation for his building.[22]

Departing Jews expressed bitterness at having to leave their homes, cars, furniture, and businesses. Once an exit visa was applied for, a Cuban immigration official came to one's home to inventory the property and came back weeks later to see if anything had been removed. People applying for departure were known to purchase appliances or other items simply to leave them behind, for fear of being accused of selling the item before the official visit. A man with an empty grandfather clock frame bought a clock to avoid suspicion, and another repaired his broken-down car for 200 pesos so he would not be suspected of deliberately sabotaging it.[23] A visiting representative of HIAS, the welfare agency, summarized what he saw in July 1961:

> It is disastrous—the rich have left, some having foreseen the situation, but these are few. . . . All assets [have been] taken over by the government, the militia, or other bandits who have simply taken over everything which our brothers have left behind after having worked for many years, sacrificing themselves to make their way. . . . Those who remain can do nothing; business is dying for lack of merchandise, and the large industries, as well as the small ones, are being nationalized. Owners are being watched strictly.[24]

Some 70 percent of the Jewish residents of Cuba—most of them naturalized Cuban citizens—eventually left as part of the general exodus of the middle and upper classes to the United States mainland (fig. 67). Smaller numbers of Cuban Jews departed for Puerto Rico, Israel, or other parts of Latin America, especially Mexico and Venezuela. Those who desired to go to Israel were assisted by the Jewish Agency, which sent a representative to act as liaison with the Cuban government, and by the Canadian Jewish Congress, which stepped in after the United States broke off diplomatic relations with Havana.[25] Jews seeking to relocate to Israel later had the word *Repatriated* stamped in their Cuban passports. Given the hostility of Cuban authorities to citizens who left for the United States— whom they labeled *gusanos* (worms)—this represented a remarkable attitude on the part of the revolutionary government, perhaps a recognition of the fact that some of the founders of the Cuban Communist party in the 1920s had been Jews. Fidel Castro considered Jews emigrating to Israel to be "returning home." The rule restricting removal of belongings to one small suitcase per person, applied to everyone leaving the island, was waived for Jews seeking to immigrate to the Holy Land. The chartered Cubana Airlines planes that carried hundreds of Jews to Tel Aviv took household effects,

Sept 14/60   AC- 4546 H.
Fecha   Clave No.

3776/54   03063
No. Expte. Ppte.   No. Pasaporte

EL CIUDADANO: Arnold Spatz

de 61 años, empleado en Propietario
Garage El Morro. Morro 60.Hbna
y vecino de Avda de Las Misiones 62
Habana

está autorizado para abandonar el Territorio
Nacional a su entera libertad. (Válido por
un año, a partir fecha expedición).

Jefe Ndo. Agencias
Pasaportes DTI (PNR)

VISTO BUENO
Jefe Dpto. Técnico
Investigaciones (P.N.R.)

67. Exit permit to
leave Cuba, 1960.
Courtesy of Hardy
L. Spatz.

clothing, and even furniture, further evidence—at least at the outset
of Castro's regime—of favored treatment to departing Jews.[26]

Jews, of course, made up only a small part of a vast exodus of
upper- and middle-class Cubans who left during the early 1960s.
New problems arose when the U.S. Department of State closed the
U.S. consulate in Havana in January 1961. Through mid-1962, Cuban officials still permitted anyone to leave who wanted to, except for some needed professionals such as engineers and technicians; physicians in some categories were also prevented from
leaving unless they obtained individual permission. In the aftermath
of the Cuban missile crisis in the fall of 1962, the doors closed until

the Camarioca boatlift, which culminated in the Freedom Flights (1965–73) initiated by the Lyndon Johnson administration. The doors were kept half-open from 1978 on, after an agreement with President Jimmy Carter, but opened wide again with the Mariel boatlift in 1980, when 125,000 Cubans disembarked in the Florida Keys. In early 1963, a census carried out by Congregation Adas Israel and the Cuban Zionist Federation estimated that 2,586 Cuban Jews remained, representing 1,022 families, based on registration required at Passover to be allowed to purchase matzo. Most were from Havana, and two-thirds of the families were Ashkenazic in origin.[27]

Few of the exiles managed to sell their assets or leave with any appreciable funds.[28] Jews fared no better and no worse than others. Some Cuban Jewish businessmen were compensated for their companies, which were absorbed under the program of nationalization, and others, for reasons known only to the revolutionary government, were not. Members of the National Institute of Agrarian Reform (INRA) entered some businesses at gunpoint and forced owners to flee. Bank accounts were frozen and houses seized. A bomb was thrown at department store owner Charles Shapiro, one of the most prominent American Jews. Families leaving Cuba were often harassed even at the airport before emigration. Chronically sick people claimed to have been denied hospital beds. But this treatment was dished out to all so-called enemies of the Revolution, not just Jews. The American Jewish Committee in Miami and other Jewish organizations repeatedly avouched that anti-Semitism was "not a factor" in the flight of Jews from Cuba.[29]

Living conditions in Cuba rapidly deteriorated. Of those Jews who remained during the early 1960s, an Israeli diplomat estimated that 45 percent were unemployed, living off gradual sales of their possessions.[30] Tourism suffered, unemployment rose, and the United States stepped up pressures against the regime, which ultimately led to economic boycott. Within six months, the hard-line face of the regime emerged. President Manuel Urrutia Lleó was forced from office. The Communist party, named the Popular Socialist party, became the only party allowed to carry out political activity in a decree published on January 1, 1960, the first anniversary of the Revolution; Jews were permitted to join, unlike Jews in Romania and Hungary. Most of the handsome, stuccoed homes in the Miami-like Havana suburbs were seized and turned into day-care centers, hostels for young people from the countryside, or socialist-bloc embassies.[31]

Jewish schools were not explicitly curtailed, but the exodus of Cuba's Jews doomed them. Often, in fact, parents sent their children ahead to the United States for schooling while they waited a bit longer, hoping that the Revolution would falter, or that somehow they could sell their assets. The government assumed control of the Colegio Hebreo, now the only comprehensive day school in Cuba, formerly run by the Centro Israelita and normally serving 500 students. By the end of the 1960–61 school year only 200 students were left, with the high school virtually empty. Classes in the Jewish religion were still given at the Jewish school, although quietly, to the 60 Jewish students registered among the neighborhood pupils. According to the Hebrew teacher, about 60 non-Jewish children—whites, mulattos, and blacks—sat through the Jewish classes in the afternoon as a volunteer effort and were taught Yiddish and Hebrew. Tahkemoni, a day school with about 100 students, mostly from Orthodox families, did not reopen in September 1960 for lack of funds. Religious services in five synagogues (two Sephardic, two Ashkenazic, and the Reform United Hebrew Congregation) would continue during the 1970s but only for tiny clusters of worshippers; the number would dwindle to two synagogues by 1991. The Yiddish-language newspaper, *Havaner Lebn*, ceased publication on December 31, 1960, after twenty-seven years of existence. Most of its last advertising bills went unpaid because the sponsoring firms, appropriated or forced to be sold, had come under new ownership.[32] The paper's place was taken by *Yedioth-Jewish Cuba*, a new progovernment publication edited by three intellectuals, one of them the poet and writer David Autiansky.[33] Articles praised the actions of the government in helping the remaining members of the community celebrate Passover and carry out other religious activities; they also expressed anxiety. The atmosphere remained tense if ambivalent. The Jewish restaurant Moishe Pipik on Acosta Street was nationalized but continued to present its old menu.

In early 1961, aides to President John F. Kennedy's health, education, and welfare secretary, Abraham Ribicoff, estimated that three-fourths of the faculty of the University of Havana were living in South Florida, part of some 30,000 Cuban refugees clustered in the Greater Miami area by late 1960. Of these, an estimated 2,500 were

Jewish, one-fourth of the total Jewish community of Havana.[34] Refugees came on tourist visas but were granted permanent residence by the United States on arrival. The Greater Miami Jewish Federation set up a reception center at the airport, as did other welfare agencies, including the Miami archdiocese's Catholic-Spanish Center. Jewish Cubans with destinations elsewhere were aided by local welfare organizations, generally coordinated by the HIAS. (For Jewish welfare organizations, the Cuban emigrants were only a tiny part of a worldwide refugee dilemma: during 1961–62, more than 200,000 Jews were displaced from their homes, mostly in North Africa and in the Middle East.)[35] Through early 1961, about 500 Cubans continued to arrive daily in Miami. They landed in the midst of an economic recession in which some 22,000 county residents were unemployed. Welfare groups elsewhere promised help. "If we could schedule 1,000 flights, we could resettle almost all the families crowded into Miami," wrote James McCracken of the Church World Service in Cleveland, but this did not materialize, and most of the Cuban refugees remained in South Florida.[36] By 1966, more than 165,000 Cubans were estimated as having come to Dade County alone. Resettlement costs, estimated at $1,000 for each family of four, were borne by local and county agencies. The American Jewish Committee, earlier in the exodus, described the situation:

> Most of the exiles are middle-class people who arrive here [in Miami] with a very small amount of money and almost no possessions. They crowd into households and make ends meet by doubling, tripling, and quadrupling the number of people normally housed in these facilities. There is constant local fighting between the Fidelistas, Miami's permanent Cuban population of about 45,000 and the anti-Castro exiles.[37]

For the immigrants and refugees who had prospered, Cuba had represented a utopia for them and for their children. Even those who left for the United States and who gained more material success in their new country always saw Cuba as the better place. Moisés Pitchón, whose father Marco had crusaded for Jewish unity and integration of the larger Jewish community into civic affairs, said in an interview in 1983:

> We liked living in Cuba. I had already traced my whole future, even into my retirement and as an old person. . . . Whether religious or not,

I thought of myself as a Jew. And I am sure that most of the young generation there felt the same way. We did not look for anything better, because we thought we had found paradise there.[38]

Church and State under Castro

The new regime faced the church-state issue gingerly. Communist ideology clearly demanded that organized religion be deprecated, and revolutionary cadres remembered all too well the opposition to Castro's movement by most of the Catholic church hierarchy as well as by most members of Cuba's elites. Postrevolutionary historical writing emphasized the supposedly anticlerical attitudes of the fathers of Cuban independence, including José Martí, Carlos Manuel de Céspedes, and the general of the liberation army, Antonio Maceo.[39]

Given its close ties to Spain during the 1930s and 1940s, the hierarchy of the Cuban Catholic church might have been expected to harbor anti-Semitic feelings but spoke with a progressive and enlightened voice. During the colonial period, Roman Catholicism was the religion of the state, and teaching of Catholic dogma was obligatory in all schools. Catholic seminaries contributed to the growth of national awareness in the early nineteenth century, as did the colonial university, secularized in 1842 but always a center of Catholic influence.[40] In the 1950s, Father Ignacio Biain, Franciscan editor of *La Quincena*, spoke in friendly terms to Jewish audiences.[41] Jewish schoolchildren, especially in the interior (where they often attended Catholic schools), were taunted, but such acts represented ignorance, not church policy. Some priests sprinkled holy water on Jewish children in the classes in a crude effort to baptize them.

In the provinces, Jews always had gravitated to private schools run by Protestants when available.[42] In some ways provincial life blurred ethnic sensitivities more than did life in Havana: in the 1930s and 1940s, Abraham Levin's children in Agramonte in the province of Matanzas played with the mayor's children. But the Levins also drew their curtains on Passover.[43] A young woman who lived in Oriente province and who attended a church school was taunted by her classmates almost daily and had no friends. Chalón Rodríguez encountered so much hostility from both priests and fellow students in a provincial town that he hid his Jewishness so that he would not suffer, although his family was dutifully observant. When he transferred to a school run by Presbyterians, he encountered less bigotry.[44] On the other hand, Abel Holtz, who attended Jesuit school in Santa Clara, interacted socially with his fellow students and as a law student at the University of Havana ran for and was elected to the presidency of the student body.[45] In Havana, some Jews attended the Colegio Metodista Central, run by Methodist missionaries from the United States. Others attended bilingual schools (two of them were the Columbus School and the Phillips School) so that they would have advantages when they traveled or entered business. If they could afford the tuition, they went to Ruston Academy, where classes were taught in English.[46]

Confrontation between the Castro regime and the Catholic church reached a peak during the 1961 Bay of Pigs invasion. Three hundred Catholic priests were deported to Spain from Cuba. But in 1985, Castro met with church leaders during a general meeting of the episcopate, formally beginning a new relationship between the regime and the church. By that time, the ratio of priests to the population (nominally 90 percent Roman Catholic) had declined from prerevolutionary levels of 9,000 to 1 to a single priest for every 53,000 Cubans. In several ways, Castro and his comrades formalized the relative tolerance and flexibility on matters of religious expression that evolved during the 1970s and early 1980s. Seventh Day Adventists, for example, forbidden by their faith to bear arms, were quietly exempted from military service, although they were drafted as medics, drivers, and cooks. Jehovah's Witnesses, on the other hand, were jailed for refusing induction. No Bibles of any denomination were published in Cuba after 1959 although, unlike the bans in the Soviet Union and in Eastern Europe before 1990, they were permitted to be imported as long as they were distributed free.[47]

The Castro regime also softened its previously harsh stance against Afro-Cuban cults, especially the public practice of santería, a Yoruba ritual involving animal sacrifice, brought to Cuba's shores by African slaves in the nineteenth century and earlier. Castro's reasons for the change were pragmatic: in the late 1970s, Cuba was becoming militarily involved in Africa, and Castro needed to curry favor with the Afro-Cuban population as well as with diplomats from the countries of black Africa. The spiritual leader of the Yorubas, His Majesty Oba Okundade Sijuwade Olubuse II, was welcomed to Cuba in June 1987 by Castro himself as well as several members of the Cuban Politboro.[48] There were other reasons for the softening of attitude: the African presence in Cuba was given importance in the revolutionary campaign to disassociate itself from the colonial legacy of Spain and the United States.[49]

The regime treated the Jews who remained in Cuba with solicitude. Newspapers, radio, and television devoted considerable coverage to Jewish holidays and cultural events "all out of proportion to the size of the Jewish community," in the words of Maurice Halperin.[50] Castroites lent the events their own revolutionary language, presumably a sign of respect: Passover was a commemoration of "national liberation," the Warsaw Ghetto uprising an example of "heroic armed struggle against Nazi-Fascists." Cubans who traced their ancestry back to Jewish roots casually affirmed the possible connection with a modicum of pride but made no effort to embrace Judaism. Foreign visitors wearing visible Stars of David attracted no specific attention, possibly because post-Castro Cubans learned not to be drawn into compromising arguments, or perhaps because being Jewish—as opposed to being a Zionist—remained vaguely acceptable.[51]

The Catholic church was initially treated more severely than the Jewish minority. Although church property was nationalized and Catholic schools closed, seminaries and churches were kept open by Castro after 1959, the religious freedom permitted subject to the discretion of religious officials and always taking the form of self-censorship. Church spokesmen today have come to talk the language of the revolution, blaming poverty elsewhere in the world on "capitalistic excess," attacking the "counter-revolutionary" attitudes of the "privileged." This was not the case at the beginning of the revolutionary regime, when the Cuban bishops formulated and delivered at Mass a general declaration against communism. But by 1969, the church had turned to criticizing the United States for imposing suffering on the Cuban people. Conservative Spanish priests had departed with the exodus of the middle class; parochial schools were shut by decree. Francisco Oves, archbishop of Havana, described the mission of the church in Cuba to be the recognition of "the human and evangelical values which converge in Christianity and Socialism."[52]

Pent-up anger over the atmosphere of corruption at least partially explains the wave of relief that greeted Castro's seizure of power in 1959, accompanied by mobs sacking the gambling casinos and other symbols of the toppled regime's glitter. Reaction to the pre-1959 atmosphere may also explain the new regime's puritanism. The Cuban Catholic church in the 1950s as well as after the Revolution backed moral stringency; priests spoke out against the moral degeneracy of "free enterprise" governments and backed Castro's stern measures to eliminate vice. Churchmen even adopted the new language. A Cuban priest remarked in 1964 that "in moral terms, Cuba before Castro seemed the creature of its 'decadent capitalist bourgeoisie.'"[53]

The revolutionary government's relations with the church, especially with such anti-Communist church-linked organizations as Acción Católica and Agrupación Catolica Universitaria, worsened as the new regime's Communist ideology came to the fore. After the failed Bay of Pigs invasion in 1961, the number of priests and nuns in Cuba diminished from 723 to 120. State censorship extended to religious publications and radio broadcasts, although weekly half-hour radio talks in Yiddish were permitted to continue, the only foreign-language broadcasts left on the air. Private schools were nationalized and church property confiscated. Cemeteries were placed under government control; as a consequence, burial costs were assumed by the state.[54] In the mid-1980s, though, the regime lessened its pressure against organized religion, granting concessions to spiritual leaders considered sympathetic. In interviews published in a widely distributed book about Castro by Brazilian Frei Betto, *Fidel and Religion*, Castro was portrayed as "trying to reconcile Christian teaching with Marxism-Leninism."[55] The new atmosphere not only improved relations between the regime and practicing Catholics, but it spilled over into institutional relations with the remaining Jewish community.

Even during the revolutionary government's antireligious campaign, Castro bent over backwards not to persecute Jews.[56] He declared an official three-day period of mourning in late April 1963 when news came of the death of Israeli president Yitzhak Ben-Zvi. Algeria's Mohammad Ben Bella supposedly rescinded an invitation to Castro because of this action.[57] Associations with the Jewish community at the outset reflected Batista's: warm, friendly, protectively guaranteeing the right of minorities to practice their religions without interference. Jews and other religious minorities, including worshipers of African dieties (santeros), suddenly found themselves, in official rhetoric, treated as hothouse flowers, exhibited as examples of religious freedom under socialism.[58] All five synagogues continued to function, although most of their members flocked into exile; no property was taken; and Jewish religious and communal buildings as well as cemeteries were extended maintenance by the state, although, like most public buildings in Cuba, they were allowed to decay.[59]

Jewish private schools were initially exempted from the nationalization decree, although the Centro Israelita's Colegio Theodor Herzl was nationalized. Built to accommodate up to 2,000 students, in the mid-1970s its student body had shrunk to about 30. The building was then appropriated as a public school, Albert Einstein, although afternoon classes were still offered in Hebrew, Yiddish, and Jewish history, available to any students at the school who elected to take them. The government subsidized two buses to transport Jewish children to the school from distant locations. But all of these special arrangements were canceled in 1975, ostensibly for lack of interest and the shortage of teachers able to teach Jewish subjects, although two classrooms were set aside for the use of afternoon instruction in Judaism.[60] Yiddish again became the Jewish community's general language, as so many of those who elected not to leave Cuba were middle-aged or older.

By December 1961, the end of the first stage of the exodus, at least 3,800 Jews had departed Cuba and another 1,000 were readying to leave.[61] On January 1, 1962, on the third anniversary of the Revolution, a group of veteran Jewish Communists and a hundred pro-Castro Jewish students seized the marble-columned Patronato and "took control of the Jewish colony."[62] Yedioth-Jewish Cuba coeditor David Autiansky, in a speech on the occasion of Israel's fourteenth anniversary of independence in 1962, sounded a bleak note:

The celebration of this anniversary is a bit beclouded. . . . Thousands of Jews in the community here are missing. This we mourn very much. We wish to emphasize without any question that we do not encourage any departure from Cuba. We want to make it very clear that we do not criticize the Cuban Jews who have by their own free will left the country. We go on record in stating the following: those who wish to leave Cuba have a right to do so. But we regret that they make such a decision. This movement causes emotional upsets for those of us Jews who live here in peace and wish to remain in Cuba.[63]

Privately, some expressed a much greater degree of fear. A Canadian visitor to Havana in 1962 found that in individual homes, or in the privacy of a synagogue office, "anyone I met told me quite openly about the terror of the regime, the ruination of which has fallen on the country as a whole, and the brutal nature of the communist regime."

It was not only a question of having spoken to persons of middle class bourgeois origin who had been expropriated and regretted the loss of their holdings. I spoke to persons who were in no way affected by the regime. . . . What these people are distressed by (to use a mild word) is the constant terror, the uncertainty, the informing (or as they use the Hebrew word—m'seerah) that goes on. In each city block and large apartment house there exist units of a "Committee for the Defense of the Revolution" who watch people as they come and go, and who, if they don't like particularly the color of your hair or the way you conduct yourself, have the right to arrest you. You are subject to arrest under any suspicion and can be informed on by a personal enemy.[64]

When a Jewish community leader found some good words to say about the regime—that now people even from the lowest level of the population could seek an education—his wife reminded him sharply that they had to tune in Castro's televised speech earlier in the week "for fear of the servant who had asked them why they were not watching it."[65] Others suffered more personal losses. Samuel and Sara Cohen's children left for exile in South Florida in 1962, but they remained behind and celebrated the birthday in absentia of their grandson Samy (fig. 68).

By 1962 it had become obvious that Castro's Revolution would survive. Those who still considered themselves Jews adopted a new profile. Ashkenazic and Sephardic customs became conflated as the community dwindled in size. Sephardim now ate at the nationalized kosher restaurant, referring to its food as "la cuisine Yidish."[66] The ratio of Ashkenazim to Sephardim was now forty to sixty, the reverse of what it had been. More Jews proportionately now lived in the provinces; Havana's Jews, presumably more prosperous, were

68. Birthday party for absent grandchild, Havana, ca. 1963. Courtesy of Lucia Suárez.

more likely to leave. Few young Jews were left. At the other end of the scale were Jews in ill-health, supported now by international Jewish welfare agencies, and Jews with special problems. Among them was a group of 200 to 250 aging Jews who had come to Cuba in the 1920s from Turkey. Before 1959 they had made a living from itinerant peddling, but the Revolution outlawed it. They were ineligible to emigrate to the United States because they were childless. There were 72 Jews in prison for currency offenses, mostly for changing pesos to dollars. Because they had been jailed by revolutionary committees rather than under the regular legal system, there was little that could be done for them; next to political crimes, theirs was viewed as one of the most serious. It was even considered dangerous for anyone other than wives or husbands to visit them in jail.[67]

Virtually all of Cuba's Jews still identifying themselves with the community departed during the early years of Castro's socialism. Anyone who wanted to do so could, except after July 26, 1963, when all males between fifteen and fifty were held liable for military service. The oft-cited claim that nationalization of businesses and socialization of the economy, and not discrimination or anti-Semitism, was the main reason that the Jewish community left is largely accurate. The first wave left in reaction to the appropriation of hotels, banks, large businesses, and factories in 1960, and a second when small businesses were nationalized in 1968. Cuban Jews in exile excoriated Castro and his Marxist-Leninist revolution, joining their voices to the outcry of exiled Cubans who took up new lives, mostly in the United States. There was little room for moderation: few in the exile community were inclined to recognize the regime's improvements in social conditions for the poorest elements of the population, especially after Cuba's official adoption of a Third World anti-Zionist posture, which was thinly veiled anti-Semitism, in 1966.

The Cold War: Cuba and Israel

Even at the height of the cold war, a foreign observer (otherwise predisposed to find evidence of official hostility by Cuba's revolutionary government toward religious expression) admitted that the regime was "beyond criticism in its respect for and consideration of Jewish religious needs."[68] Yet young Jews were said to avoid going to synagogue for fear of damaging their careers. Advancement required membership in the Communist party and precluded the active practice of religion of any denomination. In addition, the constant barrage against Israel in the media and in Fidel Castro's speeches took its toll, creating an undercurrent of distrust and hostility toward Jews even though Cubans were less and less likely to come into contact with any as time passed.[69]

Until 1973 Cuban policy toward Israel remained cautious and neutral. Without publicity, Israel sent about twenty technicians and agricultural experts to the island, helping with projects in irrigation, fishery development, and citrus production.[70] Cubans also were sent to Israel for technical training. Many of these arrangements were made by Ricardo Subirana y Lobo, an early backer of the Fidelistas, and through the auspices of the Israel-Cuba Friendship Society, administered through the kibbutz movement.[71] Initially, Castro's government maintained Batista's policy of total support for the state of Israel. The early relationship between Castro Cuba and Jerusalem was characterized as "correct" and "almost cordial" at the official level.[72] According to Isaac Silber, former leader of the Cuban branch of the Hashomer Hatzair, the youth socialist Zionist movement, who emigrated to Israel in 1949 but revisited Cuba in the early 1960s, the original Fidelistas were much more favorably disposed toward Israel than was Cuba's orthodox pre-1959 Communist party, the pro-Soviet Communist organization. Pro-Israel Castroites included partisans of the Twenty-sixth of July movement as well as those in the Sierra Maestra group. Individual loyalists in the Partido Socialista Popular, which Castro took over in 1965—most importantly, Carlos Rafael Rodríguez—had maintained contacts with Hashomer Hatzair in the 1940s and were not antagonistic to Zionist goals.

The revolutionary government accepted resident Israeli ministers in Havana, first Dr. Yoachim Prato (1961–63), then Haim Yaari (1963–65). Yaari testified that Castro's friendliness had been extraordinary.[73] Israeli policy in those years sought to cultivate ties with nonaligned nations through programs of technical aid in an effort to counter anti-Israel propaganda from the Arab states. At one point early in 1960, Tel Aviv considered Cuba as a potential link to Third World countries, but a visit by Soviet Foreign Minister Mikoyan to Havana in February 1960 threw cold water on that initiative.

Some basis for hope remained that Cuba would not follow blindly the Moscow line during the years of Soviet hegemony over the island. Fidel Castro, after all, had grown up in Cuban cultural and intellectual circles that were sympathetic to the victims of nazism. The Cubans identified with the Israeli struggle for independence in 1948, and the Castroites initially saw Israel as a model socialist nation. Although Batista had been equally friendly, there had been no exchange of ambassadors between 1951 and 1960. Sender Kaplan of the *Havaner Lebn* served as Israel's honorary consul for several years. The Israeli consulate opened in Havana in 1952 and diplomatic relations were established in 1954, when the Israeli minister to Mexico, Joseph Kessari, presented his credentials in Cuba. Still, Cuba remained the only one of the seventeen Latin American states with representation in Israel not to send diplomats with the rank of ambassador.[74]

There were other early manifestations of friendship toward Israel, perhaps surprising because of Castro's reputation even among the Soviets as a "hotheaded man."[75] Jews requesting permission to emigrate from Cuba to Israel in 1961, as mentioned earlier, were afforded preferential treatment and permitted to take valuables and personal property with them, and Cubana Airlines flew several hundred émigrés to Israel on special flights. Even while Fidel's brother Raúl visited Egypt's President Nasser in 1960, Cuba's state-controlled press remained sympathetic to Israel. Over time, however, most of this good will evaporated, a victim of Cuba's move to consolidate its self-defined position as a Third World spokesperson. After the 1962 missile crisis, Havana blamed the Soviet Union for caving in to the United States and began to assert its own leadership with the nonaligned countries. Castro urged nonaligned countries to align themselves with socialist countries, giving particular emphasis to the need to support national liberation movements around the globe and to lend aid to peoples aspiring to independence, as in Angola, Mozambique, Belize, Puerto Rico, and, of course, Palestine.[76] Cuba watchers argued that Castro was losing popularity at home, and he needed to find an issue that would enhance his image and spread his influence internationally.[77] By resisting pressure to sever relations completely with the Jewish state, Castro demonstrated his autonomy in a way, and his embrace of the Arab League's position was always cautious and muted.

Privately, Castro was reported to admire Israel, the tenacity of its armed forces, and its struggle for independence against the British. Told by a visitor that the name Castro was common among Spanish marranos, he is said to have asked one of his aides, Nuñez Jiménez, to check his ancestry; the finding was that his father's (Angel Castro's) side of the family from Galicia may possibly have been converted Jews. His mother, Lina Ruz, was of Lebanese origin. A joke circulated in Cuba by anti-Castroites noted that, given his mother's origins, El Líder, educated by Jesuits, would have been an ideal member of the rightist Lebanese Christian Falange.[78] Voices on Israel's Left, in turn, reciprocated his sympathetic posture. "For us," a MAPAM (United Workers' Party) spokesman, Mordechai Nahumi, said in 1963, "this [Cuban] revolution is also a symbol, because, while it is socialist, at the same time it is free of some of the negative phenomena which in the past accompanied the development of socialism in some countries."[79] Castro was heard to consider Arab governments with which he dealt duplicitous. But from his ideology, a pro-Arab, pro-Palestinian position flowed naturally. Palestinian fighters were welcomed as brothers-in-arms against imperialism and as fellow *guerrilleros*. As Yoram Shapira points out, the "legitimization of the terrorist organizations as a national liberation movement" meant that Cuba would have to take a stand against Israel, and with the radical/progressive Arabs against the so-called moderate/reactionary Arabs as well.[80] In an interview with a Mexican journalist published in *Granma*, Castro revealed his frustration over the issue: "The Federal Republic of Germany has been paying Israel cash compensation for the Nazis' genocide against the Jews," he declared. "Who is paying compensation for the deliberate destruction of our people's lives and riches throughout the centuries?"[81]

Castro obtained major political mileage at the First Tricontinental Conference of Solidarity with the Peoples of Asia, Africa, and Latin America, which he hosted in Havana in early January 1966. At this conference, efforts by Arab governments to brand Zionism as racist came to fruition. Most Latin American countries went along with the resolution condemning Zionism as "an imperialist movement by nature" whose methods were "racist and fascist." The conference also censured the state of Israel, although reportedly some governments later questioned the actions of their representatives, who were for the most part left-wing nationals. Castro himself was reported to have been embarrassed by the anti-Zionist resolution, which drew sharp opposition from "Jewish leftist groups" (the term applied by a foreign observer), who blasted the proponents of the anti-Zionist resolution as "war-mongers." High Cuban officials emphasized to Jerusalem that the Cuban government did not consider Cuba alone responsible for resolutions adopted at the Tricontinental Conference "and was not committed to them." Cuban publications containing the text of the Tricontinental Conference "often omitted the resolution adopted against Zionism and the State of Israel."[82]

For a time after the 1968 Second General Conference of Latin American Bishops at Medellín, Colombia, Cuban intellectuals supported the statement of the conference that the despair of Latin American peoples was linked to the historic suffering of "Israel of old." Out of this concept, in 1971, came the arguments of liberation theology, first enunciated by the Peruvian priest Gustavo Gutiérrez.[83] The movement complemented the Castro regime's emphasis on popular mobilization and opened a path by which the Cubans could sidestep their hostility to organized religion by championing the power of the poor in history and the virtues of cross-cultural solidarity. Cuba now actively identified itself with Third World opposition to imperialism and neocolonialism. Antagonism to the state of Israel began to harden, made worse by the fact that the Israeli government was publicly identified with the government side in many countries challenged by national liberation struggles. In Central America, Israel became a major supplier of arms to right-wing dictatorships from Guatemala to Panama.

Cuba's diplomatic relations with Jerusalem continued to deteriorate, although Castro attempted to demonstrate Cuba's autonomy from Moscow by still refusing, alone among the Communist bloc except for Rumania, to break relations with Israel.[84] The Cuban leader, in an interview with *New Statesman* and *Nouvel Observateur* correspondent K. S. Karol, replied to criticism from pro-Moscow Latin American Communist party delegates: although Cuba objected to Israel's actions, he said, it also recognized Israel's right to exist. "True revolutionaries," he explained to Karol, "would never threaten a whole country with extermination."[85] But at the same time, *Granma* and the rest of the Cuban press came to rely almost entirely on Arab and Soviet sources for news of the Middle East. *Granma*'s language was typical: "As long as the voice of the

Palestinian combatants—expressed through their AK-10s, bazookas and mortars—is not heeded and respected, there will be no solution in the Middle East."[86] Havana formally broke with Jerusalem at the Conference of Non-Aligned Nations at Algiers in September 1973, a month before the Yom Kippur War.

Where Cuban diplomats had previously muted their attacks on the state of Israel, the rhetoric now escalated. Before the war, most African countries and Guyana cut off relations with Israel, and the Arab bloc mounted heavy pressure on Castro to do the same. Cuban political analysts for the first time publicly endorsed the militant Palestinian cause, calling Palestine Liberation Organization (PLO) fighters guerrilleros and likening them to Castro's Twenty-sixth of July movement. Havana now declared its support of "progressive" Arabs against "reactionary" Arabs.[87] Cuba sent an armored brigade to Syria to instruct Palestinian fighters. Cuban officers in June 1973 allegedly trained South Yemeni pilots to fly the then-advanced MIG-21 jet fighters.[88] At the Fourth Summit Conference of Non-Aligned States three months later, Libya's Muammar al-Qaddafi complained that Cuba was not truly a nonaligned nation because it had joined the Soviet orbit. Castro's abrupt announcement at the summit meeting of his decision to break with Israel likely represented his effort to demonstrate his ideological agreement with the members of the Arab League.[89] Cuban officers and troops were sent to Angola, worked with Libya to run a military training program in Somalia, and cooperated with Idi Amin's regime in Uganda.[90]

Cuba also began to act as the principal supporter in the region of the PLO's campaign for full diplomatic status. Anti-Israel and anti-Zionist proclamations became routine, issued even in settings with nothing to do with the Middle East. Yassir Arafat was awarded the National Order of the Bay of Pigs (Playa Girón) by President Osvaldo Dorticós on a visit to Havana in 1974. By this time, Israel had become a "central issue" in Cuba's anti-imperialist campaign.[91] Cuban Foreign Office officials took prominent roles in UN agencies and subgroups organized to aid the Palestinian cause: the United Nations Relief and Works Agency for Palestine Refugees (UNRWA), the Regional Seminars on the Question of Palestine, and, later, the United Nations Committee on the Exercise of the Inalienable Rights of the Palestinian People (UNCIR). Cuba's support remained mostly verbal, however; between 1950 and 1984, Cuba's total contribution to UNRWA was only 2 percent of Argentina's and 3 percent of Mexico's.[92]

In some ways, playing the PLO card backfired for Cuba. While this stance won praise from the Arab and nonaligned countries, it distanced Cuba from many of its traditional neighbors. Latin American states made up more than a third of the two-thirds majority backing partition of Palestine in 1947, thereby allowing the state of Israel to come into existence. Only Guyana in addition to Cuba was willing to host meetings of the Regional Seminar on Palestine; Panama and Argentina backed out in 1981 and 1986, presumably in deference to the United States. The majority of the Latin American countries declined even to send delegates, although all of the Latin American states had voted to hold the meetings. Even though most of the participants were Guyanese or Cubans, the meetings were considered a breakthrough for the PLO cause in the Latin American and Caribbean region.[93]

The way Israelis were treated in Castro's Cuba reflected the regime's deliberate effort to treat individuals differently from Israel as a political entity. Although individual Israelis were permitted to visit Cuba and tended to be treated cordially, government radio stations frequently carried diatribes against Israel as "the Yanqui lackey." The most strident attacks were broadcast during the weekly Yiddish-language "Yevsektzia" program in the early 1960s, run by and in the name of the eighteen Jews who had been active Communists before Castro came to power. Cuban relations with the PLO became so close that Havana was accused of cooperating with Palestinian radicals in arms trafficking and of using Palestinian channels to import arms for guerrilla groups in El Salvador, Guatemala, and Chile. Havana eventually recognized the PLO formally, accepting the credentials of the PLO ambassador, Imad Jada'a, in March 1985.[94] Cuban diplomats maintained privately that the anti-Israel line was political and not linked to any bad feelings toward Jews. But among many Cubans the line was finely drawn, and confusing. Cuba's new extreme anti-Zionist policy put Cuban Jews in an awkward position, especially as the focus of their communal activities after the war had mostly been within the framework of the Zionist Federation. (Even the anti-Zionist policy was never all-embracing, however. The Cuban Zionist Federation [Unión Sionista] was permitted to continue to function openly until 1978, and permission

was granted in 1974 and 1975 to hold large, outdoor rallies in celebration of Israeli Independence Day.)[95] A veteran Cuban diplomat,
Hector Aguililla Saladrigas, claimed after his defection to the
United States that the Cuban embassy in Damascus routinely
shipped arms and ammunition to pro-Marxist groups in the Bekka
Valley.[96] Cuba quickly became one of the most strident supporters of
the radical Palestinian cause, and, following from this posture, an
implacable political opponent of the state of Israel, the "Jewish
lobby," and Zionism in the international arena.[97] The Cuban press
painted Israelis, regardless of political viewpoint, as right-wing fa-
natics determined to drive out Arabs and to expand Israeli territory
through aggression and imperialism.

Nor was any hint of pluralism permitted to survive in Cuba itself.
Many of the Cuban Jews who had stayed now distanced themselves
from Jewish communal organizations, fearing they would be labeled
Zionists by association. Fidel Castro's Revolution thoroughly and
inalterably changed the way Cubans lived. Decree laws prohibited
extravagancia, taken to include anything from clothing to surrealist
art to homosexual behavior; *predelincuencia*, literally, predelin-
quent ideas—ideological deviationism, punishable by prison up to
fifteen years; and *peligrosidad*, or dangerousness, used against "per-
ilous" intellectuals, supposed Israeli agents, fifth columnists, and
other deviants.[98] The government leveled caustic attacks against
entrepreneurs and businessmen who had prospered during the postwar years. The regime prided itself on smashing such "capitalistic
tendencies" as "commodity fetishism," "economism," abuses of
prices and profits, and other free enterprise mechanisms. Cuban
Jews, many of whom had thrived under the old system, with its
rewards for high risks and its reliance on petty (and not-so-petty)
corruption to smooth things through, were targeted not because
they were Jews but because they were seen as economic villains.[99]

Like all Cuban citizens who remained on the island, Jews were
subject to the scrutiny of the Committees of the Defense of the
Revolution, the CDRs.[100] The question of the Holocaust exacer-
bated tensions. Movies treating the subject of Jews during the war
("The Garden of the Finzi-Continis," "Sophie's Choice," and similar films) did not circulate or had their Jewish content downplayed
or entirely ignored by critics. The Holocaust period was taught in
Cuban schools as part of a required tenth-grade syllabus on the
history of world communism and movements of national liberation.

In the entire segment on the 1930s and 1940s, which included sections on World War II resistance movements, German military aggression, the war in Asia, repercussions of the war in Latin America, the end of the war, Potsdam, and the Nuremberg trials, the words "Jew," "Jewish," "genocide," and "refugee" did not appear once. There was no mention of concentration or death camps, no reference to the word *Holocaust,* although the text referred to Nazi "cruelty and sadism," the death of "54 million people" and "crimes" of Hitler, Goebbels, Himmler, and Goering.[101] An article on Auschwitz published in 1980 in *Granma* never once mentioned Jews: "Between July 14, 1940 and January 27, 1945," it stated, "more than four million persons died . . . people of different nationalities, different languages, different customs and different ideas."[102] When the word *Holocaust* was used in Castro's Cuba, many young people assumed that it referred to the atomic conflagration at Hiroshima and Nagasaki at the end of World War II. The Star of David appeared frequently in editorial page political cartoons, linked with the swastika. Israeli leaders were depicted in cartoons as Nazis, vampires, and dogs.

Even intellectuals who professed to know about Nazi victimization of the Jews addressed the theme obliquely, as if hesitant to offer their comments. Alfredo and Liliano Calviño, employees of the Cuban Film Institute in Havana, when asked what they understood about the Holocaust, responded that it had occurred at "Hiroshima and Nagasaki, where there was a bomb and many people died." When prodded with specific questions about the fate of Jews and the Nazi ovens, Alfredo, who had studied in the Soviet Union, remarked that he knew that the Nazis had held "racist" ideas against Jews as well as non-Jews. Both interviewees said that they had seen the film "Diary of Anne Frank" and read *Judgment at Nuremberg* but thought that their value was to teach "about one of the most terrible pages of human history"—also without reference to the Jewish status of the victims. Asked whether the wartime fate of European Jewry influenced the way he viewed the state of Israel, Francisco León, a Film Institute employee who, unlike his colleagues, was willing to talk about Nazi treatment of Jews (and who had visited Auschwitz during a trip to Poland) replied:

No . . . I have nothing against the Jews, but I am hostile to the Israelis, who think they can persecute the Palestinians because they, as Jews,

were victims. This gives them no right. I do not feel sympathetic because they were victims during the Second World War. . . . We cannot
deny that Jews have been murdered throughout history. But we have to
think of the rights of others affected by the creating of a Jewish
State.[103]

León, moreover, claimed that only after 1960 did the press reveal
facts about the extermination in camps of millions of "Jews and
Poles." This assertion counters all other evidence that shows that
the press before 1960 treated the issue in the same way as in the
West. It was after the Revolution that the Holocaust came to be
presented as a campaign against anti-Fascists, never mentioning
Jews.

Ironically, most of the Cubans who might have continued to harbor anti-Semitic prejudices were the first to emigrate: the former
Cuban upper class as well as the former Spanish immigrants, whose
economic conflicts with Jews in the 1920s and 1930s fueled so many
of the anti-Semitic actions of the prewar period.[104] Three thousand
Cuban Jews emigrated in the fourteen months after July 1959, including most of the leaders of Jewish communal organizations. The
Cuban Hebrew Sephardic Center inaugurated a new building in
1959 but held only one social event—a Purim party—before the
center closed down. Most of the Jews who resisted leaving were
either the older residents of the Orthodox community located in the
Old City who had loved ones buried in the cemetery, or those who
had intermarried or otherwise ceased Jewish observance.

In late 1977, Bernardo Benes, a Cuban lawyer and banker in
Miami exile whose father had begun as a peddler in Matanzas and
had become a wealthy manufacturer and businessman, started to act
as a broker between Castro and the Carter and Reagan administra-
tions to permit as many as 10,000 more Cubans to leave, many of
them political prisoners. Benes visited Cuba by his own estimate
seventy-five times between 1978 and 1986. On one of his last trips,
he carried back to Miami the Torah scrolls from the Patronato,
which he had served as a pro bono legal counsel. In 1980, Benes's
"Freedom Flights" were supplanted by the massive boatlift from the
port of Mariel, which replaced the smaller port of Camarioca as the
site from which boats carrying refugees left the island. Most of
the 100,000 refugees in this wave were lower class and mulatto or

black, in contrast to the middle-class, mostly white emigration of the early 1960s, but among them were an estimated 60 to 100 Jews. The Mariel flotilla revealed Castro's cruel side: in his eyes, the *marielitos* were unwanted human garbage, and he cleaned out his prisons and mental hospitals, dumping in the United States thousands of persons who did not fit within the criteria of approved revolutionary behavior.

Among the 1980 refugees were a thousand children and adolescents suffering from every disability from diabetes to schizophrenia. All came to South Florida, and most remained there, to the burden of the region's social agencies. The principal organization accepting responsibility for the Jewish arrivals was the Greater Miami Jewish Federation Resettlement Task Force, whose personnel had been working with earlier Soviet immigrants to the region.[105] A religious census reported that only 807 observant Jews, nearly all elderly, remained in Cuba, most of them in Havana's crumbling Old City.[106] Relations with the Cuban Communist party were formally cordial, concentrating in the 1980s on assistance for the remaining Jews.[107]

In late 1965 only 1,900 Jews still lived in Havana and another 400 in the provinces. A good portion were in their fifties and sixties. Eight families continued to worship at the United Hebrew Congregation. Most Jewish organizations except the Patronato had ceased to exist, and communal functions passed to the Cuban government. From 1960 to 1961, the Patronato incurred a deficit of $90,989, which its remaining officers asked the Joint in New York to pay off in the form of a loan.[108] Of the nearly 10,000 Jews who left Cuba, 85 percent went to South Florida; the rest went to Israel, Canada, and other Latin American countries. About half of the arrivals in Florida stayed there; the others went mostly to the New York City area. The newcomers in New York settled in Brooklyn in a neighborhood dubbed "Santos Tzoris" (Holy Misfortune), a pun on the name of the affluent Havana suburb of Santos Suárez where many had lived.[109] Fewer than a thousand resettled Cuban Jewish refugees needed relief assistance in the United States. The Ashkenazic and Sephardic communities remained separated in exile, just as in Cuba. We will likely never know the exact number of Jewish immigrants to Cuba who managed to move on to the United States between 1924 and 1959 because some entered under one or another legal guise, including marrying U.S. citizens, and others entered illegally. We do have, on the other hand, a clearer sense of how many Jews made aliya, or emigrated, to Israel. Of the 68,000 immigrants to Israel from Latin America between 1948 and 1983, 700 came from Cuba, most of them immediately after the fall of Batista.[110] The Castro Revolution created a demographic catastrophe for the colony, although it must be remembered that thousands of men and women who were born Jews but who strayed from the Jewish colony remain in Cuba but are no longer included in the annual count. By 1989, an estimated 94–96 percent of the Jewish population had departed, leaving a remnant sixteen times smaller than in 1959, mostly comprised of the elderly.[111]

With their children and grandchildren, the thousands of Jews from the Old World who had sought and received refuge in Cuba found themselves obliged to leave their homes and livelihoods again. What once again facilitated the transition was the organizational network of Jewish associations. Rabbi Gambach, for example, participated in Bet Din activities in Turkey while he lived in Barcelona, in Cuba, in Mexico City (after he left Cuba in 1960), and in the United States. Early immigrants found continuity in communal loan and burial societies, and later in the synagogues, religious schools, and cultural associations. Some of these organizations were local but most of them were affiliated with international groups such as WIZO (analogous to Hadassah in the United States) and the Zionist societies. As a result, the Jews who came to the United States were able to reaffiliate in their new homeland. Some of these organizations were generically American, like the Rotary Clubs and Masonic temples; others were virtual replicas of their Cuban counterparts, like the Latin B'nai B'rith chapter, which flourished in Miami Beach, along with two Cuban Jewish synagogues, the Sephardic Congregation of Florida, and the mostly Ashkenazic Cuban-Hebrew Congregation.

The Dwindling Community

The Castro regime's gradual championing of Third World causes made life much more awkward for those Jews who opted to remain in Cuba. The PLO maintained what amounted to full diplomatic relations with Cuba and sent representatives to the Cuban-Arabic-PLO Friendship Association, a group explicitly identified with the PLO, not simply with Cuban-Arab culture.[112] University research centers in Cuba followed the standard Third World anti-Zionist line, equating Zionism with racism. Cuba, in fact, was one of three non-Arab countries to sponsor the UN "Zionism=racism" resolution (no. 3379). "Zionism," declared the director of the Center for African and Middle Eastern Studies (CEAMO) in December 1985, "is intimately related to capitalist imperialism and would not be possible without the backing of powerful circles in the international financial oligarchy."[113] The resolution, according to the English-language *Granma Weekly Review*, revealed the "identical imperialist origins and racist structure of the Israeli Zionist regime that is occupying Palestine and the one that is exploiting the black masses in South Africa."[114]

Bohemia and other Cuban magazines and newspapers regularly published political cartoons depicting Israel's Menachem Begin as a dog wearing a collar marked with a swastika, or as a willing lackey of Ronald Reagan and Adolf Hitler.[115] Perhaps the ugliest example of Cuba's endorsement of strident anti-Zionism was the 1988 publication by the PLO of a scurrilous book by Mahmud Abbas (Abu Mazzen), *La otra cara* (The Other Face). This text, with an introduction by the PLO ambassador in Cuba, Imad Jada'a, asserts that Zionists collaborated with the Nazis and that Holocaust accounts are exaggerated and claims that Zionist Jews killed more innocent victims than the Nazis. Featuring a swastika imposed on a Star of David on its front cover, the book was widely distributed in Cuba.[116] Steps taken within the Soviet Union as early as July 1988 to reassess the Holocaust and to begin to recognize the enormity of Jewish victimization saw no counterpart in Cuba.[117] Castro-era historians typically followed the Soviet line on World War II, either ignoring the murders of Jews or submerging them in the story of Fascist atrocities, referring to Nazi victims as "antifascists" without ethnic identification.[118] Cuban historical journals and other publications devoted virtually no space to the Holocaust at any time during Castro's regime.

Still, the government claimed as open-handed policy, awarding visas to Israelis who sought to attend academic and scientific meetings in Cuba, but anti-Israel articles appeared almost daily in the Cuban press. In November 1987 a Venezuelan rabbi flew to Havana with Bishop Alfredo Rodríguez of Caracas to meet with Fidel Castro

"La otra cara: La verdad de las relaciones secretas entre el nazismo y el sionismo"

Dr. Mahmud Abbas (ABU MAZZEN)

69. Book jacket, *La otra cara* (Palestine Liberation Organization, 1988).

to appeal for the right to emigrate of five Jews previously refused exit visas; he reported that in Cuba "heroism is required in order to approach the synagogue."[119]

Two congressmen, Frederick W. Richmond from Brooklyn and Richard W. Nolan from Minnesota, visited the Patronato during the first night of Hanukkah in 1977. They shared a meal of herring, matzo, boiled eggs, bread, and Spam, the latter a pragmatic concession to food shortages in Cuba. Members of the congregation assured the visitors that there was no anti-Semitism in Cuba and that the revolutionary government placed no restrictions on religious services.[120] Observant Catholics and members of other religions faced the same difficulties as religious Jews. Young people, especially, were forced by practicality to avoid religious services, as attendance jeopardized career advancement (Communist party members were barred from attending). Cubans worked on Saturdays, and church attendance on Sundays conflicted with voluntary work brigades. Only the retired, wrote a visitor, "have the luxury of religious practice."[121] In the late 1970s, religious services were still held at the Patronato (fig. 70) as well as at Temple Chevet Ahim (fig. 71), with its wall of portraits of Herzl, Israel's Chaim Weitzman, and Fidel Castro, and at Adas Israel, but nearly all of the participants were elderly. Rarely did ten people come at any time, the minimum number needed for a full Sabbath service.

In 1979 or 1980, Bernardo Benes remembers being at the Patronato when a phone call came from an old Sephardic man from Matanzas telling him that he had just handed over the keys of the synagogue to the Fidelista CDR because he was the only one left. Government agencies made some repairs to the crumbling interior of historic Sephardic Temple Chevet Ahim on Inquisidor Street, but the other synagogues remained in disrepair (see figure 72, the Sephardic synagogue's crumbling facade in December 1991). The elegant United Hebrew Congregation building lay in ruins from neglect. Occasionally foreign rabbis came to officiate at religious services, as did an ultra-Orthodox Hasidic rabbi from Brazil's Lubavitch Beit Chabad in 1985 and 1986. In 1988, Hebrew classes for a handful of children still met, but the walls of El Patronato's Grand Synagogue, built in 1953 in mansion-filled Vedado by the affluent postwar generation, stood riddled with termites. The roof leaked, and skeletal remains of dead birds that had fallen from nests in the rafters lay on the floor of the main sanctuary. The building needed $50,000 in repairs, not likely to be forthcoming in the impoverished Cuba of the 1990s.[122] Efforts to make repairs confronted the typical dilemma in revolutionary Cuba: there were funds, but no materials. The old fruit and vegetable market at Acosta and Cuba streets—the Plaza de los Polacos—had long disappeared, along with the Jewish-owned retail stores in Habana Vieja. Adas Israel still served 120 members in 1990, and old men met there to talk and play dominos. Rather than nationalize the Centro Sefardí Synagogue, the government rented it as a practice hall for an orchestra as a way to keep it going and defray maintenance costs. "The government does what it can to facilitate a nor-

70. Templo Unión Hebrea Chevet Ahim, Havana. Courtesy of Ruth Behar.

mal Jewish life for the . . . Jews who still remain in Cuba," concluded a typical report by a visiting foreign mission to the island.[123]

Throughout the Castro period, the major responsibility for looking after the needs of the Cuban Jewish community fell to the World
Jewish Congress, mainly through its Canadian affiliate, the Canadian Jewish Congress. Canada never broke diplomatic relations with
Cuba; as a result, communications remained open, and Canadians
were not required to obtain visas to enter the country. The Canadians, as well as representatives from the Central Jewish Committee
of Mexico and some Venezuelan groups, coordinated the foreign assistance. Annually, at Passover, the Canadians sent matzos, horse-
radish, tea, chicken loaf, and ceremonial wine for the dwindling

71. Services at Patronato, 1992. Courtesy of Tequila Minsky.

numbers of observant Jews. Always the Cuban government formally pledged cooperation, which was dutifully acknowledged by the foreign bureaus. The food donated by the Canadians was allowed to be sold at a synagogue to persons registered on the Passover list. The resulting income was deposited in a community welfare fund to assist needy families and, according to the Canadian Jewish Congress representative, amounted to the "main source of revenue maintaining the Jewish institutions."[124]

Some help came from the United States as well. Foreign-born officials of U.S. Jewish agencies traveled frequently to Cuba.[125] In 1988 authorities permitted a Beechcraft private plane to land twice on Cuban soil. It was piloted by a New Jersey businessman, Jack Rosen, who carried six cases of kosher wine, boxes of matzo, and enough gefilte fish to supply two community seders held at the Patronato. The mission coincided with the visit of the first interfaith delegation to Cuba, headed by the U.S.-based Appeal of Conscience Foundation, to assess Cuba's church-state relations and to evaluate the extent of religious freedom.[126] Each synagogue received an extra portion of Passover products, a kind of incentive for congregants to attend.

72. At Temple Chevet-Ahim, 1990. By permission of Mark Asnin.

Not all efforts worked smoothly. Chicken legs were substituted for the traditional lamb shank at Passover seders because lamb was never available. A shipment of 16,500 pounds of kosher-for-Passover matzo, cooking oil, and grape juice was delayed for more than three weeks in 1986 by "bad weather" and was never unloaded, although Jewish leaders dutifully said that it had been distributed.[127] Cooking oil was especially important because the Cuban staple has always been lard. In April 1989 the government permitted a private chartered plane to fly from Miami with kosher food provided by the Appeal of Conscience Foundation.

Some Jews attempted to make peace with the Revolution and did not shy away from defending the state of Israel in public, although it often cost them their jobs. Most of these individuals, like Jack Barrocas, eventually either stopped talking openly or emigrated. A few individuals struggled to maintain tradition. Moisés Baldas led the remaining community from the early 1960s until he emigrated to Israel in 1981. Dr. José Miller Fredman, a maxillofacial surgeon and professor at the medical school, took his place as nominal leader of the community and the Patronato's president and did his best to soothe relations between the government and the dwindling community. "If at any time coldness existed with Castro," he stated to visitors in 1989, "it no longer exists."[128] A Sephardic Jew, Roberto Fliss, learned to sound the shofar used in the Yom Kippur service. In 1992, thirty-nine-year-old Moisés Asís, a man of indefatigable energy, maintained contacts with outside support groups and served as an unofficial historian for the dwindling community. His autobiography reflects the life of a man who followed a different path, but remained eminently conscious of his heritage.

Only when I was in my teens I learned about my past. At Chanukah, my mother ate pork on the eve of my birth and had an eclampsia during her partus labor: miraculously I was born and we both survived. It was on December 15, 1952, in Havana, in the first year of Batista's dictatorship. My paternal grandparents (surnames Asís and Lévy) came from Turkey and Greece, respectively. One of my maternal grandparents (surnames Córdova and Alcalá) came from Spain, the other was born in Cuba. Mine was a non-religious, non-traditional home, and my boyhood was the same as any other middle-class Cuban. My name was different, of course, I had been circumcised (something rare for Cuban boys), and I wore a *magen David* around my neck. We didn't eat pork at home or cook in non-vegetable oil, and once a year there was fast day. From my childhood I only remember a visit to the Sephardic synagogue on a Saturday morning and a Passover seder at my grandparents' and the taste of *matzoh*.

My father, being an idealist, embraced Fidel Castro's revolution with messianic fervor. He completely quit his profitable business and, until our savings became exhausted, worked day and night as an unpaid revolutionary cadre. My parents had been very poor in their childhood, and they saw the January 1959 Revolution as the repairing of all past social injustices and the elimination of poverty and discrimination. In these three decades of communism, through 1990, my father dedicated all of his time, his intelligence, and his health to the revolution, yet still had the time for university study and to write. But an idealist's home is not always comfortable for his family.

As children, we missed our father's affections and suffered the consequences of the breakdown of our home when my parents divorced. After the Revolution, our comfort disappeared, our relatives left for abroad, and our life became severely impoverished. My father's lack of personal ambitions and his honesty prevented him from reaching higher positions in the government or the Party, or a higher standard of living. Never was he rewarded; always he remained blind to his poverty and self-consuming passionate consecration to the Revolution. Although I didn't share my father's path, I learned to respect people like him and to respect any kind of idealism and honesty.

A rebel and a difficult personality from childhood, I was always maladjusted. At 14 I entered a military academy but left after a year. When classmates asked me about the Bible or about Judaism, I had no answers. A few days after my 17th birthday I was arrested and imprisoned for a year's term for "political offenses." I was still a minor, and the trial at La Cabaña's Revolutionary Court destroyed forever my faith in human justice. My criminal record stayed with me for 18 years more, because of a clerical mistake.

While I was serving my term in a forestry labor camp, I once overheard a conversation about the Middle East conflict, and an old man, an alleged communist, said: "The worst thing that Nazis did was not to kill all the Jews." Although the man was unaware of my Jewish origin, from that time I felt I was and wanted to be a Jew and that my place was with the Jews.

My life started over when I got a job as a technical draftsman and began to study after work. I married at 23, under a *chuppah* [canopy]; the entire community was invited to the wedding. My wife was not Jewish, but she has converted. Our little daughter's name is Dina Lilit.

The inevitable social isolation after my release from confinement allowed me to study a good deal and to become active in the Jewish community. I studied Hebrew and Esperanto, pursued technical subjects, wrote stories, articles, and plays, and became a member of Amnesty International. Some doors opened and other doors closed.

Although I met all requirements, I was not accepted into the Psychology program at the University of Havana, nor permitted to take a Ph.D. I continued to work as a draftsman and took degrees in Information Science and in Law. Through a fellowship from the Joint Distribution Committee, I spent six months in Argentina under a special training program at the (Conservative) Latin American Rabbinical Seminary. Although I eventually wrote ten books, more than a hundred scientific papers, and achieved international standing for my work, only my commitment to Jewish activities permitted me to be able to travel abroad a few times. Many things shaped my consciousness as a Jew: learning about the Holocaust, the eulogy in the socialist world for PLO terrorism even after the massacres in Munich and elsewhere, and my continued study of Jewish culture.

There was never anti-Semitism in Cuba. No Cuban leader ever uttered any offensive phrase or words against Jews or referred to the Jewish background of any political enemies, despite Cuba's strong political backing of the PLO and other enemies of Israel. I never saw in Cuba an anti-Semitic slogan or swastika on a wall or anywhere else. Our social situation as Jews was never worse than that of Christians and non-communist professionals and intellectuals.

My dreams have been to have a democratic and pluralistic Jewish community in Cuba, where everyone is heard, and where Jewish education has a preferential and unifying place in home and communal life. I seek to improve relations with Christians, with the State and all Cubans, and to work for an understanding between Cubans and Israelis. In 1981 I wrote a book for Cubans showing Jewish sources of human rights, social justice, and the best ideals of mankind. It was never published in spite of efforts I made to have it published abroad.

Now, in 1990, with only 635 Jews remaining—6% of the 1958 figure—intermarriage has reached 93% and assimilation is virtually complete. I still teach, as I have done since 1985, a small group of Jewish Sunday School children at "Tikkun Olam," which had been suspended in 1979. Some Fridays I lead the *kabalat shabat* services. I am very proud to be a Cuban Jew, and despite the hardships that we ten-and-a-half million Cubans face, I have inexhaustible sources of pride and social consciousness.[129]

A few institutional entities remained in 1991: the Jewish Anti-TB Society and the B'nai B'rith Maimonides Lodge, for example, which met in the former Patronato building in Vedado. Moisés Asís in 1989 and 1990 participated in the Cuban section of CEHILA, the hemispherewide association for the study of Latin American Catholicism identified with liberation theology and social action.[130] In 1987, the community organized a coordinating Jewish community structure named the Cuban Jewish Congress after the Canadian and U.S. models, to "enhance the quality of Jewish life in Cuba according to the accepted rules of Judaism."[131] But it failed, divided by internal dissention.

Ironically, one area in which Jewish Cubans who maintained their religious practices were better off than other Cubans was in meat rationing. The only private enterprise permitted in all of Cuba, in fact, was the Jewish butcher, the *shochet*, who was paid by the Jewish community during the 1970s through the Patronato and who, when they were available, slaughtered six animals weekly.[132] In 1990, Cuban families received rations of 1.5 pounds of meat and chicken every two weeks, but because the fowl arrived frozen from Bulgaria and therefore could not be made kosher, the government permitted Jewish families to receive three rations of fresh kosher meat per month.

Nonetheless, the Jewish colony as a whole neared extinction from attrition and loss of interest. When the colony's self-appointed historian, Abraham Marcus Matterín, died in 1983, his apartment, which contained thousands of clippings and other historical materials, was taken by the government.[133] At Passover in 1989, 892 persons, representing 305 families, registered to receive matzos and kosher wine. Only 7 percent of marriages in the community involved two Jewish-born partners.

Some Cuban Jews fell into step with the goals of the Revolution. A visiting Conservative rabbi from a congregation in Princeton, New

73. Site of former Jewish Market, Old Havana, 1992. Courtesy of Tequila Minsky.

Jersey, recorded the following comment from a Sephardic Jew born in Turkey who lived in Cuba from 1923 to 1928 and in the United States from 1928 to 1937, but who moved back to Cuba to open a jewelry shop:

> Rabbi, we used to have plenty to eat, whatever we wanted, and little children went hungry all over Cuba, just like they do today all over Latin America. We had all we wanted, my wife didn't have to work, she didn't have to stand in line, we didn't have rationing, but the poor went hungry. Today we don't have what we used to, but we have enough, and everybody has enough. Tell me, Rabbi, isn't that what our religion teaches?
>
> Rabbi, little girls used to walk the streets of Habana as prostitutes, and teenagers sold themselves to Americans for food and we merchants made money, not from prostitutes, God forbid, but from the system, from the atmosphere. Today there are no prostitutes, no vice, no Americans, no business. Which is better . . . ?
>
> Rabbi, you don't know how ignorant and sick the *campesino* used to be. He couldn't read, he couldn't write, he didn't have much work, he couldn't afford a doctor. Look at him today. He can read. Who taught

him? . . . There are clinics in the countryside now, and doctors, and *campesinos* live like people. *Tzelem elohim* [In the image of God], Rabbi? Do you know what that used to mean? People were so backward, so ignorant, so like animals, who could use the term? And now? They are like human beings. Doesn't our religion believe in that, Rabbi?[134]

In 1990, the number of Jews in Cuba had dwindled to roughly 305 families, most with non-Jewish spouses, in a total population of about ten million. Only fourteen families had husbands and wives both Jewish in origin. With no resident mohel on the island, Jewish boys were no longer circumcised. The last bar mitzvah in Cuba was celebrated in 1973, the last religious wedding in 1976.[135] Four out of five Jewish families lived in Havana. The community was resourceful and resilient, but there were no funds for repairs to the synagogue or for a needed facility for the elderly. A Venezuelan Jewish center provided a van to transport children to Sunday school and old people to synagogue services. There was some feeling of optimism in the aftermath of the government's better relations with organized religion after the mid-1980s. "Now children don't feel afraid to say they believe and they are Jewish," noted Adela Dworin, the librarian for the Patronato's 13,000-book collection.[136] "There's more religious freedom than five or ten years ago." With a Jewish star in its rusted grillwork, the white-tiled kosher butcher shop at 708A Cuba Street survived, distributing the three-quarters of a pound rations of beef per person per month, the only butcher shop in Cuba not run by the state. The old Flor de Berlin bakery still baked bread, although no longer of the European variety familiar to the immigrants.

Change continued to buffet the dwindling community. Cubans, especially younger ones, grew increasingly indifferent and insensitive to the meaning of Jewishness; intellectuals nonchalantly called foreign Jews who spoke against the Castro regime "Israelites," a tainted epithet because of the reviled status of the state of Israel. The sweeping reforms in Eastern Europe immediately affected the Jewish community because Cuba's traditional suppliers there stopped shipping food to Cuba. The men who attended daily prayer services at Adas Israel were given breakfast each day; the synagogue had become a kind of substitute old-age home. A community kiddush was also held weekly at the Patronato, after lay-conducted services.

With the collapse of the Berlin Wall and the exhaustion and death of state communism throughout the world, changes seemed to be inevitable, although initially Cuba remained unmoved. The cultural atmosphere continued frozen. No copies of the Bible were on sale, either the Hebrew Old Testament or the New. The films of Hector Babenco, Pedro Almodóvar, and dozens of others remained proscribed, although some were shown to a select few at film institutes. Major figures of world literature remained banned, from Cuban exiles Cabrera Infante and Heberto Padilla to Milan Kundera, Vaclav Havel, and Nobel laureate Czeslaw Milosz to all Latin American writers deemed Fascist, including Jorge Luis Borges and Mario Vargas Llosa.[137] The line that formerly separated anti-Zionism from anti-Semitism grew more fine: newspapers in late 1990 published political cartoons depicting Israeli soldiers wearing the Jewish star superimposed on the swastika, mistreating Palestinians.[138] Cuba was the only member of the UN Security Council to refuse to back the use of force against Saddam Hussein, demanding that the United Nations first condemn Israel for the death of Palestinians at the Temple Mount and require that Israel withdraw from occupied territory as a precondition to discussing the Gulf crisis.[139]

Nonetheless, there was some movement on the international political front. In mid-1990, Cuba quietly opened a channel of communication with Tel Aviv for the first time since Castro broke off relations seventeen years earlier. Latif Dori, a senior member of Israel's independent Marxist MAPAM party, visited Havana as an official guest after years of being turned down for visas. MAPAM's ties to Cuba went back to its merger with Hashomer Hatzair, the socialist youth movement that had been strong in Cuba before the Jewish colony melted away. Dori, the head of a MAPAM party committee for creating dialogue between Israelis and Palestinians, who had been jailed in Israel because of his contacts with the PLO, was obviously more acceptable to the Cubans than other Israeli politicians. Nonetheless, he represented a Zionist party within the Israeli political mainstream.[140]

Cuba also received several visits by Mike Harari, the retired Israeli intelligence officer who had served as senior adviser to Panama's deposed strongman, General Manuel Noriega. Harari, who met with Fidel Castro several times, reportedly discussed "the opening of diplomatic and commercial relations between the two countries," according to the United Army's Joint Debriefing Center in Panama.[141] Also in 1990, the semi-official Cuban Institute of Friendship with Peoples hosted an Israeli political scientist affiliated with the Truman Institute at the Hebrew University of Jerusalem as well as the University of California at Los Angeles, Dr. Edy Kaufman, and his wife. Other Israelis attended scientific, artistic, and other international congresses in Cuba on a nonofficial basis throughout the 1980s.[142]

For Cuban citizens, memories of Jews became more distant, frozen into vague stereotype. By 1990, 60 percent of the Cuban population had been born after the 1959 Revolution. "Jews were called *polacos*, regardless of where they had come from. We associated them with business, petroleum, being millionaires. They sold handmade clothing, on Muralla Street. . . . I once had a girlfriend in high school who was from a Jewish family," said Alfredo Calviño, "but I don't think about this kind of category anymore. I never say any more 'So-and-so is a santeria cultist; so-and-so is a Seventh Day Adventist.' It's not part of our vocabulary anymore."[143]

The remnants of the Jewish community shared the forced austerity of the "special peacetime period," the regime's name for the post*glasnost* years.[144] Jewishness for years had not been a comfortable fit in post-1959 Cuban society, where most Cubans defined themselves by what they opposed: anti-imperialists, anti-deviationists, and so on.[145] Changing times did not bring moderation. The more the Communist world crumbled, the deeper Castro retreated into hard-line intransigence. On December 16, 1991, Cuba was one of twenty-five states (the Arab bloc minus Kuwait, along with North Korea, Vietnam, and a handful of Third World countries still fighting the battles of the crumbling past) to vote against rescinding the UN resolution equating Zionism with racism. Still, the Cuban government, for the first time in two decades, in April 1991 allowed the Jewish community to celebrate Israeli Independence Day. The last restrictions on Cuban Jewry were being lifted, but at a time when the community had shrunk to a shadow of its former self. In October 1991, the Communist party lifted its ban on religious believers joining the party. But only a minority of Cubans had

74. Elderly woman on balcony, Old Havana, 1991. Courtesy of Ruth Behar.

been party members even before the retreat of communism elsewhere in the world, and the new policy did not entice many Jews to
join.[146]

By the 1990s, the average age of observant Cuban Jews had
climbed well beyond sixty. Decisions in behalf of the Jewish community still had to be approved by the Ministry of Religious Affairs,
which in 1990 was headed by Dr. José Felipe Carneado, a lawyer and
journalist and member of the 126-member body of the Central Committee of the Cuban Communist party. Although he and his government had been publicly supportive, outsiders believed that many
Jews in Cuba have not identified themselves as such because "it is
not helpful to be a Jew and have a government job dependent on the

Cuban Communist Party." The publication by the Cuban Ministry of Culture of the hate-filled *La otra cara* illustrated the contradictory aspect of Havana's professed abhorrence of religious discrimination of any kind.[147] Jews lived just like other Cubans, "suffering from the same lack of basic foods and goods," in the words of Moisés Asís.[148] To some, to have survived at all in the face of the exodus of all Cuban Jews who wanted to leave was a kind of miracle. To others, the miracle seemed merely a sad curiosity, a museum exhibit, a shadow.

8 ✡ LESSONS OF THE CUBAN JEWISH EXPERIENCE

Fate played a trick on the Jews who had made Cuba their home. With the exception of the Central European Jewish refugees, almost all of whom managed to enter the United States after temporary transit in Cuba for a year or less, the Jews who were the most successful in accommodating to Cuban life and who had prospered within it were the very same persons who found themselves obliged to leave after the Cuban Revolution. The stories of those who remained under the institutional umbrella of the Jewish community are well known; less so are the experiences of the thousands of Jews mostly from Eastern Europe who used Cuba as a stepping-stone to the United States before 1924, or the hundreds and possibly thousands who found ways to enter as permanent residents of the United States after Congress imposed restrictive quotas in 1924, by marrying U.S. citizens or otherwise finding loopholes in the immigration system. These individuals for practical necessity remained silent, and their stories may never be known. Finally, we understand less about those persons born to Jewish parents who did not choose to leave Castro's sovietized Cuba.[1] The dwindling colony of elderly practicing Jews is known about, of course, in part through the efforts of foreign Jewish welfare agencies to assist them and in part because the Castro government earmarked them for compassionate treatment. We know less about those secular individuals who stopped considering themselves Jews, or who converted to other religions, or who dropped away.

When the immigrants arrived in the early years of the twentieth century, there was no host community to greet them. Just as elsewhere in the region, the few Jews who had come to Cuba earlier had been almost entirely absorbed by their host societies; even though the early twentieth century witnessed several waves of Jewish arrivals, the numbers are overshadowed by other migrant populations, especially from the various regions of Spain but also from Jamaica, the Arab Middle East, China, and elsewhere. Jews totaled slightly more than 1 percent of the national population only in Argentina and Uruguay; in Cuba and the rest of Latin America, where a total of a quarter-million Jews immigrated from the Old World, the Jewish population never approached 1 percent of the whole. Furthermore, outmigration of Jews from Cuba as well as from Latin America in general always exceeded outmigration from the United States or Western Europe, and more Jews from Latin America (although not Cuba) resettled in the state of Israel than from any other part of the Diaspora.[2]

The Cuban experience differed from that of other places in Latin America where Jews emigrated. There were few differences in terms of the ethnic composition of the general population: Cuba, like most of the region, was more than half racially mixed, with another 11 percent wholly African in origin and 1 percent Chinese. Cuba achieved independence eight decades after most of its regional neighbors, however, and then only under U.S. military occupation and heavy political and economic pressure. Prejudice existed against Jews and other outsiders, but it was not institutionalized; more often than not it was petty, as in the case of the extra abuse handed out to Jewish, Asian, and Spanish arrivals at Tiscornia documented by Miguel Barnet, a non-Jew.[3] The island's colony of American Jews, complacent and completely Americanized, never assimilated at all. Among the Creole elite, only Spanish roots counted in the island's society. Americans and Europeans were allowed to do business and make their fortunes, but the new aristocracy remained aloof.[4] Cubans prided themselves on their Castilian inheritance; immigrants from other regions of Spain, especially Galicia, were treated as foreigners.

Another significant difference was the fact that while the several components of Cuba's Jewish colonies remained institutionally stable and relatively small in size (see Appendix), thousands of Jews who had come to the island seeking to emigrate did so, creating an atmosphere of constant flux within the neighborhoods in which the immigrants settled. During the early 1920s, for example, although the Jewish population remained at about 5,000, 7,000 more Jews entered each year between 1921 and 1923, and as many as 20,000 in 1924 alone, the year that the United States closed its doors. Not only did almost all of these temporary residents leave Cuba within a relatively short time, but even after emigration to the United States became legally almost impossible, extralegal emigration from Cuba continued during the 1930s and 1940s. So the permanent Jewish community functioned in the midst of what must have been a highly unstable atmosphere. As long as Cuba functioned as this kind of an immigration hotel, wages paid by Jewish employers could be kept artificially low, community-based efforts to provide social services were overwhelmed, and the effort by community leaders to organize permanent institutions was difficult if not hopeless. Still another difference was the fact that many of those Jewish immigrants who intended to stay in Cuba, especially Sephardic families, settled in provincial towns and cities, not in Havana, the capital. This did not occur nearly as readily in other Latin American countries, where most Jewish immigrants found homes in the major cities.

Immigrant groups in Cuba, of course, did generate their own support system, an infrastructure providing physicians, dentists, insurance brokers, newspaper editors, lawyers, and every other kind of English-speaking professional and semiprofessional service for the thousands of foreigners residing in Cuba who did not speak Spanish as their first language. Affluence and economic success, however, did not mean social parity with the Creole elite: directories of socially prominent Cubans published in the first decades after independence never listed persons with Jewish surnames, although some families of non-Spanish origin did appear.[5] In the rest of Latin America, notably in the case of Portuguese Jews in Venezuela and the Dominican Republic and of Alsatian Jews in Mexico, where Jews did gain unencumbered access to the upper classes, they were absorbed and lost their Jewish identity.[6] In Cuba, however, the 1950s saw sons and daughters of former immigrant Jews beginning to enter the professions and making their mark as industrialists and merchants. Although they remained affiliated with Jewish communal organizations and married overwhelmingly within their own religious community, they were making substantial progress on the road to economic parity in tolerant Cuba, an island nation indelibly colored by the legacy of its recent colonial heritage and by the realities of its close proximity, culturally as well as geographically, to the U.S. mainland. But no Jews entered politics, and no political parties ever addressed minority concerns in their platforms until 1959. Latin American culture, a perceptive observer has noted, tended to be based on philosophies that had been rejected by Jews and that were hostile to them.[7]

Cuban society's tolerance of newcomers and the general nonchalance about ethnic and racial intermarriage tended to increase pressures for assimilation, a fact that did not please Jewish communal leaders. Black immigrants, most of whom came to rural areas, faced strong economic and social discrimination, and the large numbers of Chinese who had come to the island were excluded from most social clubs and voluntary associations. But Chinese men often married Cuban women, and the passage of time softened the perception that the Chinese clung to their old ways. Spanish male immigrants also married Cuban women, and in any case the cultural differences between these two groups were not great. For Jews it was another matter. Religious tradition required marriage within the Jewish faith as well as patterns of behavior that revolved around the home, communal associations, and making a living. Although Cuba's Roman Catholic church was organizationally weak—there was only one priest for every 10,000 persons—"being Catholic" characterized "being Cuban."[8] This meant that although Cuban social behavior was not constrained by Catholic strictures, joining the majority tacitly meant joining the dominant religion. Jews who found the more open and permissive society around them appealing and who affected those life-styles soon found themselves on the outside. The fact that all of the immigrant groups numbered more men than women acted to speed up the process of assimilation, although, unlike in the United States, in Cuba it was never complete enough to integrate the immigrant entirely. Most foreigners and their children still called themselves Spanish, or Jewish, or Chinese, even decades after their arrival on the island. Ethnicity became sufficiently softened to the point that it came to be used in terms of endearment— "mi china," "mi polaca," "mi negrita".[9] But the distinction remained, which some thought was a good thing.

Jewish (as well as non-Jewish) Cubans have long argued that anti-

Semitism was imported, in differing degrees, by North American tourists, who influenced hotel managers not to accept Jewish guests, by Spanish Falangists, and by Nazi German propagandists during the 1930s. It is certainly true that Cuba's overlay of U.S. culture and its dependency on tourism as well as on trade with the United States provided the island with a far different atmosphere than elsewhere in Latin America. Supporters of the Cuban Revolution have also contended that the virulent anti-Israel rhetoric launched by the PLO and Arab League during and after the early 1970s was not directed at Jews. This hollow claim is weakened by the near-total ignorance about Judaism and the Holocaust of young Cubans whose school texts never once mention that Jews were killed in Europe during World War II. Yet Cuba was a relatively open society, not a place where xenophobia took root, even among political conservatives and nationalists, as was the case in the Southern Cone and Mexico.

Because Cuba was neither a pluralistic democracy nor a country where official institutions fostered assimilation (as did the public school system in the United States, for example, in the first part of the twentieth century), members of its Jewish population retained their identity with their national and cultural origins. The Jewish refugees from Central Europe who came in large numbers to Cuba between 1938 and 1942 remained almost completely segregated from every sector of Cuba's Jewish colony except the small American Jewish group, with which the refugees mingled at cultural events. Relations between the German-speaking refugees and other Jewish groups were cold and in some cases tinged with bad feelings. By the 1950s, although marriages between Sephardim and Ashkenazim occurred with greater frequency and although their Cuban-born children spoke Spanish as their first language, both groups remained inner-directed and isolated from one another. This pattern continued even into exile; the old communal lines remained fixed in South Florida and the other places where the Cuban Jews took up new lives. Proportionately, somewhat more Sephardic Jews than Ashkenazic were among the roughly one thousand self-acknowledged Jews who opted to stay in Cuba under Castro. They were collectively less affluent and less likely to be considered nuisances or enemies by the revolutionary regime.

Commentators on Latin American Jewry have puzzled over the reasons for the persistence of anti-Jewish ethnic stereotypes in contemporary Latin American culture, especially in places like Cuba where traditional Catholicism was actively practiced only by a small proportion of the population. "The pervasive hostility and suspicion with which minorities are characterized in Latin American popular culture and the reluctance to extend national identity to minority group members appear to reflect more than inherited prejudice and Catholic tradition," Gilbert Merkx reminds us.[10] Some explanations for this attitude include the fact that suspicion of outsiders occurs when there are weak national institutions that treat citizens universalistically, and where dependence on family and client-based in-group networks remains a mechanism of self-protection.[11] In Cuba, as elsewhere, no matter how far children of Jewish parents drifted in the direction of assimilation, no longer regarding themselves as Jews, non-Jewish Cubans still so regarded them. This was true before 1959, and it continued to be true after the Revolution.[12]

Jews arriving in Cuba experienced disorientation stemming from a myriad of factors. Some of the first culture shocks were innocent enough—their first glimpse of black people, the strange foods, the climate and humidity. Other factors affecting the immigrants were more insidious, including downward pressures on mobility and employment that forced East European Jews, 80 percent of whom had been employed in artisan crafts in the Jewish Pale, to take up peddling in the absence of industrial jobs in Cuba. Downward pressures also affected Ashkenazic women who in Europe had worked as seamstresses but who in Cuba found few opportunities for this kind of work. Ashkenazim emigrated alone or in families less closely knit than the Sephardic family clans that often migrated together from the same Turkish or Moroccan city or province to a provincial town or Havana neighborhood, providing a safety net if not security for their members. "Prostitution," Judith Laikin Elkin argues, writing about Latin America in general, "was the feminine counterpart of peddling, in that women with no tangible resources supported themselves selling a product the public desired." Her statement, however, applies to Argentina and Brazil much more than to Cuba, where far fewer European women were imported to work in what Jewish immigrants to Cuba euphemistically called the "white business."[13]

Almost everything about Cuba was strange and bewildering for the newcomers. Some had intended to go elsewhere: they had purchased passage to South American countries but liked what they

75. Newspaper vendor on park bench. Courtesy of Norbert Adler.

saw of Havana from shipboard as they approached its port, disembarked, and stayed. Osher Schuchinsky, who was born in the Polish shtetl twenty-eight kilometers from Bialystok, arrived when he was nineteen with thirty dollars stuffed in his socks. He paid four dollars a week for the right to sleep on an iron cot in a rented room shared by five others. All available space was put to use, and he slept in the center of the room. Later, he wrote a story in Yiddish about a dream in which his mother came to the room, asking him why he had not written letters to her. He replied: "What will I tell you: that I didn't eat yesterday? You want me to deceive you? I cannot find work. I owe for one week, so the restaurant I go to doesn't let me eat any more."[14]

Although Schuchinsky's experiences were harsh, he never forgot that conditions had been far worse in Eastern Europe. In response to a query about his feelings about Cuba, he said:

Cuba was a beautiful land. It is my second homeland; it was embroidered in my heart. It was more than beautiful. For a person who lived in a small Polish town, where life was more primitive, when you came to Cuba you became free. Not only free, but you were welcomed. You came from hatred. Things changed somewhat years later, when the

Jewish immigrants began to establish stores: some Cubans began to think: "They come and they are taking over." But earlier it was beautiful. We were called Germans—before Hitler, when it was a mark of respect. In Cuba, we were even permitted to become a member of the clinic at the Spanish hospital. We came to Cuba and began new lives.[15]

Schuchinsky wrote several autobiographical short stories in Yiddish treating similar themes. Shloimke, arriving in Cuba with thirty dollars and a relative on the far side of the island, roams Havana, in awe of the mixture of gaiety and sordidness of Cuba street life, especially its sexual side. Shloimke is befriended by a priest, who finds for him a Polish-Spanish dictionary, and eventually goes off to the interior to work as a hand laying railroad track. He meets Jewish shopkeepers in Camagüey and opens his own store. He discovers that much of the garment industry in Havana is already run by men with names like Grinfeld and Feldshtein. He offers credit to his customers; he plays the charada. A Cuban woman, Marisol, whom Shloimke hires, falls in love with him, but he resists marrying her, returning, instead, to Havana. He continues to feel hopelessly uprooted and nostalgic for Poland, although life there, he remembered, held out little more than suffering.

In the United States, immigrants learned to discard their foreign mannerisms and to seek Americanization while at the same time preserving and even strengthening their identity as Jews within a pluralistic society. Cuban Ashkenazim not only clung to their Yiddish culture when they arrived but worked communally to strengthen it, teaching Yiddish to children, supporting Yiddish theater and newspapers, and maintaining contact with Yiddish-speaking movements in the United States and Europe. The Sephardim maintained their Ladino culture and their religious orthodoxy but more easily adjusted to Cuban Spanish when they needed it than did Yiddish speakers.

Pressures to acculturate in the early days of immigration, of course, affected Ashkenazic as well as Sephardic Jews. Ruth Behar's Polish grandfather, Moishe (Máximo) Glinsky, lived in the tiny town of Agramonte, near Matanzas, where his was the only Jewish family. When another family arrived, the Glinskys were called "los polacos viejos," and the new family "los polacos nuevos." Máximo belonged to the Lions' Club in Agramonte and was accepted into the "cream of Agramonte society."[16] Jewish families living under these circumstances practiced Jewish customs as best they could—in rural areas Jewish families traveled long distances on the major holy days to be with other Jews—but some eventually shed their Jewish identity; others moved to larger cities where they could find religious training for their children.

Except in rural Catholic schools, where priests still spoke of "Christ-killers," Sephardic Jews were typically confused with Christians and Muslims from the Ottoman Empire, also called turcos by Cubans. Arab immigrants to Cuba generally arrived one or two decades before the Jews (Maronite Catholics, for example, began to flee Syria and Lebanon during the 1880s because they were subject to persecution by Muslims and others). Therefore, at first, these groups were rivals as merchants and peddlers, exacerbating tensions between peoples whose life-styles shared much in common.[17] In Cuban cities, especially in Santiago on the east coast and in the Old City of Havana where many Jews and Syrio-Lebanese Muslims and Christians settled, relations tended to be formally cordial, especially during the 1950s when living standards improved for both groups of immigrants.

Every immigrant to Cuba, of course, fared differently. All were individuals: immigration history often overlooks the remarkable variation in personality, motivation, and factors caused by chance in any group, even if backgrounds were similar. Each family's history, moreover, reflects the sum of encounters and events conditioned by choices: of occupation, of marriage partners, of affiliation. In Cuba new Jewish arrivals could stay in Havana or take their chances in the provinces. Men, especially if they were unencumbered by family responsibilities, could take risks, often disappearing for years, or dropping out altogether. Cuba, more open than other Latin American societies, afforded many such opportunities. Although Jewish life in Cuba was close-knit within each of the distinct Jewish groups, a higher percentage of Cuban Jews abandoned their Jewish identity through assimilation than elsewhere in the hemisphere. Young people tended to drift further from family and community; older people tended to stay put, even in the face of strong pressures to leave.

Adaptive Strategies

Despite all hardships, the Jews who came to Cuba survived the adjustment stage successfully. They achieved integration, an intermediate stage in which they continued to be regarded as an alien ethnic group, even under Castro.[18] Assimilation is the condition in which individuals are no longer regarded as members of a special ethnic group, although they may share its values. With Cuban Jews, assimilation never occurred except in the case of individuals who stopped being considered Jews. Jews in Cuba sought economic advancement, not political prerogative or cultural visibility. For their own reasons, most found it more comfortable to live within the protective confines of the Jewish community than to strike out and become Cubans first and Jews second, the pattern followed by most Jews in the United States. We do not know if Cuban society would have permitted this because few Jews tried to assimilate to that degree.

All minority immigrant groups to Latin America employed a combination of strategies to cope with obstacles on the path to assimilation. At least ten distinct strategies were adopted by some or most persons at different times in each group's history. These were: (1) withdrawal after culture shock; (2) self-segregation; (3) radicalization; (4) resistance to assimilation; (5) borrowing from the host society; (6) isolation within a Jewish infrastructure; (7) outmigration; (8) occupation alienation; (9) caution and conservatism by leaders; and (10) emphasis on education.[19]

Withdrawal after Culture Shock. Tropical America produced reeling impressions, especially for the Eastern European immigrants. Many of the Sephardic and most of the Ashkenazic Jews had come from terrible poverty; even artisans in the Jewish Pale lived in squalor. They came from living quarters in the semidarkness of cellars or in hovels with wet walls and floors. Onerous taxes aimed solely at Jews drove many to the brink of insolvency.[20] At first Cuba dazzled the eye, but then the heat, the biting insects, the strange language, and the limitations on making a living hit hard. In the words of two immigrants from Poland:

On my first night in Havana I went to walk on San Isidro Street, where women were selling themselves openly, sitting behind glass windows, calling to passersby for their attention. I was unprepared for this: I was of another morality. I thought: "How can girls sell themselves like animals?" I remember the big stores selling liquor in which girls were sitting, drinking with the American Marines. The girls drank Coca Cola, and the Marines drank and paid for schnapps. I remember the impression when I first saw the pianola on the street and a black-colored man dancing. I never saw a black man before. He was diseased, but he was dancing with real talent.[21]

I was wearing a jacket which my parents had to pay for after I left Poland, and it had a closed collar. It was so hot that sometimes it burned my skin, but I had to wear it because I thought, "How can I throw it out if they still have to pay for it on credit?" You don't understand, you don't know what it will be like to come to such a place. . . . You left a home, parents, sometimes brothers, a bed, your village, you left a life. And here you find yourself speechless, without words, in a strange new type of life. Instead [of] a life, I would call it a tragedy.[22]

For most, desolation did not last. Other strategies helped the bewildered newcomers adapt to their new environment and cope with their new lives. Cuba and the New World were far more tolerant and welcoming than the countries from which the emigrants had fled. Newcomers saved every available cent to send for brothers, sisters, cousins, and elderly relatives, a chain migration pattern that strengthened family ties and provided an internal support system.[23] But some succumbed to what they found to be insurmountable obstacles. Pale-skinned youths from Poland contracted malaria or fell to other ailments brought on by the lowering of their resistance after sixteen- and eighteen-hour work days, mostly in the broiling sun. Some peddlers in rural areas were robbed and beaten; some never returned from the work gangs for which they had signed up in desperation when no other work in the capital was available.

Self-Segregation. Immigration followed serial patterns. Family members and migrants from the same villages or provinces followed one another, with the newcomers often moving into flats shared by earlier arrivals until the more affluent moved out, creating space for still newer arrivals. Old Havana was the destination of the majority, who found apartments clustered on or near Oficios and Obispo streets in the neighborhood anchored by the San Francisco Convent, a structure thought to have been built by a marrano, Bishop Juan Laso de la Vega y Cancina.[24] Portuguese Sephardim lived near the Nuestra Señora de las Mercedes Convent, a building supposedly constructed with funds forcibly collected from Jewish refugees from

76. Havana street scene. Courtesy of Norbert Adler.

Dutch-occupied Brazil in the 1650s.[25] Some peddlers—Ashkenazic and Sephardic—acquired enough capital to open quincallas along Sol, Muralla, Bernaza, and Teniente Rey streets. Up to at least the Second World War, both East European and Sephardic Jews ghettoized themselves by choosing to live and work in these Old Havana neighborhoods. Within the Old City they rarely interacted, except at the Jewish Market.

Another form of self-segregation took the form of taking leave of (if not banishing) individuals who converted to Catholicism through marriage or who otherwise entered mainstream Cuban society without preserving their Jewish ties. One reason for the difficulty in counting the island's Jewish population at any given time was that the community wrote off persons who were born Jewish but who did not maintain institutional ties. Many more "Jews" (as they were considered by non-Jewish Cubans) remained in Cuba after the 1959 Revolution than Jewish institutional sources acknowledged, because these mostly were people who had drifted from the fold.

Many Catholic Cuban families, in fact, had one or more grandparents (usually a grandfather) who had been born Jewish and converted, or (as in case of Jacobo Adato Levy, the Sephardic maternal grandfather of Ileana Ros-Lehtinen, South Florida's first Cuban-American member of Congress) who married a Jewish woman but whose children converted. Adato had come to Cuba in 1918 from the town of Kirklisse, northwest of Istanbul, with a brother and a sister. In 1924, he married Sara Menache Lilo, who had been born in the Turkish capital, in Sagua la Grande in Las Villas province. The couple had three children, two daughters and a son. Eventually, all three married non-Jews and converted to Catholicism. Adato remained active in Jewish affairs all his life, serving as a director of the Chevet Ahim's cemetery, which was constructed in 1942, and being instrumental in the construction of the Sephardic Community Center in Vedado in the 1950s (see figure 77, the cornerstone laying in October 1957, in which an arrow identifies Adato).[26] Presumably his children and their families were not listed as Jews in estimates of the size of Cuba's Jewish population, because one was only considered Jewish as long as one remained affiliated institutionally.

Reactions to family members who took spouses of another religion varied. Observant Jews, in keeping with Orthodox law, cut off

77. Cornerstone laying, Centro Hebreo Sefaradí, 1954. Courtesy of Rabbi Nesim Gambach.

all ties, reciting the prayer for the dead for the brother or sister or son or daughter who strayed. But in most cases, family members who married Catholics or otherwise left Judaism simply passed from the world of their birth into the new world of the Cuban mainstream. In the case of a few families, relations remained good: Jacobo Adato, for example, attended the Catholic weddings of his two eldest children; he was unable to attend that of the third, who married in Miami, because he remained in Cuba until his death in 1969.[27] For most families, though, religious conversion led to permanent separation.

Radicalization. Cuban life in the early 1920s was so fragmented into ethnic and linguistic groups that a separate Yiddish-speaking Communist party cell founded in 1925 by Cuban intellectuals and students functioned for years. Most affluent Cubans were unaware of the volatile political views of the Yiddish-speaking immigrants. Some considered themselves Bundists, Social Democrats who opposed communism and the Second International; others sympathized with Trotskyism, socialist Zionism, anarchism, or a polyglot mixture of these radical causes. The American Jewish businessmen were horrified, and they worked within the larger Jewish community to dampen what they considered leftist excesses. In the absence of industrialization there was no perceived threat from syndicalists or other radicals, and the newcomers did not advocate strikes or labor stoppages. Labor Zionism was strong among the East European Jews, although the movement was factionalized among several groups with different ideological positions, including Betar, a precursor of the modern Israeli Likud party. Zionism made few inroads among Sephardic Jews, not surprising given that the Unión Sionista, the major Zionist organization, remained Yiddish speaking into the 1950s. The Jewish Socialists and Communists of the 1920s ended up ostracized from the mainstream Cuban Jewish community.

Cuban-Jewish intellectuals identified with members of the mainstream Cuban intellectual community who advocated progressive causes. The Jewish B'nai B'rith Lodge headed by Marco Pitchón, whose family came from Turkey, lionized Cuban patriot José Martí for his opposition to racism and for his advocacy of a distinctive Cuban nationalism independent of the smothering presence of the United States. Martí, who raised funds for his revolutionary cause among members of the Tampa and Key West Jewish communities during visits in 1892, was always honored by Jewish groups in Cuba.[28]

Resistance to Assimilation. The tightly knit nature of the separate groups within Cuba's Jewish colony hindered assimilation, not that absorption into the larger society ever was a goal of the Jewish community. As a byproduct of the Landsmanschaft attitude that characterized the Jewish population of all of Latin America, strong affiliation with Jewish-rooted communal groups—social, philanthropic, educational, and, to a relatively minor degree, religious—had the effect of deterring youths within the community from assimilation. Membership in Jewish organizations was as important for women as for men: in fact, women's groups in Cuba, anchored by the WIZO, had more members.[29] Cuban Jews seeking to penetrate the mainstream could not do so as easily in Cuba as in the United States, where one could anglicize one's name, rid oneself of foreign or regional accents, or affect Brooks Brothers grooming. In Cuba, social status depended much more on long aristocratic lineage. The exception was when non-Catholics of light skin married into a Cuban Catholic family: they tended to be accepted immediately, but only with the understanding (by both groups) that a line had been crossed and that there was no turning back. Crossing the line meant leaving one's origins behind. In Latin American countries such as Argentina and Brazil where the process of assimilation was relatively open, the strategy of resistance to full assimilation annoyed some tolerant non-Jews, who accused Jews of maintaining their "secret pride" and of remaining "enigmatic and suspicious."[30] There is less direct evidence of this in Cuba, where intellectuals rarely commented on questions of assimilation.

Isolation within a Jewish Infrastructure. The lack of rabbinic authority in Cuba and a corresponding lack of religiosity among the East European immigrants tended to emphasize philanthropic and social activity as well as the Russian- and Yiddish-language cultural activities that flourished in the 1920s and into the 1930s. Judith Elkin notes that the Latin American-Jewish kehillot (communities) were derived from European models based on the need for unity in face of external pressures. Therefore, the kehillah did not function as a forum for the free interplay of opinion, although many debates on Jewish issues occurred within the Patronato.[31] By the mid-1930s, more than fifty Jewish organizations banded together and hired an executive secretary, Sender Kaplan, to represent them collectively and to coordinate activities as a low-profile lobbying association. The Jewish groups never attempted to exert pressure when there was danger of retaliation, however; the watchword was caution, and those who did not agree were excluded.

The psychological need to obtain the comfort afforded by ethnic enclaves likely helped first-generation immigrants to accept sweat-shop working conditions and the degradation of peddling. As the old ethnic clubs (Landsmanschaften) began to die out, they were replaced by business associations such as Havana's Jewish Chamber of Commerce. Social clubs became the primary Jewish institutions, anchored by the Patronato, the lavishly appointed center for ceremonies, community dinners, and cultural events. Social affinity preserved the structure of ethnicity in a comfortable manner.[32] In the prosperous 1950s, some Cuban Jews imitated the behavior of the American Jewish colony by becoming "American" while living in Cuba, just as upper-class non-Jewish Cubans did. Many Cubans did business with firms in the United States, necessitating frequent travel; others sent their children to summer camps or to private schools in the United States; some even bought property in Florida or invested their savings in dollars. Cuban Jews did this as well, choosing Jewish camps and businesses (but not usually schools) when possible. These choices contributed to the persistence of the stereotype of Jews as outsiders, although few cared about the consequences. Poorer Cuban Jews mixed more with their non-Jewish neighbors and fellow workers, but economic improvement was generally accompanied by hardening of an enclave mentality.

The degree to which Jewish identity survived regardless of individual life histories is remarkable. Fabio Grobart, long a Communist and the only person of Jewish origin to belong to the central committee of the Cuban Communist party after the Revolution, maintained a deliberate distance from the Jewish community, whose leaders were embarrassed by and hostile to him and his radical comrades. But when Grobart's wife (and later, his son) died, he discreetly approached community leaders for permission to bury them according to Jewish ritual. Both were interred in the Ashkenazic cemetery in Guanabacoa.[33]

Caution and Conservatism among Leaders. Even during the darkest days of the *St. Louis* crisis, leading Jewish spokesmen preferred to work behind the scenes. They responded to eruptions of Nazi-slanted anti-Semitic propaganda over the radio by discreetly sending delegations to the chief of state or to Colonel Batista when one of his surrogates held power. Psychologists and historians of immigration know that living under paternalistic governments encourages dependency and compliance.[34] Lacking democratic protections and living in the midst of a society known for its differential, uneven application of justice and police brutality, Cuban Jews accommodated to the status quo by adopting the unspoken attitude of making the best of whatever political reality was in force at the moment. Jews, as well as most other Cubans, were glad to see Machado ousted in 1933, but after that time the heads of Jewish organizations cared little who was in power; they dealt with each administration pragmatically, to protect and extend their community's interests, conforming to the norms of the elites whose standard of comfort they wished to reach. By the 1950s, the immigrant Jews and their children had become deproletarianized members of the middle class.

On the whole, Jewish leaders in Cuba behaved much the same way as Jewish leaders elsewhere in Latin America. Isaac Gotlib, representing the World Jewish Congress, visited Central and South America from November 1953 to March 1954. In his summary report, he noted that "all communities visited by me display much weariness and apathy toward Jewish problems."[35]

Borrowing from the Host Society. As in other parts of the hemisphere, Cuban Jews adopted stances more consistent with local practice than with progressive trends elsewhere. The exception was the community's emotional support of the state of Israel, although only a small percentage of Cuba's Jews before 1948 were active Zionists. The Jewish colony remained strictly divided into subgroups based on language and national origin, but an accommodation of sorts was achieved in the 1950s with the establishment of the Patronato and its consolidation as a social-more-than-religious institution, employing a cantor, not a rabbi. One measure of the new status of the Patronato was that, although its leadership remained Ashkenazic, for the first time in Cuba families joined from all three of the major Cuban Jewish groups—the Americans, the Ashkenazim, and the Sephardim. Progressive forms of Judaism did not prosper in Cuba, although the American United Hebrew Congregation was nominally Reform. Sephardic Jews remained religiously observant, in contrast to Ashkenazim, who became increasingly secularized, although they preserved some outward forms of Jewish observance: observing the holy days, holding seders, sending their children to religious school.

Cuba's political stagnation under the corrupt and live-and-let-live regimes of Batista and of his political opponents, when they were able to take power, lulled the island's Jews into believing that somehow things would never change. Being ninety miles from the United States also influenced Cuban Jews' behavior. Access to the mainland permitted affluent Cuban Jews to visit regularly and, in some cases, to prepare, if unknowingly, for their eventual departure from Cuba. But their sense of security in Cuba and the existence of a psychological escape valve deepened the community's reliance on its Cuban roots. This was different from the experience of other Jewish communities in Latin America, which at least by the 1970s were no longer as homogeneous socioeconomically and more apt to accept diversity in life-styles and attitudes.[36] Prerevolutionary Cuba remained a kind of museum, a comfortable place, and as a result the Cuban Jewish community became more Cuban, not less.

Outmigration. At least half of the Jews who arrived in Cuba before 1930 left for the United States, legally before 1924 and surreptitiously after that date. Nearly all of the Jewish refugees from nazism departed Cuba by the end of the war. Some flourished by becoming part of Cuba's imported diamond industry. A few Cuban youths, mostly members of Zionist organizations, emigrated to Israel after 1948.[37] In the 1960s virtually the entire community identifying itself as Jewish left, except for the elderly, the intermarried, the very poor, families with sons of draft age barred from emigrating, and a few parents whose children had become involved in the Revolution.

A sense of impermanence, the fear of having someday to uproot and move again, lingered even among Cuban Jews who became economically successful and who firmly considered themselves Cubans. Ruth Behar's parents, only in their late twenties when they left revolutionary Cuba for the United States, declined to buy a piano for their daughter because they thought it wiser to buy a "more portable instrument, like the accordion or the guitar, an instrument you could take anywhere."[38] The first generation of Jewish immigrants to Cuba during and after World War I likely felt the same way. Having to learn a new language, never achieving mastery of it, having to accommodate to the unwritten and sophisticated sets of codes of behavior in new lands was hard enough, but these Jewish families had to cope with outmigration twice in three generations.

Occupational Alienation and Creativity. Economic reality during the 1920s and 1930s forced the immigrants to work in menial occupations in which they were not experienced, or to establish new businesses. American Jews, some East European Jews, and a handful of Sephardim started workshops and small factories, which eventually revolutionized the production of cheap clothing. Most manufacturing enterprises run by Jews, however, came to be owned by Ashkenazim. By the 1950s, Jewish-owned factories represented a substantial share of the nation's domestic production of shoes, clothing, and other consumer commodities. The shoe industry arose to supply the island where previously no shoes at all had been manufactured domestically; Spanish merchants had held a monopoly on shoe sales, relying entirely on imported goods. The lack of interest among native-born elites in entrepreneurship left the way open for immigrants to reach new markets.

Entrepreneurship at all levels involved dubious business practices. Importers had to pay customs inspectors thousands of dollars for shipments of merchandise they brought into the country—part of a system in which the inspectors then falsified declarations of value in order to be able to siphon off the difference for themselves. According to import merchants, corruption in Cuba extended to the presidential palace itself, where during the 1940s the family of the chief of state took its cut of the illegal fees. La botella, receiving employment sinecures through connections, was another reason Jews were unable to gain status as insiders. Only persons with connections received coveted positions in the public or private sector.

Such jobs often required little or no work but paid well. Cuban Jews, unlike their counterparts in the United States and Canada, saw no point in striving to enter mainstream professions or the bureaucracy. As the system remained relatively closed to outsiders, they channeled their energies into commerce.

Not all of the immigrants' children prospered. Most Jewish families remained poor through the mid-1940s. During the 1950s, charitable associations cared for about 150 poor families of Ashkenazic backgrounds and perhaps 80 Sephardic families. Some former immigrants remained on the margin, working as petty tradesman. There was a higher rate of intermarriage in this group than among the more affluent. In Argentina, more than a third of the Jewish community remained in the working class into the third generation; many others who had managed to rise fleetingly out of the working class actually slid back, experiencing downward mobility and economic failure.[39] Had Cuba's Jews not emigrated en masse after 1959 and had the Revolution not occurred, this pattern might have repeated itself in some form on the island.

Emphasis on Education. Jews from the beginning channeled their resources into education for their children, secular as well as religious. As the Jewish communities prospered, more of the children prepared to study for the professions. At the time of the Revolution, many Cuban Jewish youths had entered or were ready to enter university-level faculties of law, medicine, pharmacy, architecture, and engineering. But a higher percentage of the immigrants' children were ready to enter their parents' businesses, or otherwise to join the commercial sector. Cuba's generation of the 1950s had no counterpart for its peers in the United States, who would enter the Peace Corps, study academic science or public interest law, or take graduate degrees to enter university-level teaching and research.

Oscar Handlin, one of the first historians to measure the human impact of immigration, described the experience as an abrupt, irreparable break with the past, therefore traumatic and potentially devastating because it brought alienation, emotional instability, and loss of self-esteem.[40] But revisionists, including Handlin himself, have found the original premise to be unduly pessimistic. Not all psyches were shattered by the emigration of the Jews, and some amazingly successful adjustments were made. Immigrants brought with them values and hopes that strengthened them. Most of the newcomers to Cuba—Jews as well as non-Jews—accomplished the transition without significant symptoms of personal maladjustment or breakdown of family life.[41] In Cuba and throughout Latin America, Jews managed to cope even though fear during the first decades of the immigrant experience preserved old feelings of mistrust, and their small number limited their ability to stop perceiving themselves as alien. It would be unfair to fault Cuban Jews for inflexibility or for accommodating to the political and social system when their options were so severely limited. If one-third remained poor, another two-thirds elevated themselves to economic heights undreamed of by their parents and grandparents.

Strong feelings of nationalism have historically translated into anti-Semitism. This was the case of Mexico after 1910, Argentina in the early years of the century and especially in 1919 (when the hemisphere's only pogrom occurred in Buenos Aires), Peru and Chile during the 1920s, Brazil during the 1930s, and Costa Rica in the 1940s and early 1950s. Anti-Semitism occurred sporadically in Cuba, although it never captured the mood of the larger population and was always the product of foreign instigators: Nazis and Spanish Falangists before the Second World War, and the Arab bloc, and notably the PLO, a generation later.

Although few Cubans opposed Jewish immigration based on fear of ideological incompatibility or on institutional anti-Semitism, affluent Cubans wondered how easily the new arrivals would be absorbed. The Cuban government provided few welfare services and did not aid the indigent. Further, there were the ways the East European immigrants dressed and comported themselves. Most of the immigrants seemed to speak incomprehensible languages, wore the heavy shtetl shirts and trousers they had brought with them, and stood out conspicuously in the languid, tropical setting. The English-speaking Jews reacted in the same manner as the German Jews who had arrived in the United States before 1900 and who were dismayed at the public image of the Yiddish-speaking immigrants from Eastern Europe. The United Hebrew Congregation raised some $7,500 by May 1921 through its Ezra society but otherwise did not become involved in the problems of the new arrivals. Most of the Ashkenazic immigrants improved their economic position by their own hard work, without charitable aid.

Cuba's twentieth-century history of welcoming immigrants reflected a combination of factors, including the elite's nonchalance about the lower-class population, especially if it were not dark-skinned. Most of the immigrants who stayed in Cuba worked hard, despite xenophobic legislation during the late 1920s and early 1930s aimed at them, and eventually worked their way up the economic ladder. Cuba's Jewish residents differed somewhat from other immigrant groups, but in many ways their experience was similar. For persons fleeing from economic or political distress or from religious persecution, Cuba represented a haven made even more attractive by the elite's laissez-faire attitudes and by the lack of institutionalized discrimination. Cuba's status as a quasi-colony of the United States up through the Castro revolution contributed to the island's uniqueness. From the immigrants' perspective, this was not altogether bad, and the proximity to the United States added to possibilities for economic advancement.

Foreign representatives of Jewish organizations often expressed their frustration at what they considered the community's apathy and lack of commitment to Jewish issues. Within the community, however, Judaism was defined differently than in the United States. For one thing, few Cuban Jews practiced traditional Judaism. Their affiliation was more cultural and ethnic, for the most part restricted to membership in communal and social organizations. Cuba's atmosphere before 1959 was not unlike, in some ways, the U.S. South before the civil rights movement. Jews in the South lived comfortably, but always as outsiders, and always subject to the whims of a harsh political system of which they wanted no part.

A good portion of the Jews who came to Cuba, especially immediately after World War I and again in the case of the German-speaking refugees from nazism, never considered it more than a way station. Many of the immigrants were disoriented by Cuba's throbbing heat and by a society in which to survive one had to master a system based to a large degree on unwritten rules and understandings. The immigrants who chose to remain or who had no other choice came to view Cuba as a reasonable host, a place where they could raise their children nominally as Cubans in an environment structured to preserve their distinct identity as Jews, but where language and cultural differences separated one generation from another and traumatized members of the first immigrant generation in ways from which many never recovered. After 1959, things changed again, absolutely. Ninety percent of Cuba's Jews left, although Castro and his government bent over backward to avoid anti-Semitic actions in spite of Cuba's closeness with Third World causes during and after the 1970s, and despite the fact that the Cuban Jews who left did so because they shared the same economic status and attitudes about the Revolution as all other departing Cubans. In small ways related to dietary laws and their desire to maintain a religious school, the remnant of Cuba's Jewish community in the early 1990s received special treatment given to few other minority groups in Cuba. This was due in part to foreign pressure, but mostly to the regime's desire to show its sensitivity to such matters.

In a speech at a banquet held at the Patronato in 1956, Moisés Mitriani paid homage to the thirty years of sweat and hard work performed by the members of his parents' generation of immigrants, which had culminated, he told his listeners, in the fact that his ten-year-old son, born in "this dear Cuba," was able to be present under favored circumstances, a recipient of that legacy of sacrifice.[42] Fate and Cuban history soon showed that national stability was little more than a facade during the 1950s, one that would end abruptly a few years later. Given how far most of the immigrants had come, it was no wonder that they would fix the memory of Cuba in positive and nostalgic terms in their minds, a paradise lost, even if the solid prosperity most had achieved during the 1950s turned out to be fleeting. Ironically, the same Jews barred from entering the United States as undesirable aliens by immigration officials fearing an influx of Jews in the 1920s and 1930s were welcomed as refugees from Castro's Cuba, concealing, as it were, "their 'true' Jewish identity behind the mask of a 'false' Cuban identity." Cuban Jews came to Miami and to New York as Cubans, not as Jews.[43]

Appendix

Estimates of the Size of Cuba's Jewish Population, 1910–1992

1910–17   1,000–2,000 Ashkenazic Jews plus 2,000–4,000
          Sephardic Jews; many of the Ashkenazim stay about a
          year until they can get papers permitting entry to the
          United States.

1919   2,000 Jews estimated to be residing in Cuba; most
          Ashkenazim and some Sephardim leave within a year
          or so of entry for other destinations, usually the
          United States.

1921–24   5,000 Jews, with 7,000 per year entering between 1921
          and 1923 and nearly 20,000 in 1924. Nearly all leave
          for the United States or for Mexico (where they later
          depart for the United States).

1925–35   Closing of U.S. immigration doors causes permanent
          Jewish colony in Cuba to stabilize at about 4,000
          (Ashkenazic and Sephardic); 4,000 more Ashkenazic
          Jews emigrate to Cuba during these years. Many are
          "lost" through assimilation; some gain entry to the
          United States illegally. Jewish community data count
          only 2,500 in "total" Jewish colony.

1930   U.S. consul claims 14,000 Jews who entered Cuba
          since 1924 left for the United States, some with legal
          papers but most extralegally.

1936–38   5,000 German-speaking Jewish refugees enter through
          mid-1938; those with family in the United States able
          to pledge financial support permitted to leave Cuba for
          United States.

1938–39	500 more refugees enter each month. Most continue to wait less than a year before admittance to the United States. About 5,000 German-speaking Jewish refugees live in Cuba in April 1939 (1,100 classified as "destitute"). *St. Louis* and other ships' passengers holding landing permits are turned back, but others holding regular visas are permitted to enter on ships that arrive later. Total Jewish population numbers about 16,500, mostly settled in Havana except for 3,500 scattered in provincial capitals and towns.
1940	Somewhat less than 2,000 more refugees enter Cuba.
1941–early 1942	About 1,000 refugees enter Cuba.
1942–45	8,000 refugees wait to be admitted to the United States; almost all leave by war's end.
1951	Permanent Jewish population estimated at 10,000.
1959	Permanent Jewish population estimated at 10,000–12,000, two-thirds of Ashkenazic origin. Persons born Jewish but not acknowledged as Jews by preference or as a result of complete assimilation are not counted.
1960–62	4,800 Cuban Jews leave Cuba under Castro regime.
late 1965	2,300 Jews remain in Cuba (1,900 in Havana; 400 in provinces), estimated from those who register to receive Passover supplies and who therefore acknowledge their Judaism.
1992–93	Fewer than 1,000 acknowledged Jews remain in Cuba.

Notes

CHAPTER I. DIASPORA IN THE TROPICS

1. Stanley Hordes and a team of anthropologists, linguists, and sociologists affiliated with the New Mexico–based Association of Crypto-Jewish Studies are pursuing long-range, systematic research on these secret Jews, some of whose descendants continue to practice Jewish ritual in the 1990s, although they do not recognize it as such. See his paper, "The Sephardic Legacy in New Mexico: A History of the Crypto-Jews," presented at the Sixth Conference of the Latin American Jewish Studies Association, College Park, Maryland, Oct. 6, 1991.

2. Haim Avni, "Jews in Latin America: The Contemporary Jewish Dimension," 9–10.

3. Throughout this work, I refer to Jews who have moved from the United States to Cuba as the "American Jews." *Censo de Población: Cuba*, table 28, "Ciudadanía de los Extranjeros en la población total de Cuba: 1899 a 1953" (Havana, 1953), 80, courtesy of Omar J. Cuan.

4. Harry O. Sandberg, "The Jews of Latin America," 84.

5. Good recent biographies of José Martí include Christopher Abel and Nissa Torrents, eds., *José Martí: Revolutionary Democrat*, and Peter Turton, *José Martí, Architect of Cuba's Freedom*. See also "Los Judíos en Cuba," *Revista Bimestre Cubana* 45, no. 3 (May–June 1940): 467; José Martí, *Obras completas*, 4:167–68; Marifeli Pérez-Stable, "In Pursuit of Cuba Libre," 33; Medea Benjamin, "Things Fall Apart," 26. In 1990 the UJC "plastered the walls of Havana" with the slogan in graffiti (Benjamin, "Things Fall Apart," 26). Lewis Fine, a Jewish resident of Key West, also lent support to Martí. See Sandberg, "Jews of Latin America," 84.

6. They were Manuel Hadida, Martin Kohn, Jacob Heller, Isidore Lirriano, Manuel Jessel, Louis Jurick, Maurice Schecter, Joseph Steinberg, Emile Berkowitz, Adolph Dynner, and Alexander Freedman. It was estimated that there were about 100 Jews in Cuba at this time. See United Hebrew Congregation/Temple Beth Israel, *Golden Anniversary, 1906–1956*, 9–10 (hereafter *Golden Anniversary*).

7. See Glen Westfall, *Key West; Cigar City USA* (Key West: Monroe County Historical Society, c. 1980).
8. Miguel Barnet, *Gallego*, 110.
9. Louis A. Pérez, Jr., *Cuba and the United States: Ties of Singular Intimacy*, 123. Also see Moisés Asís, "El Judaísmo Cubano durante 30 años de Revolución (1959–1989)," 39.
10. Benjamin Keen, *A History of Latin America*, 414–15.
11. See Harry Viteles, *Report on the Status of the Jewish Immigration in Cuba.*
12. Natalie (Nena) Lyons, interview, Coral Gables, Florida, April 28, 1990. Lyons is Herman Beller's daughter and Henry Engler's granddaughter. See George Weinberger, "The Jews in Cuba," 1.
13. Sandberg, "Jews of Latin America," 84.
14. Isaac Gotlib, "Report on Cuba," World Jewish Congress (November 1953), Box H93, American Jewish Committee Archive, Cincinnati (hereafter AJC Archive).
15. See Demetrios Basdekis, *Unamuno and the Novel*, 20.
16. Rhoda P. Rabkin, *Cuban Politics: The Revolutionary Experiment*, 9. I am grateful to Maritza Corrales for pointing out that Columbus's *Diario de Navegación* gives the date of landing as October 28; other sources claim that it was October 27.
17. See, for example, Max J. Kohler, "Los Judíos en Cuba," 2–5; C. R. Markham, ed., "Journals of Columbus during His First Voyage"; Leizer Ran, ed., *Comunidad hebrea en tierra Cubana: Almanaque commemorativo del 25º aniversario del Centro Israelita de Cuba: 1925–1950.*
18. Sender Kaplan, Raul Moncarz, and Julio Steinberg, "Jewish Emigrants to Cuba, 1898–1960," 295.
19. Jeffrey A. Kahn, "The History of the Jewish Colony in Cuba," 7–8; Judith Laikin Elkin, *Jews of the Latin American Republics*, 8–9.
20. Moisés Asís, letter to author, Havana, September 24, 1990. Asís started his career in Cuba as a specialist on bees; Maritza Corrales, letter to author, Havana, August 18, 1991.
21. Merivale, cited by Robert L. Paquette, *Sugar Is Made with Blood. The Conspiracy of La Escalera and the Conflict between Empires over Slavery in Cuba*, 29; Manuel Moreno Fraginals, *El Ingenio: Complejo económico social cubano del azúcar*, 80–96.
22. Rebecca J. Scott, *Slave Emancipation in Cuba: The Transition to Free Labor, 1860–1899* (Princeton, N.J.: Princeton University Press, 1985), 9.
23. See Kenneth F. Kiple, *Blacks in Colonial Cuba, 1774–1899* (Gainesville: University Presses of Florida, 1976).
24. For the role of race in the development of Cuban nationality, see Franklin W. Knight, "Slavery, Race, and Social Structure in Cuba During the

Nineteenth Century," in *Slavery and Race in Latin America*, ed. Robert Brent Toplin (Westport, Conn.: Greenwood, 1974), 204–27.

25. Lee Hockstader, "Castro Has No Exit," *Washington Post* (October 6, 1991), C1.

26. Roloff's Jewishness, however, is disputed, according to Margalit Bejarano, the Israeli historian. Joseph Steinberg, who raised money for Martí, was appointed by Tomás Estrada Palma as "Captain of the Army of Liberation"; other volunteers and filibusterers included Captain Kaminsky, "formerly a peddler in Florida," and Horace (Horacio) Rubens, a Jewish attorney from New York. See Elkin, *Jews of the Latin American Republics*; Eduardo Weinfeld, *Enciclopedia Judaica Castellana*, "Cuba," 252–69. See also Dionisio Castiel, "Algunos Apuntes sobre la Contribución de los Hebreos al Desarrollo de Cuba," 59–60. Also, "Los Judíos en Cuba," 467, and, especially, Fermín Peraza Sarausa, *Diccionario Biográfico Cubano*, 5: 71.

27. Louis A. Pérez, Jr., *Cuba: Between Reform and Revolution*, 121–25. See the same author's "'Fin de Siècle' Cuba," 33–37. For an analysis of press censorship against the larger background of nineteenth-century Cuban history, see Larry R. Jensen, *Children of Colonial Despotism: Press, Politics, and Culture in Cuba, 1790–1840*.

28. See Scott, *Slave Emancipation in Cuba*, 285.

29. Louis A. Pérez, Jr., *Lords of the Mountain: Social Banditry and Peasant Protest in Cuba, 1878–1918*, xvi.

30. Louis A. Pérez Jr., "Cuba, c. 1930–59," 419.

31. See Paul W. Drake, "From Good Men to Good Neighbors: 1912–1932," 10–11.

32. See Rabkin, *Cuban Politics*, 13–15.

33. On the cultural legacy of U.S. domination, see Carol Damian; "Amelia Peláez," *Latin American Art* 3, no. 2 (Spring 1991): 27.

34. See Julia P. Herzberg, "Wilfredo Lam," 18–25.

35. Moisés Pitchón, interview, Miami, February 1985. The Pitchón family, from Turkey, lived in Oriente province during the first two decades of its Cuban residence.

36. For a Cuban version of the political history of the period, see Diana A. Abad Muñoz, "Cuba: La Revolución de 1895," 97–102.

37. Pérez, *Lords of the Mountain*, 19. See also Pérez, *Cuba: Between Reform and Revolution*, esp. 206–7.

38. On the issue of race in Cuban politics, see Thomas T. Orum, "The Politics of Color: The Racial Dimension of Cuban Politics during the Early Republican Years, 1900–1912," Ph.D. diss., New York University, 1975.

39. Moisés Asís, interview, Miami, December 18, 1991. José R. Alvarez

Díaz, ed. *A Study on Cuba: The Colonial and Republican Periods. The Socialist Experiment*, 5. See also Edouard Calic, *Ohne Maske*, 118.

40. Waldo Frank, *Cuba: Prophetic Island*, 106.
41. Basil Woon, *When It's Cocktail Time in Cuba*, 179, 175. Woon pointedly noted that Heller and Charles Berkowitz, whom he also describes, were Jews, although he identified others neutrally as "Irish," "British," or "American."
42. Michael Kenny, "Twentieth Century Spanish Expatriates in Cuba: A Sub-Culture?" 85–86.
43. John H. Parker, *Yankee, You Can't Go Home Again*, 29.
44. Those who did not know any better called all Spanish immigrants gallegos, whether or not they came from Galicia.
45. Parker, *Yankee*, 28.
46. See Daniel J. Elazar, *Jewish Communities in Frontier Societies*, 93. Jewish and Syrio-Lebanese peddlers provided credit to their customers wherever they were, including the New Mexico Territory in the United States as early as the 1860s. See Henry J. Tobias, *A History of the Jews in New Mexico*, 65–66.
47. Elkin, *Jews of the Latin American Republics*, 104; Tobias, *Jews in New Mexico*, 65–66.
48. Centro Israelita, *The 25th Anniversary of the Centro Israelita* (Havana: Centro Israelita, 1950), 99–145. Copy provided by Alberto Rodríguez.
49. For a scholarly analysis of Judezmo, the spoken language of the Iberian Jews in North Africa, Morocco, and the successor states of the Ottoman Empire, see Paul Wexler, "Ascertaining the Position of Judezmo within Ibero-Romance," 162–95.
50. Aron Rodrigue, *French Jews, Turkish Jews: The Alliance Israélite Universelle and the Politics of Jewish Schooling in Turkey, 1860–1925*, 25. See also Mair José Benardete, *Hispanic Culture and the Character of the Sephardic Jews*.
51. Turkey also provided safe haven for 1,500 German Jews fleeing nazism. Many were professors; in fact, they played a major role in Turkey's postwar university system. Information provided by Professor Steven Rosenthal, University of Hartford.
52. Margalit Bejarano, "Los Sefaradíes, pioneros de la inmigración judía a Cuba," 108–9.
53. *Bulletin de l'Alliance Israélite Universelle*, no. 29 (1904), 165.
54. Bejarano, "Los Sefaradíes," 108–9.
55. Boris Sapir, *The Jewish Community of Cuba*, 14–15. The two colonies used the same graveyard until 1924 but practiced different rituals; in 1942, the Sephardim purchased their own land, adjacent to the older

cemetery. See *Havaner Lebn*, November 22, 1935, 8; Bejarano, "Los Sefaradíes," 113–14.

56. Judrun Kraemer, *The Jews in Modern Egypt, 1914–1952* (Seattle: University of Washington Press, 1989), 191.

57. See Rodrigue, *French Jews, Turkish Jews*, esp. 47–120.

58. Michel Arbitol, "The Encounter between French Jewry and the Jews of North Africa, 1830–1914," 52.

59. L'Alliance Israelite Universelle, cited in Rodrigue, *French Jews, Turkish Jews*, 78.

60. Interview with Sender Kaplan, Miami, November 9, 1991.

61. Ruth Behar, "Juban América," 9.

62. David Blis, "Los Chutos Modernos," *Bohemia* 35 (October 1918): 4.

63. Cuban Congress, Senate, *Senate Record*, May 12, 1919, 37: 9.

64. See Haim Avni, "The Origins of Zionism in Latin America," in Judith Laikin Elkin and Gilbert W. Merkx, eds., *The Jewish Presence in Latin America*, 144–45.

65. David Blis, "Memoirs," 18–19; Kahn, "Jewish Colony," 21.

66. Ena Habif, interview, Miami, April 10, 1991. The rabbi was Gershom Maya.

67. Victor Perera, "Growing Up Jewish in Guatemala," *Echad: An Anthology of Latin American Jewish Writings*, 71. Perera's parents came from the same community as many Sephardim who came to Cuba, and their family customs were essentially the same during the early years when his father was a peddler.

68. Interview with Isidoro Behar, "Hotel Cuba" project, 1984, transcript in University of Miami Otto G. Richter Library Archives and Collections (hereafter Richter Library).

69. Like the term *gallego*, applied indiscriminately to Spanish immigrants, the term *polaco* in time was used to refer to any foreigner who was not American, Spanish, black, or Chinese. Information provided by Sara Sánchez.

70. Overall immigration to Cuba averaged 30,000 annually from 1908 through 1918; in 1919 it jumped to 80,488, to 340,241 in 1920 and 148,361 in 1921. By 1922 it had dropped to 20,184, although it picked up again in 1923–24, reaching 85,285 in that year before dropping dramatically after that time. See Susan Schroeder, *Cuba: A Handbook of Historical Statistics*, table 4.9, 111.

71. Horace M. Kallen, *Frontiers of Hope*, 194–97; Eugene Sofer, *From Pale to Pampa: A Social History of the Jews of Buenos Aires*, 25.

72. Elkin, *Jews of the Latin American Republics*, 105.

73. Kaplan, Moncarz, and Steinberg, "Jewish Emigrants to Cuba," 297.

1. Bernardo Benes, interview, Miami, March 13, 1990.
2. Schroeder, *Cuba*, table 4.9, 111.
3. Elkin, *Jews of the Latin American Republics*, 54–55.
4. See Kohler, "Los Judíos en Cuba," 127.
5. Barnet, *Gallego*, 53.
6. Margalit Bejarano, "Cuba as America's Back Door: The Case of Jewish Immigration," 485–486.
7. *Encyclopaedia Judaica*, vol. 15 (1972), 1611.
8. See the videotaped documentary by Robert M. Levine and Mark D. Szuchman, "Hotel Cuba."
9. Polish consul general in New York, cited by Marcin Kula, "La emigración polaca en Cuba en el período de entre guerras," 144. The term used was *Negroes*.
10. There were two higher levels: *cuentaniks* and *clientelchiks*. The distinctions depended on the kind of merchandise sold and the sales arrangements. See Elkin, *Jews of the Latin American Republics*, 103.
11. Ibid., 106.
12. *Havaner Lebn*, October 12, 1934, cited in ibid.
13. Judith Laikin Elkin, "A Gallery of Former Jews," 38.
14. This policy culminated in 1926 with the Verdeja Act, which reduced production by 10 percent. See Wyatt MacGaffey, "Social Structure and Mobility in Cuba," 95. Sugar prices jumped from 4 cents per pound in 1916 to 9.1 cents in February 1920 to 22.5 cents by mid-May. By December the price fell to 3.75 cents, the prewar level. See Keen, *History*, 422.
15. See K. Lynn Stoner, "Ofelia Domínguez Navarro: The Making of a Cuban Socialist Feminist," 127.
16. Jaime Suchlicki, *Historical Dictionary of Cuba*, 168.
17. Lowry Nelson, *Rural Cuba*, 162–73.
18. *Comercio* (Havana), August 7, 1927, 1.
19. Louis A. Pérez, Jr., "In Defense of Hegemony: Sumner Welles and the Cuban Revolution of 1933," 28–29.
20. Elkin, *Jews of the Latin American Republics*, 106.
21. Ibid., 112–13.
22. Dr. Felix Reyler, interview, Miami Beach, May 26, 1991; Kaplan, Moncarz, and Steinberg, "Jewish Emigrants to Cuba," 299.
23. As did Moishe Aaron Glinienski, whose name was changed to Máximo Glinsky, who arrived in Havana in 1924. See Ruth Behar, "Death and Memory: From Santa María del Monte to Miami Beach," 346–84; Ruth Behar, letter to author, Ann Arbor, Mar. 12, 1991.

24. Cristina García, *Dreaming in Cuban*, 43.
25. Behar, "Juban América," 2–3.
26. Isidoro Behar, interview, Miami Beach, February 16, 1985.
27. Vivian Ferrin, interview, Miami, April 9, 1992.
28. *Kubaner Yiddishe Yontefbleter-Pesach Blat: Cubana Hebreo, Periódico Festival,* cited by Kahn, "Jewish Colony," 37–38.
29. Maurice Lewis, report to the Jewish Committee for Cuba, March 4, 1927, cited by Kahn, ibid., 40; José Raij, interviewed by Andrew Speyer, Miami, November 14, 1990.
30. Kahn, "Jewish Colony," 41.
31. The proprietor, who used a typewriter to produce his paper, was Chaim Pinchas Berniker. Information provided by Sender Kaplan.
32. Information provided by Sender Kaplan. See also Sapir, *Jewish Community of Cuba,* 36.
33. See YIVO, "Going Home," esp. 8.
34. See *Almanaque conmemorativo de la Caja de Préstamos de la Asociación Femenina Hebrea de Cuba.* The Caja was founded in 1937.
35. Edward J. Bristow, *Prostitution and Prejudice: The Jewish Fight against White Slavery, 1870–1939,* 7, 112–13.
36. Information provided by Stanley and Rachel Wax, Coral Gables, Florida, February 18, 1991. The leaders included Elena Goldstein, Ana Pincus, Emma Lipschultz, Ana Dizik, and Nina Segal, one of its first presidents.
37. Hugh Thomas, *Cuba or the Pursuit of Freedom,* 578.
38. See José Schnaider, "Der erster antiyidisher oifruf en Cuba," *Havaner Lebn–Vida Habanera,* September 21, 1935, 3.
39. See Alberto Lamar Schweyer, *La Crisis del Patriotismo: Una teoría de las inmigraciones,* 84–89; Rosalie Schwartz, *Lawless Liberators: Political Banditry and Cuban Independence;* Ortíz cited by Carolina Amram, "The Assimilation of Immigrants in Cuban society during the 1920s and 1930s," 6–8.
40. Irwin F. Gellman, *Good Neighbor Diplomacy: United States Policies in Latin America, 1933–1945,* 18.
41. Sapir, *Jewish Community of Cuba,* 34.
42. See Kaplan, Moncarz, and Steinberg, "Jewish Emigrants to Cuba," 299.
43. Pérez, "Cuba, c. 1930–59," 423.
44. Information provided by Roberto E. Hernández, Miami, December 19, 1990.
45. Margalit Bejarano, "The Deproletarization of Cuban Jews," 58.
46. Amram, "Assimilation of Immigrants," 76.
47. Osher (Jaime) Schuchinsky, interview, 8VB, 135–160, Richter Library.
48. Amram, "Assimilation of Immigrants," 77.

49. Elkin, *Jews of the Latin American Republics*, 112.
50. Pérez, "In Defense of Hegemony," 30–31.
51. See *Diario de la Marina*, editorial, September 12, 1927, 2; September 15, 1927, 1.
52. See the allegation in *Mercurio* (Havana), September 26, 1927, 1, that immigration officials since 1923 had defrauded the government of $1 million by not turning over fees charged to newcomers.
53. For the dictator's side of the affair, see Gerardo Machado, *Ocho Años de Lucha*. His nationalist position is spelled out in his *Por la patria libre*. The Left's position is summarized in *El Socialista* (Madrid), May 9, 1933, 1.
54. Pérez, "In Defense of Hegemony," 32–36. Years before, Welles summarized his personal justification for a behind-the-scenes approach in "Is America Imperialistic?" 414. See also Pérez, *Cuba: Between Reform and Revolution*, 264; Gellman, *Good Neighbor Diplomacy*, 18–19.
55. See Manuel Pedro González, "A Selective Bibliography of the Cuban Revolution against Machado (1928–1933)," 209–31.
56. Guiteras's 1933 attack on a military barracks near Santiago de Cuba may have inspired Castro's attack against the Moncada barracks. See Rabkin, *Cuban Politics*, 15.
57. Pérez, *Cuba: Between Reform and Revolution*, 270. See also Justo Carrillo, *Cuba 1933: Estudiantes, yanquis y soldados* (Coral Gables: Graduate School of International Studies, University of Miami, 1985).
58. See, for example, *Alma Mater* (Havana), November 7, 1933, 1.
59. Pérez, *Cuba: Between Reform and Revolution*, 275; see also 264–75.
60. Telegram, Sumner Wells to Ambassador Jefferson Caffery, January 6, 1934, *Foreign Relations of the United States. Cuba, 1933–1934*, vol. 5, 837.00/4577a; telegram, Caffery to Acting Secretary of State, January 15, 1934, 837.00/4606, ibid. (Washington, D.C.: Department of State, 1967).
61. Photograph of signing of abrogation of Platt Amendment dated May 1934, in Justo Carrillo collection, Richter Library.
62. See *Mercurio* (Havana), August 8, 1927, on the arrest of the president of the Camagüey Rotary Club on suspicion of Communist activities.
63. Pérez, "In Defense of Hegemony," 31.
64. Wyatt MacGaffey and Clifford R. Barnett, *Twentieth-Century Cuba: The Background of the Castro Revolution*, 24.
65. Osher (Jaime) Suchinsky, interview, Miami Beach, November 11, 1985; *Havaner Lebn*, September 22, 1933, 6; Bejarano, "Deproletarization," 61.
66. Kenny, "Spanish Expatriates," 86.
67. See José Carlos Sebe Bom Meihy, interviewed by Neil Macaulay, Gainesville, Fla., November 30, 1988, in Bom Meihy, *A Colônia Brasilianista:*

História Oral de Vida Acadêmica (São Paulo: Nova Stella, 1990), 210.
Fidel Castro's father was a gallego expatriate. See also Barnet, *Gallego,*
esp. 62–70.
68. Kenny, "Spanish Expatriates," 91.
69. Bejarano, "Deproletarization," 60; Amram, "Assimilation of Immigrants," 50.
70. Pérez, *Cuba: Between Reform and Revolution,* 282.
71. See *Diario de la Marina,* August 23, 1934.
72. *Hoy,* July 4, 1939, 3.
73. Jacques Rieur, "The Jewish Colony of Cuba," 2.
74. Alvarez Diaz, *A Study on Cuba,* 297, 437.
75. Speaker of the House Garriga was quoted in *Hoy* on October 13, 1939, 3, as saying that people expected Batista to intervene to impose enactment of congressional bills he favored. See also *Hoy,* July 5, 1939, 3.
76. See Jerry W. Knudson, "Anti-semitism in Latin America: Barometer of Social Change," *Patterns of Prejudice* (London), 6, no. 5 (September–October 1972): 9; Arnold Roller, "The Jews of Cuba," 258.
77. Margalit Bejarano, "The Problem of Anti-semitism in Cuba, 1944–1963," ms. courtesy of author; Salvador Díaz Versón, *El Nazismo en Cuba.*
78. Zeev Raboniwitz, interviewed by M. Bejarano, Tel Aviv, May 22, 1985; *Havaner Lebn,* March 17, 1922, 19; *Kubaner Bleter,* December 1, 1938, 23–24, cited in Bejarano, "Deproletarization," 67.
79. *Havaner Lebn,* September 1, 1933, 6.
80. Bejarano, "Deproletarization," 63–64.
81. Suchinsky interview, October 15, 1990.
82. Sender M. Kaplan, interview, Miami Beach, February 10, 1991.
83. Harold D. Sims, "Cuban Labor and the Communist Party, 1937–1958: An Interpretation," 44–45.
84. For Brazil, see Robert M. Levine, *The Vargas Regime, 1934–1938;* for Mexico, see Alan Knight, "Mexico, c. 1930–46," 3–82.
85. Sims, "Cuban Labor," 45. Cooperation between Batista and the Communists lasted until 1944, when he again broke tradition and held honest elections.
86. Amram, "Assimilation of Immigrants," 26.
87. MacGaffey, "Social Structure and Mobility in Cuba," 96–97; Amram, "Assimilation of Immigrants," 14–15.
88. Alvarez Díaz, *A Study on Cuba,* 306.
89. "Filantropía," ms. provided by Rabbi Nesim Gambach, n.p., n.d. *Boletin Informativo de la Beneficencia "Bikur-Holim."*
90. Margalit Bejarano, "Antisemitism in Cuba under Democratic, Military, and Revolutionary Regimes, 1944–1963," 32.
91. One of the best accounts of this period is Alistair Hennessy's "Cuba,"

101–58. See Havana *Post*, October 17, 1933, 1–2; November 11, 1933, 1; November 13, 1933, 1.

92. Rabbi Meir Lasker, interview, Elkins Park, Pennsylvania, November 14, 1989.

93. See Bristow, *Prostitution and Prejudice*; Donna Guy, *Sex and Danger in Buenos Aires.*

94. Bertha Pappenheim, *Jewish Association for the Protection of Girls and Women. International Conference*, 97.

95. See Dr. W. Berger, "Gibt es für Cuba eine Judenfrage?" (Joint Defense Committee, New York, c. 1944), 132, ms. courtesy of Dr. Hannah Wartenberg.

96. Rivero's family controlled three newspapers, including *Diario de la Marina*. See *Cuba en la Mano: Enciclopedia Popular Ilustrada* (Havana: n.p., 1940), 994–95.

97. One of its leaders was a congressman, Adelardo Valdés-Astolfi. Information provided by Roberto E. Hernández, Miami, December 19, 1990.

98. Lasker interview, *Golden Anniversary*, 20.

99. The Sephardim opened a new synagogue, the Ashkenazi Centro Israelita reasserted itself as the leading voice of the community at large, and even the Kultur Farain began to operate again, under the new name Yiddishe Geselschaft far Kunst un Kultur, the Jewish Association for Art and Culture, with headquarters on Zulueta Street.

100. During the 1950s a commemorative volume on the history of the Great Synagogue of Ostrog was published in Yiddish in Buenos Aires, including photographs.

101. José and Esther Winer, interviews, Miami, October 27, November 23, 1990.

102. Bejarano, "Cuba as America's Back Door," 483; *New York Times*, March 12, 1926, 5; September 16, 1927, 25; *Havaner Lebn* (Havana), February 24, 1933, 4.

103. When Solomon Suchlicki, Greenstein's brother, had his first son, he named him Jaime after his nephew. Jaime Suchlicki went on to become an accomplished historian of Cuba. José Winer, interview, October 27, 1990.

CHAPTER 3. REFUGEES FROM NAZISM

1. Kaplan interview, February 10, 1991. *Havander Lebn* succeeded the Centro Israelita's *Oifgang* (1927–30). Its founders were the Cuban Jewish poets Oscar Pinis, Carlos Schwarzapel, and Eliezer Aronowsky.

2. Sender Kaplan, interviewed by Berta and Matthew Lemberger, Miami, July 1, 1991.

3. See Jeff H. Lesser, "Continuity and Change within an Immigrant Com-

munity: The Jews of São Paulo, 1924–1945," *Luso-Brazilian Review,* 25, no. 2 (1988): 45–58.

4. Ruth G. Weitzenkorn, letter to author, Lakeland, Fla., June 9, 1991.
5. See David S. Wyman, *Paper Walls: America and the Refugee Crisis, 1938–1941,* 35–37. For an overview of policies on immigration for refugees, see Haim Avni, "Mexico: Immigration and Refuge," v–ix.
6. Felicia Rosshandler, *Passing through Havana: A Novel of a Wartime Girlhood in the Caribbean.* Although fiction, the book is based on the author's experience as a German-Jewish refugee.
7. Memorandum on European Refugees in Cuba, March 17, 1939, 837.55J/1 CF; Harold S. Tewell, American Consulate, Havana, to U.S. Ambassador to Cuba J. Butler Wright, April 1, 1939, 837.55J/2, U.S. National Archives (hereafter NA). Irwin F. Gellman, "The *St. Louis* Tragedy," 144–56, esp. 145–46.
8. Total support was estimated at $4 million in 1939. See Gellman, "The *St. Louis* Tragedy," 146.
9. For Nazi pressures on Jews to leave, see Arthur Prinz, "The Role of the Gestapo in Obstructing and Promoting Jewish Emigration," *Yad Vashem Studies* (Jerusalem) 2 (1958): 205–18; Joseph Tenenbaum, "The Crucial Year 1938," 49–77.
10. Richard Mainzer, Havana, to Dr. Hans Morgenthau, December 3, 1946; letters from Matilde Gruen to her daughters, Havana, Fall 1941–June 1942, Leo Baeck Institute Archive, New York (hereafter Baeck Archive).
11. See Mechener, "Memoirs," which includes family photographs and photocopies of all of the telegrams, official papers, and other materials generated in the desperate effort to get the Mecheners' son out of occupied France.
12. Letter to Dr. Adolph Mechener and family, mailed from Vienna, Baeck Archive.
13. Eric D. Kohler, "Byways of Emigration: Panama, the Canal Zone, and Jewish Rescue Efforts, 1919–1941," *Holocaust Studies Annual,* 89–91. See also Yehuda Bauer, *My Brother's Keeper. A History of the American Jewish Joint Distribution Committee, 1929–1939;* Raul Hilberg, *The Destruction of the European Jews;* Lucy Dawidowicz, *The War Against the Jews.* See also Richard Brietman, *The Architect of Genocide: Himmler and the Final Solution,* 55.
14. Ilsa Mittel-Ashe, letter to author, Stanford, Conn., January 5, 1991.
15. Quoted by Sheldon L. Richman, "Mr. Mencken and the Jews," 411. Mencken's attitudes toward Jews have been hotly debated, for his *Diary* and other writings contain often scurrilous anti-Semitic references. But he had the courage to speak out against the conspiracy of silence on the refugee issue when most others did not.
16. See Liane Reif-Lehrer's statement in the Boston *Globe,* May 22, 1989,

13. Dr. Reif-Lehrer was a five-year-old passenger on the *St. Louis*. Her cousin, Leon Klinghoffer, one of the only members of her family to escape the Holocaust, was murdered by PLO terrorists when his wheelchair was thrown from the deck of the hijacked *Achilles Lauro* nearly a half-century later. See also Boston *Sunday Globe*, October 20, 1985, A27.

17. David Schoenbrun, *New York Times Book Review*, June 30, 1974, 28. Canada's uncooperative stance is outlined in Irving Abella and Harold Troper, *None Is Too Many: Canada and the Jews of Europe, 1933–1948*. The book title is derived from a Mackenzie King response to a question about how many Jewish refugees should be permitted to enter.

18. Wyman, *Paper Walls*, 37.

19. Havana *Post*, December 1, 1938, 1.

20. Mittel-Ashe letter, January 5, 1991. In response to entreaties from individuals and organizations beseeching the U.S. embassy in Havana to help, officials wrote that they had been instructed to act by the Department of State and therefore could do nothing. See Ambassador J. Butler Wright, Havana, November 3, 1938, to the International Workers' Order, New York, roll 50, *Confidential U.S. Diplomatic Post Records, Central America and the Caribbean: Cuba, 1930–1945* (hereafter *Confidential Records*).

21. Mittel-Ashe letter, January 5, 1991.

22. According to Sender Kaplan, because they held papers, they were interned in concentration camps but were generally not sent to crematoria.

23. Morris Branfman, interview, April 9, 1987, Center for Holocaust Studies, Brooklyn, transcript RG 1641.

24. Juan Chongo Leiva, *El Fracaso de Hitler en Cuba*, 14. Leiva cites the names of other German agents, including a Cuban colonel, Andrés Pedro Golowchenco (whose Russian-sounding name appears dubious). Lunin later was apprehended by the Cuban counterespionage agency, Servicio de Inteligencia de Actividades Enemigas (SIAE) and confessed to his work as a German spy. Some doubt has been cast on the extent to which Lunin was integrated into the German spy network. See Alton Frye, *Nazi Germany and the American Hemisphere, 1933–1941*. See also Stanley E. Hilton, *Hitler's Secret War in South America, 1939–1945*.

25. The most active U.S. agent was Colonel Ross E. Rowell of Naval Intelligence, who arrived in Cuba in April 1939. He was stationed at the U.S. embassy. See Gordon Thomas and Max Morgan Witts, *Voyage of the Damned*, 35. According to Thomas and Witts, Rowell's report S/N R-233-39 enumerated the Abwehr strength in Cuba as "about sixty agents"; reports R-304-39 and R-236-39 identified Hoffman and Julius Otto Ott, the owner of the Swiss Home Restaurant, as the major agents.

26. See confidential memorandum, Williard L. Beaulac, First Secretary, U.S. Embassy, Havana, to Secretary of State, Washington, D.C., November 5, 1938, NA.

27. On Cuban volunteer participation in the Spanish civil war see Pablo de la Torriente Brau, *Peleando con los Milicianos,* and R. Nicolau González, *Cuba y la Defensa de la Republica Española (1936–1939).* On the anti-Fascist Spanish refugees, see Merle Linda Wolin, "Hollywood Goes Havana," 12. The *Herald Tribune* article by its Havana correspondent, Jack O'Brien, was translated and published as "Las actividades del fascismo en Cuba" in *Mediodía.*

28. As related by his son, General Manuel Benítez, interviewed by Vicki Luna, Miami, November 15, 1991.

29. This was Decree 55 (January 13, 1939). Within the Jewish community there was a sense that Laredo Brú's obstinacy may have derived in part from a personal experience: an angry break with industrialist Charles Shapiro, whose lawyer Brú had been. Arón and Saulo Yukem interview, Miami Beach, May 9, 1991.

30. Walter Lippmann, letter to author, Rio Grande, P.R., March 30, 1991.

31. Norbert Adler, letter to author, Binghamton, N.Y., July 24, 1990. For the legislation that forced Jews to leave without assets, see, for example, *Verordnung über den Einsatz jüdischen Vermögens,* v. 03.13.1938, *Reichsgesetzblatt* 1938, I, S. 1909, NA, and *Akten zur Deutschen Auswärtigen Politik* (hereafter *Akten*), S. 787 (on Goering's instructions of 01.24.1939 concerning forced Jewish emigration).

32. Mittel-Ashe letters, January 5, February 7, 1991. At one point, her uncle and his wife were interned in Tiscornia for almost a week and became ill there. The official, Ilsa Mittel-Ashe maintains, "demanded and got $50—and a kiss—and released they were."

33. Ruth G(oldschmidt) Weitzenkorn, letter to author, Lakeland, Fla., June 9, 1991.

34. See, for example, copy of permit signed by Manuel Benítez González for Oscar and Regina Schwartz, refugees from Germany on the *St. Louis.* Apr. 5, 1939, Joint Distribution Committee Archive, New York City (hereafter, JDC Archive).

35. Spatz's family had obtained their visas through the Gabrylewicz and Volpe agency. Hardy L. Spatz, letter to author, Charlotte, NC, July 3, 1991.

36. Carlos and Uva Márquez Sterling, interview, 14VA, March 26, 1985, Richter Library; Hardy Spatz, interview, Miami, November 6, 1990.

37. Norbert Adler, letters to author, Binghamton, N.Y., February 15, April 11, July 24, 1990; statement prepared by Mr. Adler for the Berlin Museum, August 1990. For an excellent photographic inventory of German

Jewish life before Hitler came to power, see Nachum T. Gidal, *Die Juden in Deutschland von der Roemerzeit bis zur Weimarer Republik.*

CHAPTER 4. THE SS *ST. LOUIS* INCIDENT

1. Telegram, Secretary of State Hull, November 22, 1938, 8 P.M., received at U.S. Embassy, Havana.
2. See roll 50, *Confidential Records.*
3. Report, E.O.B. [Ellis O. Briggs] to Sumner Welles, December 16, 1938, NNDG 775096, NA, reminding Welles that he had said this to lawyer Lawrence Berenson, a personal friend of Colonel Batista's and the former head of Havana's American Chamber of Commerce, who was very active in attempting to convince Cuban officials to give sanctuary to more refugees.
4. See *Confidential Records*, especially memoranda circulating in November and December 1938. U.S. embassy officials sent copies of translations of editorials in the *Diario de la Marina* opposing Jewish emigration to Cuba with accompanying evaluations sympathetic to the would-be emigrants (for example, *Diario de la Marina*, November 30, 1938).
5. See *Akten*, Bd. V, 78off.
6. The earliest detailed account of the *St. Louis* is Mark Wischnitzer's *To Dwell in Safety: The Story of Jewish Migration since 1800*, 197–200.
7. Gellman, "The *St. Louis* Tragedy," 147.
8. Decree 937, *Gazeta Oficial* (Havana), 1, esp. article 1.
9. Kaplan interview, July 1, 1991.
10. *Berliner Jüdische Rundschau* (Berlin), March 3, 1939, 216. This newspaper, circulated among the Jewish community in Berlin, noted that often Cuban immigration authorities granted reductions of this sum, "by sometimes only demanding a payment of $60–100 and obtaining a guarantee for the remainder through a special insurance policy."
11. Harold S. Tewell, "European Refugees in Cuba" (Communique no. 311, March 17–18, 1939, 16–18, State Department File 811.11/855).
12. Thomas and Witts, *Voyage of the Damned*, 37. See also U.S. Department of State, Memorandum on European Refugees in Cuba, June 8, 1939, RG 59, 837.55J/51, and Memorandum of the Division of the American Republics, June 12, 1939, RG 59, 837.55J/63, NA.
13. Stanley Kauffmann, "At Sea," 20.
14. Cabin class program, *St. Louis*, Hamburg-Amerika Line (provided by Lutz Krätzschmar).
15. A family of three emigrating to the United States could carry 60 reichsmarks, or $24. See *Verordnung für Devisenbewirtschaftung vom*

22. *December 1938. Reichsgesetzblatt*, I, S. 1851. Personal goods could be shipped abroad after first being inspected to prevent smuggling of currency. Containers of such goods, called *Judenkisten*, were stored all over German harbors awaiting shipment (information provided by Lutz Krätzschmar).

16. See Hans Herlin, "Das Rote J," *Der Stern*, 1961 (clipping provided by Gunter W. Cohn).

17. Thomas and Witts, *Voyage of the Damned*, 50–51.

18. Rachel and Martin Koeppels, interview, June 3, 1989, South East Florida Holocaust Documentation and Education Center, Miami.

19. Memorandum, Frank N. Trager to Morris D. Waldman, American Jewish Committee, New York, August 30, 1939, JDC Archive (hereafter Trager memorandum); *American Jewish Yearbook* 41 (1939–40), "Review of the Year 5699," 355–56; Kahn, "Jewish Colony," 64.

20. Laura L. Margolis, Havana, to Cecilia Razovsky, Executive Director, National Coordinating Committee, Joint Distribution Committee, New York, May 23, 1939, JDC Archive.

21. One of the results of the meetings was the formation of a short-lived People's Committee, which JDC representatives from the United States complained was controlled by "the leading Jewish Communists in Cuba." See Trager memorandum, 10.

22. Dionisio Hashid to Rabbi Nesim Gambach, August 19, 1978 (provided by Rabbi Gambach). The Comité functioned for some years but gradually diminished its activities. Rabbi Gambach's informant claimed that the reason was that the Centro Israelita did not want to yield its position as the primary voice for Cuban Jewry. The de facto spokesman for the community was Adolph H. Kates, a Belgian Jew well connected through business to the Americans and to the Maduros and some of the older, established families on the island.

23. Milton D. Goldsmith, Joint Relief Committee, Havana, to Joseph J. Schwartz, Joint Distribution Committee, New York, September 7, 1939, JDC Archive; Trager memorandum, 13. There were 2,200 Jewish refugees, but half were self-sufficient, living on funds sent by family members in the United States and Canada.

24. Diary from aboard ship written by Albert Eskenazy, provided by Dr. Martin Lackner; Hilde Rothold Backow, interview, March 10, 1990.

25. One of the crew members, Carl Glissmann, was interviewed at length by Lutz Krätzschmar in Hamburg, who provided me with a transcript. See also Albert Eskenazy memoir, translated by Martin Lackner, 6, ms courtesy of Martin Lackner (hereafter, Eskenazy memoir).

26. Eliot Lefkowitz, "The Double Crossing." See also Henry L. Feingold, *The Politics of Rescue: The Roosevelt Administration and the Holo-*

caust, 1938–1945, 64–65. Captain Schroeder's role is analyzed in a book first published in 1984 by a free-lance writer who spent years tracking down survivors of the ship, Hans Herlin (*Die Reise der Verdammten: Die Tragoedie der St. Louis*). Also, Leah Kadden, letter to author, Chicago, January 24, 1991.

27. Thomas and Witts, *Voyage of the Damned,* 88–90. Benítez interview, November 15, 1991; Abe Resnick, interview, Miami Beach, April 2, 1991.
28. Milton D. Goldsmith to Cecilia Razovsky, Havana, October 27, 1939, JDC Archive; Kohler, "Byways of Emigration," 92.
29. Telegram, German Legation, Havana, to Foreign Office, Berlin, T. No. 1111/39, Havana, May 25, 1939. Citation provided by Lutz Krätzschmar, Hamburg. Translation assistance from Dr. Hannah Wartenberg and Dr. Susan E. Cernyak-Spatz.
30. Trager memorandum, 7.
31. Cited in Thomas and Witts, *Voyage of the Damned,* 106. Rivero died in 1944. In 1954, when the *Diario de la Marina* published its special issue (no. 559) commemorating the 125th anniversary of the newspaper, it included an apologetic biographical statement about Rivero saying that his support of fascism had been based on his belief that it was the only realistic defense against the Communist menace.
32. *Diario de la Marina,* November 30, 1938, translated and cited by U.S. Embassy, J. Butler Wright, Ambassador's Report to Secretary of State Hull, November 30, 1938, *Confidential Records.*
33. Translated and cited by U.S. Ambassador J. Butler Wright, ibid.
34. *Havana Post,* May 30, 1939, 10.
35. See *Cuba To-Day* (Havana), July 11, 1939, 4.
36. See Koeppels interview, June 3, 1989.
37. *Cuba To-Day,* June 1, 1939, 4, quoting the daily paper *País,* May 31, 1939.
38. Eskenazy memoir, 8. Rabbi Lasker, in his eighties, recollected in an interview with the author that a young girl had died aboard ship, but there is no evidence to support this.
39. Hilde Rothold Backow, interview, Longboat Key, Fla., March 10, 1990.
40. Eskenazy memoir. See also *New York Times,* June 3, 1939, 1. *Bohemia* on June 11, 1939, published an emotional plea, "A la Habana ha llegado un barco," focusing on the story of "Max Ludwig," "delirious and ravished with pain" in a Havana hospital. Translated manuscript in RG 3344, JDC Archive.
41. Coert du Bois, U.S. Consul General, Despatch no. 1017, May 31, 1939, Havana, "Jewish Refugee Situation in Habana," U.S. Consulate General, Havana, State Department File 811.11-General, NA.

42. Meyer Lansky's widow maintained this after his death. Information provided by Michael Fooner, Miami, May 20, 1991. See also Thomas and Witts, *Voyage of the Damned,* 221. The story about wearing crosses, which is unlikely to be true, is reported in Herlin, *Die Reise der Verdammten,* 90. The names of only two of the passengers permitted to land, Mr. and Mrs. Ludwig Baruch, were disclosed in the press. See *Havana Post,* May 30, 1939, 10.

43. *Havana Post,* May 30, 1939, 4.

44. Deborah Lipstadt, *Beyond Belief: The American Press and the Coming of the Holocaust, 1933–1945,* 116–17.

45. *Cuba To-Day,* June 7, 1939, 4, citing *Avance* and other daily newspapers; partial transcript of Berenson visit, undated, JDC Archive. See also Barry J. Konovitch, "The Fiftieth Anniversary of the *St. Louis:* What Really Happened," 204–6.

46. Summary of Advisory Committee to the Joint Relief Committee Report, Trager memorandum, 14.

47. Newspaper reports summarized in *Cuba To-Day,* May 31, 1939, 2; May 26, 1939, 4; June 1, 1939, 4–5.

48. Despite the failure of his mission, Berenson remained close to Batista until Batista's exile in 1959. Berenson personally accompanied the fallen dictator to the Dominican Republic. Statement by Louis Stanley Berenson, nephew of Lawrence Berenson, Miami Beach, February 2, 1989, cited by Konovitch, "Fiftieth Anniversary," 205.

49. *Discusión,* June 5, 1939, 1.

50. Trager memorandum, 8.

51. Extracted from a letter from Rabbi Meir Lasker in Philadelphia to the Jubilee Committee, *Golden Anniversary,* 21.

52. Rabbi Lasker was not universally respected during the years he was in Cuba: the representative of the JDC snidely described him in August 1939 as "a young Rabbi who has traveled widely but who does not seem to have profited too greatly by his travels." Trager memorandum, 8.

53. *Chicago Daily Tribune,* June 2, 1939, 2.

54. *Hoy* (Havana), June 2, 1939, 1.

55. Liesl Joseph Loeb, interview, South East Florida Holocaust Documentation and Educational Center, June 3, 1989; statement by Dr. Oscar Schwartz, a *St. Louis* passenger, "Abschnitt: Von Tage der Auswanderung aus Deutschland bis zur Landung in London, 13 Mai 1939–21 Juni 1939," Baeck Archive.

56. Summary Report, James N. Rosenberg to JDC, June 15, 1939, RG 3344, JDC Archive.

57. Information provided by Herbert Karliner, Miami, December 9, 1990.

See also Mary Voboril, "Haitians' Plight Reminiscent of Voyage of the *Damned*," *Miami Herald*, November 17, 1991, K1, 3.

58. Richard Breitman and Alan M. Kraut. *American Refugee Policy and European Jewry, 1933–1945*, 72.

59. For example, telegram, *St. Louis* Passenger Committee to Prime Minister Neville Chamberlain, June 9, 1939, British Public Record Office, London (transcript provided by Lutz Krätzschmar; translation by Susan E. Cernyak-Spatz).

60. Adolph H. Kates, Havana, to David M. Bressler, Joint Distribution Committee, New York, June 10, 1939, and see also S. L. Maduro, Havana, to David M. Bressler, June 10, 1939, both in RG 3344, JDC Archive. Also, Leni Yahil, *The Holocaust: The Fate of European Jewry, 1932–1945*, 119. This source indicates that some of the passengers not taken by Britain, France, Belgium, or Holland were sent back to Germany. There is no evidence for this assertion.

61. Negotiations were carried out by Morris C. Troper, the JDC's European chairman stationed in Paris. See Arthur D. Morse, "Voyage to Doom," 67.

62. June 15, 1939, quoted in Thomas and Witts, *Voyage of the Damned*, 283.

63. *New York Times*, June 19, 1939, 4. See also Shlomo Kless, "The Rescue of Jewish Children in Belgium During the Holocaust," 275–87; *Gazet van Antwerpen* (Antwerp), June 19, 1939, 1–2. Citations provided in Lutz Krätzschmar, letter to author, Hamburg, May 1, 1991.

64. See Robert E. Dallos, "Sequel," 16–17; Krätzschmar to author, May 1, 1991.

65. Leah Kadden, letter to author, Chicago, January 24, 1991. The Kaddens were reunited in the United States in January 1946. Their father, who had preceded them to Cuba and who had been waiting there when the *St. Louis* arrived, remained in Cuba until allowed to enter the United States. He never spoke about his Cuban experience, although his daughter knows that, with his family interned in Europe, it was most difficult.

66. This was during the first phase of Nazi policy (expelling Jews from Europe). The second phase, the "Final Solution" (seeking to destroy all Jews), was adopted in 1941. Thomas and Witts, *Voyage of the Damned*, 301–2; Backow interview, March 10, 1990.

67. Eskenazy memoir, 14.

68. Habif interview, April 10, 1991.

69. See Reif-Lehrer, "Memoir," Boston, April 1988, 94.

70. "Refugees Land at Last," *Southampton Daily Echo* (U.K.), June 22, 1939, 1.

71. See Bernard Wasserstein, *Britain and the Jews of Europe, 1939–1945*, esp. chapter titled "The Home Front."

72. For Captain Gerhard Schroeder's recollections of the voyage, see his memoir, *Heimatlos auf Hoher See.*

73. See *Dagens Nyheter* (Stockholm), June 2–20, 1939; *Goteborgs Handels*, June 2–21, 1939, University of Uppsala Library, Uppsala, Sweden. Translation provided by Paul Levine.

74. *Diario de la Marina*, June 2, 1939, 1.

75. Ted Stone, letter to the *New York Times*, June 23, 1992, A14. The letter writer also claimed that the then U.S. ambassador, Joseph P. Kennedy, had "talked Britain into taking in" an allotment of refugees from the ship. There is no historical evidence to document that this happened.

76. Yahil, *The Holocaust*, 119.

77. *Dagens Nyheter* (Stockholm), June 2, 1939, 6; June 3, 1939, 7; *New York Times*, June 3, 1939, 1.

78. *New York Times*, June 5, 1939, 1, 4.

79. *New York Times*, editorial, June 8, 1939, 24. No follow-up information was disclosed about the fate of these refugees.

80. Thomas and Witts, *Voyage of the Damned*, 303.

81. See *Diario de la Marina*, June 4, 1939, 1; June 6, 1939, 3; June 8, 1939, 1. The *Diario* articles were written in a fairly neutral tone and did not cast racist aspersions. Opposition to admitting the refugees was explained on the basis of Cuba's poverty and inability to absorb newcomers. Information provided by Carolina Amram Bush, Coral Gables, Fla., May 15, 1986.

82. *Información*, May 26, 1939, 1; *Diario de la Marina*, May 18, 1939, 1; *País*, May 31, 1939, 1.

83. Winer interview, November 23, 1990.

84. Breitman and Kraut, *American Refugee Policy*, 71; *Havana Post*, May 28, 1939, 1. The article, by Jimmy Canel, offered sympathy: "Many cried unabashedly as a near-hysterical youth fought his way through the crowd in an attempt to reach his aged parents. His fist full of bills, he cried at port police, 'They have no money! They need bills!' Port authorities unbent, and permitted the son and parents to meet for a few brief seconds at the gangplank. A kiss, a few words, and they were separated again."

85. Rabbi Nathan Witkin, interview, Sarasota, March 6, 1990; Woodrow de Castro, interview, Miami, March 2, 1990. Eric D. Kohler provides a detailed account of the events in Panama in "Byways of Emigration," 89–118. See also telegram, George Andrews (U.S. Consul General, Panama) to Cordell Hull, September 10, 1940, "134 Aliens Shipped

from Quarantine Station to U.S.A.," Panama *American*, September 16, 1940, cited by Kohler, 117.

86. *Pariser Tageblatt* (Paris), no. 1031, June 24, 1939, 224. Citation provided by Lutz Krätzschmar.
87. The book appeared in 1974, the motion picture in 1977.
88. Kaplan interview, February 10, 1991.
89. Habif interview, April 10, 1991.
90. Coert du Bois, American Consul General, Havana, to Mr. Billikopf, address unknown, September 30, 1939, JDC Archive. Du Bois had held lesser positions in the consulate general since 1937. The JDC's Frank N. Trager praised du Bois as a "fair, courteous, wise official" (Trager memorandum, Conference Register of Havana Trip, August 12–25), 2.
91. For documentation on behind-the-scenes efforts in the United States to rescue more refugees, see the JDC archives in New York City, including correspondence between petitioners and Professor Hans Morgenthau of the University of Chicago. Dutch author and playwright Jan de Hartog also popularized the story of the *St. Louis* in his *Schipper naast God*.
92. Charlotte Frank, letter to author, Prairie Village, Kans., September 12, 1990. Frank's story is typical. She arrived in Cuba in February 1939 with her mother, 50, and uncle, 62, on the SS *Iberia*; her father, 63, came a month earlier on the SS *Orinoco*. He had been released from a concentration camp and told to leave Germany as soon as possible. They lived in a boardinghouse for two weeks with other refugees, then rented a house. Frank does "not recall" associating with Cubans.
93. Wischnitzer, "The Historical Background of the Settlement of Jewish Refugees in Santo Domingo," 46 n.3.
94. Virgilio Trujillo's statements are discussed in C. Hoepelman, *Nuestra Vida Exterior: notas sobre historia diplomática dominicana, 1844–1950*. Ciudad Trujillo: Arte y Cine, 1951, 312–13.
95. Russell H. Fitzgibbon, ed., *The Era of Trujillo, Dominican Dictator. By Jesús de Galíndez*, 212–17; Albert C. Hicks, *Blood in the Streets: The Life and Rule of Trujillo*, 168–69.
96. Freda Kirchwey, "Caribbean Refuge," 466–68.
97. See Virgílio Ferrer Gutiérrez, *Luperón, Brida y Espuela* (Havana: n.p., 1940), cited in Wischnitzer, "Historical Background," 49, nn. 11–12.
98. Published in the monthly bulletin of the Alliance Israélite Universelle in Paris, in the *Allgemeine Zeitung des Judentums* in Germany, and in the Russian Jewish weekly, *Voskhod*, in St. Petersburg.
99. Wischnitzer, "Historical Background," 45–58.
100. Evian proceedings communicated to the League of Nations, July 15, 1938, printed as C.224, M.143, 1938, 12, cited in ibid., 46.

101. Josef David Eichen, *Sosúa: Una colonia hebrea en la República Dominicana*, 22–27, passim; Siegfried Katsch, Elke-Maria Katsch, and Henry P. David, *Sosúa-Verheissenes Land*.

102. See Efraim Zadoff, "Un Análisis Comparativo de las Redes Educativas Judías de México y Argentina, 1935–1955," 129–30.

103. See Elkin, *Jews of the Latin American Republics*, 158–59; Alicia Gojman de Backal, "Minorías, Estado y Movimientos Nacionalistas de la Clase Media en México. Liga Antichina y Antijudia (Siglo XX)," 174–92.

104. Haim Avni, *Antisemitism under Democratic and Dictatorial Regimes: the Experience of Latin American Jewry*. Anita Brenner wrote in an article submitted to the *Nation* (but not published) that at the last minute the word *judío* had been removed from banners, replaced by words like *evil merchant, foreigners, invaders*, and *Israelite*. Cited by Avni, 13.

105. Comité Judío Americano, *Comunidades judías de latinoamérica*, 107; Tovye Meisel, "Yidn in Meksike" (*Algemeine Entsiclopedia* 5 (1957): 410), cited by Judith Laikin Elkin, "The Reception of the Muses in the Circum-Caribbean," 294.

106. See Harriet Sara Lesser, "A History of the Jewish Community of Mexico City, 1912–1970," Ph.D. diss. (Jewish Theological Seminary and Columbia University, 1972), cited by Elkin, "Reception of the Muses," 293. Also see H. A. Walter, *Deutsche Exilliteratur 1933–1950*, 291–380, and W. Kiessling, *Exil in Lateinamerika* (Frankfort, 1981), cited by David Bankier, "Los Exilados Alemanes en Mexico y sus Vinculos con la Comunidad Judía (1942–1945)," 79–89.

107. Avni, "Mexico," 40–41.

108. See *The Jewish Survey* 2, no. 5 (September 1942): 22–23; Avni, "Mexico," 42, citing State Department correspondence, 840.48 (Refugees 2244), note of September 6, 1940.

109. Dr. Luis Glaser, interview, Coral Gables, Fla., March 13, 1990.

110. Norbert Adler to Günter Cohn, Binghamton, N.Y., February 15, 1990.

111. Ibid.

112. Rieur, "Jewish Colony of Cuba"; Günter W. Cohn, letter to author, Miami, June 3, 1990.

113. Elkin, *Jews of the Latin American Republics*, 85.

114. John Mendelsohn, *The Holocaust*, vol. 7, *Jewish Emigration: The S.S. St. Louis Affair and Other Cases*, i.

115. Statement of unidentified *Navemar* passenger to Rieur, "Jewish Colony of Cuba," 18.

116. Ibid., 18–20.

117. Leo Baeck Institute, *LBI News*, no. 58 (Summer 1990): 7; Cohn letter,

June 3, 1990; Margalit Bejarano, letter to author, Jerusalem, April 10, 1991.

118. Alex Weissberg, *Desperate Mission: Joel Brand's Story* (New York: Criterion Books, 1958). Montello is discussed in Jenö Lévai, *Zsidósors Magyarországon* (Jewish Fate in Hungary) (Budapest: Magyar Teka, 1948).

119. Information on the Mandel brothers and Raoul Wallenberg in Dr. Peter P. Tarjan, memorandum to author, February 28, 1990, with translated excerpts from the third edition of Jenö Lévai, *Raoul Wallenberg* (Budapest: Magyar Téka, 1989), 93. The first two editions of this book, published in 1948, were bought out within two months; the third was confiscated by Hungarian authorities but reissued in 1989.

120. Randolph L. Braham, *The Politics of Genocide: The Holocaust in Hungary*, 2:1120.

121. Braham, *The Politics of Genocide*, 2:714. In October 1990, a former KGB officer revealed to the press that Wallenberg had been shot inside the Soviet Union in 1947 for refusing to become a Soviet agent.

122. See Erich Kulka, "Auschwitz Condoned," citing correspondence from Mantello. In Braham, *The Politics of Genocide*, nn. 81 and 92, 729–30.

123. Lowell Gudmundson, "Costa Rican Jewry: An Economic and Political Outline," in Elkin and Merkx, *Jewish Presence*, 219. See also Jacobo Schifter Sikora, Lowell Gudmundson, and Mario Solera, *El judío en Costa Rica*.

124. Gudmundson, "Costa Rican Jewry," 220–23.

125. Lowell Gudmunson notes that, although the Cortés-Effinger era was easily targeted for its "vaguely pro-Nazi symbolism," Calderón's administration actually carried out more stringent measures that affected Jewish residents of Costa Rica. See "Costa Rican Jewry," 224–25. See *La Tribuna* (San José), May 17, 1940, 1, 7.

126. Translated by Lowell Gudmundson from *Diario de Costa Rica*, October 9, 1946, 1, 8.

127. *La República* (San José), October 26, 1955, 7, cited by Gudmundson, "Costa Rican Jewry," 228 n. 26; also Padre Francisco Herrera, "The Holy Church Takes the Side of the Jews," *Diario de Costa Rica*, March 2, 1960, 12.

128. See Yehuda Bauer, *American Jewry and the Holocaust: The American Jewish Joint Distribution Committee, 1939–1945*, 45–64.

129. Rolf Wartenberg, "My Salvador Experience," letter to author, Miami, October 12, 1990.

130. See Arthur Prinz, "The Role of the Gestapo in Obstructing and Promoting Jewish Emigration."

131. See Gerhardt Neumann, "German Jews in Colombia: A Study in Im-

migrant Adjustment," esp. 387. Columbia closed its doors to would-be immigrants from Central and Eastern Europe in 1939.

132. Nathan Goldberg, "Immigration Attitudes of Mexicans: An Insight," 3; *Inter-American Monthly*, December 1942.

133. Lasker interview, November 14, 1989, and Spatz interview, November 4, 1990. Details about German spy operations in the hemisphere, including its Transocean News Agency, may be found in Alton Frye's *Nazi Germany*, 101–4.

134. Caio de Lima Cavalcanti, interview, Rio de Janeiro, November 11, 1964. Many of the valuables he took as bribes were converted to cash in Europe, but he also shipped back to Brazil large amounts of property, which he showed me in a boastful manner.

135. Lisa Fittko, *Mein Weg über die Pyrenaen: Erinnerungen*, 247.

136. John F. Morley, *Vatican Diplomacy and the Jews during the Holocaust, 1939–1943*, 18–22. Copies of the correspondence in the original languages are reprinted in Pierre Blet et al., *Le Saint Siège et les victimes de la guerre. Mars 1939–Décembre 1940*, esp. 45, 63–64, 386–89, 427, 433, 524. See also Ethel Volfzon Kosminsky, *Rolandia, a Terra Prometida: Judeus Refugiados do Nazismo no Norte do Paraná* (São Paulo: Centro de Estudos Judaicos, FFLCH/USP, 1985).

137. See Mgr. Tardini, Secrétaire d'Etat, Vatican, January 4, 1940 (A.E.S. 159/40 orig.), in Blet et al., *Le Saint Siège*, 213–24.

138. Cardinal Maglione to Mgr. Besson, head of the Swiss Catholic mission in Berne, Vatican, November 7, 1939 (A.S.S. 7079), in Blet et al., *Le Saint Siège*, 180–81.

CHAPTER 5. THE WAR YEARS

1. Elkin, "Reception of the Muses," 296–97.

2. Dr. Hannah Wartenberg, interviewed by Werner Stahl, Wantaugh, N.Y., May 26, 1991.

3. See Nathan Eck, "The Rescue of Jews with the Aid of Passports and Citizenship Papers of Latin American States," *Yad Vashem Studies*, no. 1 (1957): 125–52.

4. The Joint Distribution Committee in October 1939 estimated that between 5,000 and 6,000 German refugees had landed in Cuba prior to the *St. Louis*. See Trager memorandum, 3.

5. Michel Mendelson obituary, *Miami Herald*, January 21, 1992, B3, quoting George Mendelson, Michel's son.

6. Hardy L. Spatz, letter to author, Charlotte, N.C., July 23, 1990.

7. See Elkin, "Reception of the Muses," 296–97.

8. Bishop Rummel, text of telegram to Joint Distribution Committee,

enclosed with "Special Bulletin," Memo #11, Joint Distribution Committee, May 6, 1942, JDC Archive. Dr. García Montes in Havana as well as Adolph H. Kates, one of the American Jews, also lent personal assistance. See J. C. Hyman, New York, to Lawrence Berenson, May 12, 1942, and to Adolph H. Kates, May 25, 1942, JDC Archive; Augusta Mayerson, Director, Migration Department, National Refugee Service, New York, to Robert Pilpel, JDC, September 24, 1942, JDC Archive, New York, all RG 3344.

9. Dr. Adolph Mechener, "Memoirs," typewritten draft, ch. 25, 340, Baeck Archive.

10. For example, *Berliner Jüdische Rundschau* (Berlin), April 21, 1939, 217–18.

11. See Robert Pilpel, New York, to Charles H. Jordan, Joint Relief Committee, Havana, May 7, 1942, RG 3344, JDC Archive.

12. Elkin, "Reception of the Muses," 89. The professors included Boris Goldenberg in sociology, Heinrich Friedlander in economics, and Desiderio Weiss in languages.

13. Felix Reyler, interview, Miami Beach, May 26, 1991. Thousands of Turkish Jews resident in France also were rescued. See Eck, "The Rescue of Jews," 126; *Proceedings of the Trials of War Criminals before International Military Tribunal* (Washington, DC: U.S. Government Printing Office, 1945), 16:332.

14. Uva Márquez Sterling comment to Mark D. Szuchman, Miami, 1985. Her husband, Carlos Márquez Sterling, held the posts of minister of labor and president of the House of Representatives. In 1940, he led seventy-six delegates in drafting a new constitution, considered one of the most sweeping for its time. See *Miami Herald*, May 4, 1991.

15. Information provided by Professor Javier Figueiroa, San Juan, P.R., February 11, 1989.

16. For example, *Hoy* (July 5, 1939, 3) reported that "Israel Sarovich and Izaac Zark" had thrown 150 Guanabacoa workers out of work by moving their factory to Marianao.

17. Trager memorandum, 5.

18. See Phillip Block, Executive Director, American ORT Federation, to Hugo Semler, October 19, 1942, YIVO Archive. The ORT worked through the existing Joint Relief Committee.

19. *Unterwegs (En Camino): Revista de los Refugiados Hebreos de Cuba,* was subtitled *V . . .,* files in YIVO Archive, New York. The editor was Günter W. Cohn. The word *unterwegs* means "in transit" in German.

20. These are from the ten items in the weekly list, "Uebertragung der englischen Aufgabe," in *Unterwegs,* June 19, 1942, 12. Some of the ads were placed by Ashkenazic firms but written in German. At least one

ad appeared in the 1942 Rosh Hashanah edition (September 11, p. 14) placed "in behalf of a Cuban friend of our publication."

21. See, for example, "The Situation of Surviving Jews in Europe," *V . . .*, no. 47, March 19, 1945, 4–5; and "10 Jahre Aufbauarbeit in Suedamerika," *V . . .*, no. 50, August 22, 1945.
22. Weitzenkorn letter, June 9, 1991.
23. Günter W. Cohn, letter to author, N. Miami Beach, August 14, 1990.
24. Natalie Lyons, interview, Coral Gables, Fla., April 28, 1990. Many Germans, although personally clean, were not used to taking baths more than once or twice a week.
25. Mittel-Ashe letter, January 5, 1991.
26. Weitzenkorn letter, June 9, 1991.
27. *Unterwegs*, June 19, 1942, 4.
28. Kaplan interview, February 10, 1991.
29. Adler letter, April 17, 1992.
30. Trager memorandum, 4.
31. Weitzenkorn letter, June 9, 1991.
32. William Solomon, interviewed by Linda Lurie, Miami, October 12, 1982. The Solomons came on the SS *Iberia*, the last ship to enter Havana in 1939 before the SS *St. Louis*.
33. Francis (Franzi) Mechener to Dr. Adolph Mechener, December 13, 1938, Baeck Archive.
34. Werner Stahl estimated that 90 percent of the refugees became involved in diamond production. Wartenberg interview, May 26, 1991.
35. I am indebted to Hardy Spatz for his colorful and detailed explanation of Cuba's refugee diamond industry. Letter to author, November 4, 1990, Charlotte, N.C.
36. Sara Reed, interviewed by Keith Frostad, Miami, May 7, 1990.
37. *Unterwegs*, June 19, 1942, 7; fund raising letter, Amadeo Pacifico, President, Asociación Italo-Cubana Antifascista, Havana, September 1944, YIVO Archive; *El País* (Havana), June 18, 1942.
38. Günter W. Cohn notes that Kaden was married to a Jewish woman and had a child by another. Letter to author, Miami, March 8, 1990.
39. See *El País* (Havana), June 18, 1942. Werner Stahl, from a wealthy Berlin family, married a Cuban girl he had met as a student at the Ruston Academy.
40. June 9, 1939, 1. Harrison was described as a "retired scientist."
41. Fernando Ortíz, "Defensa Cubana Contra el Racismo Antisemita," 97–107. Ortíz was president of the Asociación Nacional Contra las Discriminaciones Racistas. See María del Carmen Rivero, "The Jewish Experience in Cuba," 6–7.
42. See, for example, the translation of Alberto Aaron's "The Liquidation

of the German Jews," reprinted in Spanish from *World Christianity and Contemporary Jewish Record* (New York) in *Ultra*, no. 39 (1939): 251–54.

43. Cited by Michael Mashburg, "Documents Concerning the American State Department and the Stateless European Jews, 1924–1944," *Jewish Social Studies* 23 (Winter/Spring 1977): 164–65.

44. Kahn, "Jewish Colony," 69. See also Kula, "La emigración polaca," 131–149.

45. Díaz Versón, *El Nazismo en Cuba*, 14–15.

46. E.W.T. [Major E. W. Timberlake], Report 5550, Military Attaché's Office, U.S. Embassy, Havana, March 17, 1938, 820.02, in *Confidential Records*.

47. Before the war broke out, and before Cuba joined the United States and the Soviet Union in the anti-Nazi alliance, Batista was strongly criticized by foreign observers for legalizing the Communists. See Duncan Aikman, *The All-American Front*, 179.

48. One of his ministers, Dr. Santiago Rey Pernas, married a Cuban Jewish woman, Berta Ziegenhirt. Information provided by Roberto E. Hernández, Miami, January 19, 1990.

49. *Diario de la Marina*, December 14, 1941, 3 (on the Isle of Pines detention camp); December 18, 1941, 20 (on the arrest of Japanese fishermen); January 4, 1942, 1 (on the arrest of German nationals). Citation provided by Omar Cuan. DiVivanco was arrested by Cuan's grandfather, Lieutenant Antolín Falcón.

50. Norbert Adler, Binghamton, N.Y., to Günter Cohn, February 15, 1990, provided by G. Cohn.

51. Elkin, "Reception of the Muses," 297–98.

52. American Jewish writers and David Wyman have claimed that considerable anti-Semitism existed, coloring U.S. policy, but others have offered a more dispassionate and perhaps balanced view. I am indebted to Dr. Bernard Wasserstein for this observation.

53. Telegram, Spruille Braden to Cordell Hull, Havana, January 11, 1944, Diplomatic 1944C, Spruille Braden Papers, Columbia University (hereafter Braden Papers), naming Nestor Carbonell as involved. Citation provided by Ignacio Klich, London.

54. Telegram, Braden to Hull, Havana, January 11, 1944, Braden Papers.

55. Breitman and Kraut, *American Refugee Policy*, 137; memorandum, Messersmith to Hull, June 28, 1941, RG 59, 811.111/2275, NA.

56. Braden to Avra Warren, Havana, December 2, 1943, File Correspondence, Diplomatic 1943U–Z, Braden Papers.

57. From United States Embassy, Havana, August 1, 1944, File Correspondence, Diplomatic 1945Ne–P, Braden Papers.

58. Díaz Versón, *El Nazismo en Cuba*, 53.

59. J. Pando González, bureau chief of the Prensa-Publicidad, statement to press, Havana, May 13, 1941.

60. Melville Bell Grosvenor, "Cuba–America's Sugar Bowl," 23.

61. Kaplan interview, February 10, 1991.

62. Pérez, *Cuba: Between Reform and Revolution*, 283.

63. Bejarano, "Antisemitism in Cuba," 33.

64. Pérez, *Cuba: Between Reform and Revolution*, 284. See also E. Vignier and G. Alonso, *La corrupción política y administrativa en Cuba, 1944–1952*.

65. Sender M. Kaplan, "Jewish Robinson Crusoes," *Havaner Lebn*, October 12, 1934. Kaplan worked as secretary of the association of Cuba's thirty-six Jewish organizations, which was headed by Herman L. Beller.

66. See the short stories of Abraham Dubelman, *Oif Kubaner Erd*, cited by Elkin, *Jews of the Latin American Republics*, 88.

67. Spatz interview, November 6, 1990. See also Rieur, "Jewish Colony of Cuba," 40.

68. Schuchinsky interview, Miami Beach, February 27, 1985.

69. Campaña de Emergencia Pro-Palestina, Comité del Keren Hayesod, "Programa de la Velada," November 3, 1936, YIVO Archive.

70. Adler letter, July 24, 1990.

71. Fittko interview, March 30, 1990.

72. Maritza Corrales, letter to author, Havana, January 2, 1992.

73. See *Unterwegs*, June 19, 1942, 9. See also "Casa 'La Isla' advertisement in the same issue, 7.

74. Hardy Spatz, letter to author, Charlotte, N.C., November 2, 1990.

75. Information provided by Dr. Robert Kirsner.

76. See Abraham Matterin, "Martí y las discriminaciones raciales" (Havana: Ediciones de la Agrupación Cultural Hebreo-Cubana), cited by Elkin, *Jews of the Latin American Republics*, 89; and the Sephardic writer and civic activist Marco Pitchón's *José Martí y la compresión humana, 1853–1953*.

77. Kahn, "Jewish Colony," 74.

78. As related to Golo Mann, cited in Gordon A. Craig's review of Mann's *Reminiscences and Reflections: A Youth in Germany* (New York: Norton, 1990), *New York Times Book Review*, September 16, 1990, 15. Hahn opposed Zionism, as did many right-wing German Jews, especially followers of Naumann's movement.

79. Koeppels interview, June 3, 1989.

80. Fittko, *Mein Weg über die Pyrenaen: Erinnerungen*, 222–23. Translation by Hannah Wartenberg.

81. Fittko, *Mein Weg,* 276–69, 267–68.
82. Walter Lippmann, interview, Melbourne, Fla., February 25, 1991.
83. "Noticias de la Filarmónica," Havana, March 10, 1943, 1–4. Ticket prices for a Micha Elman concert, for example, ranged from $15 for a box for six to 50 cents for the second balcony. Before Kleiber's arrival, the director of the Philharmonic was Paul Csonka, an Austrian Jew married to a non-Jewish Austrian soprano, who before the war divorced him and returned to Europe. Csonka spent the war in Cuba as director of the orchestra's choir. Information courtesy of Günter W. Cohn. See also Federico Heinlein, "Recordando a Erich Kleiber," 222–41.
84. *Golden Anniversary,* 25.
85. Fittko, *Mein Weg,* 268; Lisa Fittko, interviewed by Hannah Wartenberg, Chicago, March 30, 1990.
86. Lasker interview, November 14, 1989.
87. Spatz interview, November 6, 1990.
88. Lasker interview, November 14, 1989; Ernst Martel, interviewed by Hannah Wartenberg, Chicago, March 10, 1989; Gunter Kosse, interview, Atlantis, Fla., January 29, 1992.
89. Weitzenkorn letter, June 9, 1991.
90. Amram, "Assimilation of Immigrants," based on interviews with former teachers at Havana's Instituto Edison.
91. See Víctor Mitrani, "A mis Correligionarios y a las Colectividades Hebreas de Cuba!" flier, Havana, 1942. Marco Pitchón bitterly blamed Sender Kaplan's *Havaner Lebn* for fostering "reactionary," "defamatory," and "criminal" disunity. Marco Pitchón, open letter to Unión Sionista de Cuba, January 25, 1945, YIVO Archive.
92. See Patrik von zur Muehlen, *Fluchtziel Lateinamerika: Die deutsche Emigration 1933–1945: Politische Aktivitäten und soziokulturelle Integration,* 264–67. The first news of the extermination of Jews in Nazi camps reached the West through London in May 1942. See Martin Gilbert, *Atlas of the Holocaust,* 98–99. José Barcia argues that it took considerably longer for the information to reach South America, specifically Argentina. See his "Cómo los argentinos conocieron el Holocausto judío," 36–37.
93. Fittko, *Mein Weg,* 281.
94. Leizer Ran, interview, Jackson Heights, N.Y., November 25, 1989.
95. See, for example, open letter from Albert Hartman, General Chairman, Joint [JDC] Committee in Cuba, October 10, 1945, JDC Archive.
96. See open letter from Joint [JDC] Comité de Campaña en Cuba, Havana, September 1945. The Joint was headed by David H. Brandon, one of the leaders of the UHC, and its board included representatives from both Sephardic and Ashkenazic groups, including Isidoro Abravanel, Isaac

Behar, David Chajmovich (president of the ORT), David Utianski, and Juan Habib.

97. Alberto Hartman, President, Cuban Joint Campaign, to David Chajmovich, President, ORT de Cuba, Havana, October 15, 1945, YIVO Archive.

98. The U.S. military attaché claimed in March 1938 that some 4,000 "men of Spanish blood" in Cuba were Falangists. See Major E. W. Timberlake, Military Attaché, Report 5550, Havana, March 17, 1938, *Confidential Records.*

99. Related by Fittko, *Mein Weg,* diary entry, "End of the War." Also, Dr. Mario Llerena, interviewed by Dr. Robert Kirsner, September 11, 1989, Miami.

100. Fittko, *Mein Weg,* diary entry, "End of 1944."

101. Mittel-Ashe letter, January 5, 1991.

102. For two examples of the more typical response, see Leonardo Senkman's "Argentina's Immigration Policy during the Holocaust (1938–1945)," 155–88, and Miguel Feldman, "El caso del Conde Grande y la política inmigratoria uruguaya," 35–55.

103. Wyman, *Paper Walls,* 211, also 169–210. See Louis Sobel, "Jewish Community Life and Organization in Latin America," 180.

104. Weitzenkorn letter, June 9, 1991.

CHAPTER 6. "LA GLORIA ERES TÚ"

The title of this chapter is the title of a popular Cuban ballad, "Heaven Was You," by José Antonia Méndez.

1. The Cuban delegate to the Vatican helped speed the process. Rabbi Dow Rozencwaig, interviewed by Omar Cuan, Miami Beach, December 14, 1989.

2. Isaac Gotlib, "Summary Report on I. Gotlib's Tour of Latin American Countries," World Jewish Congress, New York, June 21, 1954, translated from Yiddish, Box H219/4, AJ Archives.

3. Resnick interview, April 2, 1991.

4. Fanny Portnoy, interview, Bronx, November 26, 1990; Hilda Robinsky, interview, Miami Beach, February 3, 1991.

5. Seymour B. Liebman, interview, Miami, March 24, 1985. See also his "Cuban Jewish Community in South Florida," 239, 243; "Ashkenazi and Sephardi," in memorandum, B. G. Kayfetz, Canadian Jewish Congress, Central Region, to United HIAS Service, November 16, 1962, RG 3344, JDC Archive.

6. See the Lyceum and Lawn Tennis Club collection of *Memorias* and other documents, Richter Library.

7. The founder was Morris Berezdivin, a clothing manufacturer who had left Minsk for Cuba with his family when he was fourteen years old. See his obituary, *Miami Herald*, April 3, 1991, B6.
8. Dionisio Castiel, a Sephardic Jew, graduated a few years earlier from the law school but did not practice law before the Cuban bar. Felix Reyler, interview, Miami Beach, May 26, 1991.
9. Immediately after the 1959 Revolution Reyler was named to the bench because many sitting judges and some of the eighty-four judicial candidates ahead of him were dismissed. Reyler interview, May 26, 1991. He also was skeptical when other Cuban Jews told of anti-Semitism, observing that this was because they had not shed their "ghetto mentality."
10. See *Habana: Guía General*, 126–27; Yukem interview, May 9, 1991.
11. Parker, *Yankee*, 23.
12. Yukem interview, May 9, 1991.
13. Stanley Wax, letter to author, Miami, February 27, 1991.
14. Corrales letter, January 2, 1992.
15. Moreno Habif, interview, Coral Gables, Fla., April 9, 1991.
16. Samuel Oberstein, M.D., interviewed by Alberto Rodríguez, Miami, January 14, 1991.
17. List compiled from business directories of Havana in 1950 by Alberto Rodríguez, Miami, January 1991. Sender Kaplan, who sold advertising in his newspaper to store owners, remembers that there were at least 300 in 1936 and probably more by 1950.
18. Fanny Seinuk, interviewed by Alberto Rodríguez, Miami, December 21, 1991; interviewed by author, Forest Hills, New York, February 1, 1991.
19. Mendel Kochanski, "The Jewish Community in Cuba," 26.
20. Martin Mayer, letter to author, Miami Beach, August 18, 1990.
21. José Raij, interviewed by Andrew Speyer, Miami, November 13, 1990.
22. Fittko interview, March 30, 1990.
23. Spatz interview, November 6, 1990.
24. Raquel Wax, interview, Miami, November 4, 1990.
25. Entertainers at Lansky's Hotel Riviera included Vic Damone, Cantinflas, and Abbott and Costello. Robert Lacey, *Little Man: Mayer Lansky and the Gangster Life*, 227–36. See also Lester Velie, "Suckers in Paradise: How Americans Lose Their Shirts in Caribbean Gambling Joints," *Saturday Evening Post*, March 28, 1953, cited by Lacey, 225–26.
26. See Robert J. Cox, "Palatial Embassy: Symbol of Decline," in *Inside Cuba*, 10.

27. Robert McNally, Coral Gables, Fla., letter to *New Times* (Miami), November 21–27, 1990, 2.

28. Ludwig Bemelmans, "The Best Way To See Cuba," 70. See also Irving Louis Horowitz, "A Response," 15–16.

29. For an example of racist attitudes toward black employees, see Parker, *Yankee,* 48.

30. Bemelmans, "The Best Way," 73.

31. Kochanski, "Jewish Community in Cuba," 25.

32. Spatz letter, July 3, 1991.

33. Max Lesnick, interviewed by Alberto Rodríguez, Miami, November 7, 1990. The Big Five clubs were the Biltmore Yacht and Country Club, Havana Yacht Club, Miramar Yacht Club, Vedado Tennis Club, and Casino Español. See *New York Times,* April 3, 1991, B5.

34. Nelson, *Rural Cuba,* 227.

35. Bemelmans, "The Best Way," 216.

36. Related to Erna Fergusson, *Cuba* (New York: n.p., 1946), 104, cited by Pérez, *Cuba and the United States,* 212. The country club's park, developed and managed by the Trust Company of Cuba, was one of the most elegant in the world. See Woon, *Cocktail Time,* 94.

37. *Almanaque Hebreo* (1950), 168. He attended courses there at the Institute for Traffic and Training as well as safety education at the Center for Safety Education at NYU.

38. Story confirmed by Athletic Information Office, University of Miami. The University of Havana also played exhibition games with teams from the University of Tampa and Rollins College during the 1930s and 1940s.

39. Ruby Hart Phillips, *Cuba: Island of Paradox* (New York: n.p., 1959), 357–58, cited by Pérez, *Cuba and the United States,* 211.

40. P. Quintana, quarter-page advertisement, *Almanaque Hebreo: Vida Habanera,* vol. 8 (Havana: Editorial Vida Habanera, 1950), 338.

41. See memorandum, B. C. Kayfetz, Canadian Jewish Congress, Central Region, to United HIAS Service, November 16, 1962, report of visit to Havana, October 19–26, 1962, RG 3344, JDC Archive (hereafter Kayfetz memorandum).

42. Pérez, *Cuba: Between Reform and Revolution,* 299. Much of the discussion about Cuba's economy in the 1950s is drawn from Pérez's chapter, "The Eclipse of Old Cuba."

43. Ibid., 303–4.

44. Ibid., 304–5; Arthur M. Schlesinger, Jr., *A Thousand Days,* 173.

45. Kochanski, "Jewish Community in Cuba," 25–26.

46. See *Havaner Lebn,* November 30, 1946, 1; December 25, 1946, 3;

Kubaner Yiddishe Wort, January 11, 1946, 1; April 5, 1946, 1; letter from Adrian Spies, "Made in the U.S.A.," *Commentary* 1, no. 6 (April 1946): 88–89.

47. Parker, *Yankee*, 52.
48. The architect, Acquiles Capablanca, visited several Jewish centers in the United States while planning the structure. See memorandum, Joseph Kage, National Executive Director, Canadian Jewish Congress, to Saul Hayes, Executive Vice-President, CJC, Montreal, c. March 1961, 5, JDC Archive.
49. *Rescue*, Winter 1952, 15, cited by Bejarano, "Antisemitism in Cuba," 45 n. 33.
50. In the late 1950s, the Orthodox (Ashkenazic) synagogue in Old Havana, Adas Israel, was rebuilt at a cost of a quarter of a million dollars. See report, Joseph Kage, National Executive Director, Canadian Jewish Congress, to Saul Hayes, Executive Vice-President, CJC, Montreal, March 14, 1961, JDC Archive.
51. For example, at the testimonial banquet held in 1956 to honor Primitivo Ramírez Medina, guests included Dr. Rafael Guas Inclán, vice president of the republic, Félix O'Farrill, president of the Club Atenas, and Eudaldo Gutiérrez Paula, vice-dean of the Colegio Provincial de Periodistas, as well as Patronato president Herman Heisler. Clipping, FAMA Press Service, Havana, October 18, 1956, courtesy of Primitivo Ramírez.
52. Gotlib, "Report on Cuba," 7. One body, the Comité Central/Consejo Central, functioned between 1939 and 1947, but it dissolved. Among the fifty delegates to the WJC-sponsored congress in November 1954 were representatives from the Patronato, Centro Israelita, the Zionists, the Kehilla, the 700-member Jewish Women's Organization, the Committee to Fight TB, the Chamber of Commerce, the Writers' Union, and several synagogues.
53. Gotlib, "Report on Cuba," 6. The groups were the Protectora de los Tuberculosos y Enfermos Mentales and the Asociación Femenina Hebrea de Cuba.
54. Ibid., 5; Ileana Ros-Lehtinen, letter to author, Washington, D.C., April 14, 1992.
55. See *Der Gruntshteyn (La Primera Piedra)*.
56. Kochanski, "Jewish Community in Cuba," 26. Also, Dr. Berta Savariego, interviewed by Keith Frostad, Coral Gables, Fla., May 1, 1990.
57. For example, ORT directors were invited on October 12, 1952, to a mass celebrating the 460th anniversary of the discovery of America at the Havana Cathedral. Leizer Ran Collection, YIVO Archive.

58. "Los Latinos in the Promised Land," *Miami Herald*, July 12, 1991, E1–2.

59. Max Lesnick, interviewed by Margalit Bejarano, Miami Beach, c. 1984. Information provided by M. Bejarano.

60. Pérez, *Cuba: Between Reform and Revolution*, 289.

61. Lacey, *Little Man*, 223.

62. Ironically, this was not always true for their children. The son of Bernard Barker, one of the more distinguished presidents of the United Hebrew Congregation, was Bernard Barker, Jr., arrested in the Watergate burglary in Washington, D.C., in the 1970s.

63. For the history of the armed forces' conflict with Batista, see John Dorschner and Roberto Fabricio, *The Winds of December*. A broader view of the political opposition is provided by Charles D. Ameringer, "The Auténtico Party and the Political Opposition in Cuba," 327–51.

64. Some, including Bernardo Benes, did. Bernardo Benes, interview, Miami, January 30, 1991.

65. Portell Vilá, interviewed by Margalit Bejarano, Miami, June 13, 1984, cited in Bejarano, "Antisemitism in Cuba," 38.

66. See Nahman Solowiejczyk, "Ashkenazim y Sefaradim," 43–44.

67. Pro-Zionist community organizations in Cuba date back to the 1920s. See, for example, *El Estudiante Hebreo*, a monthly publication started in 1929 under the direction of Fiodor Valbe.

68. Ofelia Domínguez, *50 años de una vida*, 455–72, and her memoirs about prison life, *De seis a seis*. See, for example, brochure circulated by the Círculo Universitario Hebreo de Cuba (July 15, 1947) announcing a pro-Israel cultural program at the Unión Hebrea Chevet Ahim, featuring Dra. Ofelia Domínguez Navarro as speaker; "Manifesto al pueblo cubano por un Comité Pro Palestina," *El Avance Criollo*, April 14, 1944; Bejarano, "Antisemitism in Cuba," 33; Bejarano letter, April 10, 1991. See also Stoner, "Ofelia Domínguez Navarro," 119–40.

69. Information provided by Stanley and Rachel Wax, Coral Gables, Fla., February 18, 1991.

70. Bejarano, "Antisemitism in Cuba," 34.

71. Enrique Trinchet, *Jirones Cubanos (Conozca la política, cierta prensa, el comercio judío y español y la didáctica como son: tumores nacionales)*.

72. Bejarano, interviews with members of the Garazi family, Miami, March 1, 9, 1987, in "Antisemitism in Cuba," 34.

73. Lasker interview, November 14, 1989. The amount donated probably was closer to $1,000. Bejarano letter, April 10, 1991.

74. Ignacio Klich, "Latin America and the Palestinian Question," 3. See

also Yoram Shapira, "Latin American Political Parties and Israel," 23–24; and Benno Weiser, "The Pro-Zionism of Latin America," 17.

75. Clark Clifford with Richard Holbrooke, "The Truman Years," 70.

76. See Moshe A. Tov, *El Murmullo de Israel*, 152–53; *Havaner Lebn*, May 4, 1948, cited by Bejarano, "Antisemitism in Cuba," 35. Margalit Bejarano notes that Belt, based on his record as Havana's mayor in the mid-1930s, had been considered sympathetic to Cuban Jews.

77. Cuba's formal recognition of the state of Israel came on January 14, 1949, the decree signed by Minister Carlos Hevia y Reyes Gavilán in the presence of Israel's representative, Dr. Solomon Rosenthal. See *Redención* (Havana), March 1949, 74.

78. Quoted in *Havaner Lebn*, November 13, 1984, 1; *Kubaner Yiddish Wort*, November 17, 1948, 4, cited by Bejarano, "Antisemitism in Cuba," 36.

79. "Combatientes a Israel en el 1948," list of the nineteen volunteers, many of whom were Sephardic. List provided by Rabbi Nesim Gambach, Miami Beach, April 6, 1990. Sender Kaplan recollects that there were thirty-one, not nineteen, although some went to organize settlements, not to fight (interview, Miami Beach, March 26, 1991).

80. Habif interview, April 10, 1991. See also Harry Eisner, *American Veterans of Israel Newsletter*, November 15, 1986, 2.

81. Ramírez (who later adopted the name Abraham ben Abraham) directed the program. It was underwritten financially by Nahman Solowiejczyk, Andrés Dworin, and Ezequiel Gimelstein. Primitivo Ramírez, letter to author, Corona, N.Y., December 19, 1990.

82. Ibid; Abraham Luski, interview, Charlotte, N.C., October 28, 1990; Spatz interview, November 6, 1990. Primitivo Ramírez divorced, married another Jewish woman, and divorced her. In 1990 he was living in Corona, Queens. See also David Jay Bercuson, *The Secret Army*, on the larger effort to supply arms.

83. *Tiempo*, June 10, 13, 14, 15, 17, 22, 1952, from the Leizer Ran Collection, YIVO Archive; Spatz interview, November 4, 1990.

84. Stanley Wax, an American in the textile business who had been stationed in Cuba as a soldier during the war and who had married a Sephardic Cuban woman, and Dr. Felix Reyler, an attorney, coordinated the merchants' committee and its activities. Stanley Wax, interview, Coral Gables, Fla., February 18, 1991.

85. Bejarano, "Anti-Semitism in Cuba," 8.

86. Bemelmans, "The Best Way," 73. Few of even the wealthiest immigrant Jews in Cuba were rich enough to consider membership, even had they been invited.

87. Bemelmans, "The Best Way," 73; Bejarano, "Anti-Semitism in Cuba,"

11, citing Alfred Padula, "The Fall of the Bourgeoisie, Cuba, 1959–1961" (Ph.D. diss., University of New Mexico, 1974), 8–25.

88. Bejarano, "Anti-Semitism in Cuba," 11.

89. Gustavo Kates and members of his family were listed in the *Registro Social de la Habana* and in the *Libro de Oro de la Sociedad Habanera* throughout the 1950s. See, for example, *Libro de Oro: 1956* (Havana: Ed. Lex, n.d.), 391.

90. *Golden Anniversary,* 14–15.

91. See Rabbi Everett Gendler, "Holy Days in Havana," 17.

92. Castiel, "Algunos Apuntes," 60; Moreno Habif and Ena Habif, interviews, Miami, April 10, 1991.

93. The system is described in detail in interviews with Moisés Pitchón and Osher (Jaime) Schuchinsky, Richter Library. See, for example, tapes Pitchón 2B and Schuchinsky 4A-B; also Vignier and Alonso, *La Corrupción Política Administrativa,* an indictment not so much of the system of corruption as of government failures to provide for the poor and to administer in good faith.

94. Rieur, "Jewish Colony of Cuba," 14, 19.

95. See, for example, the advertisement in the Yiddish-language *Shtral* (Havana, December 1940) for the "Our Lady of Carmen" Clinic, "Serving the Cuban Hebrew Colony." The clinic, a full-service hospital, also sent its physicians on house calls. YIVO Archive.

96. Foreign Policy Association, *Problems of the New Cuba. Report of the Commission on Cuban Affairs,* 38–39; Rieur, "Jewish Colony in Cuba," 40. In the 1950s the association expanded its work to include the mentally ill.

97. Bemelmans, "The Best Way," 66; Roberto E. Hernández and Raúl da la Cruz, "Cuestionario Cultural Cubano," Miami-Dade Community College, Wolfson Campus, March 26, 1990 (ms., privately distributed).

98. List, "Professionales," provided by Dr. José Achuily, February 10, 1991; also, Chuili Levy, "Noticiero Médico Hebreo-Cubano," 25. The magazine also reprinted caricatures of "Jewish personalities interpreted by Cuban artists," not as a protest but in appreciation. The issue cited reproduces Massaguer's caricature of Vladimir Horowitz, "the most eminent 'virtuoso' of our times" (supplement C). See also Pérez, *Cuba and the United States,* 230–31.

99. Jacobo Timmerman, *Cuba: A Journey,* 94.

100. See the photographs of Constantino Arias, the house photographer of the Hotel Nacional, documenting the lavish as well as the mundane aspects of the good life, as George Black writes, with a sense of irony that (likely) escaped his subjects. Arias was interviewed in 1984 by Marucha and Sandra Levinson, with excerpts from the videotape

sound track published in Black's *Cuba: A View from Inside. 40 Years of Cuban Life in the Work and Words of 20 Photographers*, 25.

101. MacGaffey, "Social Structure," 102; Charles E. Chapman, *A History of the Cuban Republic*; International Bank for Reconstruction and Development, *Report on Cuba, Findings and Recommendations of an Economic and Technical Mission Organized by the IBRD* (Washington, D.C.: IBRD, 1951); Byron White, "Cuba and Puerto Rico: A Case Study in Comparative Economic Development Policy."

102. MacGaffey, "Social Structure," 102; Chapman, *History of the Cuban Republic*, 556.

103. Rivero, "Jewish Experience in Cuba," 8; Guillermo Cabrera Infante, *La Habana para un Infante Difunto*, 83–85.

104. Darcia Moretti, *Los Ojos del Paraíso*, c. 1990.

105. Abel Holtz, interviewed by Hannah Wartenberg, Miami, March 5, 1990.

106. Hon. Lily M. Montagu to Rabbi Solomon, London, November 7, 1957, Solomon Collection, Richter Library.

107. Solomon Collection, undated but probably early 1959, Richter Library. Rabbi Solomon arrived in the fall of 1958.

CHAPTER 7. A SECOND DIASPORA

1. *American Jewish Year Book: 1962*, vol. 63 (New York: American Jewish Committee, 1962), 482. Community sources later claimed that there had been as many as 14,500, but without documentation. See *American Jewish Year Book: 1969*, vol. 70 (New York: American Jewish Committee, 1969), 238; Lavy Becker, "Cuban Jewry Today," 11.

2. The figures must have been rough, as they omitted all other categories. We know that there were small numbers of engineers, physicians, bureaucrats, and others engaged in white-collar occupations. Survey cited in MacGaffey and Barnett, *Twentieth-Century Cuba*, 42. See also Maurice Halperin, *The Taming of Fidel Castro*, 238.

3. Bejarano, "Antisemitism in Cuba," 12; Avni, *Antisemitism*, 15.

4. See Fred Ward, "Inside Cuba Today," 32.

5. Parker, *Yankee*, 6.

6. Ernesto "Ché" Guevara de la Serna, who was Argentine and trained in dermatology, also served in the Sierra Maestra.

7. David J. Kopilow, *Castro, Israel, & the PLO*, 15. Silber became a member of Kibbutz Gaash, founded in 1951 by Latin American Jewish socialists and, in 1991, one of the few kibbutzim still following socialist precepts. See "Los Latinos in the Promised Land," E1–2.

8. Gertrude Miller, "The Cuban Connection," 10.

9. Avni, *Antisemitism*, 15; see also Bejarano, "Antisemitism in Cuba," 39–41; Halperin, *The Taming of Fidel Castro*, 90–92; Norma Orovitz, "Cuban Judaism," *Miami News*, July 27, 1978, 16.

10. See Thomas, *Cuba*, 576, 597, 697; Tad Szulc, "Two Reds behind Scenes," *New York Times*, March 10, 1962, clipping file, AJC Archives.

11. Goldenberg, "Foreword," 7. Dr. Bernardo Benes recalls Goldenberg as his most inspiring schoolteacher during the late 1940s (interview, January 30, 1990).

12. Szulc, "Two Reds behind Scenes," 4.

13. See M. Kraicer to James P. Rice, Executive Director, United HIAS Service, Tel Aviv, February 26, 1964, describing an interview with the ambassador at the Cuban embassy in Herzliah, outside Tel Aviv, RG AR3344, JDC Archives.

14. Information provided by Moisés Asís, interview, December 18, 1991.

15. Bejarano, "Antisemitism in Cuba," 40. See Jorge García Montes and Antonio Alonso Avila, *Historia del Partido Comunista de Cuba*; Abraham Dubelman, "Cuba," 481–85.

16. Yoram Shapira and Edy Kaufman, "Cuba's Israel Policy: The Shift to the Soviet Line," 22, citing *Haaretz*, February 26, 1960.

17. Ibid., 23–24. For a survey of Cuban-Soviet relations, see Cole Blasier, *The Giant's Rival: The USSR and Latin America*.

18. For the Cuban view, see Oscar Pino-Santos, *La Oligarquía Yanqui en Cuba*.

19. Armando Hart Davalos, "The Traditions behind a Socialist World View," 22, citing V. I. Lenin, *Collected Works*, vol. 20 (Moscow: Progress Publishers, 1937), 24.

20. Bemelmans, "The Best Way," 66.

21. Wax interview, February 18, 1991.

22. Lavy Becker, letter to author, Montreal, August 16, 1991.

23. Kayfetz memorandum, 8.

24. Marek Schindelman to Rice, President, United HIAS Service, July 1961, trans. Carmen Roman, RG AR3344, JDC Archive.

25. See, for example, Geoffrey Wigoder, "The Jewish Scene," *Jerusalem Post*, June 5, 1962, 4; "Difficult Times for Cuban Jewry," 1, published by the Canadian Jewish Congress.

26. Moisés Levin, interview, Miami Beach, February 8, 1991; Netanel Lorch, commentary in Haim Avni, *Antisemitism*, 40–41; Bejarano, "Antisemitism in Cuba," 40.

27. Press release, Jewish Telegraph Agency, Havana, September 26, 1963, 3, AJC Archive.

28. Bernardo Benes's wealthy father managed to convert $50,000 in Cuban currency into dollars before he left, but he left much more in Cuba, Benes interview, January 30, 1991.

29. See, for example, memorandum, Seymour Samet to S. Andhil Fineberg, John Slawson, and others, American Jewish Committee, Miami, January 4, 1961, 2, AJC Archive; Bejarano, "Antisemitism in Cuba," 15.

30. Bejarano, "Antisemitism in Cuba," 40, citing interview with the Israeli ambassador Haim Yaari.

31. See Frances FitzGerald, "A Reporter at Large: Slightly Exaggerated Enthusiasms," 148; *New York Times*, August 9, 1966.

32. *American Jewish Year Book: 1962*, vol. 63 (New York: American Jewish Committee, 1962), 483–84.

33. The others were Eliezer Aronowsky and Nissan Yoeli, an Israeli employee of the Jewish agency from a MAPAM kibbutz who had come to Cuba to teach Hebrew and stayed to teach at the nationalized Albert Einstein School. See Abraham Dubelman, "Jewish Life in Cuba under the Castro Regime," manuscript of translated text in RG AR3344, JDC Archive. Moisés Baldas, the head of Zionist Union, was responsible for the publication. See also Kayfetz memorandum, 11.

34. *New York Times*, February 4, 1961, AJC Archive; U. O. Schmeltz, P. Glikson and S. J. Gould, eds., *Studies in Jewish Demography: Survey for 1972–1980;* memorandum, Danzig to Samet, New York, Dec. 16, 1960, American Jewish Committee; confidential memorandum, Rice, Executive Director, United HIAS Service to Dr. John Slawson, American Jewish Committee, New York, March 23, 1961, YIVO Archive.

35. Press release, Jewish Telegraph Agency, Geneva, October 29, 1962, AJC Archive. See also *Jewish Times* (Philadelphia), February 17, 1961; *New York World Telegram and Sun*, January 4, 1961; *New York Times*, February 4, 1961.

36. James McCracken, quoted in "Speaking of People," broadcast press release from the Institute of Human Relations, American Jewish Committee, New York, March 1962, 1–2, AJC Archive. See also Jacob Schatzky, *Yiddische Yichuvim en Latin Amerika* (Buenos Aires, 1952), 185.

37. Memorandum, Samet to Danzig, American Jewish Committee, December 16, 1960, AJC Archive.

38. M. Pitchón, tape 2B 639–680, Richter Library.

39. Some revisionists also painted Céspedes as an opportunist who freed Cuba's slaves so that they could be used to fight the Spanish. Carlos Moore, cited by Alfonso Chardy, "Heresy or History," *Miami Herald*, December 7, 1990, E1–2.

40. *New Catholic Encyclopedia*, s.v. "Cuba," 516.

41. Bejarano, "Antisemitism in Cuba," 10, citing Rev. I. Biain, "Religión y Etica," *Bene Berith Fragmentos* (Havana) 5, no. 51 (March 1956), edited by Marco Pitchón.

42. Roberto E. Hernández, interview, Miami, December 19, 1990.

43. Behar, "Juban América," 8.

44. Chalón Rodríguez, tape 12A, Richter Library.

45. Abel Holtz, interviewed by Dr. Hannah Wartenberg, Miami, March 6, 1990.

46. Pupils studied mathematics and, of course, English, in English, the rest of their subjects in Spanish. Information provided by Günter W. Cohn. Also, Habif interview, April 10, 1991.

47. A. Kamorin, "The Church Itself Has Changed," 27–28.

48. Rabkin, *Cuban Politics*, 190.

49. Dr. Ruth Behar, letter to author, September 25, 1991.

50. Halperin, *The Taming of Fidel Castro*, 240.

51. See Timmerman, *Cuba: A Journey*, 64–65. Timmerman attributed the lack of curiosity about his Jewishness to Cubans under Castro being "verbally immobilized. Frozen."

52. See, for example, James Higgins, "New Church in New Cuba," *Commonweal*, July 28, 1972, 399–402. The best overview of the church under Castro is Margaret E. Crahan's "Cuba, Religion, and Revolutionary Institutionalization," 207–29.

53. Oscar Tisyera, *Cuba marxista vista por un católico*, 167; Frederick C. Turner, *Catholicism and Political Development in Latin America*, 110.

54. Bejarano, "Antisemitism in Cuba," citing Juan Clark, *Religious Repression in Cuba* (Coral Gables, Fla.: Cuban Studies Project, Institute of Interamerican Studies, 1986), 3–12, 20–21. See also Halperin, *The Taming of Fidel Castro*, 238–40; Kopilow, *Castro, Israel, & The PLO*, 16.

55. A critical view of Castro's change of heart about the Catholic church and his endorsement of liberation theology concepts is provided by Voice of America, U.S. Intelligence Agency, Office of Research and Policy, Radio Martí Program, *Cuba Annual Report: 1985*, esp. 9.

56. This understanding was repeatedly stressed by officials of the AJC in reports on the exodus of Jews from Castro's Cuba to the United States. See, for example, the exchange of letters between Danzig and Samet, with copies to Slawson, AJC President, December 16, 1960, January 4, 13, 1961, and Máximo Yagupsky to Simon Segal, January 18, 1961, YIVO Archive. Yagupsky chides HIAS for having assumed that Castro's policies were anti-Semitic. He suggests that AJC help the Cuban Jews form a "Landsmanschaft" in Miami, along the lines of the organi-

zations started by German refugees during the war, so that the Jews might be able to distance themselves from the "Castristas" and "anti-Castristas" and therefore not be "misinterpreted by U.S. officials."

57. Halperin, *The Taming of Fidel Castro*, 242.

58. See, for example, Margaret Randall, *Women in Cuba: Twenty Years Later*, 98. One exception was the Jehovah's Witnesses, persecuted (and finally banned) as counterrevolutionary reactionaries because of their refusal to accept medical treatment and to salute the flag. See Randall, 98–99.

59. See memorandum, Segal to Hannah Desser, American Jewish Committee, Mexico City, October 10, 1966, AJC Archive.

60. Bejarano, "Antisemitism," 17.

61. Memorandum, Seymour Samet, Miami, to David Danzig, American Jewish Committee, New York, December 16, 1960, AJC Archive.

62. Kahn, "Jewish Colony," 88. They soon lost interest, however, and returned the building to the remaining skeletal Patronato board.

63. David Autiansky, quoted by Dubelman, "Jewish Life in Cuba"; Kayfetz memorandum, 3.

64. Kayfetz memorandum, 6.

65. Ibid., 9.

66. Ibid., 13.

67. Ibid., 7–8. Eventually most of the seventy-two were released or sentenced to terms averaging 6 years.

68. Gendler, "Holy Days in Havana," 19.

69. Clifford Krauss, "The Jews of Cuba: Reduced in Number, Adept at Improvising," *Wall Street Journal*, February 21, 1986, 4; Alfonso Chardy, *Miami Herald*, September 22, 1990, 4B, citing Cuban exile Frank Calzon on the "anti-Jewish climate" created by Castro's opposition to Israel.

70. For a report on a visit of a Cuban delegation to Israel in 1983, see *New Outlook* (Tel Aviv), June–July 1983, 48–49.

71. Dopilow, *Castro, Israel, & the PLO*, 15; Halperin, *The Taming of Fidel Castro*, 242.

72. Paul Jacobs, "Letter from Cuba," *New Outlook*, March–April 1975, 41, cited by Harris O. Schoenberg, "Betrayal of an Ideal: Cuba's Campaign Against Israel," May 1977, 1, ms, Anti-Defamation League Archive, New York (hereafter ADL Archive); Pérez, *Cuba: Between Reform and Revolution*, 378.

73. Yaari, interviewed by Margalit Bejarano, 1981, cited in Bejarano, "Antisemitism in Cuba," 17.

74. Bejarano, "Antisemitism in Cuba," citing Consejo Plenario Sionista, *Cuba-Israel*, in Utiansky Collection, Institute of Contemporary Jewry,

Jerusalem; Miller, "The Cuban Connection," cited by Yoram Shapira, "The Arab-Israeli Conflict," 157.

75. The phrase was used by Nikita S. Khrushchev. See his *Khrushchev Remembers: The Glasnost Tapes.*

76. Rozita Levi, *Cuba in the World*, 147–48. For a discussion of the role of Left-oriented militants from other countries who came to Cuba to help build communism during this time, see the bitter memoir by Pierre Golendorf, *7 Años en Cuba*. Golendorf turned against Castro and was imprisoned for thirty-eight months before being returned to Paris.

77. Schoenberg, "Betrayal," 1.

78. Benes interview, January 30, 1991. For a general discussion of Fidel Castro's origins and personal attitudes, see Georgia Anne Geyer, "Castro: the 'Knowable' Dictator," 37–49.

79. *Revolución* (Havana), May 6, 1963. Nahumi was a correspondent for *Al Hamishmar* of Tel Aviv. See Halperin, *The Taming of Fidel Castro*, 243.

80. Shapira, "The Arab-Israeli Conflict," 156.

81. Fidel Castro, interviewed by Regino Díaz, editor of the Mexican newspaper *Excelsior*. Reprinted in *Granma Weekly Review* (April 7, 1985) and in *Fidel Castro: Speeches 1984–1985* (New York: Pathfinder Books, 1985), 227–28.

82. See memorandum, Buenos Aires office, American Jewish Committee, to Dr. Hannah Desser, New York, May 4, 1966, AJC Archive; also Edy Kaufman, letter to author, Los Angeles, July 20, 1990; Shapira and Kaufman, "Cuba's Israel Policy," 24.

83. See Marc H. Ellis, "Holocaust Theology and Latin American Liberation Theology: Suffering and Solidarity," 584–97.

84. Yoram Shapira, "Cuba and the Arab-Israeli Conflict," 153; Shapira and Kaufman, "Cuba's Israel Policy," 24, citing *Israel un tema para la izqierda*, 2d ed. (Buenos Aires: Editorial Nueva Sión, 1968), 218–19, 290.

85. *Israel un tema*, 291, cited by Shapira and Kaufman, "Cuba's Israel Policy," 25.

86. A. Zapata, editorial, *Granma*, on the second anniversary of the Six Day War (June 5, 1969), cited by Shapira and Kaufman, "Cuba's Israel Policy," 32. See also "Barbarie de los ocupantes," *Verde Olivo*, March 21, 1971.

87. Shapira and Kaufman, "Cuba's Israel Policy," 26, citing Carlos Lechuga, "Olor a pólvora," *Bohemia*, March 8, 1968. See also the collected writings and speeches of Ernesto (Che) Guevara, *Che Guevara and the Cuban Revolution*, esp. 326.

88. *New York Post*, June 26, 1973, 2; Robert Peters, in *Frankfurter Allge-*

meine Zeitung, quoted in Latin American Jewish Congress, *Information Bulletin* (Buenos Aires), no. 232, September 13, 1974.

89. *New York Times,* September 10, 1973, 1, 6; Shapira, "The Arab-Israeli Conflict," 157; *Granma,* quoted in *Maariv,* September 10, 12, 1973.

90. Some doubt has been cast on the extent to which Cuban specialists trained PLO in military and intelligence matters. The main source of the allegation was an article in the London weekly *Foreign Report* (November 28, 1979), which the Israeli scholar Ignacio Klich claims was "highly inaccurate" ("Latin America and the Palestinian Question," 7). But the report was used as the basis for several articles emphasizing Cuba's role in training guerrillas. See, for example, Eileen Scully, "The PLO's Growing Latin American Base"; Morton M. Rosenthal and Raquel Schuster-Herr, "PLO Activities in Latin America," 13.

91. Shapira, "The Arab-Israeli Conflict," 158; *Washington Post,* April 3, 1974, and *New York Times,* March 5–6, 1977, cited by Schoenberg, "Betrayal," 3. Also see Schoenberg's memorandum, "The UN Palestinian Committee and its Report" (New York: B'nai B'rith International Council, 1976); Maurice Zeitlin, "Cuba and the PLO" (*Nation,* March 20, 1976, 338.

92. Total Latin American support for UNRWA over the 1950–84 period was a modest $750,000, much less than the amounts given by the United States and other industrialized nations, but more than any other bloc. See *Report of the Commissioner-General of the United States Relief and Works Agency for Palestine Refugees in the Middle East,* Supplement no. 13, reproduced in Klich, "Latin America," 32.

93. Ibid., 1–2.

94. Voice of America, *Cuba Annual Report: 1985,* 24.

95. Shapira and Kaufman, "Cuba's Israel Policy," 28. By the 1980s the federation had ceased to exist.

96. Weapons of U.S., Israeli, or Italian manufacture were said to be favored because they would help disguise "socialist involvement" in the trafficking. Cuban military advisers also allegedly trained Palestinians as frogmen, in weapons use, and in techniques of falsifying passports and engaging in clandestine correspondence. See "Cuban Diplomat Defects," *Washington Post,* January 26, 1989, clipping file, Anti-Defamation League of B'nai B'rith, New York.

97. See, for example, the transcript of the "Eighteenth United Nations Seminar on the Question of Palestine," Palacio de las Convenciones, Havana, December 15–17, 1987, under the auspices of the UN Division for Palestinian Rights, a meeting mostly hostile to Israel but that included participation by retired Israeli general Mattityahu Peled of the Peace Now movement.

98. Anthony Kerrigan, "Literacy, Yes. Books, No," *The Issue is Cuba*, no. 5 (April 1990): 26, originally published as an occasional paper by the Helen Kellogg Institute for International Studies, University of Notre Dame, 1988.

99. For a summary of the regime's attitudes, see Seng Xiaopeng, "Process of Rectifying Errors and Negative Tendencies in Cuba," 63–64.

100. See Timmerman, *Cuba: A Journey*, 22–23.

101. Roberto Lagar Quintero, Teresita Bacallao Reyes, Bárbara Rafael Vázquez, Raquel Guevara Pérez, and Gladys Avila Molina, *Historia del Movimiento Comunista, Obrero y de Liberación Nacional y Cubano (1917–1945), 10 grado* (Havana: Editorial Pueblo y Educación, c. 1987).

102. *Granma Weekly Review,* March 2, 1980, 12, cited by Kopilow, *Castro, Israel, & the PLO,* 25.

103. Francisco León, interviewed by Sandra Levinson, Havana, December 16, 1990.

104. See Bejarano, "Antisemitism," 18–19.

105. Richard Yaffee, "900 Cubans Remain," *London Jewish Chronicle,* July 18, 1980, clipping file, ADL Archive.

106. Josh Friedman, "A Dwindling Community," *Miami Herald,* Dec. 26, 1983, part 2, 3. The figure of 807 was so precise because it represented the total number of Jews who registered at the Patronato to receive packages of matzo and kosher meat from Canada.

107. On March 18, 1985, Dr. José Felipe Carneado, the director of the Division of Religious Affairs of the Central Committee of the Cuban Communist party, met with Patronato officials and pledged to maintain the remaining synagogues and Jewish cemeteries. Comment by Adela Dworin of the Patronato, reported in *Los Angeles Times,* December 1984, cited in Jarkow Institute for Latin America of the Anti-Defamation League of B'nai B'rith, *Latin American Report,* May 1985, 7.

108. Memorandum #816, Boris Sapir to Moses A. Leavitt, American Jewish Joint Distribution Committee, New York, February 1, 1961, 1. A similar appeal was made to the JDC to cover the deficit of the Colegio Hebreo del Centro Israelita de Cuba.

109. Kahn, "Jewish Colony," 90. Miramar was the most affluent and desirable of the suburban neighborhoods in which Jews lived in Havana. Some 140,000 Cubans between 1961 and 1977 flew to Spain, with 10 percent remaining. It is not known if any Jews formed part of this group. See Michael R. Marrus, *The Unwanted: European Refugees in the Twentieth Century,* 369–70.

110. Sergio Della Pergola, "Demographic Trends of Latin American Jewry," in Elkin and Merkx, *Jewish Presence,* 120–21.

111. Asís, "El Judaísmo Cubano," 39.

112. Jarkow Institute, *Latin American Report*, 7.

113. Armando Entrialgo, director of CEAMO, symposium, "Zionism and the International Community," December 1985, cited in ibid., April 1986, 8.

114. *Granma Weekly Review*, January 18, 1976.

115. *Bohemia*, September 24, 1982, 65; March 9, 1983. See Kopilow, *Castro, Israel, & the PLO*, 22–23.

116. Mahmud Abbas, *La Otra Cara: La verdad de las relaciones secretas entre el nazismo y el sionismo*. Copy provided by Professor Edy Kaufman, director, Harry S Truman Research Institute, Hebrew University of Jerusalem; Larry Luxner, interview, San Juan, March 8, 1990. The Ministry of Culture must approve all books published in Cuba. Other virulently anti-Semitic books published under Arab League auspices were sold widely in Cuban bookstores, including: Tony Fernández's *Sionismo: el fascismo de la estrella de David*; Nabil Khalil's *Propagandistas del terror*, published by the PLO; Domingo Amuchástegui's *Palestina, Dimensiones de un conflicto*; the GEIS's (Group for Study and Information on Zionism) *Simposio sobre la ingerencia sionista en América Latina*; and Walid Zayed Massis's *Palestina . . . Arde el Silencio*.

117. The reassessment in the Soviet Union came two years before the attempted putsch against Mikhail Gorbachev and included opening sealed archives in Moscow to representatives of the U.S. Holocaust Council. See Judith Miller, *One by One by One*, 162–63.

118. See Zvi Gitelman, "History, Memory, and Politics: The Holocaust in the Soviet Union," 23–37, esp. 23.

119. Rabbi Pynchas Brener of Unión Israelita, Caracas, and president of the Committee of Relations between Synagogues and Churches in Venezuela. See Jarkow Institute, *Latin American Report*, Winter 1987, 6.

120. Ann Crittenden, "Jews in Cuba," *New York Times*, December 12, 1977, clipping courtesy of Rabbi Nesim Gambach.

121. Bill Aron, *From the Corners of the Earth: Contemporary Photographs of the Jewish World*, 72.

122. Mimi Whitefield, "Jews in Cuba: The Fragile Flame," *Miami Herald*, December 9, 1990, H-4.

123. Rabbi Lavy Becker, Honorary National Vice-President of the Canadian Jewish Congress, "Inter-Office Information," Canadian Jewish Congress, October 3, 1975; see also Lisa Aronson Fontes, "Castro, Cuba and the 800," *Present Tense* 13, no. 1 (August 1985): 41–46.

124. Ben G. Kayfetz, "Cuban Jews in Need," 22. The annual cost of the shipment was estimated in 1900 to be $20,000. See Mimi Whitefield,

"Jews in Cuba: The Fragile Flame," *Miami Herald*, December 9, 1990, H-1, 4.

125. For example, Jacobo Kovadloff, an Argentine citizen, represented the AJC and made frequent trips to Cuba.

126. "Mitzvah Plane," *Canadian Jewish News*, April 7, 1988, 3.

127. Statement by Ian Kagedan, religious affairs director of the CJC. The truth was admitted later by a member of the Patronato, Raquel Markizer, and confirmed by a visitor from Toronto, April 16, 1987, in Jarkow Institute, *Latin American Report*, July 1987, 5. See also Janice Arnold, "Matzoh for Cubans Delayed," *Canadian Jewish News*, April 30, 1987, 3.

128. Jarkow Institute, *Latin American Report*, June 1989, 4; Congressman Bill Green, "The Jewish Diaspora in Cuba," *Congressional Record*, April 27, 1989, no. 50.

129. Paraphrased, with permission, from Moisés Asís, letter to author, Havana, March 1990.

130. Moisés Asís, letter to author, Havana, November 23, 1989. At the same time, he was refused permission to attend the 10th World Congress on Jewish Studies in Jerusalem and the 13th Maccabiah in Israel, although a small group of eight Cubans was permitted to attend.

131. "Mandate of Cuban Jewish Congress," 1987, courtesy of Dr. Edmond Y. Lipsitz, Executive Director, Canadian Jewish Congress, Toronto.

132. Becker, "Cuban Jewry Today," 11–12, and "Cuban Jewry, 1973," 21–22, clippings provided by Rabbi Becker.

133. William R. Long, "Judaism Withers in Cuba as Youths Abandon Faith," *Miami Herald*, January 11, 1985, B4. Matterín's clippings and some other materials are available to researchers at the Havana City Archives.

134. Gendler, "Holy Days in Havana," 22. Jacobo Timmerman, however, observed quite a number of prostitutes (called *jineteras* [jockeys] or *cubanas fleteras* [taxi-girls] in and around hotels occupied by tourists). See Timmerman, *Cuba: A Journey*, 88–93. Prostitution was in fact authorized under government supervision but the practice was well beyond police control.

135. Asís, "El Judaísmo Cubano," 43; "Cuba's Jews Face Shortages," 7 (based on interview with M. Asís); Behar, "Juban América," 21 n. 6.

136. Whitefield, "Jews in Cuba," H4.

137. Kerrigan, "Literacy, Yes," 15–27.

138. Larry Luxner, interview, San Juan, October 8, 1990.

139. *New York Times*, November 28, 1990, 2. Secretary of State James Baker's conversation with Cuban officials at the United Nations on this date was the first such meeting in more than thirty years.

140. One of Hashomer Hatzair's leaders in Cuba was Yitzhak Silber, a Castro classmate who emigrated to Israel in 1940. See Kopilow, *Castro, Israel, & the PLO*; Alfonso Chardy, "Cuba Makes Quiet Overture to Israel," clipping from *Miami Herald*, July or August 1990, provided by Dr. Henry Green. Also, Jarkow Institute, *Latin American Report*, October 1990, 4–5.

141. *Cuba Update* 11, no. 4 (Fall 1990): 36.

142. Courtesy of Moisés Asís.

143. Paraphrased from Sandra Levinson, interviews with Francisco León and Alfredo Calviño, Havana, 1990.

144. Christian Jaurena, *Libération* (Paris), cited in *World Press Review*, April 1991, 53.

145. See Ramón A. Mestre, "Reading the Music," 29.

146. "Cuba's Jews Face Shortages," 7.

147. Luxner interview, March 3, 1990.

148. Moisés Asís, interviewed by Tom Sawicki, in "A View from Havana," 5.

CHAPTER 8. LESSONS OF THE CUBAN JEWISH EXPERIENCE

1. The phrase is Judith Laikin Elkin's, "Is There a 'Jewish Interest' in Latin American Politics?" 61.

2. Gilbert W. Merkx, "Jewish Studies as a Subject of Latin American Studies," in Elkin and Merkx, *Jewish Presence*, 5, 7.

3. See Barnet, *Gallego*.

4. For a Cuban view of the island's early history, see Rafael Hernández and Haroldo Dilla, "Political Culture and Popular Participation in Cuba," 38–54.

5. See, for example, William Belmont Parker, ed., *Cubans of To-Day*.

6. Merkx, "Jewish Studies," 5.

7. Elkin, *Jews of the Latin American Republics*, 10; Robert M. Levine, "Adaptive Strategies of Jews in Latin America," in Elkin and Merkx, *Jewish Presence*, 72.

8. Amram, "Assimilation of Immigrants," 11; Lowry, *Rural Cuba*; Leslie Dewart, *Cristianismo y Revolución*.

9. See Amram, "Assimilation of Immigrants," vi–ix.

10. Merkx, "Jewish Studies," 9.

11. Eric R. Wolf and Edward C. Hansen, *The Human Condition in Latin America* (New York: Oxford University Press, 1972), 200–204, 350–58.

12. Moisés Asís, letter to author, Jerusalem, January 26, 1992.

13. Elkin, *Jews of the Latin American Republics*, 108. Her analysis applies more accurately to Argentina and Brazil than to Cuba, where fewer single Jewish women emigrated.

14. Osher Schuchinsky, interviewed by Shlomit Oz, Miami Beach, October 8, 29, 1990. See also Bejarano, "Deproletarization," 57–59.
15. Paraphrased from transcript of Schuchinsky interview, October 29, 1990.
16. Behar letter, September 25, 1991.
17. Victor A. Mirelman, "Sephardic Immigration to Argentina Prior to the Nazi Period," in Elkin and Merkx, *Jewish Presence*, 24.
18. See Lars Henrik Ekstrand, "Migrant Adaptation: A Cross-Cultural Problem," *Educational and Psychological Interactions* 59 (January 1977): 14, citing Eisenstadt and others.
19. Levine, "Adaptive Strategies," 72, 73–82. Parts of this section appeared in somewhat different format in that essay.
20. Sofer, *From Pale to Pampa*, 20.
21. Iser Szuchman, interview, transcribed for Levine and Szuchman, *Hotel Cuba*.
22. Osher (Jaime) Schuchinsky, interview, transcribed for ibid.
23. See Suzanne Ziegle, "Family Unit and Internal Migration," *International Migration Review* 11, no. 3 (Fall 1977): 326; Dorothy E. Mandel, "Aspects of the Adaptive Process in Migration" (Ph.D. diss., United States International University, San Diego, 1982).
24. Maritza Corrales reminds us that this bishop is often confused with the chronicler Garcilazo de la Vega (El Inca), born in Peru in 1540 of a Spanish father and an Inca princess.
25. The story may well be false. Plans for the construction of a convent on the site were drawn up as early as 1637, but nothing was built until 1755, and that a convent of another name. The present-day Nuestra Señora de las Mercedes was constructed in 1865–67. Maritza Corrales, letter to author, Havana, August 18, 1991.
26. Marco Pitchón stands in the white guayabera and trousers next to the speaker in the photograph.
27. Telefaxed communication, Ileana Ros-Lehtinen to author, May 4, 1992. Jacobo Adato worked between 1960 and 1969 with a Jewish organization in Switzerland to help elderly and sick Jews leave Cuba if they wished.
28. See Abraham Marcus Matterín, *Martí y las discriminaciones raciales* (Havana: Ediciones de la Agrupación Cultural Hebreo-Cubana, 1953).
29. Information provided by Dr. Haim Avni, Jerusalem.
30. The Argentine socialist leader Juan B. Justo, writing in the Jewish magazine *Vida Nuestra*, cited by Sofer, *From Pale to Pampa*, 35.
31. Judith Laikin Elkin, "The Evolution of the Latin American-Jewish Communities," in Elkin and Merkx, *Jewish Presence*, 316.
32. Elkin, "Evolution of the Latin American-Jewish Communities," 313.
33. Information provided by Jacobo Kovadloff, College Park, Md., October 6, 1991.

34. Edgar Goldstein, "Psychological Adaptations of Soviet Immigrants," *American Journal of Psychoanalysis* 39, no. 3 (1979): 258.

35. Gotlib, "Summary Report."

36. See Leonardo Senkman, "Between Revolution and Reaction," *Jewish Frontier*, 10–13.

37. See Della Pergola, "Demographic Trends," 85–133.

38. Behar, "Juban América," 1.

39. Sofer, *From Pale to Pampa*, 96.

40. Oscar Handlin, cited in Corinne Azen Krause, "Urbanization without Breakdown," *Journal of Urban History* 4, no. 3 (May 1978): 302.

41. See Krause, "Urbanization without Breakdown," 292–94, and Jean-Claude Lasry and John J. Sigal, "Influences sur la santé mentale de la durée de séjour, de l'instruction, du revenue personnel, et de l'age, chez un groupe d'immigrants," *International Review of Applied Psychology* 25, no. 3 (1976): 215–23.

42. Moisés Mitriani, speech in honor of Arón Mindik, his son-in-law, Patronato, Havana, March 9, 1956. Copy provided by Rabbi Nesim Gambach, Miami Beach, April 6, 1990.

43. Behar, "Juban América," 5.

Selected Bibliography

Abad Muñoz, Diana A. "Cuba: La Revolución de 1895." In *Historia del ciclo de las revoluciones de España y América Latina (1790–1917)*." Edited by Manfred Kossok and Sergio Godoy Vilaboy, 97–102. Havana: Universidad da la Habana, 1990.

Abbas, Mahmud [Abu Mazzen]. *La Otra Cara: La verdad de las relaciones secretas entre el nazismo y el sionismo*. Translated by Usama Ahmed Khalil. Havana: PLO, 1988.

Abel, Christopher, and Nissa Torrents, eds. *José Martí: Revolutionary Democrat*. Durham: Duke University Press, 1986.

Abella, Irving, and Harold Troper. *None Is Too Many: Canada and the Jews of Europe, 1933–1948*. Toronto: Lester and Orpen Dennys, 1982.

Aikman, Duncan. *The All-American Front*. New York: Doubleday, Doran, 1940.

Akten zur Deutschen Auswerten Politik. Serie D (1937–1945), Baden-Baden, 1953.

Almanaque conmemorativo de la Caja de Préstamos de la Asociación Femenina Hebrea de Cuba. Havana: n.p., 1952.

Alvarez Díaz, José R., ed. *A Study on Cuba: The Colonial and Republican Periods. The Socialist Experiment*. Coral Gables: University of Miami Press, 1965.

Ameringer, Charles D. "The Auténtico Party and the Political Opposition in Cuba." *Hispanic American Historical Review*, 54, no. 3 (May 1985): 327–51.

AMILAT. *Judaica Latinoamericana: Estudios Histórico-Sociales*. Jerusalem: Editorial Universitaria Magnes and Hebrew University, 1988.

Amram, Carolina. "The Assimilation of Immigrants in Cuban Society during the 1920s and 1930s." Master's thesis, University of Miami, 1983.

Amuchástegui, Domingo. *Palestina, Dimensiones de un conflicto*. Havana, n.p., c. 1980.

Arbitol, Michel. "The Encounter between French Jewry and the Jews of

North Africa, 1830–1914." In *The Jews of Modern France*, edited by Frances Malino and Bernard Wasserstein. Hanover, N.H.: Brandeis University Press–University Presses of New England, 1985.

Aron, Bill. *From the Corners of the Earth: Contemporary Photographs of the Jewish World*. Philadelphia: Jewish Publication Society, 1985.

Asís, Moisés. "El Judaísmo Cubano durante 30 años de Revolución (1959–1989)." *Coloquio* (Buenos Aires), no. 22 (1989), n.p.

Avni, Haim. *Antisemitism under Democratic and Dictatorial Regimes: The Experience of Latin American Jewry*. Translated by Aryeh Rubinstein. Jerusalem: Institute for Contemporary Jewry, 1986.

_____. "Jews in Latin America: The Contemporary Jewish Dimension." In AMILAT, *Judaica Latinoamericana: Estudios Histórico-Sociales*. Jerusalem: Editorial Universitaria Magnes and Hebrew University, 1988.

_____. "Latin America and the Jewish Refugees: Two Encounters, 1935 and 1938." In *The Jewish Presence in Latin America*, edited by Judith Laikin Elkin and Gilbert Merkx, 45–49. Boston: Allen and Unwin, 1987.

_____. "Mexico—Immigration and Refuge." *Working Papers, Latin American Program, The Wilson Center*. Washington, D. C.: Wilson Center, 1989.

_____. "The Origins of Zionism in Latin America." In *The Jewish Presence in Latin America*, edited by Judith L. Elkin and Gilbert Merkx, 135–56. Boston: Allen and Unwin, 1987.

Bankier, David. "Los exilados Alemanes en Mexico y sus Vínculos con la Comunidad Judía (1942–1945)." In AMILAT, *Judaica Latinoamericana: Estudios Historico-Sociales*, 79–89. Jerusalem: Editorial Universitaria Magnes and Hebrew University, 1988.

Barcia, José. "Como los argentinos conocieron el Holocausto judío." *Todo es Historia* (Buenos Aires) 148 (1979): 36–37.

Barnet, Miguel. *Gallego*. Madrid: Ediciones Alfaguara, 1981.

Bartolomé, Leopoldo José. "The Colonos of Apostles: Adaptive Strategy and Ethnicity in a Polish-Ukrainian Settlement in Northeast Argentina." Ph.D. diss., University of Wisconsin, Madison, 1974.

Basdekis, Demetrios. *Unamuno and the Novel*. Berkeley: University of California Press, 1967.

Bauer, Yehuda. *American Jewry and the Holocaust: The American Jewish Joint Distribution Committee, 1939–1945*. Jerusalem: Institute for Contemporary Jewry and Wayne State University Press, 1981.

_____. *My Brother's Keeper. A History of the American Jewish Joint Distribution Committee, 1929–1939*. Philadelphia: JDC, 1974.

_____, ed. *Remembering for the Future: Working Papers and Addenda*. Vol. 3. *The Impact of the Holocaust and Genocide on Jews and Christians*. Oxford: Pergamon, 1989.

Becker, Lavy. "Cuban Jewry, 1973." In *World Jewry*, 21–22. New York: World Jewish Congress, 1973.

———. "Cuban Jewry Today." In *World Jewry*, 11–12. New York: World Jewish Congress, 1971.

———. "Report on [the] Jewish Community of Cuba," Canadian Jewish Congress, Toronto, June 1975. Typescript.

Behar, Ruth. "Death and Memory: From Santa María del Monte to Miami Beach." *Cultural Anthropology* 6, no. 3. (Summer 1991): 346–84.

———. "Juban América." Forthcoming in special issue on "Literature, History, and Anthropology in/about Latin America," *Poetics Today*. Manuscript.

Bejarano, Margalit. "Antisemitism in Cuba under Democratic, Military, and Revolutionary Regimes, 1944–1963." *Patterns of Prejudice* 24, no. 1 (1990): 32–46.

———. "Cuba as America's Back Door: The Case of Jewish Immigration." In *The History of the Jewish People*. Vol. 2., 481–88. Jerusalem: World Union of Jewish Studies, 1990.

———. "The Deproletarianization of Cuban Jews." In AMILAT, *Judaica Latinoamericana: Estudios Histórico-Sociales*. Jerusalem: Editorial Universitaria Magnes Press and Hebrew University, 1988.

———. "Los Sefaradíes, pioneros de la inmigración judía a Cuba." *Rumbos en el Judaísmo, el Sionismo e Israel*, no. 14 (1985): 107–22.

———. "Religion y Etica." *Bene Berith Fragmentos* (Havana) 5, no. 51 (March 1956), n.p.

———. *Religious Repression in Cuba*. Coral Gables, Fla.: Cuban Studies Project, Institute of Interamerican Studies, 1986.

Bell, Grosvenor Melville. "Cuba—America's Sugar Bowl." *National Geographic* January 1947, 2–25.

Bemelmans, Ludwig. "The Best Way to See Cuba." *Holiday* December 1957, 65–75.

Benardete, Mair José. *Hispanic Culture and the Character of the Sephardic Jews*. 2d ed. New York: Sepher-Hermon, 1982.

Benjamin, Medea. "Things Fall Apart," *NACLA Report on the Americas* 24, no. 2 (August 1990): 26.

Bercuson, David Jay. *The Secret Army*. New York: Stein & Day, 1984.

Binyan, Narciso. "Arabs and Armenians in Latin America." *Patterns of Prejudice* 13, no. 6 (November–December 1979): 5–11.

Black, George. *Cuba: A View from Inside. 40 Years of Cuban Life in the Work and Words of 20 Photographers*. New York: Center for Cuban Studies, 1985.

Blasier, Cole. *The Giant's Rival: The USSR and Latin America*. Rev. ed. Pittsburgh: University of Pittsburgh Press, 1988.

Blet, Pierre, Robert A. Graham, Angelo Martini, and Burkart Schneider.

Le Saint Siège et les victimes de la guerre. Mars 1939–Décembre 1940. Rome: Libreria Editrice Vaticana, 1972.

Blis, David. "Memoirs." *Havaner Lebn–Vida Habanera* 21 (February 1936): 18–19.

Boletin Informativo de la Benefiencia "Bikur-Holim." Havana: Beneficiencia "Bikur-Holim," 1959.

Bom Meihy, José Carlos Sebe. *A Colônia brasilianista: história oral de vida acadêmica.* São Paulo: Nova Stella, 1990.

Branfman, Morris. *In Pursuit of Freedom.* New York: Shengold, 1991.

Braham, Randolph L. *The Politics of Genocide: The Holocaust in Hungary.* Vol. 2. New York: Columbia University Press, 1981.

Breitman, Richard. *The Architect of Genocide: Himmler and the Final Solution.* New York: Knopf, 1991.

Breitman, Richard, and Alan M. Kraut. *American Refugee Policy and European Jewry, 1933–1945.* Bloomington: Indiana University Press, 1987.

Bristow, Edward J. *Prostitution and Prejudice: The Jewish Fight against White Slavery, 1870–1939.* New York: Schocken, 1983.

Buell, Raymond. *Problems of New Cuba.* New York: Foreign Policy Association Press, 1935.

Bulletin de l'Alliance Israélite Universelle, no. 29 (1904), 165.

Burkett, Elinor. "Los Latinos in the Promised Land." *Miami Herald,* July 12, 1991, E1–2.

Cabrera Infante, Guillermo. *La Habana para un Infante Difunto.* Barcelona: Seix Barral, 1979.

Calic, Edouard. *Ohne Maske.* Frankfurt: Societats-Verlag, 1968. (Spanish edition: *Hitler sin máscara; conversaciones secretas.* Barcelona: Plaza & Janés, 1975).

Canova, Enrique C. "Cuba—The Isle of Romance," *National Geographic,* September 1933.

Castiel, Dionisio. "Algunos Apuntes sobre la Contribución de los Hebreos al Desarrollo de Cuba." *La Voz de Marianao* (Havana). Edicion Anual del Centro Israelita del Termino de Marianao, 1949–1950, 59–60.

Centro Israelita. *The 25th Anniversary of the Centro Israelita.* Havana: Centro Israelita, 1950.

Chapman, Charles E. *A History of the Cuban Republic.* New York: Macmillan, 1927.

Chuili Levy, José A. "Noticiero Médico Hebreo-Cubano." *Israelia* 3, no. 9 (September 1952): 25.

Clifford, Clark, with Richard Holbrooke. "The Truman Years." Part 1. *New Yorker,* March 25, 1991, 70.

Comité Judío Americano. *Comunidades judías de latinoamérica*. Buenos Aires: Candelabro, 1970.

Confidential U.S. Diplomatic Post Records. Central America and the Caribbean: Cuba, 1930–1945, by E. W. Timberlake. Frederick, Md.: University Publications of America, 1985.

Corbitt, Duvon Clough. "Chinese Immigrants in Cuba." *Far Eastern Survey* 13, no. 4 (July 12, 1944): 130–32.

―――. "Immigration to Cuba." *Hispanic American Historical Review* 22 (May 1942): 280–308.

―――. *Study of the Chinese in Cuba, 1847–1947*. Wilmore, Ky.: Asbury College, 1971.

Cox, Robert J. "Palatial Embassy: Symbol of Decline." In *Inside Cuba*. Washington, D.C.: Freedom House, 1990.

Crahan, Margaret E. "Cuba, Religion, and Revolutionary Institutionalization," in *Social Cuba: Past Interpretations and Future Challenges*, edited by Sergio G. Roca, 207–29. Boulder, Colo.: Westview, 1988.

Cuban Economic Research Project. *A Study on Cuba: The Colonial and Republican Periods: The Socialist Experiment*. Coral Gables, Fla.: University of Miami Press, 1965.

"Cuba's Jews Face Shortages." *WJC International Report*, February–March 1992, 7.

Dallos, Robert E. "Sequel." *People Weekly*, February 14, 1977, 16–17.

Dawidowicz, Lucy. *The War Against the Jews*. New York: Holt, Rinehart & Winston, 1975.

de la Torriente Brau, Pablo. *Peleando con los Milicianos*. 2d ed. Havana: Editoria Política, 1987.

Der Gruntshteyn (La Primera Piedra). Edición Extraordinaria Conmemorativa de la Colocación de la Primera Piedra de la Casa de la Comunidad Hebrea de Cuba. Havana: Artprint de Pascual y Gutsztat, 1951.

Detlev, J. K. Peukert. *Inside Nazi Germany: Conformity, Opposition, and Racism in Everyday Life*. Translated by Richard Deverson. New Haven: Yale University Press, 1987.

Dewart, Leslie. *Cristianismo y Revolución*. Barcelona: Editorial Herder, 1965.

Díaz Versón, Salvador. *El Nazismo en Cuba*. Havana: Obrapia, 1944.

"Difficult Times for Cuban Jewry." *Congress Bulletin* (Montreal) 15, no. 4 (April 1961): 1.

Domínguez, Ofelia. "Manifesto al pueblo cubano por un Comité Pro-Palestina." *El Avance Criollo*, April 14, 1944.

―――. *De seis a seis*. Mexico City: n.p., 1937.

―――. *50 años de una vida*. Havana: Instituto Cubano del Libro, 1971.

Dorschner, John, and Roberto Fabricio. *The Winds of December.* East Rutherford, N.J.: n.p., 1980.

Drake, Paul W. "From Good Men to Good Neighbors: 1912–1932." In *Exporting Democracy: The United States and Latin America: Themes and Issues,* edited by Abraham F. Lowenthal. Baltimore: Johns Hopkins University Press, 1991.

Duarte Oropesa, José. *Historiología Cubana Desde 1898 hasta 1944.* Vol. 2. Miami: Ediciones Universales, 1974.

Dubelman, Abraham. "Cuba." In *American Jewish Yearbook: 1962,* 482–84. New York: American Jewish Committee, 1963.

Eck, Nathan. "The Rescue of Jews with the Aid of Passports and Citizenship Papers of Latin American States." *Yad Vashem Studies* 1, no. 1 (1957): 125–52.

Eichen, Josef David. *Sosúa: Una colonia hebrea en la República Dominicana.* Santiago, Dominican Republic: Universidad Católica Madre y Maestra, 1980.

Elazar, Daniel J. *Jewish Communities in Frontier Societies.* New York: Holmes & Meier, 1983.

———. *The Sephardim Today.* New York: Basic Books, 1989.

Elkin, Judith L. "A Gallery of Former Jews." *Commentary* 92, no. 6 (December 1991): 38–45.

———. "Is There a 'Jewish Interest' in Latin American Politics?" *Patterns of Prejudice* 24, no. 2–4 (1990): 60–74.

———. *Jews of the Latin American Republics.* Chapel Hill: University of North Carolina Press, 1980.

———. "The Reception of the Muses in the Circum-Caribbean." In *The Muses Flee Hitler: Cultural Transfer and Adaptation, 1930–1945,* edited by Jarrell C. Jackman and Carla M. Borden, 291–302. Washington, D.C.: Smithsonian Institution Press, 1983.

Elkin, Judith L., and Merkx, Gilbert W., eds. *The Jewish Presence in Latin America.* Boston: Allen and Unwin, 1987.

Ellis, Marc H. "Holocaust Theology and Latin American Liberation Theology: Suffering and Solidarity," In *Remembering for the Future,* edited by Yehuda Bauer, 584–97. Vol. 1. *Jews and Christians during and after the Holocaust.* Oxford: Pergamon Press, 1989.

Feingold, Henry L. *The Politics of Rescue: The Roosevelt Administration and the Holocaust, 1938–1945.* New Brunswick, N.J.: Rutgers University Press, 1970.

Feldman, Miguel. "El caso del Conde Grande y la política immigratoria uruguaya." *Hoy es Historia* 1, no. 6 (October–November 1984): 35–55.

Fernández, Tony. *Sionismo: el fascismo de la estrella de David.* Havana: Editorial de Ciencias Sociales, 1981.

Fidanque, E. Alvin. *Kol Shearith Israel: Cien años de vida judía en Panama, 1876–1976*. Panama City: n.p., 1977.

Fittko, Lisa. *Mein Weg über die Pyrenaen: Erinnerungen*. Munich: Carl Hanser, 1985.

FitzGerald, Frances. "A Reporter at Large: Slightly Exaggerated Enthusiasms." In *The New Cuba: Paradoxes and Potentials*, edited by Ronald Radosh. New York: Morrow, 1976.

Fitzgibbon, Russell H., ed. *The Era of Trujillo, Dominican Dictator*. By Jesús de Galíndez. Tucson: University of Arizona Press, 1973.

"Five Martyrs." *Dos Naie Kubaner Yiddish Vort*, May 1963, 19–22.

Foreign Policy Association. *Problems of the New Cuba. Report of the Commission on Cuban Affairs*. New York: Foreign Policy Association, 1935.

Fox, John P. "German and European Refugees, 1933–1945: Reflections on the Jewish Condition under Hitler and the Western World's Response to their Expulsion and Flight." *Refugees in the Age of Total War*, edited by Anna C. Bramwell, 69–85. London: Unwin Hyman, 1988.

Frank, Waldo. *Cuba: Prophetic Island*. New York: Marzani, 1961.

Frye, Alton. *Nazi Germany and the American Hemisphere, 1933–1941*. New Haven, Conn.: Yale University Press, 1967.

Gambach, Rabbi Nessim. "Filantropía." *Boletín Informativo de la Beneficencia "Bikur-Holim."* Havana: Beneficencia "Bikur-Holim," 1959.

García, Cristina. *Dreaming in Cuban*. New York: Knopf, 1992.

García Montes, Jorge, and Antonio Alonso Avila. *Historia del Partido Comunista de Cuba*. Miami: n.p., 1970.

Gellman, Irwin F. *Good Neighbor Diplomacy: United States Policies in Latin America, 1933–1945*. Baltimore: Johns Hopkins University Press, 1979.

———. "The *St. Louis* Tragedy," *American Jewish Historical Quarterly* 41, no. 2 (December 1971): 144–56.

Gendler, Rabbi Everett. "Holy Days in Havana." *Conservative Judaism* 23, no. 2 (Winter 1969): 15–24.

Genizi, Haim. *American Apathy: The Plight of Christian Refugees from Nazism*. Ramat-Gan, Israel: Bar-Ilan University Press, 1983.

Geyer, Georgia Anne. "Castro: the 'Knowable' Dictator." In *The Cuban Revolution at 30*, 37–49. Occasional Paper #29. Washington, D.C.: Cuban-American Foundation, 1989.

Gidal, Nachum T. *Die Juden in Deutschland von der Roemerzeit bis zur Weimarer Republik*. Hamburg: Bertelsmann Lexikon, 1988.

Gilbert, Martin. *Atlas of the Holocaust*. London: Michael Joseph, 1982.

———. *The Holocaust: Maps and Photographs*. New York: Holt, Rinehart & Winston, 1986.

Gitelman, Zvi. "History, Memory, and Politics: The Holocaust in the Soviet Union." *Holocaust and Genocide Studies* 5, no. 1 (1990): 23–37.

Gojman de Backal, Alicia. "Minorías, Estado y Movimientos Nacionalistas de la Clase Media en México. Liga Antichina y Antijudía (Siglo XX)." In AMILAT, *Judaica Latinoamericana: Estudios Histórico-Sociales,* 174–92. Jerusalem: Editorial Universitaria Magnes and Hebrew University, 1988.

Goldberg, Nathan. "Immigration Attitudes of Mexicans: An Insight." *Rescue* 2 (July–August 1945): 3–101.

Goldenberg, Boris. "Foreword." *The Cuban Revolution and Latin America.* London: Allen and Unwin, 1965.

Golendorf, Pierre. *7 Años en Cuba.* Esplugas de Llobregat, Spain: Plaza & Janes, 1977.

Gondi, Ovidio. "La Hispanidad in Hitler's Service." *Free World* 3, no. 1 (June 1942): 61–65.

González, Manuel Pedro. "A Selective Bibliography of the Cuban Revolution against Machado (1928–1933)." *Revista Bimestre Cubana* 50 (1942): 209–31.

Guevara, Ernesto (Che). *Che Guevara and the Cuban Revolution.* Leichhardt, Sydney, Australia: Pathfinder Books, 1987.

Guy, Donna. *Sex and Danger in Buenos Aires.* Lincoln: University of Nebraska Press, 1991.

Habana: Guía General. Havana: Cuban Reception Committee to the U.S.W.V. 30th National Encampment, 1928.

Halperin, Maurice. *The Taming of Fidel Castro.* Berkeley and Los Angeles: University of California Press, 1981.

Hart Davalos, Armando. "The Traditions behind a Socialist World View." *World Marxist Review* 33, no. 1 (January 1990): 22–25.

Hartog, Jan de. *Schipper naast God.* Antwerp: De Sikkel, 1960.

Heinlein, Federico. "Recordando a Erich Kleiber." *Revista Musical Chilena.* Reprinted in *Revista Bimestre Cubana* 54 (January–June 1958): 222–41.

Hennessy, Alistair. "Cuba." In *The Spanish Civil War, 1936–1939: American Hemispheric Perspectives,* edited by Mark Falcoff and Fredrick B. Pike, 101–58. Lincoln: University of Nebraska Press, 1982.

Herlin, Hans. *Die Reise der Verdammten: Die Tragoedie der St. Louis.* Frankfurt/W-Berlin-Wien: Ullstein, 1985.

Hernández, Rafael, and Haroldo Dilla. "Political Culture and Popular Participation in Cuba." *Latin American Perspectives* 18, no. 2 (Spring 1991): 38–54.

Herzberg, Julia P. "Wilfredo Lam." *Latin American Art* 2, no. 3 (Summer 1990): 18–25.

Hicks, Albert C. *Blood in the Streets: The Life and Rule of Trujillo.* New York: Creative Age, 1949.

Higgins, James. "New Church in Cuba." *Commonwealth,* July 28, 1972, 399–402.

Hilberg, Raul. *The Destruction of the European Jews.* Chicago: University of Chicago Press, 1967.

Hilton, Stanley E. *Hitler's Secret War in South America, 1939–1945.* Baton Rouge: Louisiana State University Press, 1981.

Horowitz, Irving Louis. "A Response." In *The Cuban Revolution at 30.* Occasional Paper #29. Washington, D.C.: Cuban-National Foundation, 1989.

International Bank for Reconstruction and Development. *Report on Cuba, Findings and Recommendations of an Economic and Technical Mission Organized by the IBRD.* Washington, D.C.: IBRD, 1951.

Italiaander, Rolf. *Juden in Lateinamerika.* Tel Aviv: Olamenu, 1971.

Jackman, Jarrell C., ed. *The Muses Flee Hitler: Cultural Transfer and Adaptation, 1930–1945.* Washington, D.C.: Smithsonian Institution Press, 1983.

Jensen, Larry R. *Children of Colonial Despotism: Press, Politics, and Culture in Cuba, 1790–1840.* Tampa: University Presses of Florida, 1988.

Kahn, Jeffrey A. "The History of the Jewish Colony in Cuba." Ordination thesis, Hebrew Union College–Jewish Institute of Religion, 1981.

Kallen, Horace M. *Frontiers of Hope.* New York: Liveright, 1929.

Kamorin, A. "The Church Itself Has Changed." *Izvestiya* (Moscow), November 29, 1988. Reprinted in special issue of *Religion in Communist Dominated Areas* (edited by Blahoslav Hruby and Olga S. Hruby) 28:1 (Winter 1989): 27–28.

Kaplan, Sender M., Raúl Moncarz, and Julio Steinberg. "Jewish Emigrants to Cuba, 1898–1960." *International Migration* 28, no. 3 (September 1990): 295–310.

Katsch, Siegfried, Elke-Maria Katsch, and Henry P. David. *Sosúa-Verheissenes Land.* Dortmund: Arbeitsunterlage 38/39 zur Lateinamerikaforschung, n.p., n.d.

Kauffmann, Stanley. "At Sea." *New Republic,* December 20, 1976, 20.

Kayfetz, Ben G. "Cuban Jews in Need." *Ottawa Jewish Bulletin and Review,* September 11, 1987, 22.

Keen, Benjamin. *A History of Latin America.* 4th ed. Boston: Houghton-Mifflin, 1992.

Kenny, Michael. "Twentieth Century Spanish Expatriates in Cuba: A Sub-Culture?" *Anthropological Quarterly* 34, no. 2 (April 1961): 85–86.

Kerrigan, Anthony. "Literacy, Yes, Books, No: A Personal Report from Cuba." *The Issue Is Cuba,* no. 5 (April 1990): 15–27.

Khalil, Nabil. *Propagandistas del terror.* Havana: Palestine Liberation Organization, c. 1980.

Khruschev, Nikita S. *Khruschev Remembers: The Glasnost Tapes.* Edited and translated by Jerrold L. Schecter with Vyacheslav V. Luchkov. Boston: Little, Brown, 1990.

Kirchwey, Freda. "Carribbean Refuge." *Nation,* April 13, 1940, 466–68.

Kless, Shlomo. "The Rescue of Jewish Children in Belgium during the Holocaust." *Holocaust and Genocide Studies* 3, no. 3 (1988): 275–87.

Klich, Ignácio. "Latin America and the Palestinian Question." *Research Report,* nos. 2/3. London: Institute of Jewish Affairs, January 1986.

Knight, Alan. "Mexico, c. 1930–46." In *The Cambridge History of Latin America,* edited by Leslie Bethell, 3–82. Vol. 7. Cambridge: Cambridge University Press, 1990.

Knudson, Jerry W. "Anti-semitism in Latin America: Barometer of Social Change." *Patterns of Prejudice* 6, no. 5 (September–October 1972): 1–11.

_____. "The Bolivian Immigration Bill of 1942: A Case Study in Latin American Anti-Semitism." *American Jewish Archives* 22, no. 2 (November 1970): 138–58.

Kochanski, Mendel. "The Jewish Community in Cuba." *Jewish Frontier* 18, no. 9 (September 1951): 26–27.

Kohler, Eric D. "Byways of Emigration: Panama, the Canal Zone, and Jewish Rescue Efforts, 1939–1941." *Holocaust Studies Annual,* edited by Sanford Pinsker and Jack Fishel, 89–118. Vol. 1. Greenwood, Fla.: Penkevill, 1983.

Kohler, Max J. "Los Judíos en Cuba." *Revista Bimestral de la Sociedad Económica del País* 10 (July–August 1920): 2–5.

Konovitch, Barry J. "The Fiftieth Anniversary of the *St. Louis:* What Really Happened." *American Jewish History* 74, no. 2 (Winter 1989–90): 203–9.

Kopilow, David J. *Castro, Israel, & the PLO.* Washington, D.C.: Cuban-American Foundation, 1984.

Kraemer, Judrun. *The Jews in Modern Egypt, 1914–1952.* Seattle: University of Washington Press, 1989.

Kranzler, David. *Japanese, Nazis & Jews: The Jewish Refugee Community of Shanghai, 1938–1945.* New York: Yeshiva University Press, 1976.

Kula, Marcin. "La emigración polaca en Cuba en el período entre guerras." Translated by Jorge Ruiz Landizábal. *Revista de la Biblioteca Nacional José Martí* 22 (1980): 131–49.

Kulka, Erich. "Auschwitz Condoned." *Wiener Library Bulletin* 23, no. 1 (Winter 1968–89): 729–30.

Lacey, Robert. *Little Man: Mayer Lansky and the Gangster Life.* Boston: Little, Brown, 1991.

Lagar Quintero, Roberto, Teresita Bacallao Reyes, Bárbara Rafael Vázquez, Raquel Guevara Pérez, and Gladys Avila Molina. *Historia del Movimiento Comunista, Obrero y de Liberación Nacional y Cubano (1917–1945)*. 10th grade. Havana: Editorial Pueblo y Educacíon, 1987.

Landstreet, Barent. *Cuban Population Issues in Historical and Comparative Perspective*. Ithaca, N.Y.: Cornell University Press, 1976.

Langer, Lawrence L. *Versions of Survival: The Holocaust and the Human Spirit*. Albany: State University of New York Press, 1982.

Lefkowitz, Eliot. "The Double Crossing." Chicago: Holocaust Memorial Foundation of Illinois and Loyola University of Chicago, 1989. Videotape.

Leiva, Juan Chongo. *El Fracaso de Hitler en Cuba*. Havana: Editorial Letras Cubanas, 1989.

Lerner, Natan. "Nationalism and Minorities in Latin America." *Patterns of Prejudice* 11, no. 1 (January–February 1977): 17–22.

Levi, Rozita. *Cuba in the World*. Edited by Cole Blasier and Carmelo Mesa-Lago. Pittsburgh: University of Pittsburgh Press, 1979.

Levine, Robert M. "Adaptive Strategies of Jews in Latin America." In *The Jewish Presence in Latin America*, ed. Judith L. Elkin and Gilbert Merkx, 71–84. Boston: Allen and Unwin, 1987.

———. *The Vargas Regime, 1934–1938*. New York: Columbia University Press, 1970.

———, ed. *Windows on Latin America: Understanding Society through Photographs*. Coral Gables, Fla.: SECOLAS, 1987.

———, and Mark D. Szuchman. "Hotel Cuba." Coral Gables, Fla.: University of Miami, 1985. Videotape. Distributed by University of Illinois Film Service, Urbana, Ill.

Lewis, Morris. *Report of the Director of the Jewish Committee of Cuba*. Havana: Jewish Committee of Cuba, March 1927.

Liebman, Seymour B. "Cuban Jewish Community in South Florida." In *American Jewish Yearbook, 1969*, 238–46. Vol. 70. New York: American Jewish Committee, 1969.

Lipstadt, Deborah. *Beyond Belief: The American Press and the Coming of the Holocaust, 1933–1945*. New York: Free Press, 1986.

Lowenstein, Sharon. *Token Refugee: The Story of the Jewish Refugee Shelter at Oswego, 1944–46*. Bloomington: Indiana University Press, 1986.

Lowry, Nelson. *Rural Cuba*. Minneapolis: University of Minnesota Press, 1950.

Lyceum y Lawn Tennis Club. *Memoria*. Havana: Siglo XX, 1929–30, 1930–31, 1931–32, 1932–33, 1939, 1943–45.

MacGaffey, Wyatt. "Social Structure and Mobility in Cuba." *Anthropological Quarterly* 34, no. 2 (April 1961): 95.

MacGaffey, Wyatt, and Clifford R. Barnett. *Twentieth-Century Cuba: The Background of the Castro Revolution*. Garden City, N.Y.: Doubleday, 1965.

Machado, Gerardo. *Ocho Años de Lucha*. Miami: n.p., 1982.

———. *Por la patria libre*. Havana: n.p., 1926.

Malino, Frances. *The Jews in Modern France*. Hanover, N.H.: Brandeis University Press–University Presses of New England, 1985.

Mann, Peggy. "When the Holocaust Could Have Been Stopped." Chicago *Sun-Times*, April 23, 1978, 116.

Markham, C. R., ed. "Journal of Columbus during His First Voyage." London: *Hakluyt Society Publications* no. 86, n.d.

Marrus, Michael R. "Recent Trends in the History of the Holocaust." In *Remembering for the Future: Working Papers and Addenda*, edited by Yehuda Bauer, 2640–54. Vol. 3. *The Impact of the Holocaust and Genocide on Jews and Christians*. Oxford: Pergamon, 1989.

———. *The Unwanted: European Refugees in the Twentieth Century*. New York: Oxford University Press, 1985.

Martí, José. *Obras completas*. Vol. 4. Havana: Editorial Nacional de Cuba, 1963.

Mendelsohn, John. *The Holocaust*. Vol. 7. *Jewish Emigration: The S.S. St. Louis Affair and Other Cases*. New York: Garland, 1982.

Mestre, Ramón A. "Reading the Music." *Hemisphere* 2, no. 3 (Summer 1990): 29.

Miller, Gertrude. "The Cuban Connection." *Jerusalem Post Magazine*, September 14, 1973, 10–11.

Miller, Judith. *One by One by One*. New York: Simon & Schuster, 1990.

Moore, Carlos. "Heresy or History." *Miami Herald*, December 7, 1990, E1–2.

Moreno Fraginals, Manuel. *El Ingenio: Complejo económico social cubano del azúcar*. Havana: La Prensa Cubana, 1978.

Moretti, Darcia. *Los Ojos del Paraíso*. Coral Gables: North-South Center, University of Miami, 1991.

Morley, John F. *Vatican Diplomacy and the Jews during the Holocaust, 1939–1943*. New York: KATV Publishing, 1980.

Morse, Arthur D. "Voyage to Doom." *Look*, November 28, 1967, 67.

Nelson, Lowry. *Rural Cuba*. Minneapolis: University of Minnesota Press, 1950.

Neumann, Gerhardt. "German Jews in Colombia: A Study in Immigrant Adjustment." *Jewish Social Studies* 3 (1941): 387.

Nicolau González, Ramon. *Cuba y la Defensa de la Republica Española (1936–1939)*. Havana: Editorial Política, 1981.

O'Brien, Jack. "Las actividades del fascismo en Cuba." *Mediodía*, April 18, 1939.

Orovio, Naranjo. *Cuba vista por el emigrante español.* Madrid: n.p., 1987.

Ortíz, Fernando. "Defensa Cubana Contra el Racismo Antisemita." *Revista Bimestre Cubana* 44, no. 3 (June 1939): 97–107.

Pappenheim, Bertha. *Jewish Association for the Protection of Girls and Women. International Conference.* June 22–24, 1927. Official Report. London: Jewish Association for the Protection of Girls and Women, 1927.

Paquette, Robert L. *Sugar Is Made with Blood. The Conspiracy of La Escalera and the Conflict Between Empires over Slavery in Cuba.* Middletown, Conn.: Wesleyan University Press, 1988.

Parker, John H. *Yankee, You Can't Go Home Again.* Miami: privately printed, 1984.

Parker, William Belmont, ed. *Cubans of To-Day.* New York: Putnam, 1919.

Perera, Victor. "Growing Up Jewish in Guatemala." *Echad: An Anthology of Latin American Jewish Writings,* edited by Robert Kalechofsky and Roberta Kalechofsky, 71–80. Marblehead, Mass.: Micah Publications, 1980.

Pérez, Louis A., Jr. *Cuba: Between Reform and Revolution.* New York: Oxford University Press, 1988.

_____. *Cuba and the United States: Ties of Singular Intimacy.* Athens: University of Georgia Press, 1990.

_____. "Cuba, c. 1930–59." In *The Cambridge History of Latin America,* edited by Leslie Bethell. Vol. 7, *1930 to the Present,* 419. Cambridge: Cambridge University Press, 1990.

_____. "'Fin de Siècle' Cuba," in Robert M. Levine, ed. *Windows on Latin America: Understanding Society through Photographs,* edited by Robert M. Levine, 33–57. Coral Gables, Fla.: SECOLAS, 1987.

_____. "In Defense of Hegemony: Sumner Welles and the Cuban Revolution of 1933." In *Ambassadors in Foreign Policy: The Influence of Individuals on U.S.–Latin American Policy,* edited by C. Neale Ronning and Albert Vannucci. New York: Praeger, 1987.

_____. *Lords of the Mountain: Social Banditry and Peasant Protest in Cuba, 1878–1918.* Pittsburgh: University of Pittsburgh Press, 1989.

Pérez-Stable, Marifeli. "In Pursuit of Cuba Libre." *NACLA Report on the Americas* 24, no. 2 (August 1990): 33.

Pino-Santos, Oscar. *La Oligarquía Yanqui en Cuba.* Havana: Editorial Nuestro Tiempo, 1975.

Pitchón, Marco. *José Martí y la comprensión humana, 1853–1953.* Havana: P. Fernández, 1957.

Prinz, Arthur. "The Role of the Gestapo in Obstructing and Promoting Jewish Emigration." *Yad Vashem Studies* 2 (1958): 205–18.

Rabkin, Rhoda P. *Cuban Politics: The Revolutionary Experiment.* New York: Praeger, 1991.

Ran, Leizer. *Comunidad hebrea en tierra Cubana: Almanaque commemorativo del 25° aniversario del Centro Israelita de Cuba: 1925–1950.* Havana: Havaner Leben, 1951.

———. "Cuba." In *Algemeine Entsiclopedia* 5 (1957): 421–36.

Randall, Margaret. *Women in Cuba: Twenty Years Later.* New York: Smyrna, 1978.

Reif-Lehrer, Liane. "Memoir," Boston *Globe,* April 1988, 94.

———. "With Freedom, Unsettling Memories." Boston *Globe,* November 26, 1989, A43.

Richman, Sheldon L. "Mr. Mencken and the Jews." *American Scholar* 59, no. 3 (Summer 1990): 407–11.

Rieur, Jacques. "The Jewish Colony of Cuba." Joint Distribution Committee, New York, 1942. Manuscript.

Rivero, María del Carmen. "The Jewish Experience in Cuba." Coral Gables, Fla., July 1990. Manuscript.

Rodrigue, Aron. *French Jews, Turkish Jews: The Alliance Israélite Universelle and the Politics of Jewish Schooling in Turkey, 1860–1925.* Bloomington: Indiana University Press, 1990.

Rolandia, a Terra Prometida: Judeus Refugiados do Nazismo no Norte do Paraná. São Paulo: Centro de Estudos Judaicos, FFLCH/USP, 1985.

Roller, Arnold. "The Jews of Cuba." *Menorah Journal* 17, no. 3 (December 1929): 258.

Rosales, Martín. "Tiscornia, Ante-Sala de Cuba." *Carteles* 22, no. 48 (November 30, 1941): 30–33.

Rosenthal, Morton M., and Raquel Schuster-Herr. "PLO Activities in Latin America." *Anti-Defamation League of B'nai B'rith International Report,* New York, May 1982.

Rosshandler, Felicia. *Passing through Havana: A Novel of a Wartime Girlhood in the Caribbean.* New York: St. Martin's/Marek, 1984.

Salvídar, José David. "The Dialectics of Our America." In *Do the Americas Have a Common Literature?* edited by Gustavo Pérez Firmat, 62–84. Durham: Duke University Press, 1990.

Sandberg, Harry O. "The Jews of Latin America." *The American Jewish Yearbook, 5678. September 17, 1917 to September 6, 1918,* 35–104. Philadelphia: Jewish Publication Society of America, 1919.

Sapir, Boris. *The Jewish Community of Cuba.* New York: Jewish Teachers' Seminary and People's University, 1948.

Sarausa, Fermin Peraza. *Diccionario Biográfico Cubano.* Vol. 5. Coral Gables, Fla.: Ediciones Anuario Bibliográfico Cubano, 1955.

Sawicki, Tom. "A View from Havana." *Jerusalem Report,* January 16, 1992, 5.

Schlesinger, Arthur M. *A Thousand Days.* New York: Houghton-Mifflin, 1965.

Schmeltz, U. O., P. Glikson, and S. J. Gould, eds. *Studies in Jewish Demography: Survey for 1972–1980.* Jerusalem: Institute of Contemporary Jewry, 1983.

Schroeder, Gerhard. *Heimatlos auf Hoher See.* Berlin: Beckerdruck, 1949.

Schroeder, Susan. *Cuba: A Handbook of Historical Statistics.* Boston: Hall, 1982.

Schwartz, Rosalie. *Lawless Liberators: Political Banditry and Cuban Independence.* Durham, N.C.: Duke University Press, 1989.

Schweyer, Alberto Lamar. *La Crisis del Patriotismo: Una teoría de las inmigraciones.* Havana: Editorial Martí, 1929.

Scully, Eileen. "The PLO's Growing Latin American Base." *Heritage Foundation Backgrounder* (Washington), August 2, 1983.

Senkman, Leonardo. "Argentina's Immigration Policy during the Holocaust (1938–1945)." *Yad Vashem Studies* 35 (1991): 155–88.

―――. "Between Revolution and Reaction." *Jewish Frontier* 48, no. 3 (March 1981): 10–13.

Serpa, Enrique. *Contrabando.* 1927. Reprint. Havana: Editorial Arte y Literatura, 1975.

Shapira, Yoram. "The Arab-Israeli Conflict." *Granma,* quoted in *Maariv,* September 10, 1973.

―――. "Cuba and the Arab-Israeli Conflict." In *Cuba in the World,* edited by Cole Blasier and Carmelo Mesa-Lago, 153–68. Pittsburgh: University of Pittsburgh Press, 1979.

―――. "Latin American Political Parties and Israel." *Jewish Frontier,* March 1981, 23–24.

Shapira, Yoram, and Edy Kaufman. "Cuba's Israel Policy: The Shift to the Soviet Line." *Cuban Studies/Estudios Cubanos* 8, no. 1 (January 1978): 22–35.

Shell, Marc. "Marranos (Pigs), or from Coexistence to Toleration." *Critical Inquiry* 17, no. 2 (Winter 1991): 306–35.

Sikora, Jacobo Schifter, Lowell Gudmundson, and Mario Solera. *El judío en Costa Rica.* San José, Costa Rica: Editorial Estatal a Distancia, 1979.

Simon, Kate. *Bronx Primitive.* New York: HarperCollins, 1989.

Sims, Harold D. "Cuban Labor and the Communist Party, 1937–1958: An Interpretation." *Cuban Studies/Estudios Cubanos* 15, no. 1 (Winter 1985): 44–45.

Smith, Wayne S. *The Closest of Enemies.* New York: Norton, 1987.

Sobel, Louis. "Jewish Community Life and Organization in Latin America." *Jewish Social Service Quarterly*, 20, no. 4. (June 1944): n.p.

Sofer, Eugene. *From Pale to Pampa: A Social History of the Jews of Buenos Aires.* New York: Holmes & Meier, 1982.

Solowiejczyk, Nahman. "Ashkenazim y Sefaradim." In *Der Gruntshteyn (La Primera Piedra)*, 43–44. Translated from the Yiddish. Edición Extraordinaria Conmemorativa de la Colocación de la Primera Piedra de la Casa de la Comunidad Hebrea de Cuba. Havana: Artprint de Pascual y Gutsztat, 1951.

Stone, Robert. "Havana Then and Now: Revisiting a City Once Again in History's Straits." *Harper's*, March 1992, 36–47.

Stoner, K. Lynn. "Ofelia Domínguez Navarro: The Making of a Cuban Socialist Feminist." In *The Human Tradition in Latin America: The Twentieth Century*, edited by William H. Beezley and Judith Ewell, 119–40. Wilmington, Del.: Scholarly Resources, 1987.

Suchlicki, Jaime. *Cuba: From Columbus to Castro.* 2d ed. Washington, D.C.: Pergamon-Brassey's, 1986.

_____. *Historical Dictionary of Cuba.* Metuchen, N.J.: Scarecrow, 1983.

Tenenbaum, Joseph. "The Crucial Year," *Yad Vashem Studies* 2 (1958): 49–77.

Tewell, Harold S. "European Refugees in Cuba." In *The Holocaust.* Vol. 7. *The S.S. St. Louis Affair and Other Cases.* New York: Garland, 1982.

Thomas, Gordon, and Max Morgan Witts. *Voyage of the Damned.* New York: Stein & Day, 1974.

Thomas, Hugh. *Cuba, or the Pursuit of Freedom.* New York: Harper & Row, 1971.

Timberlake, E. W. *Confidential U.S. Diplomatic Post Records, Central America and the Carribean: Cuba, 1930–1945.* Frederick, Md.: University Publications of America, 1985.

Timmerman, Jacobo. *Cuba: A Journey.* New York: Knopf, 1990.

Tisyera, Oscar. *Cuba marxista vista por un católico.* Buenos Aires: Jorge Alvarez, 1964.

Tobias, Henry J. *A History of the Jews in New Mexico.* Albuquerque: University of New Mexico Press, 1990.

Tov, Moshe A. *El Murmullo de Israel.* Jerusalem: n.p., 1983.

Trinchet, Enrique. *Jirones Cubanos (Conozca la política, cierta prensa, el comercio judío y español y la didáctica como son: tumores nacionales).* Havana: n.p., 1947.

Turner, Frederick C. *Catholicism and Political Development in Latin America.* Chapel Hill: University of North Carolina Press, 1971.

Turton, Peter. *José Martí, Architect of Cuba's Freedom.* London: Zed, 1986.

United Hebrew Congregation/Temple Beth Israel. *Golden Anniversary, 1906–1956*. Havana: United Hebrew Congregation, 1956.

Vignier, E., and G. Alonso. *La corrupción política y administrativa en Cuba, 1944–1952*. Havana: Instituto Cubano del Libro, 1963.

Viteles, Harry. *Report on the Status of the Jewish Immigration in Cuba*. New York: Joint Distribution Committee, February 1925. Mimeo, YIVO archives, New York.

Voice of America, U.S. Intelligence Agency, Office of Research and Policy, Radio Martí Program. *Cuba Annual Report: 1985*. New Brunswick, N.J.: Transaction Press, 1988.

von zur Muehlen, Patrik. *Fluchtziel Lateinamerika: Die deutsche Emigration 1933–1945: Politische Aktivitäten und soziokulturelle Integration*. Bonn: Neue Gesellschaft, 1988.

Walter, H. A. *Deutsche Exilliteratur, 1933–1950*. Vol. 4. Stuttgart: n.p., 1984.

Ward, Fred. "Inside Cuba Today." *National Geographic*, January 1977, 32.

Wasserstein, Bernard. *Britain and the Jews of Europe, 1939–1945*. Oxford: Oxford University Press, 1979.

Weiser, Benno. "The Pro-Zionism of Latin America." *Jewish Frontier*, October 1948, 17.

Weissberg, Alex. *Desperate Mission: Joel Brand's Story*. New York: Criterion, 1958.

Welles, B. Sumner. "Is America Imperialistic?" *Atlantic Monthly*, September 1924, 414.

Wexler, Paul. "Ascertaining the Position of Judezmo within Ibero-Romance." In *Vox Romana: Annales Helvetici Explorandis Linguis Romanicis Destinati*, edited by J. Jud and A. Steiger, 162–95. Bern: Francke, 1977.

White, Byron. "Cuba and Puerto Rico: A Case Study in Comparative Economic Development Policy." Ph.D. diss., University of Texas, 1959.

Wischnitzer, Mark. *To Dwell in Safety: The Story of Jewish Migration since 1800*. Philadelphia: Jewish Publication Society of America, 1948.

_____. "The Historical Background of the Settlement of Jewish Refugees in Santo Domingo." *Jewish Social Studies*, 4, no. 1 (1942): n.p.

Wolin, Merle Linda. "Hollywood Goes Havana." *The Issue Is Cuba*, no. 8 (April 1990), 12.

Woon, Basil. *When It's Cocktail Time in Cuba*. New York: Liveright, 1928.

Wyman, David S. *Paper Walls: America and the Refugee Crisis, 1938–1941*. Amherst: University of Massachusetts Press, 1968.

Xiaopeng, Seng. "Process of Rectifying Errors and Negative Tendencies in

Cuba." In *Latin American Studies* 1 (1990): 63–64 (Beijing: Institute of Latin American Studies, Chinese Academy of Social Sciences, 1990).

Yahil, Leni. *The Holocaust: The Fate of European Jewry, 1932–1945.* Translated by Ina Friedman and Haya Galai. New York: Oxford University Press, 1990.

Yans-McLaughlin, Virginia. *Family and Community: Italian Immigrants in Buffalo, 1880–1930.* Ithaca, N.Y.: Cornell University Press, 1977.

———, ed. *Immigration Reconsidered: History, Sociology, and Politics.* New York: Oxford University Press, 1977.

YIVO Institute for Jewish Research. "Going Home: How American Jews Invent the Old World." New York: YIVO Institute for Jewish Research, 1989. Brochure.

Zadoff, Efraim. "Un Análisis Comparativo de las Redes Educativas Judías de México y Argentina, 1935–1955." In AMILAT, *Judaica Latinoamericana: Estudios Histórico-Sociales.* Jerusalem: Editorial Universitaria Magnes and Hebrew University, 1988.

Zayed Massis, Walid. *Palestina . . . Arde el Silencio.* Havana: n.p., 1990.

Index

naque Hebreo, 207; arduous conditions faced by, 30–36; cemetery of, 299, 312–13n.55; characteristics of, xv, 17, 29–51, 69–75, 288, 301; cold relations of, with German-Jewish refugees, 158–59, 182; first attorney of, 194; foods of, 70; intentions of, to leave Cuba for United States, 20; men outnumber women among immigrants, 17; most from Poland and Russia, 33; names changed in Cuba, 39; poverty among, 302; prosper, 301; relationship of, with Sephardim, 185, 226, 265; schoolroom of (photo), 45; socialism popular among, 23, 26, 46, 51, 61, 189; study for professions, 200; trapped in France, 152; unions of, 51; women, 288. *See also* Kultur Tsenter

Asís, Moisés, xv, xvii; observations of, about Jewish life in Cuba, 273–76, 282; refused permission to travel, 353n.130; rejected by University of Havana, 275

Asociación de Jovenes Hebreos de Cuba. *See* YMHA

Asociación Feminina Hebrea de Cuba, 45. *See also* Froien Farain

Auerbach, Morris, 198

Aufbau: advertisements in, by Jews seeking news about relatives, 186; read in Cuba, 84, 155; read in Mexico, 138

Australia: racial preference policies of, 81

Austria: *Anschluss*, 84, 98, 150; Austrian Jews in U.S., 91; Austrian refugees in Mexico, 138; Free Austria Association, 165;

refugees seek to leave, 102, 125; Vienna, 84, 92, 97

Auténticos. *See* Cuban Revolutionary Party

Autiansky, David, 246, 252

Autos da fé. *See* Jews: historical persecution of

Avni, Haim, 25

Axis countries: consulates in, 150; transmigrants barred from, 152

Balboa, 121, 130. *See also* Panama (Canal Zone)

Baldás, Moisés, 242, 273

Banks in Cuba: Banco Nacional, 35; First National City Bank of New York, 35

Barker, Bernard, Jr., 341n.62

Barnet, José A., 55

Barnet, Miguel, 284

Barouch family, 4

Batista y Zalvidar, Fulgencio, 54 (photo); approached by Lawrence Berenson, 118–20, 322n.3, 325n.48; closes doors of Cuba to refugees, 152; collaborates with Céspedes, 53; emerges as power behind 1933 revolution, 55, 58, 60, 75; façade of stability of, 216; heavy-handedness of, 219; issues new visas for Jews, 152; and labor, 62, 74; laissez-faire economic system of Cuba under, 235; outlaws Nazi and Falange parties, 168; Pax Batistiana, 60; political stagnation under, 300; as president, 59, 167–68, 170, 216; promotes social reform, 58; protests against Céspedes government, 53; pro-U.S., 239; relationship of, with Benítez, 112; as "Second Batistato," 215–16, 221,

Handlin, Oscar, 302
Harari, Mike, 279
Hashomer Hatzair. *See* Zionism
Haskalah. *See* Judaism
Havana, 3, 4 (photo), 7; archbishop of, 152; Chamber of Commerce, 83, 113; electric utilities in, 4, 13; Inquisition established in, 9; Jewish Market in, 129, 294; Obispo Street, 38 (photo); Old City (Old Havana), 7, 14, 43, 155, 196–97, 264, 291, 293–94; Prado Promenade, 39 (photo)
Havana Post, 65; office of, catches fire, 74; pleads for compassion for refugees, 118
Havaner Lebn: advertising in, 388n.17; attacked, 80; called reactionary, 366n.91; closes, 246; founded, 60, 177; political outlook of, 214, 257; replaced by *Yedioth-Jewish Cuba*, 246, 252; thrives, 179, 223. *See also* Kaplan, Sender M.
Hays-Quesada Treaty, 120
Hebrew Immigrant Aid Society (HIAS), 5, 42, 125, 130, 133, 140, 145, 153, 190, 243, 247; criticized, 347n.56
Hebrew language. *See* Languages (Hebrew)
Heller, Nathan I., 16
Herzl, Theodor, 269; Theodor Herzl School, 42–43. *See also* Zionism
Heydrich, Reinhard, 98. *See also* Nazis
HIAS (also known as HICEM). *See* Hebrew Immigrant Aid Society
Hitler, Adolph: and Cuban concentration camps, 15; final solution of, 129; impact of, on Cuba, 79–

149; Jews flee from, 132, 152; statue of, covered, 110; students admire, 65; takes power in Germany, 79, 146. *See also* Nazis; Germany
Hoffman, Robert, 93, 113
Holland: accepts some of *St. Louis* passengers, 124; Caribbean colonies of, 1; generous to refugees, 188; Jews emigrate from, to Cuba, 176; Jews transported to Germany by Nazis, 126; passengers land at Rotterdam, 126; quarantine station at Heijplaat, 126; receives refugees from nazism, 89; Westerbork camp in, 126
Holocaust, 79, 99, 138, 189; monument to, 193; news about, 155, 165–66, 185–86, 233; news of, disbelieved, 185; not associated with Jews, 262–64, 287; reassessed in Soviet Union, 267, 352n.117. *See also* Germany; Nazis
Holtusen, Claus-Gottfried, 108
Holtz, Abel, 232–33, 249
Holy Inquisition, 20; last victim of, 9
Honduras, 120
Hornedo, Alfredo, 205
Hostos, Eugenio, 134
Hull, Cordell: actions regarding refugees, 82, 102, 169; as secretary of state, 54, 82
Hungary: anti-Jewish laws of, 142; Free Hungary Association, 165; Jews banned from Communist Party in, 245; Jews from, in Cuba, 176; Jews from, in Mexico, 138; Mantello rescue operation of Jews in, 142–43, 146–47; refu-

Hungary (continued)
gees seeking to leave, 81; revolution in 1848, 12. See also Wallenberg, Raoul

Iberia. See Portugal; Spain
Immigrants: apolitical tendencies of, 61; assimilation and coping strategies of, 32–33, 56–57; come to Cuba, 1–59; conditions worse in Europe for, 289–90; find loopholes in laws, 228; hardships faced by, 24–27, 30–33; numbers of, 59, 150, 313n.70; upward social mobility of, 191; wage structures of, 49
Immigration Department of Cuba. See Benítez Valdes, Manuel
Immigration and Naturalization Act. See United States (restrictions on immigration into)
Inner history (intrahistoria), 8
Instituto de La Habana, 64, 196
Instituto del Vedado, 6, 196
Intergovernmental Committee on Refugees, 108. See also Evian-les-Bains Conference
International Refugee Committee (London), 90
Isleños, 56
Isle of Pines, 120, 182
Israel: Cubans identify with, 257; Cubans visit, 348n.70; emigration to, 7, 243, 265–66; established as state, 25, 192, 218–20, 237; formally recognized by Havana, 342n.77; friendship of, with Prío Socarrás, 220; "Israelites," 278; Likud Party in, 296; MAPAM party in, 258, 279, 346n.33; ministers to Cuba named, 256; and deteriorating re-

lations with Cuba, 252–65; sells arms to Central America, 259. See also Palestine; Zionism

Jabotinsky faction. See Zionism
Jacksonville, 3, 5
Jada'a, Imad. See PLO
Jamaica, xv; accepts Jewish refugees, 147; accepts refugees from Cuba, 78; prejudice against, in Cuba, 17, 33–34, 51–52, 229; workers from, 10–11, 16, 284
Jehovah's Witnesses: persecuted, 249, 348n.58
Jewish Chamber of Commerce: organization of, 61, 236, 298
Jewish (Joint) Relief Committee, 83, 93, 101, 108–10, 115. See also American Jewish Joint Distribution Committee (JDC)
Jews: historical persecution of, 2, 9. See also Jews in Cuba; Judaism
Jews in Cuba: apathetic, 299; attacked, 65; called "Germans," 34; compared to U.S. southerners, 304; considered uncharitable, 141; definitions of Jewishness, 288; depart Castro's Cuba, 7, 77–78, 217, 232–82, 300, 305; downward mobility of, 302; emotional ties of, to Israel, 299; enclave mentality among, 298; and entertainment industry, 66, 74–75; "Eskimo Pie" nickname for, 34; estimated size of community of, in various years, 7, 26, 30, 35, 47, 175, 236, 243, 252, 265, 276, 278, 284–85, 307–8, 344n.1, 351n.106; excluded from some careers, 230; fear militancy, 253; hostility of,

to Arabs, 25; as immigrants, 1–78; impact of Cuban Revolution on, 240–82; intermarriage among, 7, 25, 42, 78, 175–76, 191, 202, 275–76, 287; internal divisions blurred among, 200; lack models of rabbinic authority, 192; last bar mitzvah of, 278; leave Cuba extralegally, 265–66, 283–85; lessons of experience in Cuba, 283–305; little support from, for Castro's movement, 216; modest interest of, in Zionism, 299; occupations of, 74, 236; outmarriage among, 173, 296–97; racial attitudes of, 14, 73–74, 191, 202; reasons some remain under Castro, 264–65, 276–78, 287; as refugees, 2, 79–188; relations of, with Cuban heads of state, 299; treatment of, under Revolution, 240–83; urged to stay, 252; women of, in community, 226, 297; worship by, prohibited, 3; worship services of, 2, 60, 276. See also Adaptive strategies of Jews in Cuba

Johnson, President Lyndon: policy of, toward Cuban refugees, 245

Joint. See American Jewish Joint Distribution Committee (JDC)

Judah, Noble Brandon, 2. See also Brandon, Jacob (Jack)

Judaism: Jewish Law, 1; secret practice of, in Christian countries, 9. See also Jews in Cuba

Judezmo (Judeo-Spanish), 20

Judíada: as derogatory term for Jews, 47. See also Polacos; Turcos

Junta Revolucionaria Cubana (Tampa), 3

Kadden, Leah, 125–26

Kallen, Horace, 26

Kaplan, Rabbi Zvi, 30, 31 (photo); performs interracial marriage, 221

Kaplan, Sender M., xiii–xiv, 30, 60–61, 173, 215 (photo), 298; arrested, 80; as publicist, 223; as Zionist, 220, 257

Karliner family, 110–12, 111–12 (photo), 115–17 (photo); Herbert as St. Louis passenger, 123

Kates, Adolph H., 124, 323n.22; awarded decoration, 225

Kawama Club, 210

Kennedy, John F., 246. See also Bay of Pigs invasion

Kennedy, Joseph, 123, 327n.75

Keren Hayesod. See Zionism

Kessari, Joseph, 257

Key West, 3–5; Cuban Revolutionary Club in, 3, 296–97; proximity of, to Cuba, 8, 229; refugees passing through Cuba come to, 91

King, William Lyon Mackenzie. See Canada

Klappers. See Peddlers

Klein, Martin, 237

Klinghoffer, Leon, 320n.16

Knesset Israel: merged with Adas Israel, 211

Korean War: Jewish volunteers in, 215

Kristallnacht, 85, 91, 101, 117

Kultur Farain-Unión Cultural Hebrea: leads strikes against Jewish industrialists, 51; organized, 46; reopens, 318n.99; repressed, 56. See also Yiddish culture

Kulturgruppe. See Yiddish culture (Yiddishe Kulturgruppe)

own side of story, 316n.53; public appearances of, 73; relationship of, with University of Havana, 63–64; second presidential term of, 47; U.S. and downfall of, 52–53

Madagascar: as possible haven for Jewish refugees, 89

Maduro family, 2, 323n.22; reputed to be involved in *St. Louis* negotiations, 120–21

Magoon, Charles E., 13

Mahmud Abbas. *See* Abbas, Mahmud (Abu Mazzen)

Manasse, Herbert, 127

Mandel, Joseph, 142

Mantello, Georges: helps Jews escape Hungary, 142–43, 146–47

MAPAM party, 258, 279, 346n.33. *See also* Israel

Marchena family, 2

Margolis, Laura, 83, 108–9

Mariel boatlift, 264–65

Marivale, Herman, 10

Marmorstein, Naum, 46

Márquez Sterling, Manuel, 55

Marranos, 1, 8

Martí, José: attitudes of, about Judaism, 179; envisions racially united Cuba, 47; forest in Israel named for, 223; good relationship of, with American Jews, 2–3; Jews contribute to monument for, 219; José Martí University, 196; lionized, 296–97

Matanzas province: early Jewish settlement in, 21, 76–78; site of, described, 11; Jewish life at, during 1930s and 1940s, 175, 248–49, 290–91

Matterín, Abraham Marcus, 276

May, Hugo, 200

Maya, Rabbi Gershon, 40

Maydl Heim residence, 32. *See also* Ashkenazic Jews

Mayer, Louis B., 80

Mayer, Martin, 200

Mechner family, 84–85

Mediterranean Jews. *See* Sephardic Jews

Mencken, H. L., 86; attitudes of, toward Jews, 319n.15

Mendieta, Carlos, 55

Mendieta, Pedro, 104

Menocal, Mario García, 62

Mexico: accepts large numbers of refugees from Spanish Civil War, 65, 147; accepts some Jewish refugees, 85; aids elderly Cuban Jews, 270; Alsatian Jews in, 285; anti-Semitism in, 136, 303; Ashkenazic community in, 137; Cárdenas government, 137; during Spanish colonial empire, 1; impact of Depression on, 136; Jewish community in, 136–38; Jewish immigrants from Poland in, 69, 167, 289–93; Jews from Cuba emigrate to, 243; preference of, for Christians, 137; refugees in, read *Aufbau*, 138; schools in, 43, 136, 138; Sephardic community of, 136; support of, for Spanish Republic, 65; Syrian Jews emigrate to, 21, 236; V. L. Toledano role in, 137

Miami: aids refugees from Cuba, 247; accepts arrivals as Cubans, not as Jews, 305; businessmen from, 209; Cubans traveled to, 63, 229; food sent from, 273; Havana resembled, 206; rally at Bayfront Park in, 166; refugees from nazism come to, 188; *St.*

Miami (continued)
  Louis off Miami Beach, 123, 129;
  synagogues on Miami Beach,
  266. See also Mariel boatlift
Milanés, Oscar Caíñas, 96, 222
Miller Fredman, Dr. José, 273
Miramar: as goal for immigrants,
  197, 211; as most affluent sub-
  urb, 351n.109
Miramar Yacht Club, 6. See also
  "Big Five" clubs
Mittel-Ashe, Ilsa, xiv, 86, 91–92,
  96, 158; grateful for freedom,
  187–88
Mizrachi, Carlos, 237
Molton, Lothar, 111
Montagu, Lily H., 234
Moriscos, 20
Morocco, 17, 74
Moros. See Turcos
Moshe Pipik restaurant, 177, 246
Mosse, George, xv
Mulattos, 73
Muslims: expelled from Spain, 20

Nasser, Gamal Abdul, 239, 257
National Council of Jewish
  Women, 42, 162
National Origins Act. See United
  States: restrictions on immigration into
Navemar, SS, 140–41, 141
  (photo)
Nazis: Abwehr network, 92–93,
  113, 128; Batista opposes, 62;
  brutality of, reported, 65, 85–87;
  come to power in Germany, 79;
  Gestapo, 98, 104, 108, 122, 126,
  168; Party of, in Cuba (Asociación Nazista de Cuba), 67, 92;
  party of, in U.S., 167; persecute
  Jews, 6, 85–86, 182; propaganda

success of, 133; send anti-
Semitic materials to Cuba, 52;
spies of, in Cuba, 92, 104, 128,
168, 232, 320n.24; spies of, in
Latin America, 168–70,
331n.113; sterilization of prisoners by physicians of, 126; supporters of, in Cuba, 218–19. See
also Germany; St. Louis, SS
Networking, 31
New Christians: defined, 8–9, 20;
  help finance Columbus's voyages,
  9; settle in New World, 9
New Orleans, 3
Nightclubs, 74–75, 76 (photo), 178,
  203, 231; Tel Aviv Bar, 221
"Ninety-Eighters," 5
Northern Rhodesia: as possible haven for Jewish refugees, 90
Novograd (Stolik), 238
Nyasaland: as possible haven for
  refugees, 90

Obispo Street, 27, 38 (photos)
Oifgang, 43
Orbita, SS. See Orduña, SS
Orduña, SS, 104–5, 120–21; pas-
  sengers of, transferred to Orbita,
  130–31; saved, 131
Organized crime, 203. See also
  Lansky, Meyer
Oriente Province: Jewish immi-
  grants in, 21, 175, 236
Orinoco, SS, 95–96, 108, 328n.92
ORT Foundation, 154, 183, 186,
  340n.57
Ortíz, Fernando, 166
Osachki, Enrique Oltuski, 237
Otra Cara, La, 267, 268 (photo),
  282. See also Abbas, Mahmud
Ottoman Empire. See Turkey (Ot-
  toman Empire)

Poland (continued)
    Rabbi Lasker in, 65; refugees
    from, 130; as source of Jewish
    prostitutes, 66; trapped members
    of army of, accepted into Mexico,
    147; unemployment and hard-
    ships among Jews in, 26–27
Polar Brewery, 4
Porra, porristas. See Machado y
    Morales, General Gerardo
Portugal: expels Jews, 1, 6, 20, 23;
    receives refugees during World
    War II, 127; refuses Angola as ha-
    ven for Jews, 89
Potemkin (battleship), 69
Prato, Yoachim, 256
Prío Socarrás, Carlos, 173, 189,
    216, 220; honesty of, 231
Projan, Benhamin, 16
Prostitution: curtailed, 353n.134;
    Jews engaged in, 25, 66; as major
    industry in Cuban cities, 14,
    173, 203, 209, 231; specialty
    brothels, 203; "white slave
    trade," 66

Qaddafi, Muammar al, 260
Quakers: aid refugees in Cuba, 183
Quincallas, 19. See also Peddlers

Raft, George, 203. See also Casinos
Ramírez, Primitivo, xiv, xvi, 74,
    222 (photo), 342nn.81–82; fights
    for Israel, 220–21; honored,
    340n.51
Rashi letters, 20
Razovsky, Cecilia, 119
Reagan, President Ronald: associ-
    ated with Menachem Begin by
    Cuban media, 267
Refugees from nazism, 6, 80–101;
    adaptation problems of, 180–83;

consider Cuba a way station,
304; cultural life of, 336n.83;
emigrate to U.S., 189, 300, 304;
life of, in Cuba, 79–187, 200,
308, 323n.23; Rivero's newspapers oppose, 66, 79, 113–14;
strategies of, 84–85; women
among, 182–83. See also Diamond industry
Reich, Otto, 165
Revolution, Cuban, 235–82; attacks "Jewish lobby," 262; bans
religious believers, 280; blames
Soviet Union, 257; censors films,
279; courteous to Jewish citizens, 255–56, 280–81, 283; foreign policy of, 259; frowns on
homosexuals, 262; and historical
hegemony of Soviet Union, 257;
idealists embrace, 274; outlaws
peddling, 255; policy of, toward
Israel, 255–62, 278–80; restricts
departure of males, 255; seizes
Patronato, 252; supports anti-
colonialism, 257; threatens non-
conformists, 253. See also Castro, Fidel; Soviet Union; Twenty-
sixth of July movement
Revolution, French. See France
(French Revolution)
Rexist movement: in Belgium, 125.
See also Belgium
Reyler, Felix, 43, 193
Rivero, Count Nicolás, 67
Rivero, José Ignacio (Pepín), 67;
anti-Semitism of, 79, 113–14;
defense of record of, 324n.31
Rodriguez, Lalo, 72
Rodriguez, Primitivo, 171
Rolloff, Akiva, 12
Romania: emigrants to U.S. from,
3; Jews banned from Communist

Party in, 245; refugees from, 84, 176

Roncalli, Angelo, 147

Roosevelt, Franklin D.: and Jewish refugees, 86, 89, 135, 188, 233; and *St. Louis*, 122, 166; warned about Cuba, 54

Roosevelt, Theodore (Teddy), 4, 13; at San Juan Hill, 16

Rosen, Joseph A., 135

Rosenberg, James N., 135

Rosenberg, Philip, 224–25

Ros-Lehtinen, Ileana, xvi, 294–95. *See also* Adato Levy, Jacobo

Rothschilds: admitted to Mexico as non-Jews, 138; counsel *St. Louis* passengers on behavior, 126; negotiates with French Foreign Office, 123

Rubens, Horace, 3

Russia: Bialystock, 30; czars in, 1, 6; Jews as artisans in, 288; Pale settlement, 66, 68, 134, 288; revolution of, 30, 69; White Russia, 29; Zhukov's army, 190. *See also* Soviet Union

Ruston Academy, 5, 192, 196, 238, 333n.39. *See also* Education in Cuba

Ruz, Lina, 258

Sagua la Grande province. *See* Las Villas province

Saint Augustine (Fla.), 9

St. Louis, SS: aftermath of return of, 166–67; Batista fails to respond to, 211; conditions on board, 114–15; as "errant vessel," 140; fate of passengers on, xiv, 129, 320n.16, 325n.42; memory of, 166; Panama connection to, 120–21; passenger committee

on, 127; psychological impact of, 131–33, 139, 299; publicity brochure from, 106–7; saga of, xv, xvii, 102–49, 162, 223; suicide attempted on, 116–17, 324n.40; symbolic importance of, 131–33; telegram denying permission to disembark from, 114. *See also* Refugees from nazism

Sandberg, Harry, 7

Santa Clara Province, 21, 175, 194, 232–33, 237, 249

Santa Cruz, Agustín Morell de, 9

Santeria, 36

Santiago de Cuba, 11, 22 (photo), 92

Santos Suárez, 197, 211; nicknamed "Santos Tzoris," 265

Sapir, Boris, 48

Sapira, Rabbi Srul, 152

Sarovich, Israel, 59

Schiendick, Otto, 104–5, 113, 128

Schlesinger, Arthur M., Jr., 209

Schlesinger, Louis, 12

Schroeder, Captain Gustav: attempts to aid Jewish passengers on *St. Louis*, 122–24; authors book about experiences, 121, 323–24n.26; as captain of *St. Louis*, 104–5, 110, 115–16, 127; fears returning to Germany, 127–28. *See also* St. Louis, SS

Schuchinsky, Osher, xiii–xiv; biography of, 289–90

Scott, Rebecca J., 10

Scouting, 71

Semler, Hugo, 154

Sepharad, 1, 20. *See also* Spain

Sephardic Jews: aging remnants of, 255; alleged use of healers, 25; vs. Ashkenazim, 25, 253; become shopkeepers, 50; Bikur Holim so-

Sephardic Jews (*continued*)

ciety of, 64, 192, 226; Buena Voluntad society of, 46; community center of, 212, 226, 264, 269, 294–95; characteristics of, xv, 20, 24–26, 174, 253, 285, 291; confused with Muslims, 290; Congregación Israelita Chevet Ahim, 21, 40, 43, 70–71, 161, 174, 192, 269–70, 272, 274, 295; as earliest settlers, 175; first burial society of, 21; foods of, 253, 273; importance of family to, 186, 191; as peddlers, 22, 50; philanthropy among, 64, 208, 302; prosperity of, after World War I, 29; remain unassimilated, 265; role of women among, 25, 41, 297; size of community dwindles, 253; State of Israel and, 218

Seventh-Day Adventists, 280

Shutzfarain far Peddler. See Peddlers

Silber, Isaac, 239, 256, 344n.7. *See also* Zionism

Simchowitz, Abraham. *See* Grobart, Fabio (Abraham Simchowitz)

Sírios. *See* Turcos

Sirovich, William I., 80

Slavery, 10

Socarrás, Carlos Prío. *See* Prío Socarrás, Carlos

Sociedad Bikur Holim, 64

Sociedad Colonizadora, 82. *See also* Bolivia

Solomon, Dr. Frederick, 234. *See also* United Hebrew Congregation

Sosúa refugee colony, 82, 90, 133–36. *See also* Dominican Republic

South Africa: attacked for pro-Zionist sentiments, 267; racial preference policies of, 81

South-West Africa: as possible haven for Jewish refugees, 90

Soviet Union: Cubans study in, 263; Foreign Minister Anastas Mikoyan visits Havana, 239, 256; and *glasnost,* 280; hegemony of, over Cuba, 257; Jews depart from, 69; persecution of Jews in, 216; reassesses Holocaust, 267; relationship of, with Cuba, 239; suggests Alaska as haven for Jewish refugees, 89; support from, in Cuba, 76. *See also* Russia

Spain: Asturias, 56; Canary Islands, 56; Civil War, 64, 176; colonial wars of, 17; Cuban volunteers in, 321n.27; first rabbi in, 161; Galicia, 10, 47, 56, 284; immigrants from, in Cuba, 10, 17, 56, 68, 93; Jews expelled from, 1, 6, 23; men predominate among immigrants from, 56; receives refugees during World War II, 127. *See also* Falange; Gallegos

Spanish-Cuban-American War of 1898, 2–3, 58; blockade of Cuba during, 4; concentration camps during, 15

Spanish immigrants. *See* Gallegos

Spatz, Arnold: interned at *Schutzhaft,* 151; operates travel agency dealing in visas, 97; owns Avis agency, 199

Spatz, Hardy (Leonhard), xvi, 184 (photo); helps F.B.I., 148; story of, 151, 191–92, 199, 206, 339n.37

Stayer, Col. Morrison C., 131

United Hebrew Congregation (*continued*)
in disrepair, 269; cultural isolation of, from Cuban society, 233–34; dealings of, with Batista, 80; early years of, 3, 5, 21, 182; leaders of, 224; Reform affiliation of, 233–34, 300; wartime activities of, 152, 183. *See also* Americans in Cuba

United Nations: admits Israel, 219–20; condemns Zionism as racism, 267; Cuban role in UNRWA and UNCIR, 260–61; Division for Palestinian Rights, 350n.97; rescinds anti-Zionist resolution, 280. *See also* Belt y Ramírez, Guillermo

United States: anti-Semitism in, 65; and Batista, 62; considered imperialistic, 3; faulted for allegedly pressuring Cuba over *St. Louis*, 117–18; Immigration and Naturalization Act in, 20, 33, 82–83; influence of, 52–54, 206–7, 230–31, 296; intervenes in Cuba's War of Independence, 12; military occupation of Cuba by, 3, 12; National Origins Act in, 20; quota system of, for immigrants, 69, 81–83, 86, 91, 101, 176; relationship of, with Cuban immigration officials, 102–3; restrictions on immigration into, 20, 28, 33, 69, 86, 102; severs diplomatic relations with Cuba, 241; treatment of refugees in, 80, 129

United States State Department, 47, 60, 62, 82, 102; anti-Semitism within, 168, 334n.52; closes U.S. consulate in Havana, 244; considers refugees a security risk, 148; denies allegations about laxity, 166; instructs consulate not to help *St. Louis* passengers, 320n.20; makes no protest about *St. Louis*, 123; opposes creation of State of Israel, 219–20; suspects visa rackets, 169; sympathizes with refugees from Coert de Bois, 132, 328n.90

University of Havana: faculty flee after Revolution, 246; first Jewish students at, 183, 185, 196, 230, 249; involved in politics, 63–64; opposes Machado, 63; politicized, 275; relationship of, with University of Miami, 206

Unterwegs, 155, 332n.19

Uruguay, 10; Jewish population of, 284; and refugees, 82; ships refused landing rights in, 140

Vargas Llosa, Mario, 278

Vatican: refugee policy of, 149. *See also* Pius XII, Pope

Vedado, 206 (photo); site of German school, 67; suburb of, attractive to successful Jews, 95, 178, 197, 205, 211, 226, 269, 295

Venezuela: aids elderly Cuban Jews, 270; appeals to Fidel Castro, 267–68; Cuban Jew named U.S. ambassador to, 165; Jews flee Cuba for, 243; López Contreras allows passengers to disembark in, 136; Orinoco River Valley as possible haven for Jewish refugees, 90; per capita income, 208; Portuguese Jews in, 285

Vienna, 84, 92, 97. *See also* Austria

Villa de Madrid, SS, 84

Voyage of the Damned, 132

CPSIA information can be obtained
at www.ICGtesting.com
Printed in the USA
BVOW08s0852020117
472333BV00002B/412/P

9 781558 765214